Anthropology and Photography

Anthropology and Photography 1860–1920

EDITED BY

Elizabeth Edwards

Yale University Press · New Haven and London   1992

IN ASSOCIATION WITH

The Royal Anthropological Institute, London

Set in Linotron Bembo by Excel Typesetters Company,
Hong Kong
Printed and bound in Hong Kong by Kwong Fat Offset
Printing Co. Ltd.

Library of Congress Cataloging-in-Publication Data

Anthropology and photography 1860–1920
    edited by Elizabeth Edwards.
    p.   cm.   Includes index.
    "In Association with the Royal Anthropological
       Institute, London."
    ISBN 0–300–05168–9
    1. Photography in ethnology—Great Britain—History.
2. Ethnology—Great Britain—History. I. Edwards,
Elizabeth J.M., 1952– . II. Royal Anthropological
Institute of Great Britain and Ireland.
GN347.A59   1992
301'.028—dc20   91–41482
                                      CIP

A catalogue record for this book is available from the British
Library

Frontispiece: A photographic encounter in south-east Africa.
John H. Murray's photographic darkroom wagon on tour,
c.1880. (RAI 35833)

Contents

Foreword

When I first joined the Royal Anthropological Institute in 1974, work on the Photographic Collection — already initiated by Brownlee Kirkpatrick, our distinguished librarian — had to go through a phase of excavation from dusty basements, followed by a phase of salvage since many of the negatives were made of combustible cellulose-nitrate and had to be rephotographed.

The touring exhibition *Observers of Man*, organized by Roslyn Poignant in 1980 in association with the Photographers' Gallery, with an accompanying catalogue, was a milestone in the phase of interpretation. It was designed, however, primarily to open up the collection to public access, displaying its richness and variety.

Observers of Man was designed as a pleasing exhibition with (as Sue Davies pointed out in the catalogue foreword) 'no pictures . . . of diseased or miserable people'. To balance this impression, two disturbing images from the collection not selected for *Observers of Man* were published in the April 1980 issue of our newsletter *RAIN*: one of a shackled prisoner made to stand against an anthropometric scale, and the other a portrait (by W.L. Hildburgh) of a limbless man photographed in Madras about 1902. In retrospect, some pages of *Observers of Man* evince a comfortable exoticism, or emulsification of the fractious, which in the 1980s would be questioned with more edge. After *Observers of Man* it was clearly time to promote research into the collection that would try to analyze not merely who took a given photograph and when, but also for what purpose and in what historical context. Research of this kind would take its place in the more general 'history of anthropology' which was developing fast. At about this time Edward Said's *Orientalism* was exerting an influence on both anthropology and art history; and the historical placing of anthropology in the context of colonial empires could no longer be dismissed by anyone as merely an oedipal move to disconcert the older generation.

In 1984 the Royal Anthropological Institute was awarded a grant by the Calouste Gulbenkian Foundation for a pioneering project to research its photographic collection, under one of the Foundation's priority policies at that time, 'Educational use of archives'. The title given to the project was 'European encounters with the Third World' — echoing Talal Asad's *Anthropology and the Colonial Encounter*[1] — and a resulting publication was planned from the start. Immediate stimulus for the project came partly from a workshop at Oxford in May 1984 on 'Visual documentation of colonized peoples', sponsored by the Centre for Social History.

At the time one or two influential voices within the Institute opposed our project on the grounds that some of the Victorian past of anthropology is discreditable and has nothing to do with the humanist discipline established since Malinowski and Boas; or even that the project was not really anthropology and hence was no concern of the Institute. I believe that the current intense interest in reflexivity, in the history of our subject, and in anthropologists' field records, will fully vindicate the original decision to embark on the project.

The RAI's photographic collection, like the other major collections of this kind in Britain[2], is still seriously underfunded. Those who have worked in our collection know that it is a precious deposit of human understanding and misunderstanding, accumulated organically — for until the early 1970s no one thought of such photographs as having any financial value — and completely irreplaceable. We are now entering an age where computerization can make possible much more effective cataloguing and retrieval of images than ever before. I hope that this book will not only advance scholarly understanding of 'anthropology and photography', but also make the collection better known and eventually housed, conserved and documented to the standard that it deserves.

Acknowledgements

Thanks are due first to the Gulbenkian Foundation for their imaginative grant referred to above.

Fiona Stewart was engaged as research editor, with an advisory panel consisting of Jonathan Benthall, Roslyn Poignant and Gwyn Prins, who were later joined by Michael Hitchcock. We are grateful to Fiona Stewart for her work on the original project — both archival research and liaison with authors. In particular she succeeded in finding out historical information about some of the images through imaginative assiduity (for instance, the identification of Mary Deane in the jacket photograph), when most other researchers would have given up the task.

Unfortunately the original publication envisaged could not be realized. However, in 1989 Elizabeth Edwards agreed to review all the work done to date and to undertake the planning and editing of a new publication. She has been assisted by an editorial advisory panel consisting of Jonathan Benthall, Michael Hitchcock, Howard Morphy, Roslyn Poignant, Gwyn Prins and Marilyn Strathern. Chris Pinney, the current Chair of the Institute's Photographic Committee, has also played a supportive role.

The Institute is very grateful to Elizabeth Edwards for her outstanding work in coordinating and bringing to fruition this complex international project. We thank, too, all members of the editorial advisory panel and others who have given their encouragement, especially Roslyn Poignant, whose discerning commitment over many years to the Institute's photographic collection has been vital.

Earlier support from the British Library Board, Kodak Limited, the Pilgrim Trust, Christie's (South Kensington) Limited, the Arts Council, the Robert and Lisa Sainsbury Fund, the late Dr Audrey Richards, the Inchcape Charitable Trust Fund and the Wenner-Gren Foundation was of great help towards conserving and cataloguing the collection.

Jonathan Benthall
Director, Royal Anthropological Institute

---

1 London: Ithaca Press, 1973.
2 Principally the Pitt Rivers Museum, Oxford; University Museum of Archaeology and Anthropology, Cambridge; Museum of Mankind, London; though there are numerous smaller collections.

Editor's Acknowledgements

I SHOULD LIKE first of all to thank the editorial panel for their support throughout the project and to express my gratitude for the unfailing support and guidance of Jonathan Benthall and Ros Poignant, who did everything they could to make my editorial life easier. Especial thanks are also due to Howard Morphy, who has read, commented and advised beyond the call of duty. I should like to second Jonathan Benthall in acknowledging Fiona Stewart's research from which many contributors, including myself, have benefited. I am also indebted to the many people who, in different ways, have made this volume possible, giving freely their support, advice and comments; Richard Boddy, Jane Carmichael, Jeremy Coote, Simon Edwards, John Falconer, Jane Feaver, Gill Grant, Richard Hanson, Ray and Adi Inskeep, Monica Janowski, I.N. Jones, Schuyler Jones, Caroline Kerr, Patti Langton, Nadia Lovell, Frances Morphy, Malcolm Osman, Harry Persaud, Alison Petch, Chris Pinney, and Linda Simmie. Thanks are also due to John Todd, who produced the artwork for Plate 154, Christopher Wright who produced the index, Kate Cabrie, who typed the larger part of the manuscript, Richard Dawes, who worked on the manuscript, Patricia Rennie, the designer, and finally Robert Baldock at Yale University Press for his advice and endless patience.

E.E.

The editor would like to acknowledge the help and generosity of the following in supplying photographs:

American Museum of Natural History, New York; Asiatic Society, Bombay; Bodleian Library, University of Oxford; British Columbia Archives and Record Service, Victoria; British Library of Political and Economic Science, London School of Economics; British Museum, London; British Museum, (Museum of Mankind), London; British Museum (Natural History), London; Cambridge University Library; Institute of Ethiopian Studies, Addis Ababa; Institute of Social Anthropology, University of Oxford; Library of Congress, Washington; Mayotte Magnus; Charlie Meecham; Dedria Mohamed and Saleh-el-Din Mohamed; Museum of Archaeology and Anthropology, University of Cambridge; Museum of Contemporary Art, Power Collection Sydney; National Archives of Canada, Ottawa; National Portrait Gallery, London; Pitt Rivers Museum, University of Oxford.

All other photographs are courtesy of the Royal Anthropological Institute, London.

List of Contributors

Judith Binney is Associate Professor of History, University of Auckland.

Margaret B. Blackman is Professor of Anthropology at the State University of New York College at Brockport.

Nicholas J. Bradford was formerly Lecturer in Social Anthropology at the University of Aberdeen.

Brian W. Dippie is Professor of History at the University of Victoria, Canada.

Elizabeth Edwards is Archives Curator at the Pitt Rivers Museum, University of Oxford.

James C. Faris is Professor of Anthropology at the University of Connecticut.

The late Naziha Hamouda completed postgraduate studies at the University of Kent.

Paul Hockings is Professor of Anthropology at the University of Illinois, Chicago.

Ira Jacknis is Associate Research Anthropologist at the Lowie Museum of Anthropology, University of California, Berkeley.

Martha Macintyre is Senior Lecturer in the Department of Anthropology, La Trobe University, Victoria, Australia.

Maureen MacKenzie is Research Associate at the Communications Research Institute of Australia, Canberra.

Iskander Mydin is Curator (History) at the National Museum of Singapore.

Richard Pankhurst is Professor of Ethiopian Studies at the Institute of Ethiopian Studies, Addis Ababa.

Christopher Pinney is Lecturer in South Asian Anthropology at the School of Oriental and African Studies, University of London.

Roslyn Poignant is a writer, approach anthropological, and past Chairperson of the Royal Anthropological Institute Photographic Committee.

Gwyn Prins is Director of Studies in History, Emmanuel College and of the Global Security Programme, University of Cambridge.

Vivienne Rae-Ellis is a writer and lecturer, working extensively on Tasmanian history.

Anne Salmond is Associate Professor in Social Anthropology and Maori Studies at the University of Auckland.

Joanna C. Scherer is Anthropologist/Illustrations Researcher, Handbook of North American Indians Project, Smithsonian Institution, Washington.

H.L. Seneviratne is Associate Professor of Anthropology at the University of Virginia.

Frank Spencer is Professor of Anthropology at Queens College of the City University of New York.

Brian Street is Senior Lecturer in Social Anthropology in the School of Social Sciences, University of Sussex.

Donald Tayler is University Lecturer in Ethnology and Curator at the Pitt Rivers Museum, University of Oxford.

Jan Vansina is Professor of History and Anthropology, University of Wisconsin.

Terence Wright is Reader in Media Studies at Luton College of Higher Education.

Introductory Essays:

Historical and Theoretical Perspectives

Introduction

Elizabeth Edwards

ANTHROPOLOGY AND PHOTOGRAPHY looks at the significance and relevance of still photography created and used in British anthropology from about 1860 until 1920. This photographic material is the evidence of the early years of what has now become the sub-discipline of visual anthropology, with all the paraphernalia of its practice: specialist interest groups, conferences and journals. Thus, while addressing historical materials, this volume is also very much a response to modern recording and interpretive problems.

The visual image is possibly the dominant mode of communication in the late twentieth century and its location, establishment and integration among traditional texts rightly exercises the minds of interested scholars and practitioners. As a result historical material is coming under similar scrutiny: there is an interest in exploring its possibilities and in examining its integration as evidence of the past among more traditional forms of transcribing and transmitting anthropological information. The process is not unique to anthropology, but there has perhaps been particular resistance in anthropology because of its uneasy relationship with history. Traditional functionalist thinking, especially in Britain, and later structuralism, were based in a generally static, synchronic and ahistorical view of culture (Tonkin et al. 1989:3–4). While an 'historical perspective' was sometimes appended, history as such has not been, for the most part, an integrated part of the subject, its research or its analysis (Thomas 1989:10).[1] Despite various attempts at reconciliation (for example Evans-Pritchard 1962; Lewis 1968) it is only in recent years that anthropologically minded historians and historically minded anthropologists have bridged the gap (for example Ladurie 1980; Cohn 1987; Thomas 1989).

There are, however, good reasons for considering historical photographic material. Although sophisticated techniques for integrated visual recording, both photography and film, have been developed as part of modern anthropological method (for example Hockings 1975; Collier & Collier 1986; Caldarola 1987), historical material is just beginning to receive detailed attention.[2] There are a number of reasons for this. First, the intentions and ideology of the early makers of these images were ostensibly radically different from those of the contemporary visual anthropologist. This has created a tension and inaccessibility such that the resulting images have tended to be dismissed in rather simplistic terms. New and very different cultural and epistemological contexts make it impossible, of course, to view the material with the same conviction with which it was viewed by contemporaries. However, by subjecting the material to historical analysis we can come closer to understanding how images were constructed and perceived in the past, and can suggest ways in which they might be accommodated in contemporary analysis. This type of exercise is fraught with difficulties, for interpreting photographic images is in many ways an extremely subjective process (Skinningsrud 1987:50). However, it is hoped that these essays will show that with careful and sensitive analysis which takes into account the positioning of productive and interpretive power, these images can make an important contribution to historical and anthropological understanding.

The second reason for taking the historical perspective is related to the first. The material belongs to a period of anthropological photography which has, in broad terms, a coherence in the themes reflected and in the ideology and intentions of the photographers. Up to about the second decade of this century photography was, broadly speaking, part of the collective endeavour in the production of anthropological data. As Poignant demonstrates in her essay, committees were established to coordinate and circulate material of anthropological interest and photographs were collected, swapped and archived for the common scientific good as part of the collection of 'raw data' from all over the world for analysis at the metropolitan centre. Indeed, the last decade of the nineteenth century saw a flurry of interest in systematic approaches to photography in the work of im Thurn (1893), Portman (1896) and Haddon (1899), the latter drawing on the considerable photographic experience of the Cambridge Torres Straits Expedition of 1898.

By about 1910 or 1920 various strands which had been developing over previous decades in Britain came together and brought about a major change of direction in anthropology (Urry 1972; Stocking 1983). First was the development of professional, institutionally based social anthropology and the establishment of individual fieldwork as its central practice. Related to this was the increasing emphasis on the detailed analysis of social organization, which was not necessarily conceived as being visible in photographic terms. Thirdly, and perhaps less quantifiable but equally related, was the crisis of confidence in the analogical view of photography, argued by Pinney in this volume (Sekula 1989:372). Lastly, good photographic equipment became available to the amateur. The net consequence was that photography became just another ancillary tool in the fieldworker's arsenal. Photographs became specific to given fieldwork projects and marginal to the process of explanation rather than becoming part of a centrally conceived resource; photography, a technique perceived as recording surface rather than depth, which

was the business of the anthropologist (Malinowski 1934:461).[3]

Finally, changes in the general perception of photographs themselves have influenced the perception of historical photographs. At the time when the photographs which are the subject of this book were taken photography was viewed largely as a simple recording truth-revealing mechanism. Today it is perceived as a form of mass communication and indeed of mass participation and manipulation. Its apparent integration with the general cultural furniture of the late twentieth century has undermined its potency — the image is all-pervasive yet devalued (Hunter 1988:200; Bourdieu 1965:41–9).[4]

This volume is primarily an exercise in source criticism, and despite strong historical content it makes no attempt to present a united chronological account. The majority of the photographs discussed in this volume come from the collections of the Royal Anthropological Institute (RAI) in London, for it was the Institute which initiated the project of which the book is the outcome. However, by way of contrast, material from elsewhere has been included where contributors particularly wished to explore points relevant to the interpretation of material held by the RAI, but which could not be illustrated specifically from that collection. Two essays, those by Prins and Jacknis, in fact explore material from non-British traditions but it has been decided to include them as they make a useful contribution to the balance of the studies, while Jacknis's essay on George Hunt explores an aspect notably lacking in the British tradition. Furthermore, whereas all the images in the RAI archives were used in the British tradition, they were not necessarily produced by it, so a certain eclecticism is inevitable. The photographs were not selected for any reason other than that they reflect, in some explicable way, the relationship between the photographer and the photographed and the creation and consumption of images. As in any 'selection', the final choice is an informed personal one of the contributors. Other selections, equally valid, could have been made, but in all likelihood the analyses would have highlighted similar themes even if the specific points of reference were different. Whereas they unavoidably reflect the interpretive preoccupations of the day, the analyses should in no way be seen as predetermined through selection.

The format adopted is one of short case-studies, in which specific images or short series of images are considered in detail, rather than the analysis of the corpus of a given photographer or the photographs of a particular geographical area. The advantage of this approach is that contributors have been encouraged to concentrate on 'reading the image', supported by contextual material, rather than use photographs to exemplify general statements. If this appears at moments disjointed, it is only a reflection of photography and indeed history, which are themselves fragmentary (a point to which I shall return). Here we are working towards placing those fragments within wider structures of anthropological and historical knowledge.

The scope of the essays has been purposely, and indeed necessarily, catholic in order to give an idea of the multitude of possible interpretive strategies. The case-studies are preceded by four orientating essays which provide a framework, ranging from the empirical to the post-modern, for thinking about the relationship between anthropology and photography. They are not intended as exhaustive or definitive statements but rather they examine a series of theoretical perspectives through which the critical possibilities are highlighted.

In their introductory essays both Pinney and Poignant examine, in different ways, the anthropological perception of photography — the quest for photographic realism and certainty, the authentication of the anthropological object, and indeed the ultimate failure, in positivist terms, of these endeavours. These considerations are closely related in social terms to psychological theories of visual perception, surveyed by Wright, which inform photographic 'seeing'. These themes, which recur in different forms, are perhaps the volume's leitmotifs, for evidential value cannot be assessed without reference to a more abstract approach to the nature of photography and its historical relations. Scherer picks up these themes in a more pragmatic context in her discussion of the photograph as document, where considerations of production and consumption come to the fore.

Finally, there are two essays — more subjective views of photography and anthropology. The first, from Faris, is specifically political, the other, from Mydin, more broadly 'cultural'. As such they are selective views, framed in ways not dissimilar to the processes which circumscribe photographs themselves, for as Barthes illustrates in *Camera Lucida* (1980), responses to photography can be as personal as its creation, but can nonetheless suggest different lines of enquiry.

This book does not pretend to offer an immutable truth on the nature of historical photographs in anthropology, nor does it, or can it, offer a key to a cultural decoding — for neither exists. Although content can be quantified and evaluated in a systematic way (for example Borchert 1981) a deeper, contextual understanding is dependent on a network of encoded structures in representation. In anthropological photography these embody expressions of beliefs, assumptions and classification relating on one hand to the nature of man, and on the other, to the nature of the anthropological exercise (what David Tomas has termed 'the representational culture' (1987:1)). 'Interpretation' can equally be an expression of presupposition based in historical distance and modern disciplinary preoccupations. Although strands of representation and interpretation can certainly be identified, they cannot be neatly disentangled, for they are largely contiguous. Meaning shifts in a delicate and possibly indeterminable balance between creator, consumer, and occasionally subject. There are no boundaries, no strictly defined limits to meaning but rather a pluralism of approach and meaning suggested by both Pinney and Mydin. While this leads to interpretive complexity, it points also to the richness of the photographic record in both theoretical and evidential modes.

Historical relations and contexts

Context is, as with any historical source, crucial to the interpretation of photographs. It is not necessarily always definitive, but certainly provocative and suggestive (Levine 1989:x). Relevant to all the images in this volume are two powerful interrelated contexts, one intellectual, the other political. Firstly, perception of the 'Other', most powerfully manifested in theories of race, and secondly the expansion and maintenance of European colonial power. The cultural circumscriptions included under the modern interpretive blanket 'Western perception of the "Other"' are central to the creation and consumption of photography in the second half of the nineteenth and the first half of the twentieth centuries. Whereas the definition and labelling of these past relations is a manifestation of late-twentieth-century interpretation, past relations nonetheless comprised beliefs, values and classifications which at one level expressed themselves physically and politically, and at another were imprinted to a greater or lesser extent in images (Pinney 1990). As such this body of cultural ideas is crucial to the historian's assessment and understanding of the material considered in this volume.

One cannot do more here than summarize a complex body of ideas which has been extensively examined elsewhere (for example Gould 1981; Stepan 1982; Stocking 1987). The second half of the nineteenth century and the early twentieth century saw major colonial expansion and consolidation by the European powers. This movement brought Europeans into contact with cultural difference on an unprecedented scale. Underwriting this appropriation of most of the non-European globe and structuring responses to it was a set of assumptions concerning the superiority of the white man and the duties and rights this superiority bestowed. In parallel there developed an increasing dominance of ideas which placed value on technological and scientific achievement. In combination with a re-emergence of a more evangelical religious stance, this created a climate in which Europeans and those of European extraction in the New World could assert their assumed superiority and justify this political position scientifically. The power relations of the colonial situation were not only those of overt oppression, but also of insidious, unequal relationships which permeated all facets of cultural confrontation. Indeed this confrontation included local power relations of the white-settled lands. While this relationship was in many cases tempered at an individual level with a genuine desire for a sympathetic understanding of peoples in human terms, such intentions were inevitably confronted by the intellectual difficulties of such an endeavour, and the unequal relationship was sustained through a controlling knowledge which appropriated the 'reality' of other cultures into ordered structure. Photography was in many ways symbolic of this relationship. It represented technological superiority harnessed to the delineation and control of the physical world, whether it be boundary surveys, engineering schemes to exploit natural resources, or the description and classification of the population (Birrel 1981; Monti 1987; Falconer 1990).

The emergence of scientific anthropology was a coincidental and not unrelated part of these processes, for it was through anthropology that the power of knowing was transformed into a rationalized, observed 'truth'. Central to our concerns here are ideas of race, for these are common both to the justification and rationalization of colonial domination and to the scientific study of anthropology, which in its turn gave the weight of scientific truth to assumptions of racial character. The encompassing intellectual model during the period was evolutionism, embracing ideas such as progress, regression, recapitulation and 'archaic' survival. Central to these models was the belief in the intrinsic relationship between the physical, biological nature of man and his cultural, moral and intellectual nature. Thus culture was seen as being biologically determined. Non-European races, who appeared less accomplished technologically, were interpreted as representing the 'childhood of mankind', a phase through which European man had passed in his prehistoric and proto-historic periods in a linear progression towards 'civilization'. Through

such theories science was seen to underwrite existing power relations and social structure and at the same time to offer the white man the key to his own history (Gould 1981; Kennedy 1976). Anthropology, despite its eclectic nature in its emerging years, adopted much of its method from the biological sciences, the stress being on observation, recording and classification. On this was erected a firm structure for positive, scientific, empirical knowledge. The facts observed, namely what was allowable as 'truth', were carefully constructed. In Britain the British Association for the Advancement of Science's small book *Notes and Queries on Anthropology* (which ran to six editions between 1874 and 1951) constructed an anthropological world-view, shaped by disciplinary preoccupations which in their turn shaped the representation of culture (Stocking 1987; Tomas 1987; Edwards 1989; Coote 1987; Urry 1972). This has important implications for anthropological photography, for it largely determined what was photographed and therefore which fragments were created, and thus determined which 'facts', intentionally recorded, become historical data.

By the end of the nineteenth century the more rigid models of evolutionary thinking began to dissolve in the light of shifts in scientific thinking. There was a general movement towards a more relativist view of culture and the beginnings of extended anthropological observation in the work of those such as Boas in the United States, Spencer in Australia and Rivers and Seligman in Britain.[5] However, the cultural assumptions of racial, cultural and moral superiority were thoroughly absorbed into and perpetuated by European social and political structures and continued as a powerful supporting system both to colonial relationships and to anthropological thinking (Stepan 1982; Stocking 1987; MacKenzie 1984, 1986).

History and the photographic moment

Many analyses of historical photographs have centred around the photograph as document, as Scherer's survey reveals.[6] In using photographs in anthropology one is attempting to interpret cultural differentness through the operation of the technology (material culture objects) of the interpreting culture. This paradox is, of course, by no means unique to the creation and application of photography and the problem in wider ethnographic practice has been much discussed in recent years (for example Clifford 1983; Marcus & Fischer 1986). It is the directness of photography, its apparent reality, that is beguiling. The problem is in essence an historical or ideological one rather than a photographic or photo-historical one, for photographs are never simply evidence — they are themselves historical (Tagg 1988:65) and the complexities of the contexts of the perception of 'reality' as manifested in the creation of image intersect with the complexities of the nature of the photograph itself in great diversity. The cultural circumscription which enabled an image and determined and validated the photographic moment expresses at least a cultural 'partiality', a conception of what is 'photographable' (Bourdieu 1965; Clifford & Marcus 1986:6). On one hand subordination to a collectivist stance of social and disciplinary control has been argued (Tagg 1988; Tomas 1987; Bourdieu 1965). Nevertheless, personal circumstance, vision and intention are present within this overall framework and exist in a reflexive relationship with wider cultural frameworks (Carr 1987:32–5; Lloyd 1986:280–4). As the case studies in the volume show, particularly Tayler's essay on im Thurn, Hockings's on Rivers and Macintyre and MacKenzie on three photographers in New Guinea, individual responses in the creation of images differ considerably and while one would not argue that the individual is anything but 'of his/her culture', the application of an over-collectivist view cannot accommodate the endless diversity in the photographic record.

Central to the nature of the photograph and its interpretive dilemmas is its insistent dislocation of time and space. Sontag, in comparing photography with film, highlights this: 'A still, which allows one to linger over a single moment as long as one likes, contradicts the very form of film, as a set of photographs that freezes moments in a life or society contradicts their form, which is process, a flow in time. The photographed world stands in the same essentially inaccurate relation to the real world as stills do to movies' (1978:81). The strength and weakness of the photograph are contained within this paradox. The photograph by its very nature is 'of' the past. Yet it is also of the present. It preserves a fragment of the past that is transported in apparent entirety to the present — the 'there-then' becomes the 'here-now' (Barthes 1977:44). The very immediacy and realism of the photograph set it apart from all other mechanisms through which we have access to the past. As Barthes states, what the photograph reproduces to infinity has occurred only once: 'the photograph mechanically repeats what could never be repeated existentially' (1984:4). The repetition of arrested time is powerful for it allows the viewer to linger, imagine or analyse in a way which would not be possible in the natural flow of time.[7] It could also be argued along these lines that the photograph perpetuates the past in an insidious fashion, denying time, presenting a timeless vision, an 'ethnographic present' and as such becomes another manifestation of anthropology's atemporal discourse (Fabian 1983).

Closely related to temporal dislocation in a photographic context is spatial dislocation. In the creation of an image, photographic technology frames the world. Camera angle, range of lens, type of film and the chosen moment of exposure further dictate and shape the moment. Exposure is an apposite term, for it carries not only technical meaning, but describes that moment 'exposed' to historical scrutiny. The photograph contains and constrains within its own boundaries, excluding all else, a microcosmic analogue of the framing of space which is knowledge (Szarkowski 1966; Ardener 1989:23). As such it becomes a metaphor of power, having the ability to appropriate and decontextualize time and space and those who exist within it. The photograph isolates a single incident in history. It can make the invisible visible, the unnoticed noticed,[8] the complex apparently simple and indeed vice versa (see for example Poignant 1989). Photography aided the reification process as creations of the mind became concrete, observed realities, recorded in the mechanical eye of the camera. Through photography, for example, the 'type', the abstract essence of human variation, was perceived to be an observable reality (Edwards 1990). The inevitable detail created by the photographer becomes a symbol for the whole and tempts the viewer to allow the specific to stand for generalities, becoming a symbol for wider truths,[9] at the risk of stereotyping and misrepresentation.

Yet despite such dislocations, the undeniable authority of the photograph is grounded in its temporal and physical presence. It was there. The photograph confirms the presence and observation of the photographer and 'truth' of his account. As such, a photograph is an analogue of seen 'reality', for what was in front of the camera existed (Malmsheimer 1987:21). That type of 'bald' realism is not in question. The problem of evidential force is ultimately historical not existential (Tagg 1988:5) for, as Heider has pointed out, there are any number of 'truths' in anthropology, all valid in certain contexts and many capable of visual expression (1976:65); what is to be assessed and evaluated in using historical photographs (or indeed any images) is the ratio between fact and social input (Stott 1973:13; Gould 1981:22; Lyman 1982). The 'real' or the 'natural' or 'authentic', and the elements selected to represent that reality, depend on the status of the objects concerned within the overall classification of knowledge and the representation of those objects in a way which will be understood as 'real' by the viewer.

If then the fragmentary nature of photography presents theoretical problems, at an evidential level the problem has a certain familiarity. All history is constructed of selected fragments, a process which starts with event-registration and continues with continual retrospective assessment and reworking. Likewise, in anthropology 'significant' structures of a culture are observed, the fragments of informants recorded and the final work born of synthesis and then generalization; the fragments become moulded to a unifying account of 'culture'. So, in photography, the specific moment becomes representative of the whole and the general.

Representation and interpretation

The term 'still' photograph both describes the nature of the photograph exactly and at the same time implies a misrepresentation of its nature. While the content is indeed 'still', chemically fixed on paper, its interpretation is not. As with other forms of graphic image, viewers attribute new meaning through their own cultural experience and as such a photograph is in some ways submissive. Yet photographs are not totally passive. They suggest meaning through the way in which they are structured, for representational form makes an image accessible and comprehensible to the mind, informing and informed by a whole hidden corpus of knowledge that is called on through the signifiers in the image (Barthes 1977:36–7; Arnheim 1974:155–6; Sekula 1975; Connerton 1989:11–12). It has been argued that the photograph is an analogue of physical reality and that the assigning of meaning, interpretation, is a secondary activity. However, it may be more useful to consider the photograph as an analogue of visual experience, and as such, a culturally based ordering of the world in which the signifier and the signified are read at one and the same time. Yet the links between signifier and signified are in many ways arbitrary, codes are shifting and impermanent, so that new connections can be made and reinterpretation becomes a valid exercise. Contiguous with meaning is the 'expectation' which photography brings — the photograph itself becomes a signifier. If photography is perceived as 'reality' then modes of representation will themselves enhance that 'reality' — in other words the photograph is perceived as 'real' or 'true' because that is what the viewer *expects* to see: 'this is how it should be' becomes 'this is how it is/was'.

The patterns of representation are not easy to quantify or categorize. The technology of photography itself dates from the second quarter of the nineteenth century, but, as Wright outlines in his essay, the cultural conditions which made possible the acceptance of a photograph's 'optical knowledge' have a much longer pedigree. Photographic representation was firmly based in established pre-photographic ways of seeing (Galassi 1981). Documentary or record illustrations such as those of the 'great voyages' were viewed as something separate from 'Art' (Smith 1960; Ivins 1980:218; Seiberling 1986:47–8; Honour 1988:14), yet there is a continuity of vision, and anthropological photography should be viewed as a continuation of this illustrative tradition both in functional and representational terms. While traditional aesthetic devices for the representation of the 'Other' can be found in both figure and landscape photography (for example Lee 1985), anthropology effectively developed its own modes of representation as it attempted to use photography in a scientifically definable way (Edwards 1988, 1990; Pinney and Poignant, this volume). For example, anthropometric systems such as those advocated by Lamprey and Huxley and discussed in this volume by Spencer (Plates 60–1) were absorbed into a more general 'realist' aesthetic, and are alluded to not only in 'portrait types' (Plates 1–2) but also in photographs 'showing' or 'displaying' culture (Plate 3). More importantly they influenced the way of seeing such photographs. In a two-way process, material, itself influenced by anthropological perceptions, was absorbed into the scientific domain as being of 'anthropological interest'. (Banta & Hinsley 1986; Edwards 1988, 1990; Poignant, this volume).

Rochelle Kolodny (1978) has suggested three interconnecting models which have acted in the structuring of reality in images and although in some ways problematic, they provide at least a useful starting point in the argument. Each of the three models, which are also explanatory systems, can be broken down into four facets: assumptions about the nature of the world as defined by the role of the images, the aspects of the creating culture to which the images connect, the ideological frameworks which those images uphold and finally the function of each model or framework. The models are first 'romanticism',[10] which is concerned with the world of essences. This is translated into 'Art' and upheld by an ideology of idealism which functions as a redemptive ideology. Second is 'realism', which is concerned with the world of facts. In this model empirical reality informs science within a positivist or empirical ideology. This model has an analogous function — 'this is how it is' — a 'true' representation. Finally there is the 'documentary mode', which is concerned with the world of action in an 'inspirational'

markers of 'primitiveness' and thus of cultural distance. Pose is also used in this way. For example, the oppositional connotation of three young women posed in the western iconographical convention of the 'Three Graces' in the mode of Botticelli, (I have seen examples from Australia, South America and southern Africa) or the extensive range of photographic images derived from the exotic conventions of orientalist painting and Western male erotic fantasy (Alloula 1987; Graham-Brown 1988) (Plates 4–5). Likewise, forms and contexts of action can operate as cultural markers, for example dance as a display of the 'primitive', as suggested in Vansina's examination of photographs from the Torday expedition, and by the Western photographers' fascination with Hopi dance ceremonies (Fleming & Luskey 1986:145).

An aesthetic response does not, of course, invalidate the anthropological record (as Mead pointed out, it is pleasant to have the combination of aesthetic sensitivity and scientific fidelity (1975:5)) but the coexistence of the scientific and aesthetic begs the question of how one can establish the ratio between them. These problems are approached in different ways by Tayler and Macintyre & MacKenzie, and on a more conjectural level of associational aesthetics by

2. Portrait. Tibetan woman from Tashi-Lumpo, c.1890. Photograph by P.A. Johnston and T. Hoffman. (RAI 197)

1. Portrait. Big Mouth Hawk, Southern Arapaho, 1874. Photograph by Alexander Gardner. (RAI 856)

way. It relates to social science and technology, implying social or political comment.

While these models may be distinguished analytically, in practical terms the position is more complex. It is often the case that in the creation of a particular image more than one model may apply. Furthermore, a photograph may be interpreted according to different models at different times as new perspectives are brought to it.[11] The 'romantic' mode is perhaps most easily recognized because it is linked to a strongly aesthetic response and to notions of the exotic. For example, Macintyre & MacKenzie and Dippie discuss examples of culture represented through an aestheticizing grid. Questions of aesthetic and iconographical construction are indeed central to a number of papers, being important and sometimes unacknowledged components in visual representation in anthropology. Pinney discusses photographs of caste where items of material culture are used as

3. Displaying culture. Iban woman weaving, Sarawak, *c.*1890–1900. Photograph by Charles Hose. (RAI 11037)

Pinney and Hockings. All are looking at ways in which the structuring of the content operates to produce a range of signifiers, which position the subject in broader ideologies.

Kolodny's 'realist' and 'documentary' modes are more closely related and perhaps in the final analysis come down to intention or to the ideology which underlies the function. For example, is a photograph of a group of people in European clothing, standing in front of a decrepit traditional house, a true representation of their existence (realist), or a comment on acculturation and poor housing conditions (documentary), or indeed, by association, a comment on the corruption and passing of traditional ways (romanticism) (see for example Plate 6)? For the 'romanticist' aesthetic also comes into play in the 'realist' and 'documentary' modes, not only in the iconographical sense but also at the level of essences. It could be argued that photography such as that discussed by Blackman, Jacknis and Edwards, which was conceived as 'salvage ethnography', documenting traditional culture in the face of irreversible change,

is not necessarily purely 'documentary'. It evokes feelings of nostalgia at the passing of cultures and an aestheticized 'nobility' which transcends the 'realist' or 'documentary' mode. This may even be argued for images created in a context of overt appropriation such as the Tasmanian photographs discussed by Rae-Ellis. At this point we appear to have come full circle back to questions of fragmentation, for the detail comes to stand for general truths which are perhaps external to the dynamics of the image itself.

If the complexity of photographic meaning makes precise categorization impracticable, one can perhaps accept a simple parallel model of positive and negative images which can be used, through selected and motivated representation, to manipulate meaning.[12] The origin of such themes is to be found as visual expressions of literary and philosophical devices rather than as observed reality, but when considered in conjunction with the realist nature of the photographic image and the reifying tendencies of scientific thought these conventions take on a powerful stereotypical force. They can be seen clearly mani-

4. Samoan woman, *c.*1890. (RAI 10747)

give detailed documentation in a way which gives authority to the main body of the text. Their suggestion of personal encounter frees the subject from a categorization imposed by the generalizing tendencies of both photography and anthropological writing. Either way, the caption is being used to position the photograph and processes of interpretation are controlled through the interaction of image and text (Hunter 1988:130–42). Text may also have a narrative role, thus an amplifying function. Photographs themselves have no true narrative in the classical literary definition; they cannot forward the action, for this requires a sequence of time (Metz 1974:18–21). While they can have a form of coherence, even a series of photographs requires language or text to fill in the gaps in the narrative. Active participation in the narrative is thus not inherent in the photograph, depending rather on its relationship with other photographs or texts as Prins's essay demonstrates.

All these attributes of the photograph influence its interpretation. Nevertheless, because the photograph is assumed to be unmediated and analogical, there is a danger in photographic analysis that the retrospective construction of intention, rather than substantiable analysis, will be used to legitimate the interpretive

5. Rodiya girls, Sri Lanka, *c.*1890. (RAI 5870)

fested in nineteenth-century representations. If these stereotypical representations seem extreme (Plate 7) they are still active, though often expressed in more subtle and insidious forms (Bhabha 1983; Pinney 1989; Mydin, this volume).

The meaning of photographs can, of course, be guided or suggested by text, which further enmeshes them in a particular context. This is especially pertinent in the anthropological context, for it is often through text that an image is finally legitimated within the scientific and disciplinary domain. For example, it is through the juxtaposition of a specific representational mode and caption that the 'types' are established or that an individual can become a generality. Generalizing captions such as 'A Typical Native', 'A Native Belle', 'A Warrior' or even 'Native using Fire-Stick' function in this way. A more sophisticated version is the scene-setting generality of the 'classic' ethnographic approach: for example 'Youth' (the frontispiece of Evans-Pritchard *Nuer Religion*, 1956) or 'Group by ashes of cattle camp fire' (Plate 1b, in Buxton *Chiefs and Strangers*, 1967). Conversely, a caption can give immediacy and assurance to photography: for example in Firth *We, the Tikopia*, where captions to the photographs name individuals and

6. Swampy Cree people at Cross Lake, Manitoba, Canada, *c*.1925. "Woman on left wearing rabbit skin — these are now only used as covers not as robes but she put it on for the occasion". Photograph by Dr Stone. (Courtesy of Pitt Rivers Museum, University of Oxford. PRM.BB.AI.85)

appropriation of the image into a specific discourse (Krauss 1985:313). Thus visual analysis, as opposed to mere interpretation, is dependent on being able to assess and evaluate contextual possibilities rather than on an act of simple translation according to a 'presentist' stance (Clifford 1986:120; Asad 1986: 150–2). But although 'meaning' may theoretically be open-ended, it is also historically and culturally determined. From the moment of its creation the photograph will 'mean' something, reflecting the photographer's intention. While this meaning may remain with it, or may be recoverable through historical research, it becomes stratified (the archaeological metaphor is intentional) beneath other meanings attributed to the image. These may be in complete opposition to the photographer's intention since different bodies of knowledge are deemed significant as the photograph is used to express different preoccupations (Dolby 1979).[13] Ideas extraneous to the picture itself thus give meaning to it, both for its original audience and for subsequent generations of interpreters.

Initially, the colonial context in which both anthropology and photography functioned has been the primary contextual mode. However, it is not improbable that other, more complex contexts for analysis will emerge (or are indeed already emerging) especially as formerly colonized peoples reassert their power and repossess their own histories. It is often the very tensions in a photograph, the very circumstance of its creation which are of historical significance and these abstract qualities are documents in themselves. Colonial or anthropological presence is, in many of the photographs discussed in this volume, conspicuous by its absence in visual terms,[14] suggesting an unmediated record. As has been suggested also, the photograph invokes a timelessness. But the very fact that people are photographed is part of their history, their changing existence in a broadening world. Photographs can, with close contextual examination, be read as broad texts which reveal these 'hidden histories' rather than as individual descriptive documents. Again, much depends on the questions asked, but on examination so much appears to contradict the received, perhaps the anthropological, version of these photographs that the uncovering of 'hidden history' must surely be one of the major analytical and interpretive aims in the modern consideration of the photographs of the period under discussion. It is certainly a theme which appears in some form in almost every essay in the book.

A number of essays take a forensic approach to the internal evidence of the photograph, for it is through contextualized forensic reading that 'hidden history' is revealed. Prins establishes a photographic narrative in order to elucidate other incomplete historical narratives; Vansina and Edwards examine the way in which the colonial sub-text operates in ostensibly anthropological work; Bradford suggests ways in which the subject may have used the photographic confrontation. Indeed some photographs, such as those discussed by Pankhurst and Binney, have been repositioned, removed from the traditional anthropological paradigm, and returned to a more historically realist position, declassified in anthropological terms, and relocated in differently orientated historical discourses. Further, Hamouda shows how material created with ethnographic intent and published as such can be repositioned and reinterpreted outside the anthropological frame to elucidate other histories, in this case the oral tradition of the Auresian people in Algeria. Likewise Salmond's essay on the Te Tokanga-nui-a-noho meeting-house suggests the power of 'hidden histories' revealed, the content of the image assuming a quality of historical symbolism.

We might be led to ask in the end what is it that actually makes a photograph anthropological. At its simplest an anthropological photograph is any photograph from which an anthropologist could gain useful, meaningful visual information. The defining essence of an anthropological photograph is not the subject-matter as such, but the consumer's classification of that knowledge or 'reality' which the photograph appears to convey. Material can move in and out of the anthropological sphere[15] and photographs which were not created with anthropological intent or specifically informed by ethnographic understanding may nevertheless be appropriated to anthropological ends. But definitions of what constitutes visual anthropological information will alter according to changing perceptions of scientific objectivity and accuracy (historical photographic material has been overlooked for just this reason) (Heider 1976).[16]

The photographs in this volume span what might be described both as 'public' and 'private' expressions which to some extent parallel a scientific/non-scientific opposition. The 'public', 'scientific' record was intended to inform disciplinary concerns directly and a number of essays concern themselves with the work of such photographers as E.H. Man, Everard im

7. The extremes of stereotype. 'Fijian cannibals', c.1890. Photograph by T. Andrew. (RAI 34758)

Thurn, Emil Torday or Edgar Thurston, who were working specifically to produce anthropological data. The selection of subject and mode of representation was ostensibly made to record, document and describe within the boundaries of certain perceived standards of logical rigour and observational skill.

On the other hand there is a larger, more amorphous group which present a more 'private' record — a personal response and visual expression, created for personal interest, such as Whitfield's photographs discussed by Faris. There is also an intermediate group, 'public' photographs from other spheres — missions, colonial administrations, professional commercial photography — which were intended to communicate in some specific 'public' framework but were without anthropological intent. Again these are well represented in the volume: photographs such as the enigma of the image of the Burmese pilgrims discussed by Seneviratne, or the more politically motivated images discussed by Pankhurst and Binney. Such apparently marginal material might be viewed as being of 'anthropological interest' even if it is not perceived as being of 'anthropological intent'. It contains important aspects of lived experience which must be of interest to the anthropologist and therefore should not be ignored. Binney's comments on the Māori photographs she discusses could be usefully extended to all such material; they 'are "anthropological" in the correct sense: they are records of men in their time . . .'.

Finally, it should be remembered that although the images were collected as being of 'anthropological interest', their circulation was by no means restricted to anthropological circles. As both Street and Poignant show, scientific anthropology had popular manifestations which underlined its stereo-typing tendencies. Vansina also suggests, in a different context, ways in which photographers adapted their subject-matter and modes of representation to popular expectations. Indeed a number of the images in the RAI collection, such as im Thurn's photographs discussed by Tayler or some of the Torday Expedition material discussed by Vansina, also survive as early lantern slides. Their role in the wider dissemination of photographic images is obvious.

To move beyond a narrow disciplinary definition of anthropological photography is not without its problems. It presents a challenge of interpretation, for it requires an understanding of visual information which goes beyond the quest for the scientific do-cument to an appreciation of the broader historical relationships which are beginning to be drawn into the anthropological domain.[17]

There are strong visualist metaphors in anthro-pology—'observing', 'seeing', 'reading' — and there is the obvious analogy between the anthropologist and camera as external observer and recorder (Fabian 1983:107; Clifford 1986:11). Yet visual material itself has remained marginal. The anthropological tradition has been to look *into* culture and society whereas photographs have been looked *at*. The aim of this volume is to suggest ways in which one can look *into* photographs and through them into culture, both the culture portrayed and the representing culture. Some of the interpretive possibilities of historical photo-graphs in anthropology are explored: what is revealed is not only 'anthropology' but a reflexive history. In analyzing and trying to understand how people in the past patterned their world we may perhaps see how their patterns can be constructively integrated with our histories. In doing this we may then better appreciate how we pattern our own world and how we might illuminate histories which are yet to be articulated.

ACKNOWLEDGEMENTS

I should like to thank Roslyn Poignant, Jonathan Benthall, Marilyn Strathern and Patti Langton for their encouragement and invaluable com-ments on many aspects of this paper. My particular thanks are due to Frances and Howard Morphy for their constructive criticism and unfailing support throughout the numerous drafts.

NOTES

1 There have, of course, been exceptions: for example the work of Melville Herskovits (1938) and Hilda Kuper (1984); for a useful review of the field see Krech (1991). The main historical pre-occupation in anthropology has been with the history and his-toriography of the discipline itself (cf. Lowie 1937; Voget 1975; Stocking 1983, 1987; Kuper 1973; Evans-Pritchard 1981).

2 There have been studies of some national traditions: for example Banta & Hinsley (1986) and Theye (1989) and there is a growing corpus of journal literature.

3 Again there are exceptions, notably Bateson and Mead's famous intensive project in Bali in 1936–8 (1942). This study, a full discussion of which is beyond the scope of the volume, made photography (including film) the central method of field recording and thus subsequent analysis depended upon it. Despite the project's ambitious scale and innovative nature it had limited impact at the time and even to date, when the importance of the project has been truly recognized, it has not been emulated with quite such insight (Brigard 1975:26–7; Jacknis 1989).

4 Furthermore it might be argued that changing perceptions of historical photographs, even within academic study, have been influenced by the active interest of collectors and the art market in recent decades. 'Value' attributed in informational terms is not unrelated to 'value' in commercial terms. Related to this is a concept of 'heritage', encompassing and elevating an increasing number of manifestations of 'the past'.

5 This period was an important watershed in the use of photo-graphy in anthropology. All these anthropologists made extensive use of photography, but inter-pretive difficulties were already emerging (Jacknis 1984; Mul-vaney 1982; Pinney, this volume).

6 Scherer's survey of the photo-graph as document draws largely on American work on American traditions, for there has been a more active and extensive interest in historical photographic material in this field. However, the principles of the argument have more universal applications.

7 This feature of photography actually made possible a project such as Bateson and Mead's.

8 There are various techniques through which photography re-veals the unseen and unnoticed: shutter speeds, use of flash, infrared photography, micro-scopic photography etc.

9 This in many ways has always been the *sine qua non* of docu-mentary photography.

10 Kolodny actually uses the term 'Primitivism' but, as Peterson has pointed out (1985:165), to sustain this usage might be construed as ethnocentric. He suggests 'Romanticism' as a preferred alternative.

11 Photographs can change cat-egories and meanings through use, aestheticized through the context of interpretation: for

example, anthropometric photographs taken according to Lamprey's and Huxley's systems were recently included in the photographic exhibition *Behold the Man: the Male Nude in Photography* (Foster 1988).

12 Positive and negative images in some ways parallel earlier aesthetic themes of the 'noble savage' and the 'barbarous primitive', what Smith has termed 'hard' and 'soft' primitivism (1960:6–7).

13 Recent material can, of course, be subjected to scrutiny with equally valuable effect. Indeed modern material presents major interpretive challenges as modern equipment and filmic techniques and styles make mediation even less apparent, thus disguising the power relations further.

14 As Leach has pointed out (1989–90:41), the only two European items to appear in Malinowski's published photographs are the ethnographer's tent and his typewriter.

15 For example, the establishing of the anthropological discipline in the nineteenth century involved distancing itself from other forms of writing about the 'Other' such as travel writing (Pratt 1986:35). This can be paralleled in photography, where travel photography, although described in the photographic journals as being of 'ethnological interest' was not, on the whole, collected by anthropologists, and it is barely represented in the major anthropological archives in Britain. However, much of this material does contain material which would now be considered to be valid visual data in some aspect of anthropology or ethnohistory.

16 These judgements were institutionalized through the inclusion of the photographs in 'anthropological' archives, where they are arranged and arrayed in yet finer gradations of classification, which tended to predetermine the researcher's approach to them and to some extent prestructure their reading.

17 Christraud Geary's recent examination of the photographic record of Bamum, Cameroon, points to the riches of this approach (1988).

REFERENCES

Alloula, M. 1987. *The Colonial Harem.* Manchester: University Press.

Ardener, E. 1989. 'The Construction of History, Vestiges of Creation'. In E. Tonkin, M. Macdonald & M. Chapman (eds.) *History and Ethnicity* 22–33. London: Tavistock.

Arnheim, R. 1974. On the Nature of Photography. *Critical Inquiry* 1:149–61.

Asad, T. 1986. 'The Concept of Cultural Translation in British Social Anthropology'. In J. Clifford & G.E. Marcus (eds.) Writing Culture. 141–164. Berkeley: University of California Press.

Banta, M. & Hinsley, C. 1986. *From Site to Sight: Anthropology, Photography and the Power of Imagery.* Cambridge, Mass.: Peabody Museum Press.

Barthes, R. 1977. 'The Photographic Message'. In R. Barthes *Image Music Text.* Trans. S. Heath. London: Fontana.

— 1977. 'The Rhetoric of Image'. In R. Barthes *Image Music Text*, trans. S. Heath. London: Fontana.

— 1984 (1980). *Camera Lucida.* Trans. R. Howard. London: Fontana.

Bateson, G. & Mead, M. 1942. The *Balinese Character: A Photographic Analysis.* New York Academy of Sciences, Special Publications 2. New York: New York Academy of Sciences.

Bhabha, Homi K. 1983. The Other Question: the Stereotype and Colonial Discourse. *Screen* 24(6): 18–36.

Birrel, A. 1981. Survey Photography in British Columbia 1858–1900. BC *Studies* 52:39–60.

Borchert, J. 1981. Analysis of Historical Photographs: a method and a case study. *Studies in Visual Communication* 7(4):30–59.

Bourdieu, P. 1965. *Un Art Moyen, Essai sur les usages sociaux de la Photographie.* Paris: Editions de Minuit.

Brigard, E. de 1975. 'The History of Ethnographic Film'. In P. Hockings (ed.) *Principles of Visual Anthropology* 13–43. The Hague: Mouton.

Buxton, J. 1967. *Chiefs and Strangers.* Oxford: Clarendon Press.

Caldarola, V. 1987. 'The generation of primary Photographic Data in Ethnographic Fieldwork and the problem of objectivity'. In M. Taureg & J. Ruby (eds.) *Visual Explorations of the World* 217–39. Aachen: Edition Heredot.

Carr, E.H. 1987. *What is History?* 2nd edn. Harmondsworth: Penguin.

Clifford, J. 1983. On Ethnographic Authority. *Representations* (2):118–46.

— 1986. 'On Ethnographic Allegory'. In J. Clifford and G.E. Marcus (eds.) *Writing Culture.* 98–121. Berkeley: University of California Press.

Clifford, J. & Marcus, G.E. (eds.) 1986. *Writing Culture.* Berkeley: University of California Press.

Cohn, B.S. 1987. *An Anthropologist among the Historians and Other Essays.* Oxford: University Press.

Collier, J. & Collier, M. 1986. *Visual Anthropology.* rev. edn. Albuquerque: University of New Mexico Press.

Connerton, P. 1989. *How Societies Remember.* Cambridge: University Press.

Coote, J. 1987. *Notes and Queries* and Social Interrelations. *Journal of the Anthropological Society of Oxford* 18(3):255–72.

Dolby, R.A. 1979. 'Reflections on Deviant Science'. In R. Wallis (ed.) *On the Margins of Science: The Social Construction of Rejected Knowledge.* Sociological Review Monograph 27. Keele: University Press.

Edwards, E. 1988. 'Representation and Reality: Science and the Visual Image'. In H. Morphy & E. Edwards (eds.) *Australia in Oxford* 27–45. Oxford: Pitt Rivers Museum.

— 1989. Images of the Andamans. *Journal of the Museum of Ethnography* 1:71–78.

— 1990. 'Photographic Types': The Pursuit of Method. *Visual Anthropology* 3(2–3):235–58.

Evans-Pritchard, E. 1956. *Nuer Religion.* Oxford: University Press.

— 1962. 'Anthropology and History'. In Evans-Pritchard *Essays in Social Anthropology.* London: Faber & Faber.

— 1981. *A History of Anthropological Theory*, ed. A. Singer. London: Faber and Faber.

Fabian, J. 1983. *Time and the Other: how anthropology makes its object.* New York: Columbia University Press.

Falconer, J. 1990. 'Photography in nineteenth century India'. In C.

Bayley (ed.) *The Raj: India and the British 1600–1947.* 264–77. London: National Portrait Gallery.

Firth, R. 1936. *We, The Tikopia.* London: Allen & Unwin.

Fleming, P. Richardson and Luskey, J. 1986. *The North American Indian in Early Photographs.* New York: Harper and Row.

Foster, A. 1988. *Behold the Man: the Male Nude in Photography.* Edinburgh: Stills Gallery.

Galassi, P. 1981. *Before Photography: Painting and the Invention of Photography.* New York: Museum of Modern Art.

Geary, C. 1988. *Images of Bamum.* Washington: Smithsonian Institution Press.

Gould, S.J. 1981. *The Mismeasure of Man.* New York: W.W. Norton & Co.

Graham-Brown, S. 1988. *Images of Women: the Portrayal of Women in Photography of the Middle East 1860–1950.* London: Quartet Books.

Haddon, A.C. 1899. 'Photography'. In BAAS *Notes and Queries* 235–40. London: Anthropological Institute.

Heider, K. 1976. *Ethnographic Film.* Austin: University of Texas Press.

Herskovits, M.J. 1938. *Acculturation: a study of culture contact.* New York: J.J. Augustin Publ.

Hockings, P. (ed.) 1975. *The Principles of Visual Anthropology.* The Hague: Mouton.

Honour, H. 1988. *The Black in Western Art.* 2 vols. New Haven: Yale University Press.

Hunter, J. 1988. *Image and Text.* Harvard: University Press.

im Thurn, E. 1893. Anthropological Uses of the Camera. *Journal of the Anthropological Institute* 22:184–203.

Ivins, W.M. 1980. 'New Reports and New Vision: The Nineteenth Century'. In A. Trachtenberg (ed.) *Classic essays on photography* 217–36. New Haven: Leete's Island Books.

Jacknis, I. 1984. Franz Boas and Photography. *Studies in Visual Communication* 10(1):2–60.

— 1989. Margaret Mead and Gregory Bateson in Bali: Their use of photography and film. *Cultural Anthropology* 3(2):160–77.

Kennedy, K. 1976. *Human Variation in Space and Time.* Dubuque: Wm. C. Brown Co.

Kolodny, R. 1978. *Towards an Anthropology of Photography: Frameworks for Analysis.* MA thesis, Dept. of Anthropology, McGill University.

Krauss, R. 1982. Photography's Discursive Spaces: Landscape/View. *Art Journal* (Winter):311–19.

Krech, S. III. 1991. The State of Ethnohistory. *Annual Review of Anthropology* 20:345–75.

Kuper, A. 1973. *Anthropologists and Anthropology.* London: Allen Lane.

Kuper, H. 1984. Function History Biography. Reflections on Fifty Years in British Anthropological Tradition. *History of Anthropology* 2:192–213.

Ladurie, E. Le Roy 1980 (1978). *Montaillou.* Trans. B. Bray. Harmondsworth: Penguin.

Leach, E. 1990. Masquerade: The Presentation of the Self in Holy-Day Life. *Cambridge Anthropology* 13(3):47–69.

Lee, S.C. 1985. *John Thomson: a photographic vision of the Far East 1860–1872,* unpublished M.Litt. thesis, University of Oxford.

Levine, R.M. 1989. *Images of History: Nineteenth and Early Twentieth Century Latin American Photographs as Documents.* Durham, N.C.: Duke University Press.

Lewis, I.M. (ed.) 1968. *History and Social Anthropology* ASA Monograph 7. London: Tavistock.

Lloyd, C. 1986. *Explanation in Social History.* Oxford: Blackwell.

Lowie, R. 1937. *History of Ethnological Theory.* New York: Holt, Rinehart and Winston.

Lyman, C. 1982. *The Vanishing Race and Other Illusions: Photographs of Indians by Edward S. Curtis.* Washington: Smithsonian Institution Press.

Mackenzie, J. 1984. *Propaganda and Empire.* Manchester: University Press.

— (ed.) 1986. *Imperialism and Popular Culture.* Manchester: University Press.

Malinowski, B. 1934. *Coral Gardens and their Magic.* London: George Allen & Unwin.

Malmsheimer, L. 1987. Photographic Analysis as Ethnohistory. *Visual Anthropology* 1(1):21–36.

Marcus, G.E. & Fischer, M.J.J. 1986. *Anthropology as Cultural Critique.* Chicago: University Press.

Mead, M. 1975. 'Visual Anthropology in a Discipline of Words'. In P. Hockings (ed.) *Principles of Visual Anthropology* 3–10. The Hague: Mouton.

Metz, C. 1974. *Film Language: A Semiotics of the Cinema.* New York: Oxford University Press.

Monti, N. 1987. *Africa Then.* London: Thames & Hudson.

Mulvaney, J. & G. Walker 1982. *The Aboriginal Photographs of Baldwin Spencer.* South Yarra: John Currey O'Neil Publ.

Peterson, N. 1985. 'The Popular Image'. In I. Donaldson & T. Donaldson (eds.) *Seeing the First Australians* 164–180. Sydney: George Allen & Unwin.

Pinney, C. 1989. Other people's Bodies, Lives, Histories? Ethical Issues in the Use of a Photographic Archive. *Journal of Museum Ethnography* 1:57–68.

— 1990. 'Colonial Anthropology in the "Laboratory of Mankind"'. In C. Bayley (ed.) *The Raj: India and the British 1600–1947,* 252–63. London: National Portrait Gallery.

Poignant, R. 1989. Getting the Picture: Axel Poignant's photographic record of a threatened fight in Arnhem Land. *Journal of Museum Ethnography* 1:15–22.

Portman, M.V. 1896. Photography for Anthropologists. *Journal of the Anthropological Institute,* 25:75–85.

Pratt, M.L. 1986. 'Fieldwork in Commonplaces'. In J. Clifford and G.E. Marcus (eds.) *Writing Culture.* Berkeley: University of California Press.

Seiberling, G. 1986. *Amateurs, Photography and the Mid-Victorian Imagination.* Chicago: University Press.

Sekula, A. 1975. On the Invention of Photographic Meaning. *Artforum* 3:36–45.

— 1989. 'The Body and the Archive'. In R. Bolton (ed.) *The Contest of Meaning: Critical Histories of Photography.* Cambridge, Mass.: MIT Press.

Skinningsrud, T. 1987. Anthropological Films and the Myth of Scientific Truths. *Visual Anthropology* 1(1), 47–53.

Smith, B. 1960. *European Vision and the South Pacific 1768–1850.* London: Oxford University Press.

Sontag, S. 1978. *On Photography.* Harmondsworth: Penguin.

Stepan, N. 1982. *The Idea of Race in Science: Great Britain 1800–1960.* London: Macmillan.

Stocking, G. 1983. The Ethnographer's Magic. Fieldwork in British Anthropology from Tylor to Malinowski. *History of Anthropology* 1:70–120.

— 1987. *Victorian Anthropology*. New York: Free Press.

Szarkowski, J. 1966. *The Photographer's Eye*. New York: MOMA.

Stott, W. 1973. *Documentary Expression and Thirties America*. London: Oxford University Press.

Tagg, J. 1988. *The Burden of Representation: Essays on Photographies and Histories*. London: Macmillan Education.

Theye, T. (ed.) 1989. *Der geraubte Schatten*. Munich: Münchner Stadtmuseum.

Thomas, N. 1989. *Out of Time: History and Evolution in Anthropological Discourse*. Cambridge: University Press.

Tomas, D. 1987. *An Ethnography of the Eye*. Unpublished Ph.D. thesis, McGill University.

Tonkin, E., Macdonald, M. & Chapman, M. (eds.) 1989. *History and Ethnicity*, ASA Monograph 27. London: Routledge.

Urry, J. 1972. *Notes and Queries on Anthropology* and the Development of Field Methods in British Anthropology. *Proceedings of the RAI* 1972:45–57.

Voget, F. 1975. *A History of Ethnology*. New York: Holt, Rinehart and Winston.

Photography: Theories of Realism and Convention

Terence Wright

The language of 'reality' . . . may be the most beautiful and powerful but certainly it must in any case be about the heaviest of all languages. (Agee & Evans 1941:236)

WHILE THERE IS an element of contradiction in James Agee's view of photography as 'the language of "reality"', his choice of phrase could well be regarded as symptomatic of a polarization in photographic theory. On the one hand, the *reality* of the photograph is considered largely unproblematic, allowing 'transparent' access to subject-matter; on the other, the *language* of the image is regarded as conventional, highly constructed, its understanding determined by Western culture.

For instance, in the early days of ethnographic photography, reacting against rigid anthropometric formulations, Everard im Thurn (1893:200) argued for a fairly uncomplicated photographic realism: 'the camera . . . may be utilised by the traveller with anthropological tastes to very great advantage in securing, for exhibition to those of similar tastes who are not lucky enough to be able to travel and see for themselves, accurate records of the appearance, life, and habits of the primitive folk visited' (Plate 8).

More recently Segall, Campbell & Herskovits (1966:33) have taken the other course, in which there is nothing at all realistic about the photographic image: 'one can regard the photograph as we use it as an arbitrary linguistic convention not shared by all peoples'.

But from the outset, few would deny that photographs usually do appear extremely realistic and we can put forward two quite convincing reasons why this should be. The first of these is *instrumentality*: the authenticity of the photograph based on causal connection, by which the photograph is directly 'transcribed' from Nature. Secondly, the 'instrument' itself, the camera, is frequently called on to explain the mechanics of visual perception. Here, Sherrington (1937–8:105) has been of major influence: 'the likeness to an optical camera is plain beyond seeking. . . . The eye-ball is a little camera'. This analogy gained its strength not only from the similarities of physical structure and optical function of both eye and camera, but also from observations that the camera produces an image that approximates to that which occurs in the eye.

It might seem obvious that these two factors are closely related, yet it had not always been so. The *camera obscura* (Plate 9) had been used in astronomical studies around 1000 AD by Ibn Al-Haitham (Alhazen), who had also evolved a comprehensive theory of vision in which he described the convergence of light rays (Pirenne 1970:15). It remained for Kepler, in 1604, to be first to suggest that an eye–camera analogy might solve the classical puzzle of how objects greater than the eye itself, and at a distance, might be detected by the eye (Lindberg 1976:178–208).

Thirty-three years later, Descartes (1637:245) de-

8. *Taratoo*: the Warrau shield game, Guyana, *c*.1888. Photograph by Everard im Thurn. (RAI 605)

scribed an experiment to demonstrate the effectiveness of the analogy. To explain how the image is formed on the retina (Plate 10), the membranes from a dissected ox eye were gradually removed. When thin enough to expose the vitreous humour without it spilling out, the back of the eye was covered with a thin piece of white paper (analogous to the ground-glass screen of a plate camera). The eye was then secured in the shutter of a window — 'looking' outside. The room was darkened and an inverted image of the scene outside could be viewed 'I dare say with surprise and pleasure' (Descartes 1637:245).

The perspective system of representation, evolved from camera-like devices, has been considered the natural way of representing the environment in the Western world for the past five centuries. To a significant degree these perspective projections, in establishing a way of representing the world, had paved the way for photography. But while there may appear to be strong similarities between the representational aims and the pictorial images produced by both painting and photography, Barthes (1980) has pointed out that photography constituted a significant shift in representation. Photography resulted from the combination of two phenomena, which produced a new medium of unique character: 'the painters' camera obscura is only one of the causes of Photography; the essential one, perhaps, was the chemical discovery' (Barthes 1980:31). Nevertheless, it is generally believed that images based on this system have a strong resemblance or correspondence to the depicted object or event. Theories based on the eye–camera analogy regarded a type of photographic pictorial image as the simple unit of a retinal-based theory of visual perception. This equated the perception of the world with the perception of pictures.

Of course, the comfortable idea that the photograph shows us what we would have seen 'had we been there at the time' hardly accords with the reality. The argument for naïve realism could be easily countered by pointing out instances where photographs fail to correspond to everyday perception. However, the classical theories of perception had proposed that ambiguities of visual stimulation were to be expected. If there are difficulties of perception with photographs as simple set-ups, we should naturally expect greater difficulties in the complexity of everday life. That the retinal image is flat and reduced in size suggests we learn to perceive by association, making unconscious inferences from the

9. *Camera obscura* to demonstrate the workings of the eye: 'a darkened room, or perspective Box, in which all the Appearances that are made in the Eye are in some manner represented'. From *The Posthumous Works of Robert Hooke*, London, 1705, p. 126. (Courtesy of the British Museum (Natural History))

retinal image. The perceiver would passively infer information from a static mosaic of sensations.

These theories, assuming two-dimensional vision to be immediate, primitive or sensory, suggested that any experience of an objective world is secondary, derived or perceptual. Therefore, in spite of any problems that may arise, flat pictures such as photographs remained a primary kind of stimulus. The eye–camera analogy was established in a central role, explaining and shaping theories, both in the psychology and philosophy of perception. For Descartes it was particularly significant to his philosophy. In terms of dualism, the body/soul dichotomy was followed by the body/consciousness dichotomy. This, in turn, has implied the separation of eye and mind — consequently identifying the eye, as an organ of perception, with the camera.

In retrospect, not only was the anthropometric photography of the nineteenth century encouraged by the instrumental camera's yielding of exact mathematical data, but it was the inevitable product of a perception based on the eye–camera analogy (Plate 11). This also became so for the photography of

'cultural material' in general, which was considered to be made quantifiable by the 'transparency' of the camera.

While this theory had a major part in accounting for the *realism* of the photograph, it was also thought to explain how photographs themselves were perceived. On the condition that the spectator viewed the image monocularly from the centre of perspective, the photograph replicated the sheaf of light rays which would have been produced by the depicted objects. So, for an anthropology deeply rooted in positivism, photography offered a tempting proposition: an objective vision and collection of 'facts', facilitating systematic organization and analysis, in the service of scientific enquiry. With little interference, outside influence, nor allowing — within the photograph — room for the viewer's investigation, the photograph brought the subjects of anthropological study directly

10. Illustration of an experiment to explain the formation of the retinal images performed by Scheiner (1619) which appeared in Descartes, *La Dioptrique*, 1637. (Courtesy of Cambridge University Library)

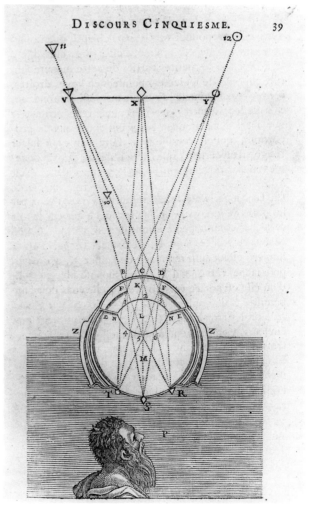

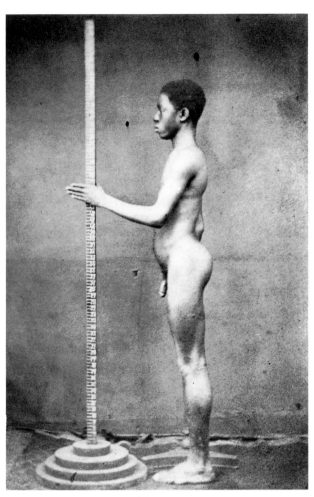

to the armchair. Although there has been the occasional exception — such as Malinowski (Plate 12), who used photography as a research device and evolved an exploratory use of the camera in the field (Wright 1991) — the positivist approach had established the general pattern for fieldwork photography: a means of transferring the location of analysis and control of the subject.

Psychological theory now rejects the retinal image as the basis of visual perception. By the late 1960s increasing attention had been placed on the action and exploration of the perceiver — a process occurring over time. James Gibson's 'commonsense' approach to the theory of perception is outlined in his *The senses considered as perceptual systems* (1966). His objections to the eye–camera analogy shift the emphasis from the passive registration of retinal images to perception based on an active engagement with the environment. Accordingly we do not need to capture the world by a picture on the retina: the visual information to perceive the world is already structured in the ambient light. The perception of the world does not depend on a succession of retinal snapshots. All we need is the ability to gather optical information, and while this optical information in the light may have been struc-

11. (*left*) Anthropometric study. (RAI 1498)

12. (*below*) Bronislaw Malinowski using the camera in his fieldwork. Photograph by Billy Hancock. (Courtesy of Mrs Helena Wayne and the British Library of Political and Economic Science, London School of Economics)

13i–ii. From *The Wood*. Photographs by Charlie Meecham. (Courtesy of the photographer)

tured by the environment it has certainly not been structured in the form of a 'picture'. So while the eye of a vertebrate may be shown to bear an image, it is not particularly significant for the wider activity of visual perception. Incidentally, this perceptual theory, dependent on 'information pick-up', can also explain how insects manage with their 'compound' eyes: a different mechanism for sampling environmental information yet one which produces no 'picture'. The perceiver's experience and self-determination of changing stimulation indicates an objective world. Perception considered in terms of its active, exploratory nature is seen as a process that occurs over time. It is the transformations in a total pattern of stimulation that specify the properties of the world:

> *A natural stimulus for . . . perception has the following characteristics. First, it always has some degree of adjacent order. Second, it always has some degree of successive order. And third, it always therefore has some component of non-change and some component of change.* (Gibson 1966:40)

The adjacent order is described by Gibson as referring to the spatial pattern of stimulation. The successive order refers to the temporal structure of stimulation. The characteristic of non-change/change is the transformations that occur in those adjacent and successive orders. So instead of dealing with the flat pictorial arrays of traditional visual perception, it now means that most important in determining our perception of the environment is our ability to detect changes in time and space. When a photograph is taken the camera samples a similar but limited amount of information available in the ambient light and arrests the transformations (Plates 13i–ii). Thus the latent photographic image is imprinted in a state of permanent non-change.[1]

13ii.

Gibson's theoretical shift, away from the positivism of psycho-physics, rejecting the laboratory setting in favour of the organism's natural environment, was not entirely unheralded. The Gestalt psychologists in the 1920s had first attempted to explain perception as holistic: other than as a mosaic of independent sensations. But Gibson goes on to develop what he called the 'ecological approach to visual perception' (1979). In his rejection of abstract concepts of mathematical space, he turns his attention to the influence of environmental layout on behaviour, finally to coin the term *affordance*.

The medium, substances, surfaces, objects, places, and other animals have affordances for a given animal. They offer benefit or injury, life or death. This is why they need to be perceived. (Gibson 1979:143)

Gibson's approach is partly indebted to evolutionary theory, which has influenced his focus on two main points. First, adaption is relative to a particular environment. So to understand the function of a specific character the organism must be considered within its usual habitat. Secondly, natural selection operates on the whole organism and not on its parts. These conditions have meant that perception cannot be studied completely unless the subject is able to operate in its natural setting, and perceptual processes have evolved to cope with problems that are specific to that organism in its natural environment.

If Gibson's theory of perception is adopted many of the illusions that point to the fallibility of perception disappear. In the psychology laboratory the success of the most convincing demonstrations of perceptual unreliability depend on the perceiver being forced into the role of a passive spectator. This usually entails viewing, from a distance through a peep-hole, an artificial display of indeterminate ground. Under such cramped conditions perception is subject to error. In

14. Bagjok skull trophies, Congo, 1909. Photograph by Bombeeke for the Torday Expedition. (RAI 7934)

everyday perception we do not encounter abstract forms, objects are not floating in a void, but they themselves are textured and are set against a textured ground surface (Plate 14). Besides, if we do see something that we are unsure of, we are usually free to investigate the situation further. So walking around, and perhaps handling, a puzzling object becomes an all-important part of perceiving it. In the laboratory setting the subject is usually denied this aspect of visual perception. The implications of this for perceiving photographs are clear.

In this new context the differences, rather than the similarities, between perceiving objects in the world and their pictorial representations become especially relevant. So the attempt to displace pictorial images from their central position in the theory of perception has led to an awareness of the special problems of visual representation.

> Psychologists and artists have misled one another; we have borrowed the so-called cues for depth from the painters, and they in turn have accepted the theory of perception we deduced from their techniques. (Gibson 1967:20)

The criticisms of the eye–camera analogy, the status of illusions in psychological experiments, the consideration of the organism in its environment, and criticisms of the argument from illusion all point to a new theory of perception. In this ecological approach to perception the emphasis moves to investigating the kinds of information available to the moving, actively engaged perceiver: perception not based on a fixed punctate image.

Any connection between the psycho-physiological approaches to perception and the equally rigid formulations of nineteenth-century anthropology might well be attributed to the common influence of positivism. One could also make a tentative proposition: that in the 1920s the same cultural climate encouraged the Gestalt psychologists' rejection of positivism, characterized by Köhler's 'single viewpoint for psychology . . . the world as I find it, naïvely and uncritically' (1929:1); and Malinowski's development of *participant observation*, in which the 'imponderable yet all important facts of actual life are part of the real substance of the social fabric' (1922:19). But, however valid those explanations might be, there is no doubt about the current interest in photographic representation from both areas of study; and the acquisition of information from photographs and other such representational pictures must be regarded as a rather special mode of perception. The question can now be addressed: if photographic images do not form the basis of visual perception, are they secondary, derived phenomena with characteristics that are very different from the way we perceive the world?

Nelson Goodman (1968) believes that photographs, and other pictorial images based on linear perspective systems, are so unlike 'normal' perception that they are entirely conventional. Closely akin to language, as arbitrary systems of representation, they only appear realistic because we have learned to see them as such. Thus pictorial realism is relative to the historical period and society in which the images serve (Plate 15):

> a picture, to represent an object, must be a symbol for it, stand for it, refer to it . . . almost anything can stand for anything else . . . [it] depends not upon imitation or illusion or information, but inculcation. (Goodman 1968:5, 38)

Indeed there are many examples within *chirographic*[2] representation — 'involv[ing] a graphic tool of some sort for the hand–eye system' (Gibson, 1979:272) — which do place a heavy reliance on symbolic representation. However, the camera, when sampling environmental information, cannot be so easily directed. This means that photography offers the viewer a range of interpretive possibilities different from chirographic representations. For instance, Fox Talbot had been quick to point out that:

> *the operator himself discovers on examination, perhaps long afterwards, that he had depicted many things he had no notion of at the time. Sometimes inscriptions and dates are found upon the buildings, or printed placards more irrelevant, are discovered upon their walls.* (Talbot 1844)

Nevertheless, Goodman's theory, which suggests there is no intrinsic relation between the picture and its referent, can be seen as a development of earlier views — though these tended to be restricted to chirographic practices. Steinberg (1953) states that there is no technical skill involved in imitating nature; the skill lies in the ability to reproduce graphic symbols to a set of conventions. Arnheim (1954:117) believes that it may be only a matter of time before modern 'unrealistic' depictions will appear 'realistic'. This depends more on the attitude of the spectator than on the picture itself. According to Arnheim, 'this "artistic reality level" may shift quite rapidly. Today we can hardly imagine that only a few decades ago the Cézannes and Renoirs looked offensively unreal.' Similarly, for Goodman, representation is a matter of choice on behalf of the artist and habit on the part of the observer. As for systems of representation, such as perspective, they produce images which have no causal relation to their referents:

> *the behavior of light sanctions neither our usual nor any other way of rendering space; and perspective provides no absolute or independent standard of fidelity.* (Goodman 1968:19)

For some theorists of photography (for example Burgin 1975) this has made Saussure's brand of semiology — based on the arbitrary nature of signs — particularly attractive. Other recent approaches have also adhered to a theory of representation relying on 'the truly conventional nature of photographic communication' (Sekula 1982:87).

In an attempt to find authority for this belief, anthropology has been called on to provide evidence. And Herskovits has been thought to demonstrate the arbitrary nature of the photograph conclusively:

> *The anthropologist Melville Herskovits shows a Bush woman a snap-shot of her son. She is unable to recognise the image until the details of the photograph are pointed out. . . . The Bush woman 'learns to read' after learning first that a 'reading' is the appropriate outcome of contemplating a piece of glossy paper. Photographic 'literacy' is learned.* (Sekula 1982:85)

The procedure seems straightforward, and on it Sekula rests his case. But Herskovits, along with other proponents of cross-cultural studies in visual

15. *The Zodiac Man*, fourteenth century manuscript illustration. (Courtesy of the Bodleian Library, University of Oxford. MS. Ashmole 5, f.34v)

perception, has been criticized on a number of points regarding the images used, the design of the experiment, and the methods of evaluation — these have been outlined elsewhere (Miller 1973; Wright 1983). From the anthropological point of view, they more often display a total disregard for the subject's own cultural background. For instance, few even consider whether the pictorial traditions of the subject's culture might act so as to counter any 'natural' realism of the photograph. As Judith Gutman (1982) has shown, these traditions certainly seem to influence the photography of 'other cultures': in her examples (to which I shall return) Indian photographs have retained the organizational space of Indian painting.

However, to return to cross-cultural studies, the researchers frequently interpret puzzlement as perceptual inability. For Herskovits (1948:381) the Bush woman 'turned a photograph this way and that, in attempting to make sense of the shadings of greys on the piece of paper she held'. And if we return to Gibson — his *Observations on Active Touch* (1962) — there is nothing at all unusual in the Bush woman's reaction to a novel object. It does not necessarily signify puzzlement, rather a positive systematic curiosity in which the perceptual abilities of the hands accompany and underlie visual sensitivities. Besides, turning the plate 'this way and that' could help to solve the puzzle of how the image may have come into being, how an illusion had been achieved. For the experimenter, it is already agreed that photographs are unusual objects, which is why they had been singled out for special investigation.[3]

This leaves largely unresolved the issue of innate abilities for photographic perception. Although we are left uncertain as to whether the 'language of pictures' is or is not learned, a simple recognition of photographed objects does seem to be achieved extremely rapidly. While this is certainly not completely arbitrary, other aspects of the photograph may require the viewer to resort to linguistic abilities and, with regard to cross-cultural studies, part of the understanding of the image may depend on the viewer being literate. This is not necessarily limited to the influence of the caption on the image, although certain aspects of pictorial construction and meaning may draw on the viewer's reading ability. So literacy may determine whether the viewer understands some pictorial elements which hitherto had been regarded as essentially 'visual'. Even Segall, Campbell & Herskovits (1966:33) had to admit that the conventionalist position is by no means clear-cut: 'It is interesting that the experience of anthropologists shows that motion pictures are almost universally perceived without trouble and that coloured prints are also.'

There is, however, another approach to the issue. Although theories of photographic convention — the 'language' of photography — have been used to counter 'realist' beliefs, it is an argument based on the same Cartesian dualist theory of perception as the eye–camera analogy. There are, for example, strong similarities between the sensation-based theory of perception and Goodman's symbolic-based theory of representation. For Gregory (1970:26), 'the same data can always "mean" any of several alternative objects . . . the number of possibilities is infinite'; while for Goodman (1968:5) 'almost anything can stand for anything else'. From these viewpoints, we could be forgiven for assuming that photographs *and* everyday visual perception rely on conventions/ unconscious inferences imposed on, or constructed

from, limited amounts of data. Oddly enough, this brings us back to where we started: a position almost identical to the 'realist' belief, where there is little difference between getting information from photographs and perceiving the world. This is perhaps most clear in the work of Gregory (1970, 1971) in which uncritically he uses photographs and other visual images to illustrate a theory of perception based on the Cartesian 'argument from illusion'. Consequently, this return to a theory of visual perception equated with retinal/photographic images cannot begin to address the unusual nature of photographic representation.

In contrast, Gibson's *Ecological Approach to Visual Perception* (1979) suggests the photograph re-presents not the objects that appeared in front of the camera, but part of the environment's optical structure. At the same time the *modus operandi* of the camera creates elements in the photograph that constitute a deviation from optical correspondence. As such we could consider them conventionalized.

The representation of movement in the still image is a good example of how representational convention has been adopted to overcome the inadequacy of a photograph to depict movement 'naturally'. The photograph's limited correspondence to the appearance of the environment acts with pictorial conventions such as the blur, which can indicate movement, to form the photographic system of representation. Unlike movie-film, still photography cannot use movement itself to represent, say, moving figures. According to Gibson (1966:40), in the environment 'motion is immediately detected . . . not deduced from change of position'. But with photographs, either we have to deduce movement from the position of the figure, or from its context. Another method of deduction is from multiple images — by noticing change of position or viewpoint. Thirdly, we may have learned to recognize the convention of the blurred subject or its background (Plate 16). But here the position is by no means clear.

C.S. Peirce's (1940) trichotomy — *icon, index, symbol* — has certainly been influential and has proved to be a useful approach to systems of visual representation (see also Pinney, this volume). As summarized by Eagleton (1983:101):

> *There was the 'iconic', where the sign somehow resembled what it stood for (a photograph of a person, for example); the 'indexical', in which the sign is somehow associated with what it is a sign of (smoke with fire, spots with measles), and the 'symbolic', whereas with Saussure the sign is only arbitrarily or conventionally linked with its referent.*

16.   Mary Douglas rides a scooter. Photograph by Mayotte Magnus. (Courtesy of the photographer).

Nonetheless, it does remain difficult to fit photography comfortably into Peirce's scheme. The correspondence of visual information may account for the iconic characteristics of the photograph. However, our deduction of movement from the position of the figure, or from its context, relies on the index. Yet the photographic blur would seem to be both index and symbol: partly derived through causal connection — as a 'trace'; yet perhaps signifying partly from convention. Either requires a somewhat specialist knowledge of photography's cause and effect — of movement, light, shutter speed, emulsion — or simply 'learning the rule'.

That a single photograph may display two or more indices of movement clearly suggests that any workable theory of photography must abandon the opposition of naïve realism and conventionalism. Instead we can propose a theory of 'natural correspondences' between the photograph and the perceived environment which operates in conjunction with pictorial conventions. Many such conventions emanate from the properties of photography itself. In photography, as with other systems of representation, pictorial correspondences and conventions do not oppose each other but act together to form such a system. Perhaps any choice to be made for using one representational system rather than another resides in the correspondences with the perceived environment that forms the basis of that system; or even in the ways in which the system may be able to compensate for its lack of metaphor in a particular area — the medium's ability to compensate for this through adapting to convention. Essentially this questions the counterpositioning of the photograph and reality.

This suggests, as does Gutman's work on nineteenth and early-twentieth-century Indian photography, that other factors may be even more important than realism and convention in offering any complete graphic possibilities into the chirographic domain, it appears they placed less emphasis than might a Westerner, on the contrast between the two-dimensional picture plane and the scene represented in depth.

If, like Gibson, we reject the retinal image as a basis for visual perception, and propound the active, exploratory role of the perceiver, the speculations of the traditional theorists of perception might simply be adopted to explain photographic phenomena, since retinal/photographic images formed the basis of their theories. However, there may be further objections to the eye–camera analogy. Not only do the recent theories indicate that seeing the world is nothing like looking at a photograph, but also that any characteristics attributed to the retinal-image theory have little in common with photography.

When viewing a photograph we are always aware that whatever we perceive in the image is mediated (Plate 17) in its creation and reception (see Edwards, this volume). Photographs intrude on, and become part of, everyday perception. The dual awareness of realism, yet at the same time non-realism, creates a tension that is central to photographic representation.

18. Anthropological portrait: Tama Bulan Wang, Kenyah chief, Sarawak, *c.*1890–1900. Photograph by Charles Hose. (RAI 11038)

17. Photographing: Santos Maranjo. Photograph by Barbara Freire-Marreco, 1912. (Courtesy of the Pitt Rivers Museum, University of Oxford. PRM. B10. 38A)

account of photographic representation. In this instance, as in Western photography, cultural factors have determined the significance of the environmental information that is 'extracted' for pictorial purposes. For example, Indian photographers:

> compressed space, used unique patterns of composition, and radically altered uses of light. Until now we have been so culturally root-bound that we have generally considered European, or Western images as the 'standard' for all photographic imagery. (Gutman, 1982:15)

Such differences in photographic style derive from a choice of precise and particular sets of optical information which are in keeping with the traditions of Indian painting. If at times this necessitated painting on to the photograph, extending the range of photo-

19. Pictorial Investigations. Photograph by Terence Wright.

When viewing a portrait we experience the image as if we were seeing the sitter, while our awareness of the medium constantly reminds us we are not doing so (Plate 18). While this position, close to the phenomenological standpoints of Sontag (1977) and Barthes (1980), tends to incline towards the abstract, Pirenne (1970) demonstrates how this operates in practice.

In his *Optics, Painting and Photography*, Pirenne outlines some of the conditions that can most fully enhance the realism of a photograph and other perspective-based depictions. These we briefly encountered with reference to anthropometric photography and other uses of the camera to collect ethnographic data. That the viewer remains at the centre of perspective is of key importance. However, most usually we do not view photographs from this position, nor monocularly — here our subsidiary awareness of the picture-plane of a photograph, our awareness of the photograph as an object — enables us to compensate for the optical distortions that we would expect to arise (Plate 19).

Until recently theorists of photographic perception have felt it necessary to confront the fact that although photographs appear to be very similar to the things they represent, they are totally different physically. Peirce (1940) had defined the picture (photo) as an 'icon', in view of its 'common qualities' with its object 'in some respect or capacity'. Umberto Eco (1970:32), in the belief that 'it is necessary to be trained to recognise the photographic image', disagrees: 'a simple phenomenological inspection of any representation, either a drawing or a photo, shows us that an image possesses none of the properties of the object represented'.

Both seem to miss the point. Eco is correct that it 'possesses none of the properties of the object', but, in the light of Gibson's theory, the picture changes. For the camera, in sampling some of the ambient light, enables the photograph to provide a limited amount of *information* about the photographed environment.

The new theories of perception point to photography as a special system of representation that employs both conventions and 'correspondences' with the event or environment recorded. The extreme conventionalist position seems to be that photographic representation has nothing to do with the way things appear in the world. But even if the claim for photographic convention by Sekula and others is overstated, their work still has the virtue of concentrating attention on the cultural aspects of photography.

Besides, Peirce did refer to two types of icon: the *image* and the *diagram*. Again this does not provide a very sharp division among representations, with the image displaying the 'simple qualities' of the object and the diagram, the relation of the parts. But, for the photograph, it may point to the ways that visual information is laid out within the camera's format.

Conclusion

The late 1960s and early 1970s had experienced something of a cultural rebellion against an academicization which had tended to favour form and style over use and function. Paralleled by the critique of structuralism in anthropology 'as being too distant from the intentionality and experience of social actors' (Marcus & Fischer 1986:29), Gibson's psychological theory rejected intellectualist explanations of visual perception. This ecological approach to perception led in turn to a new emphasis on the problems of photographic representation. Meanwhile the practice of photography itself was initiating renewed interest in photographic theory. The 'transparency' of photography had been challenged in a wave of 'reflexivity' which questioned the photograph's relation to reality and had begun to investigate the medium's scope and limitations. Such changes in attitude constituted a move away from the objectivist view of the photo-

PRACTICAL TRAINING IN PERSPECTIVE DRAWING: FIRST STUDIES FOR A HORSE AND CARRIAGE

20. 'Practical training in perspective drawing: first study for a horse and carriage,' *c*.1905. (From J.A. Hammerton (ed.) *Peoples of All Nations*, n.d., vol. 4 p.2422.)

21. Monk of the German Trappist Mission directing the pose, Mariannhill, Southern Africa, *c*.1895. (Courtesy of Pitt Rivers Museum, University of Oxford. PRM. B10. 38A)

graph as a simple record, to a position which accentuated the social and cultural determinants of the photographer's motivations, accompanied by the viewer's active exploratory and interpretive approach to the information available in the photograph.

For Western culture in general, theories of visual perception have guided our assumptions of how we might understand the world, but they have also had a strong influence on how it should be represented and consequently have predicted how we should view those representations (Plate 20). For anthropology in particular, these theories are reflected in our appropriation and subsequent viewing of the images of 'others' (Plate 21). This not only gives an important emphasis to the need to understand the terms in which photographic representation was established in the past, but calls us to question our own working theory, our own historical and cultural standpoints, before we begin to address photographs showing 'other cultures'.

NOTES

1 The 'invisible' image on exposed but undeveloped film which is revealed by development.

2 Gibson adopts the term 'chirographic' for images that are drawn. They are a direct result of human mediation in contrast to photographic images with optical/chemical origins (see Barthes 1980:31).

3 There do not appear to be any photographs surviving from the early experiments and it could well be purely a matter of print quality whether a photograph is seen as a clear depiction of its subject, or as shadings of grey on a flat piece of paper.

REFERENCES

Agee, J. & Evans, W. 1941. *Let us now praise famous men*. Boston: Houghton Mifflin.

Arnheim, R. 1954. *Art and visual perception*. Berkeley and Los Angeles: University of California Press.

Barthes, R. (1980) 1982. *Camera lucida*. Trans. R. Howard. London: Jonathan Cape.

Burgin, V. (1975) 1982. 'Photographic practice and art theory'. In V. Burgin (ed.) *Thinking Photography* 39–83. London: Macmillan.

Descartes, R. (1637) 1954. 'The Dioptrics'. In E. Anscombe & P.T. Greach (eds.) *Descartes: Philosophical Writings*. London: Nelson.

Eagleton, T. 1983. *Literary theory*. Oxford: Blackwell.

Eco, U. (1970) 1982. 'Critique of the image.' In V. Burgin (ed.) *Thinking Photography* 32–8. London: Macmillan.

Gibson, J.J. 1962. Observations on active touch. *Psychological Review* 69:477–91.

— 1966. *The senses considered as perceptual systems*. Boston: Houghton Mifflin.

— 1967. 'Autobiography'. In E.S. Reed & R.K. Jones (eds.) *Reasons for Realism: Selected Essays of James J. Gibson*. Hillsdale, N.J.: Erlbaum. 1982.

— 1979. *The Ecological Approach to Visual Perception*. Boston: Houghton Mifflin.

Goodman, N. 1968. *The Languages of Art*. Indianapolis: Bobbs-Merrill.

Gregory, R.L. 1970. *The intelligent eye*. New York: McGraw-Hill.

— 1971. *Eye and Brain*. New York: McGraw-Hill.

Gutman, J.M. 1982. *Through Indian eyes: 19th and early 20th Century photography from India*. New York: Oxford University Press.

Hammerton, J.A. (ed.) n.d. *Peoples of All Nations*. London: Fleetway House.

Herskovits, M.J. 1948. *Man and his Works*. New York: Knopf.

im Thurn, E.F. 1893. Anthropological uses of the camera. *Journal of the Anthropological Institute*. 22:184–203.

Köhler, W. (1929) 1930. *Gestalt Psychology*. London: Bell.

Lindberg, D.C. 1976. *Theories of vision from Al-Kindi to Kepler*. Chicago: University Press.

Malinowski, B.C. 1922. *Argonauts of the Western Pacific*. London: Routledge & Kegan Paul.

Marcus, G.E. & Fischer, M.J.M. 1986. *Anthropology as Cultural Critique*. Chicago: University of Chicago Press.

Miller, R.J. 1973. Cross-cultural research in the perception of pictorial materials. *Psychological Bulletin*. 80:135–50.

Peirce, C.S. 1940. *The Philosophy of Peirce*. New York: Routledge & Kegan Paul.

Pirenne, M.H. 1970. *Optics, Painting and Photography*. Cambridge: University Press.

Sekula, A. 1982. 'On the invention of photographic meaning'. In V. Burgin (ed.) *Thinking Photography* 84–109. London: Macmillan.

Segall, M.H., Campbell, D.T. & Herskovits, M.J. 1966. *The influence of culture on visual perception*. New York: Bobbs-Merrill.

Sherrington, C.S. (1937–8) 1951. *Man on his Nature*. Cambridge: University Press.

Sontag, S. 1977. *On photography*. New York: Farrar, Straus, & Giroux.

Steinberg, L. 1953. The eye is part of the mind. *Partisan Review* 20:194–212.

Talbot, W.H.F. 1844. *The Pencil of Nature*. (unpaged). London.

Wright, T.V. 1983. Photography, realism and 'The Natives'. *British Journal of Photography* 6400. vol. 130:340–2.

— 1991. The Fieldwork Photographs of Jenness and Malinowski and the Beginnings of Modern Anthropology. *Journal of the Anthropological Society of Oxford* 22(1).

The Photographic Document: Photographs as Primary Data in Anthropological Enquiry

Joanna C. Scherer[1]

HISTORIANS SUCCESSFULLY USE PHOTOGRAPHS as documents (Hales 1984; Mejía 1987); so do sociologists (Wagner 1979; Harper 1987). It is time that anthropologists took more seriously these sources of unique information. While certain fundamental questions can be debated,[2] it is the premise of this essay that photographs can be used as primary data and as anthropological documents — not as replications of reality itself but as representations that require critical reading and interpretation (Gidley 1985:39). Neither the photograph itself as an artefact, nor the viewer's interpretation of the subject of the photograph, nor an understanding of the photographer's intention, can alone give holistic meaning to images. It is only by looking at the three as parts of a process, ideally in reference to groups of related images, that one can extract relevant sociocultural meaning from photographs. It is suggested that photographs as a body are reliable evidence open to analysis and interpretation as seen through the interrelationship of the photographer, subject and viewer.

This arena of the anthropology of visual communication includes study of the photographer's view of the Other, as well as the academic's perspective on the photographer; study of the subjects' influence over the image, as well as an analysis of the subjects themselves; and study of the viewer's construction of the Other, as well as the audience's use of the image. In sum, the researcher must approach the photograph as a social artefact, to understand the process of interaction between the producer of the image, the subject of the image, and the viewer. Proposed here is a reflexive, critical, study of photographs that contextualizes images to aid in the reconstruction of cultures.

Since the invention of photography in 1839, pictures have more often than not been subordinated to the written word. Visuals have been used to seduce (i.e. to give viewers an impression that what they are seeing is typical or exemplary of a subject) and/or to distract or amuse readers (i.e. to break up the text) rather than to convey information. To some, in fact, only 'the linguistic mode is capable of meaning' (Worth, cited in Gross 1981:32).

The visual in Western culture is often associated with intuition, art and implicit knowledge, while the verbal is associated with reason, fact and objective information (Collier & Collier 1986:169–70). 'Pictures have been seen as feminine, deceptive and irrational when compared to words, which are male, truthful and rational' (Krieger 1979:253). Thus there seems to be a difference of value between the visual and the written which is somehow rooted in basic differences of cognition between the sexes. Following this logic, it should be no surprise that a study of social science articles published in the nineteenth century revealed that those which included pictures were predominately written by women (Stasz 1979:133) and that much of the published critical analysis of historical photographs has been by women.

The preference for word or picture may turn out to reflect more than differential patterns of sensitivity of Western men and women; it may also represent a division between Western and non-Western perception. In his study of Navajo, Hall (1986:xv) concluded: 'western people . . . perceive the written word as reality and visual imagery as impression. Navajo observers . . . see photographs as literal information and language as coded interpretation'. Yet, as Hockings (1988:191) has noted, 'much of the anthropologist's subject matter is in fact language behaviour, and his most usual way of presenting it is through another language, his own'. Indeed, Margaret Mead (1975) characterized anthropology as 'a discipline of words', primarily because of anthropologists' interest in lifestyles of past times rather than the observation of contemporary events. Memory ethnography, recording directly the words of informants, became the basic mode of anthropological reportage. Unfortunately for most social scientists today, this emphasis on memory ethnography and words remains unchanged.

Photography was a mechanical by-product of the European technological revolution, the period during which scientific facts, invention, mass production, ownership of products, and conspicuous consumption began to rule in Western society. Because it was mechanical, photography was believed by many during this period to be a direct reflection of nature and reality, evidence in support of facts. Its invention was aimed at replacing reality (Hoffman, cited in Munsterberg 1982:56). The assumed reality of the photograph invested it with the illusion of 'truth' and gave it much of its power. The factual, informative value of photography would not have been possible without the mass-production capability of the photographic print (Sekula 1984:9). Photography was also early linked to the development of journalism (Schiller 1977; Sontag 1973:86), and advances in transport (Banta 1988:11). Just as the rise of journalism made information available to the masses, the growth of photography made images, especially depicting exotic places which were now accessible, available to people everywhere. Such images were widely accepted as 'real' and factual. Photographs were also used to give meaning to political, economic and social understandings, preconceptions and stereotypes. In fact, the photograph not only replicated earlier visual stereotypes but also moulded and codified these stereotypes. Indeed, what is called 'true to life' at any given time must be a stereotype in order to be recognizable (Worth 1981:183). Thereafter photography transformed the subject into an object (Barthes 1981:13) which could be individually possessed. As part of this technological revolution, photography was used extensively in the colonial effort to categorize, define, dominate and sometimes invent, an Other (Banta & Hinsley 1986; Geary 1988), and the representation became a form of cultural and legal power (Goldman & Hall 1987:148; Sekula 1984:10).

The search for 'meaning' and 'reality' in photographs is a subject that has been tackled by philosophers, art historians, social historians, aestheticians, semioticians, psychologists and sociologists, as well as by visual anthropologists. The philosophical speculations range from the existential, 'if no one ever sees a photograph, can it still be said to bear witness' (Goldberg 1984:20) — or in fact to exist at all — to the pragmatic, as in the familiar Chinese proverb: One picture is worth a thousand words. Those who deny that meaning can be found in photographs often view them as purely subjective, suggesting different meanings to different viewers (Sontag 1973:109). On a more middle ground some believe photographs can convey meaning but are incomplete messages, whose meanings are dependent on context (Sekula 1984:4). Thus a 'correct reading' depends on an understanding of the code, the caption, and the context (Gombrich 1972:86). Photographs are seen in this middle ground as symbolic of human interactions (Worth 1981; Chalfen 1987).

Unlike words, which are generally understood to be open to generalization, deduction and empirical analysis, pictures are often thought of in a phenomenological sense (Hockings 1988). Words are selective in a more precise way than images. When we see words we use our knowledge of grammar to interpret and understand them. When we see photographs there are no comparable rules to help us 'read' them, and the information within can overload the mind. Visual images, being sensory, are suspect to the anthropological community, who, like most urban dwellers, tend to be visually unsophisticated (Collier & Collier 1986:110). Despite the fact that 'vision' is used as a metaphor for 'understanding' in American folk speech (Dundes 1972), a legitimatization of visuals has not been transferred to social-science scholarship. Being perceived as a popular medium, visuals are shunned by the scientific community. Then again photographs are seen as icons of their creators, visual artefacts of what was of interest to the photographer at a moment in time, a product of the art of choice of the photographer. Such perspectives limit the research potential of photographs, dismissing them as objects of scholarly study.

Margaret Mead (1963:176) suggested that 'photographs taken by one observer can be subjected to continued re-analysis by others', and Collier expressed his belief that 'photography fixes the image for analysis and reappraisal' (Collier & Collier 1986:64). It is time to take up this challenge and show that 'information in a still photograph exists on many levels but training and systematic relating of photographic information to a careful analytic technique can keep the levels separate and the information available and useful' (Byers 1964:82). Although they are selective abstractions, we can learn to 'read' photographs (Sekula 1984:19), especially for the cultural symbols they reveal (Longo 1987:33). The photograph 'yields up those "details" which constitute the very raw material of ethnological knowledge' (Barthes 1981:28). Pictures can be treated as ethnographic documents. They need only to be contextualized socioculturally to be utilized for scholarly study.

Ethnographic photography may be defined as the use of photographs for the recording and understanding of culture(s), of both the subject and the photographer. What makes an ethnographic photograph is not necessarily the intention of its production but how it is used to inform ethnographically (see Edwards and Poignant, this volume). The research methodology for the use of ethnographic photographs in anthropological enquiry includes: (1) detailed analysis of internal evidence and comparison of photographs with other images; (2) understanding of the history of photography, including technological constraints and conventions; (3) study of intention and purposes of the photographer and the manner in which images were used by their creator; (4) study of the ethnographic subjects; and (5) review of related historical evidence, including an examination of the uses to which images have been put by others. While the analysis of specific images points to levels of detailed reading, which is an essential baseline, the value in research terms becomes increasingly apparent when these techniques are multiplied over a larger body of material. The researcher must have a large enough data base for analysis; this will frequently mean studying a majority of the images of a single photographer, or thousands of pictures of a particular people. Only then can valid research results be obtained.

The first problem in analysis of ethnographic photographs is the practical one of locating them. Images are useful to scholars only if they can be found and are accessible; they must be archived and cata-logued and means must exist for obtaining prints. Many collections of nineteenth and early-twentieth-century photographs are only beginning to be properly staffed, maintained and made available for scholars (Steiger & Taureg 1987:318–319). Specific guides for North American Indian images include Blackman (1986a), Mattison (1982, 1985), and Scherer (1981, 1990).

In the early phases of work, photography scholars are often at the mercy of the muses. Combing guides to museum collections, historical societies and library special collections located in a given geographical area, or visiting museums with associated ethnographic collections, may not always guarantee success. The researcher must deal with the often considerable limitations and biases of collections. Not only do photographers choose from among innumerable subjects what to photograph, but repositories accept or reject collections or parts of them according to idiosyncratic collection policies, thereby limiting the nature of the photographic record to be preserved (Poignant, this volume). Thus the United Methodist Church photographic archive, made between 1860 and 1925, collected a specific kind of image, reflecting 'the unity of mankind', which could be used for raising revenue for missionary efforts (Kaplan 1984; Geary 1988:138). Researchers must be aware of and make allowances for such limitations.

Photographs are of most value to scholars when they are in related groups. Then they can serve as a valuable record, for example to those investigating non-traditional subjects that are often poorly documented in early ethnographic sources such as the family; women's roles; children's position in society; popular culture at specific times and places (Peters & Mergen 1977:282) and comparison with élite values and social practices (Mejía 1987); the physical scale of an event, its spatial arrangement and the degree of individual participation (Geary 1986:100); or settlement patterns, material culture and culture change (Gidley 1985:44). Thus, over the last decade there has been a growing use of non-traditional data, and an increasing awareness that new information can be gleaned from old images.

After location, images must be subjected to detailed analysis. A methodology by which to extrapolate historical, social and cultural data from these artefacts is being developed (see Peters & Mergen 1977; Schwartz 1982; Templin 1982; Geary 1986; Blackman 1986a; Malmsheimer 1987). Accurate identification of the circumstances in which each image was made, coupled with the original documentation of who, what, where, when, by whom, why and how the image was used, provides the context for the image maker.[3] The process must include reviewing the background, especially the backdrop in the case of a studio portrait, individuals pictured, the material culture evident, the event portrayed, and spatial relations, as well as limitations of the technology at the period. Such analysis will determine who controlled the image: the subject, viewer, photographer or a combination of these.

The subject can control the content by determining costume and pose and deciding when the image is to be made. This can be seen, for example, by studying images of the same individual (Scherer 1988). The viewer can shape the image by creating the demand for the photograph and thus determining the acceptable content (Kaplan 1984; Albers & James 1990). Nineteenth-century images, for example, were usually small and inexpensive and catered to Victorian taste for escapism and possession (Hales 1988:48). In assessing the photographer's influence — in terms of methods of manipulation and selection as well as intentions — as much as feasible of the entire corpus of the photographer's work must be studied. For example, the same props or items of clothing may appear in different images (Scherer 1975). Some props may be overt cultural symbols such as North American Plains Indian signs such as tomahawks, blankets and tipis as seen in William H. Jackson's images (Hales 1988:33–4); in Bolivia such signs are the poncho, blanket and hat (Knowlton 1989); in India symbolic signs such as banyan trees were featured repetitively along with other caste-type signs (Pinney, this volume and 1990). In addition, stylistic conventions for posing subjects may be determined (Scherer 1988) including choice of vantage point, time and season photographed; and techniques to control the image through exposure duration and choice of lens (Hales 1988:49) can be found.

The photographer's use of images must be investigated. Were they copyrighted and sold to the public for entertainment or education? Were they used in mass communication to sway the public to a particular viewpoint or to motivate certain actions? If the motive of the photographer was monetary he/she would likely photograph the subject in the accepted stereotype of the day, because that is what would sell best. All photographers had an audience in mind.[4] By referring to ethnographic sources, a researcher can evaluate the basis for the photographer's choice of images — what was photographed and what not.

Historical sources such as business and city directories, census records, tax records, state, county and city records and local newspapers can be checked for documentary information on the photographs. For the nineteenth century and early twentieth century the latter are very often revealing of attitudes towards other people, and they may be very descriptive of a local photographer's activities. Professional photographers' journals of the period can be studied to determine photographic conventions and technical constraints. In general, it is patterns in the photographs that are being looked for, evidence of repeated visual conventions whose implications can then be assessed.

A multiplicity of photographers, amateur as well as professional, have worked with various ideologies and motivations. The images they created, however, cannot be understood in isolation from their agendas. It is important in evaluating the images of these expeditionary, reformist and ethnographic photographers to note that, although their goals were different, they all by necessity dominated the subjects photographed. By reconstructing their goals and intentions we can categorize and understand their photographs in the contexts in which they were created.

There seems to be a correlation between the explicit intentions of the image maker, selection process and resulting visual styles. Steiger and Taureg (1987:322) reached this conclusion by comparing images of the Bamum in Cameroon taken by missionaries with photographs taken by anthropologists. Jacknis (1984:12) came to a similar conclusion by comparing the Kwakiutl photographs of Edward S. Curtis, who made images for aesthetic purposes, with those made by O.C. Hastings for scientific purposes. In reviewing the photographs of James Mooney (Jacknis 1990) the visual record reflects the methodology and purpose of early ethnographers: participant observation over a substantial period to establish an intimate familiarity with the subjects, in order to record daily life and cultural processes. In contrast, the images of expeditionary professional photographers are usually formalized portraits and views of the outside of dwellings (Blackman 1981:64, 71–73). These photographs, made in order to 'prove' the existence of the 'discovered' natives or as proof of their 'possession' by the government representatives, are rarely informal pictures reflecting personalities. The fact that these photographers were not intimate with their subjects is evident. Similarly, the social documentary images of Joseph K. Dixon (Krouse 1990) also reflect his methodologies and purposes. He often romanticized and stereotyped the North American Indian in order to appeal to those influential in Indian reform. In addition, missionary photographers and educationalists frequently emphasized the contrast between the native represented as 'primitive', 'uncivilized' and the power of conversion to bring about 'civilization', and often used such photographs as propaganda for their value as evidence (Brown 1981; Malmsheimer 1985). Studying the oeuvre of the image maker it is possible to evaluate the intentions of a particular photographer in the context of the photographic conventions of the period.

Historical photographs can be used as primary documents, as artefacts themselves, not just as illustrations for textual information. The research potential is clearly great. Present technology gives us the means to access visual materials easily, not only in terms of locating the images physically but also in reconstructing details of the spatial ordering of sequences and related images (Frassanito 1975; Jacknis 1984; Kavanagh 1991); microanalysis of such subject-matter as dress, adornment and pose (Blackman 1986b; Scherer 1988) and understanding the politics behind such representation (Geary 1988); photogrammetric analysis (adding the dimension of depth to two-dimensional photographs) of architecture and features in and around houses (Blackman 1981:150); determining some colours of material artefacts depicted in black and white images (Holm 1985); and dating early photographs by card mounts and other internal evidence such as costumes or studio props (Pilling 1986).

In order to extract usable data about culture from historical photographs we must develop lines of enquiry that are capable of being tested. What was the purpose for which the image was made? Who possessed it? Was the photograph a result of the photographer's vision or the subject's self-image? What was the relationship between photographer and subject? What did the subject think about early photography? Were they fearful, antagonistic, or full of wonder, excitement and pleasure? Did the subjects also take photographs themselves and if so did they have a unique native vision? How did the indigenous people use photographs? Were they used in unusual ways or in more common ways, for example as a reminder of a deceased relative? What kinds of information do these photographs contain that is useful for scholars today? Do they reflect cultural change or do they depict a static historical present? Who collected, exhibited and/or wrote about these photographs?

In summary, we must learn what can be understood from the image itself and what must be obtained from associated documentary materials. Critical to the creation of hypothesis and analysis is the contextualization of the image, a study of the historical and cultural environment in which pictures were produced. This requires understanding both the photo-

grapher's culture and that of the subject. Examples of good illustrative studies include those of Blackman on late-nineteenth-century Northern and Kaigani Haida culture (1981) as well as recent cultural change, especially in architecture; Gutman (1982) on the images made by photographers in India and the non-Western cultural artefact they produced; Malmsheimer (1985, 1987) on cultural transformation as depicted in the 'before and after' photos of Carlisle Indian School students taken by J.N. Choate, and the persuasive purposes for which they were used by society at large; Geary (1988) on visual constructions of colonialism as seen in images of the Bamum in Cameroon; Albers & James (1984a, 1984b, 1985) on postcards as popular image makers, and their role in creating a predominance of Plains Indian imagery; and by Scherer (1988) in a study of the creation through photographs of a nineteenth-century Northern Paiute woman's self-image.

Many scholars have used photographs in memory ethnography. Good examples are Helm (1981) reporting on her 1979 study of status and occupation among the Subarctic Dogrib; Eber (1977) describing her use in the 1970s of images taken by the Arctic Inuit photographer Peter Pitseolak (1975); and John C. Ewers' method of gaining both rapport and cultural information from the Blackfoot (Werner 1961:57, 76). Photographs have also been used to document change in particular elements of culture, such as the clothing of North-East Winnebagos in Wisconsin (Lurie 1961); and monumental art of the Northwest Coast Haida, especially architecture, totem poles and sculpture (MacDonald 1983). Photographs have been used to help supply much-needed documentation to museum specimens, as McLendon's (1981) study of the baskets of California Pomo demonstrates. A few researchers have looked critically at the visual corpus of particular individuals such as Franz Boas and the images made by O.C. Hastings under his direction (Jacknis 1984), Edward S. Curtis (Lyman 1982), Edward H. Latham (Gidley 1979), Robert Flaherty (Danzker 1980) and Martin Chambi (Harries and Yule 1986). Others have reviewed the oeuvre of a photographer at a particular time and place in order to reconstruct historical events: DeMallie (1981) on Alexander Gardner's stereographic views of Plains Indians at the 1868 Fort Laramie treaty councils; Palmquist (1977) on photographs by Louis Heller and Eadweard Muybridge during the Modoc War 1872–3; and Frassanito (1975) on Alexander Gardner's and other photographers' images of the Gettysburg battlefield in 1863 are exemplary of this work.

Unique uses of historical photographs include a preliminary attempt to identify the tribal origins of

Plains Indian pictographic drawings by comparing them with historical photographs from the same period (Brizee 1982); Masayesva and Younger's (1983) bicultural examination of the Hopi through presentation of the work of Euro-American photographers in comparison with that of Hopi photographers; G. Roberts's (1978) investigation of sources for an authentic portrait of the Cheyenne Little Wolf; Weber's (1985) study of subject and photographer interaction revealed in the analysis of the use of artefacts of Northwest Coast Haida and Kwakiutl as depicted in photographs; and Blackman's analysis of images of the potlatch ceremony (1977).

Although use of nineteenth and early-twentieth-century photographs in anthropological enquiry has begun, there is still a great need for guides to collections and for historical studies focusing on particular photographers, situating them in their cultural milieu. We have only begun to study the visual depictions of the constructed Other but know already that they are not accurate reflections of the real world. Thus we must sort out myths of Otherness and stereotypes. We can begin to do this by learning how non-Western photographers see their society and how various cultures interpret these seemingly identical forms according to culturally specific symbolic meanings and functions (Sprague 1978a:19; Gutman 1982; Goldman & Hall 1987:14).

The serious analysis of non-Western or native photographers is a relatively untouched field, or at least unpublished in academic circles (for exceptions see Sprague 1978a, 1978b; Gutman 1982; Marr 1989). For example, North American Indians known to have left collections of still pictures are few in number: Louis Shotridge (Tlingit), who made about 475 photographs of the Tlingit and Tsimshian from about 1915 to 1932 which are preserved in the archives of the University Museum, University of Pennsylvania; J.N.B. Hewitt (Iroquois), who made about 300 photographs (mainly portraits) on Six Nation Reserve, Grand River, Ontario, Canada, which are now in the Smithsonian Institution's National Anthropological Archives; Harry Sampson (Northern Paiute), who produced a substantial collection of Washoe and Northern Paiute photos in the 1920s and 1930s which is still owned by his family; Richard Throssel (Wasco, adopted Crow), who made about 1,000 photographs of Crow and Northern Cheyenne from 1902 to 1910, which are now in the possession of the American Heritage Center, University of Wyoming; George Hunt (Kwakiutl), who photographed from about 1900 until the 1920s, and left a body of about fifty photographs (now at the American Museum of Natural History) which is currently being studied by Ira Jacknis (see Jacknis, this volume). The indigenous Native American photographers whose works are at least partially published are the Inuit Peter Pitseolak (1975; Eber 1977), whose collection of about 2,000 negatives made between the 1930s and the 1960s is housed at the Notman Archives, McCord Museum, McGill University, and the Makah photographers Daniel Quedessa and Shobid Hunter, whose work is discussed in Marr 1989.

Most collections of ethnographic photographs have been analysed by cultural outsiders. Perspectives from the inside, from indigenous photographers, both professional and amateur, would enrich our studies. We may find that there are universal human behaviours that are recorded photographically. The camera is an obtrusive instrument, especially during its first introduction to a society, 'when the image is defined as something that can be stolen from its owner' (Sontag 1973:171; Carpenter 1972:164). It transforms the subject into an object confronting the 'terror of self-awareness' (Carpenter 1972:130) or causes withdrawal of the soul and death (Worswick & Spence 1978:143). However, at a later stage there seems to be a universal eagerness to get into every picture (Werner 1961:48).

Alternatively, we may find that various cultures have unique ways of responding to photography (Goldman & Hall 1987:10). Examples include the Nigerian Yoruba highly conventionalized traditional portrait described by Sprague (1978a, 1978b); the full-face formal portrait preferred by the Chinese (Sontag 1973:172; Worswick & Spence 1978:16, 144); and the shadowless, flat, multi-interest-point, painted photograph preferred in India (Gutman 1982:15). When the camera is pointed at either an individual or group there seem to be photographic conventions that overshadow individual, ethnic and cultural differences: the subject's desire to pose (Barthes 1981:10–11; Chalfen 1987:73); to be portrayed dressed in one's best clothing, especially that which is status-revealing paraphernalia; or to include in the photograph objects that symbolize social status or identify the event. There also seems to be a cross-cultural commonality in the use of pictures as ritual relics (Beloff 1985:180) produced to commemorate important events (Kunt 1983:14; Sprague 1978a:19); in symbolic exchanges and displays of portraits; as substitutes for absent individuals; to denote relationship or hero worship; and, commonly, as mnemonic devices to commemorate events or deceased individuals.

Photographs seem to be used cross-culturally as a visual framework to situate the owner in a known place in the universe, between historical ancestors and immediate family. Perhaps photography, a mechanical invention of Europeans, creates a particular environment; one in which the individual needs and desires to possess the product — the image — and all that it symbolizes. By its very nature photography may indeed 'swallow culture' (Carpenter 1972:182), revealing universal human behaviour. Only by considering patterns of subject-matter, symbolic content and composition can we utilize as primary data the historical photographs held in vast numbers in repositories throughout the world.

NOTES

1 The ideas in this paper are explored at greater length in my introductory chapter in a special issue of *Visual Anthropology* published by Harwood Academic Publishers. (Scherer 1990). The concentration on references to North American Indians reflects this writer's interest as well as the relative richness of work in this area. However, other areas are receiving increasing attention. Photographic historians of South America (McElroy 1985; Levine 1987, 1989) are newly looking at the rich history of that region. Africanists (Sprague 1978a, 1978b; Geary 1986, 1988, 1990; Viditz-Ward 1987; A. Roberts 1988; Kaplan 1990) have aggressively begun to show serious interest in the field, as have scholars writing on the Middle East (Alloula 1987; Graham-Brown 1988; Grant 1989). Photographic historians of Asia, although having serious proponents (Worswick & Spence 1978; Worswick 1979; Gutman 1982; Banta 1988), have only begun to analyse seriously the huge numbers of photographs which exist.

2 There are numerous philosophical and pragmatic questions beyond the scope of this essay, but they are discussed in various ways by other essays in this volume. Some are: What is a documentary photograph? Can a photograph which was not made for documentary purposes be used as a document? Can we derive objective information from a photograph? If so, how? Does 'meaning' come from the photograph itself or from the viewer's interpretation of it? If photographic interpretations are dependent on the viewer's past experiences rather than representing an outside 'reality', can they be used as evidence at all? For discussion of these important questions and the pitfalls in defining 'documentary' photographs and the influence of pictorial intention and a concern with visual interest, coherence and clarity, see Snyder 1984. For discussion of where meaning in photographs comes from, see Worth (1978, 1980, 1981). In general the photograph is viewed as an artefact bound in a social process, 'an intentional use of symbolic material in ways which are shared by a group precisely for the purpose of implying and inferring meaning from signs and sign events' (Worth 1978:9, 16). Visuals are examined as cultural artefacts; the social context of their production and consumption revealing of culture (Ruby 1976:5–7, 1981:20–3).

3 It is not always possible to identify the image maker. This is partly due to the seemingly free exchange of prints and negatives between photographers, lack of strong copyright laws and means to enforce them, and the custom of selling photographic negatives with a studio (Scherer 1981:60). Authorship of the image was not a high priority among most nineteenth and early-twentieth-century photographers (Fleming & Luskey 1986:195; Robinson 1988:41).

4 Even the photographers who were considered primarily documentarians had purposes and agendas that went beyond efforts to create an objective record. For example, Jacob Riis and Lewis Hine used the camera to reveal the life of the poorer classes as a means to bring about social reform (Becker 1974:8). William Henry Jackson's landscape photographs revealed the glories of Yellowstone Park and he became a lobbyist to preserve the American wilderness (Taft 1964:300–2); his early Indian photographs, especially of Omaha in the 1860s, were dual messages revealing 'Indianness' and the positivism of assimilation which became propaganda for Indian policy (Hales 1988:27–39). The Civil War photographs — by Mathew Brady and colleagues such as Alexander Gardner, Timothy O'Sullivan, the Tyson Brothers and others — revealed the horrors of war but were in fact sometimes set up, with bodies moved about to make images more dramatic (Frassanito 1975:187–92).

5 Certainly indigenous people — especially in cultures that allowed and valued representation of human figures and had a strong tradition of figurative art — also made collections of family and community photographs which would be of anthropological value. It seems inconceivable that earlier ethnologists did not see the value of this type of native participation or that indigenous people interested in the historical preservation of their culture did not take up the recording tool of the camera. The training of native assistants in the use of the camera was encouraged in the 1960s (Werner 1961:59–60). The question remains, where are the works of these indigenous photographers and their analysis? Have they been absorbed uncredited into contemporary anthropological publications and/or records? If such collections exist, their identification is an important goal for future research.

REFERENCES

Albers, Patricia C. & James, William R. 1984a. Utah's Indians and Popular Photography in the American West: A View from the Picture Post Card. *Utah Historical Quarterly* 52(1):72–91.
— 1984b. 'The Dominance of Plains Imagery on the Picture Post Card'. In George P. Horse Capture & Gene Balls (eds.) *Fifth Annual 1981 Plains Indians Seminar in Honor of John C. Ewers* 73–97. Cody, Wyo.: Buffalo Bill Historical Center.
— 1985. Images and Reality: Post Cards of Minnesota's Ojibway People 1900–1980. *Minnesota History* 49(6):229–40.
— 1990. Private and Public Images: A Study of Photographic Contrasts in Postcard Pictures of Great Basin Indians, 1898–1919. Special issue *Visual Anthropology* 3(2–3) Picturing Cultures: Historical Photographs in Anthropological Inquiry. J.C. Scherer (ed.).
Alloula, Malek 1986. *The Colonial Harem.* Minneapolis: University of Minnesota Press.
Banta, Melissa & Hinsley, Curtis 1986. *From Site to Sight: Anthropology, Photography and the Power of Imagery.* Cambridge, Mass.: Peabody Museum Press.
Banta, Melissa 1988. 'Life of a Photograph: Nineteenth Century Photographs of Japan from the Peabody and Wellesley College Museums'. In M. Banta & Susan Taylor (eds.) *A Timely Encounter: Nineteenth-Century Photographs of Japan*: 11–21. Cambridge, Mass.: Peabody Museum Press.
Barthes, Roland 1981. *Camera Lucida: Reflections on Photography.* Trans. Richard Howard. New York City: Hill and Wang.
Becker, Howard 1974. Photography and Sociology. *Studies in the Anthropology of Visual Communication* 1(1):1–26.
Beloff, Halla 1985. *Camera Culture.* New York and Oxford: Basil Blackwell.
Berger, John et al. 1972. *Ways of Seeing.* New York: Viking Press.
Blackman, Margaret B. 1977. Blankets, Bracelets and Boas: The Potlatch in Photographs. *Anthropological Papers of the University of Alaska* 18(2):53–67.
— 1981. Window on the Past: The Photographic Ethnohistory of the Northern and Kaigani Haida.

Canada. National Museum of Man. Mercury Series. Ethnology Service Papers 74. Ottawa.
— 1986a. Visual Ethnohistory: Photographs in the Study of Culture History. In Dennis Weidman, Gerry Williams & Mario Zamora (eds.) *Studies in Third World Societies Publication* 35:137–66. Williamsburg, Va.: William and Mary College.
— 1986b. Studio Indians: Cartes de Visite of Native People in British Columbia, 1862–1872. *Archivaria* 21:68–86.
Brizee, Sandra L. 1982. Pictographs and Photographs. *The Society for the Anthropology of Visual Communication Newsletter* 10(2):1–3.
Brown, Jennifer S.H. 1981. Mission Indian Progress and Dependency: Ambiguous Images from Canadian Methodist Lantern Slides. *Arctic Anthropology* 18(2):17–28.
Byers, Paul 1964. Still Photographs in the Systematic Recording and Analysis of Behavioral Data. *Human Organization* 23(1):78–84.
Carpenter, Edmund 1972. *Oh, What a Blow That Phantom Gave Me!* New York: Holt, Rinehart and Winston.
Chalfen, Richard 1987. *Snapshot: Versions of Life.* Bowling Green, Ohio: Bowling Green State University Popular Press.
Collier, John Jr. & Collier, Malcolm 1986. *Visual Anthropology — Photography as a Research Method.* rev. edn. Albuquerque: University of New Mexico Press.
Danzker, Jo-Anne Birnie 1980. Robert Flaherty/Photographer. *Studies in Visual Communication* 6(2):3–32.
DeMallie, Raymond 1981. Scenes in the Indian Country: A Portfolio of Alexander Gardner's Stereographic Views of the 1868 Fort Laramie Treaty Council. *Montana: The Magazine of Western History* 31(3): 42–59.
Dundes, Alan 1972. Seeing is Believing. *Natural History* 81(5):8, 10–12, 86–7.
Eber, Dorothy 1977. How It Really Was. *Natural History* 96(2):70–5.
Fleming, Paula Richardson & Luskey, Judith 1986. *The North American Indians in Early Photographs.* New York: Harper and Row.
Frassanito, William A. 1975. *Gettysburg: A Journey in Time.* New York: Charles Scribner's Sons.
Geary, Christraud M. 1986. Photographs as Materials for African History: Some Methodological

Considerations. *History in Africa* 13:89–116.
— 1988. *Images from Bamum.* Washington: Smithsonian Institution Press.
— 1990. Impressions of the African Past: Interpreting Ethnographic Photographs from Cameroon. Special issue *Visual Anthropology* 3(2–3) Picturing Cultures: Historical Photographs in Anthropological Inquiry. J.C. Scherer (ed.).
Gidley, Mick 1979. *With One Sky Above Us: Life on an Indian Reservation at the Turn of the Century.* Seattle: University of Washington Press.
— 1985. North American Indian Photographs/Images (review essay). *American Indian Culture and Research Journal* 9(3):37–47.
Goldberg, Vicki 1984. A Fever of History (review of *A Vanished World*, by Roman Vishniac). *American Photographer* 12(2):16–20.
Goldman, Noelle, & Hall, Stuart 1987. *Pictures of Everyday Life: The People, Places and Cultures of the Commonwealth.* London: Comedia Publishing Group.
Gombrich, Ernst H. 1972. The Visual Image. *Scientific American* 227 (September):82–96.
Graham-Brown, Sarah 1988. *Images of Women: The Portrayal of Women in Photography of the Middle East 1860–1950.* London: Quartet Books.
Grant, Gillian (ed.) 1989. *Middle Eastern Photographic Collections in the United Kingdom.* Oxford: MELCOM.
Gross, Larry (ed.) 1981. Introduction: 'Sol Worth and the Study of Visual Communication'. In *Studying Visual Communication* 1–35. Philadelphia: University of Pennsylvania Press.
Gutman, Judith Mara 1982. *Through Indian Eyes.* New York: Oxford University Press.
Hales, Peter B. 1984. *Silver Cities: The Photography of American Urbanization, 1839–1915.* Philadelphia: Temple University Press.
— 1988. *William Henry Jackson and the Transformation of the American Landscape.* Philadelphia: Temple University Press.
Hall, Edward 1986. Foreword. In J. Collier & M. Collier *Visual Anthropology: Photography as a Research Method.* rev. edn. xiii–xvi. Albuquerque: University of New

Mexico Press.

Harper, Douglas 1987. *Working Knowledge: Skill and Community in a Small Shop*. Chicago: University of Chicago Press.

Harries, Andy & Yule, P. (directors) 1986. *Martin Chambi and the Heirs of the Inca*. Film. New York: The Cinema Guild.

Helm, June 1981. Dogrib Folk History and the Photographs of John Alden Mason: Indian Occupation and Status in the Fur Trade, 1900–1925. *Arctic Anthropology* 18(2):43–58.

Hockings, Paul 1988. 'Ethnographic Filming and the Development of Anthropological Theory'. In P. Hockings & Yasuhiro Omori (eds.) *Cinematographic Theory and New Dimensions in Ethnographic Film* 185–204. (Senri Ethnological Studies 24) Osaka: National Museum of Ethnology.

Holm, Bill 1985. Old Photos Might Not Lie, But They Fib A Lot About Color. *American Indian Art* 10(4): 44–9.

Jacknis, Ira 1984. Franz Boas and Photography. *Studies in the Anthropology of Visual Communication* 10(1):2–60.

— 1990. James Mooney as an Ethnographic Photographer. Special issue *Visual Anthropology* 3(2–3) Picturing Cultures: Historical Photographs in Anthropological Inquiry. J.C. Scherer (ed.).

Kaplan, Daile 1984. Enlightened Women in Darkened Lands: A Lantern Slide Lecture. *Studies in the Anthropology of Visual Communication* 10(1):61–77.

Kaplan, Flora 1990. Some Uses of Photographs in Recovering Cultural History at the Royal Court of Benin, Nigeria. Special issue *Visual Anthropology* 3(2–3) Picturing Cultures: Historical Photographs in Anthropological Inquiry. J.C. Scherer (ed.).

Kavanagh, Thomas 1991. Whose Village? Photographs by William S. Soule, Winter 1872–1873. *Visual Anthropology* 4(1):1–24.

Knowlton, David C. 1989. 'Viva mi Patria Bolivia': Conflicting Ethnic Images and Discourses in the Construction of Bolivian Nationalism. Paper presented at American Anthropological Association meeting, Washington, DC.

Krieger, Martin H. 1979. 'Truth and Pictures: "Fetishes", "Goodness", and "Clarity"'. In Jon Wagner (ed.) *Images of Information* 249–57.

Beverly Hills, Calif.: Sage Publications.

Krouse, Susan Applegate 1990. Photographing the Vanishing Race. Special issue *Visual Anthropology* 3(2–3) Picturing Cultures: Historical Photographs in Anthropological Inquiry. J.C. Scherer (ed.).

Kunt, Erno 1983. Photography and the Peasant. *New Hungarian Quarterly* (NS) 24(96):13–20.

Levine, Robert M. (ed.) 1987. Windows on Latin America: Understanding Society through Photographs. Special issue *South Eastern Latin Americanist*. Coral Gables, Florida: North-South Center, University of Miami.

— 1989. *Images of History: Nineteenth and Early Twentieth Century Latin American Photographs as Documents*. Durham, N.C.: Duke University Press.

Longo, Donna 1987. Towards Understanding Historical Photographs: Essays in Honor of George L. Harris. *American University. Anthropology Department. Occasional Papers* 2. Washington.

Lurie, Nancy 1961. Ethnohistory: An Ethnological point of View. *Ethnohistory* 8(1):78–92.

Lyman, Christopher 1982. *The Vanishing Race and Other Illusions: Photographs of Indians by Edward S. Curtis*. New York: Pantheon Books.

MacDonald, George F. 1983. *Haida Monumental Art: Villages of the Queen Charlotte Islands*. Vancouver: University of British Columbia Press.

McElroy, Keith 1985. *Early Peruvian Photography: A Critical Case Study*. Ann Arbor: UMI Research Press.

McLendon, Sally 1981. 'Preparing Museum Collections for Use as Primary Data in Ethnographic Research'. In Anne-Marie E. Cantwell, James B. Griffin & Nan A. Rothchild (eds.) *The Research Potential of Anthropological Museum Collections* 201–227. New York: New York Academy of Sciences.

Malmsheimer, Lonna M. 1985. 'Imitation White Man': Images of Transformation at the Carlisle Indian School. *Studies in Visual Communication* 11(4):54–75.

— 1987. Photographic Analysis as Ethnohistory: Interpretive Strategies. *Visual Anthropology* 1(1): 21–36.

Marr, Carolyn 1989. Taken Pictures:

On Interpreting Native American Photographs of the Southern Northwest Coast. *Pacific Northwest Quarterly* 80(2):52–61.

Masayesva, Victor, Jr. & Younger, Erin 1983. *Hopi Photographers, Hopi Images*. Tucson: University of Arizona Press.

Mattison, David 1982. British Columbia Photographers of the Nineteenth Century: An Annotated, Select Bibliography. *BC Studies* 52 (Winter):166–70.

— 1985. *Camera Workers: The British Columbia Photographers Directory 1858–1900*. Victoria, BC: Camera Workers Press.

Mead, Margaret 1963. 'Anthropology and the Camera'. In Willard D. Morgan (ed.) *The Encyclopedia of Photography*. Vol. 7. 166–84. New York: Greystone Press.

— 1975. 'Visual Anthropology in a Discipline of Words'. In Paul Hockings (ed.) *Principles of Visual Anthropology* 3–10. The Hague and Paris: Mouton.

Mejía, Germán Rodrigo 1987. 'Colombian Photographs of the Nineteenth and Early Twentieth Centuries'. In Robert M. Levine (ed.) Windows on Latin America: Understanding Society Through Photographs 48–61. Special issue *South Eastern Latin Americanist*.

Munsterberg, Marjorie 1982. The World Viewed: Works of Nineteenth-Century Realism. *Studies in Visual Communication* 8(3):55–69.

Palmquist, Peter E. 1977. Image-makers of the Modoc War: Louis Heller and Eadweard Muybridge. *The Journal of California Anthropology* 4(2):206–41.

Peters, Marsha, & Mergen, Bernhard 1977. 'Doing the Rest': The Uses of Photographs in American Studies. *American Quarterly* 29:280–303.

Pilling, Arnold 1986. 'Dating Early Photographs by Card Mounts and Other External Evidence: Tentative Suggestions'. In Dennis Weidman, Gerry Williams & Mario Zamora (eds.) *Studies in Third World Societies Publication* 35:167–226. Williamsburg, Va.: William and Mary College.

Pinney, Christopher 1990. Classification and Fantasy in the Photographic Construction of Caste and Tribe. Special issue *Visual Anthropology* 3(2–3) Picturing Cultures: Historical Photographs in Anthropological Inquiry. J.C. Scherer (ed.).

Pitseolak, Peter, & Eber, Dorothy 1975. *People From Our Side; An Eskimo Life Story in Words and Photographs.* Bloomington: Indiana University Press.

Roberts, Andrew 1988. Photographs and African History (review article). *Journal of African History* 29: 301–11.

Roberts, Gary L. 1978. In Search of Little Wolf... A Tangled Photographic Record. *Montana: The Magazine of Western History* 28(3): 48–61.

Robinson, Bonnell D. 1988. 'Transition and the Quest for Permanence: Photographers and Photographic Technology in Japan, 1854–1880s'. In Melissa Banta & Susan Taylor (eds.). *A Timely Encounter: Nineteenth Century Photographs of Japan* 39–51. Cambridge, Mass: Peabody Museum Press.

Ruby, Jay 1976. In A PIC's Eye: Interpretive Strategies for Deriving Significance and Meaning from Photographs. *Afterimage* 3(9):5–7.

— 1981. Seeing Through Pictures: The Anthropology of Photography. *Camera-Lucida: The Journal of Photographic Criticism* (Spring): 19–32.

Scherer, Joanna Cohan 1975. You Can't Believe Your Eyes: Inaccuracies in Photographs of North American Indians. *Studies in the Anthropology of Visual Communication* 2(2):67–79.

— 1981. Repository Sources of Subarctic Photographs. *Arctic Anthropology* 18(2):59–65.

— 1988. The Public Faces of Sarah Winnemucca. *Cultural Anthropology* 3(2):178–204.

— 1990. Historical Photographs as Anthropological Documents: a retrospect. Special issue *Visual Anthropology* 3(2–3) Picturing Cultures: Historical Photographs in Anthropological Inquiry.

— 1990. Repository Sources of Northwest Coast Indian Photographs. *Arctic Anthropology* 27(1): 40–50.

Schiller, Dan 1977. Realism, Photography and Journalistic Objectivity in 19th Century America. *Studies in the Anthropology of Visual Communication* 4(2):86–98.

Schwartz, Joan M. (ed.) 1982. The Past in Focus: Photography and British Columbia, 1858–1914. *BC Studies* 52 (Winter):5–177.

Sekula, Allan 1984. 'On the Invention of Photographic Meaning' (1974). In *Photography Against the Grain* 3–21. Halifax: The Press of the Nova Scotia College of Art and Design.

Snyder, Joel 1984. Documentary Without Ontology. *Studies in the Anthropology of Visual Communication* 10(1):78–95.

Sontag, Susan 1973. *On Photography.* New York: Dell.

Sprague, Stephen 1978a. How I See the Yoruba See Themselves. *Exposure: The Journal of the Society for Photographic Education* 16(3): 16–29.

— 1978b. Yoruba Photography: How the Yoruba See Themselves. *African Arts* 12(1):52–59, 107.

Stasz, Clarice 1979. 'The Early History of Visual Sociology'. In Jon Wagner (ed.) *Images of Information* 119–36. Beverly Hills, Calif.: Sage Publications.

Steiger, Ricabeth & Taureg, Martin 1987. 'Sleeping Beauties: On the Use of Ethnographic Photographs 1880–1920'. In Martin Taureg & Jay Ruby (eds.) *Visual Explorations of the World* 316–41. Aachen: Edition Herodot.

Taft, Robert 1964. *Photography and the American Scene: A Social History 1839–1889.* New York: Dover.

Templin, Patricia 1982. 'Still Photography in Evaluation'. In Nick Smith (ed.) *Communication Strategies in Evaluation* (New Perspectives in Evaluation 3) 121–75. Beverly Hills, Calif.: Sage Publications.

Viditz-Ward, Vera 1987. Photography in Sierra Leone, 1850–1918. *Africa* 57(4):510–17.

Wagner, Jon (ed.) 1979. *Images of Information: Still Photography in the Social Sciences.* Beverly Hills, Calif.: Sage Publications.

Weber, Ronald L. 1985. Photographs as Ethnographic Documents. *Arctic Anthropology* 22(1):67–78.

Werner, Oswald 1961. *Ethnographic Photography.* Unpublished MA thesis, Syracuse University, Syracuse, N.Y.

Worswick, Clark, & Spence, Jonathan 1978. *Imperial China; Photographs 1850–1912.* New York: Pennwick/Crown Books.

Worswick, Clark 1979. *Japan: Photographs 1854–1905.* New York: Alfred A. Knopf.

Worth, Sol 1978. Man Is Not a Bird. *Semiotica* 23(1/2):5–28.

— 1980. Margaret Mead and the Shift From 'Visual Anthropology' to the 'Anthropology of Visual Communication'. *Studies in Visual Communication* 6(1):15–22.

— 1981. 'Pictures Can't Say Ain't' (1975). In Larry Gross (ed.) *Studying Visual Communication* 162–84. Philadelphia: University of Pennsylvania Press.

Surveying the Field of View: The Making of the RAI Photographic Collection

Roslyn Poignant

THE PHOTOGRAPHS IN THE ARCHIVES of the Royal Anthropological Institute were frequently described by their collectors as of 'anthropological interest'. This essay endeavours to uncover ways in which such photographs can be seen to articulate a history of anthropology, particularly an emerging Victorian anthropology and an early-twentieth-century anthropology struggling to institutionalize and professionalize itself. It seeks to view from an ethnohistorical perspective the way in which the anthropological community absorbed, and was absorbed by, the new technology of photography that was reshaping profoundly not only the way the world was represented but also the way it was seen and comprehended. It examines how, through time, the relationship changed from a confident embrace to an arm's-length separation as the frustratingly problematic, metonymic nature of the photographic image began to be realized, and how this contributed to a more restrained employment of photography in both anthropological practice and interpretation.

The thrust of my argument is that photographs have evidential value for anthropology, in particular for a history of anthropology. By way of example, I seek first to explore the ways in which an analysis of one particular photograph elucidates one of the major givens of anthropology throughout the period under discussion: namely the insistence on the urgency of recording the *vanishing, dying, disappearing* peoples and/or their cultures before it was too late. It was an approach that helped to shape a mode of observational enquiry that produced a constructed *other*, starting from anthropology's emergence as a fact-gathering, classificatory natural science when photographs were gathered in as part of the evidence, through its Malinowskian revolution when they were frequently, but not solely, used to locate the anthropologist in his field.

On its own the print from a cracked glass plate of 'New Georgian Youths' (Plate 22i) is an easy visual metaphor for a fractured society.[1] When it is identified as having been taken in the Solomon Islands in 1893–4 by a young Royal Navy lieutenant, H.T.B. Somerville, while assigned to the Hydrographic Survey of the Pacific, and when it is recalled that he used the RAI's *Notes and Queries* to guide his anthropological observations, which were later published in the Institute's journal (1896) then, returned to its textual anchorage, this fractured image may also serve as an iconic representation of an earlier anthropology compromised by its indissoluble links with colonialism. The power of this visual metaphor flows from the paradox that, by attracting attention to the physical nature of the artefact — its material surface —

22i–ii.   New Georgian youths, Solomon Islands. Photograph by Lieutenant H.T.B. Somerville, 1893–4. Described by Somerville in his lantern-slide lecture of 1928, *Surveying the South Seas*, as: 'Here are two more young fellows, rather stiffly posed leaning against one of our coconut trees, which again shows you the slim character of the New Georgian. Their hair is fashionably lightened with lime, much as we in Europe were all poudré 150 years ago, and those lines of white lime on the face may be taken to correspond with the patches worn in those days, but here the contrast of white against black, instead of a black spot against a complexion of pearl powder and rouge. The man on the right is a considerable dandy in the matter of earrings'. (RAI 1773)

the print from the cracked plate directs attention away from the literal meaning of the image and brings into focus layers of connotative meaning, particularly those related to the nature of the signifier (Barthes 1977). But when one juxtaposes this indubitably constructed image with a print made before the plate was damaged several things happen (Plate 22ii). The most obvious one is that the transparency of the image is restored — this is a photograph of 'Two New Georgian Youths'. But as one's gaze shifts from one image to the other, the tension generated by their juxtaposition produces an effect that is analogous to an extension of photographic depth of field. It brings into focus different orders of meaning, at the level both of the signifier and the signified, and of expression and content — thus

extending the interpretive process beyond the merely metaphoric to an evidential level.

To extend the process further one can, in Somerville's case, situate the photograph within a particular text. If one first explores those meanings which attach to the signifier, the textual evidence reinforces the largely fortituous interpretation that derives from the accident of the cracked plate. And because Somerville himself chose to print from it[2] one is led to those aspects of the text that elucidate Somerville's attitudes. Not only did he consider the New Georgians doomed, he regarded their 'elimination' as being 'of no great loss to the world' — 'except from a scientific point of view' (1896:411)[3]. That this was not a prejudice he reserved for the Solomon

Islanders alone is evident from the remarks with which he prefaced his lantern-slide lecture, 'Surveying in the South Seas', given in Ireland over thirty years later. 'The surveying [of] my title,' he said, 'refers to two separate things; one . . . chartmaking; the other to the wide outlook that may be made, as from some kind of moral aeroplane, over the affairs of mankind, and the places he inhabits' (1928:1).

Thus Somerville located himself as an active agent in an expansive and confident end-of-century British imperialism. However, when one turns to those meanings that attach to the signified, then Somerville's texts provide only a thin description of New Georgian culture and of the interaction between the British surveying party and the New Georgians; it is the photograph rather than the text that prompts the questions (a subject that will be returned to later in relation to this photograph). The relationship between the visual and textual documentation is seen to be of a complementary nature rather than a matter of primacy of one over the other.

What arrives in a collection? What survives in a collection?

The object of the work is to promote accurate anthropological observation on the part of travellers, and to enable those who are not anthropologists themselves to supply the information which is wanted for the scientific study of anthropology at home. (Notes and Queries: 1874: iv[4])

Paired, these two representations of the New Georgian youths made from the same negative also project a sense of movement and the passage of time that makes them a useful visual metaphor for the whole collection. Bearing in mind the peripatetic nature of the Institute in the early years of its existence, and the removal of the collection from London during the Second World War, clearly the element of chance has played some part in what has survived. But it is not only the physical history of the collection that conveys a sense of bricolage. The assumption of the period that a photograph was not merely a semblance of a thing but the thing itself meant that many of the photographs that first entered the collection as part of that gathering of information for the armchair anthropologists to study were regarded by them as 'isolated' anthropological facts. Consequently not only those photographs that were taken by 'anthropological observers' who used *Notes and Queries* as their guide (for instance E.H. Man; see Edwards, this volume), but also those that were products of the great anthropological surveys of the last quarter of the century, such as that of the United Kingdom (see below), appear detached from their moorings until their histories are recovered.[5]

Some of the sense of fragmentation also stems from the way in which the collection was used throughout the period. There were various attempts to assemble the accumulating bank of images within a classificatory mould, and, in the 1890s, many of the photographs were made into sets of lantern slides for loan to illustrate the teaching of the new Science of Man under headings such as 'Anthropometry' or 'Prehistory', or rearranged according to broad cultural/geographical areas or aspects of material culture such as 'Charms and Amulets' or 'Primitive Canoes'. Therefore once photographs in the collection are restored to their various historical contexts, each of these earlier layers of practice may yield up its own layer of meaning.

In the examples that follow I have tried to adopt a range of interpretive strategies that exploits the polysemic nature of the photographic image in order to articulate aspects of this condensed history. My choice of particular photographs — as fragments of visual evidence — should alert the reader (and myself) to the role of my selective eye as a modifier. The selection of other fragments would have produced at least a shift in emphasis, if not a different history. Within the confines of this essay it has also been difficult to take proper account of the shifting frontiers of colonial encounter through time and space. Consequently I have followed what I see to be a line of development in which the problems relating to the integration of photography within anthropological practice surfaced mainly at home, rather than in the field, in the context of the emphasis on the body in the anthropology of the period. It is possible that the power of a facial expression to compel attention, even (or perhaps especially) when it is mediated by the photographic medium, has deflected my attention from the many views, monuments and material artefacts in the collection. In spite of these and other caveats, there emerges, from a broad survey of the contents of the collection as well as from a consideration of what is not in the collection, an awareness of both the symbiotic nature of the relationship between photography and anthropology, and the way in which particular photographs, considered individually, in groups or in series, do indeed articulate the collection's history and that of anthropology itself.

An emerging anthropology

. . . we have not adopted the term anthropology out of deference to any particular dogmas or set of opinions, or out of regard for any particular party or society, but because that term appears to be etymologically the most accurate for embracing the whole of those many studies which are included in the science of man. (Col. A. Lane Fox. 1872. Address to BAAS Dept. of Anthropology:158)

Stocking[6] has suggested that as the principal ideas that informed an emergent Victorian anthropology were developed the process can be presented as the relationship of 'three anthropological paradigms, in which ethnology is thesis; polygenism, antithesis; and evolutionism, synthesis' (Stocking 1973:cvi). In 1843 the struggle to give ethnological ideas institutional form led to the founding of the Ethnological Society. The impetus came from those of scientific inclination within the Anti-Slavery and the Aborigines' Protection Societies who wished to distance themselves institutionally from the older societies, not because they were opposed to their humanitarian goals but because their religious and political affiliations were seen by the ethnologists to compromise their scientific aspirations. The following year the putative science was at last admitted to the British Association for the Advancement of Science.

By the 1860s an essentially historical Prichardian ethnology, which had attempted to establish a typology of the diverse races of mankind, was being gradually transformed by the Darwinian revolution in scientific thought into an anthropology that applied systematic methods of classification to produce developmental models of social evolution that were in essence hierarchical. While the ethnological approach had tended to favour a single origin for mankind, some now saw the new ideas as allowing for a possible multiple origin, and others took up a strongly anti-Darwinian stance that was orientated towards a polygenist view that racial types were immutable. In 1863 those with more extreme views, led by James Hunt, broke away to form the Anthropological Society of London, while the leading exponents of the subject remained in the Ethnological Society. For the rest of the decade both these societies, their meetings and their journals, were the loci of anthropological discourse. The forum in which the proponents of this new Science of Man sought acceptance for their discipline as a science among the other sciences was the annual meetings of the British Association Sections. When, in 1866, the rebellion of the blacks in Jamaica was ruthlessly suppressed, the humanitarian impulse of the 'Ethnologicals' was strong enough for them to join in the protests. The 'Anthropologicals' took up a contrary, extremely racist stance and the conflict spilled over into the BAAS arena, where the 'Anthropologicals' attempted to set up a separate forum.[7]

The schism within the anthropological community was damaging to the scientific status of the discipline but men who held the larger issues in view, particularly Huxley, Lane Fox, Beddoe and Lubbock, struggled to heal the breach. Negotiations were protracted and centred on the name both for the field of study and for the new society (Stocking 1971). Finally, in 1871, the subject, Anthropology, defined as the 'Science of Man', was assigned a department within Biology, Section D, and the memberships of the two societies came together in an uneasy union in the Anthropological Institute. The dispute simmered on for a few more years, but the scientific party had triumphed.[8] These men belonged for the most part to a confident new professional class. They were mainly liberal by persuasion and the majority of them belonged to the Established Church, although some were nonconformists. A network of friendships and relationships united them. Most were members of more than one learned society; many of them held important positions in other British Association sections. They were part of a broader fraternity[9] within Victorian society, the 'Gentlemen of Science', whose ideas powered the engine of Progress that was propelling the British Nation towards the commanding heights of Civilization (Stocking 1987; Morrell & Thakeray 1981; Howarth 1931; Burrow 1966; Careless 1974).

'New anthropological facts'

There are several groups of photographs which came to the Institute from the earlier societies — along with their books and artefacts, and debts of the 'Anthropologicals' — that can be seen to elucidate the way in which the emerging anthropology shed its humanitarian concerns and attempted to identify and systematize anthropological facts. One of these is C.A. Woolley's set of photographs of five Tasmanian Aborigines and the fact that some of the set, particularly the frontal portrait of Trucanini, are found in almost every collection of anthropological photographs testifies both to the intense scientific speculation they aroused and to the morbid curiosity that surrounded this pitiful group of survivors (see Rae-Ellis, this volume). In retrospect it is the aesthetic framing of these images that can be seen to reflect the social attitudes of the period; the vignetting of the figures gives visual expression to the euphemism 'dying' and also sets the figures in a timeless frame. The photographer's choice of this common artistic convention signals the contemporary iconic status of these representations of 'The Last of the Tasmanians', a subject seen as worthy of display in the section devoted to Ornamental Arts at the Intercolonial Exhibition, Melbourne, in 1866 (Official Catalogue:78). The five Tasmanians were each identified by name in the exhibition, but it is the accumulative effect of the way in which each of them has been subjected to the same displinary poses — full face, three-quarter view and profile — that positions these representations within

23. *The National Picture 1985* by Geoff Parr, a Nekko print on canvas. The whole work is a transposition (in which white figures replace the Aborigines) of the unfinished painting, *The Conciliation* by Benjamin Duterreau, 1840, which depicts the meeting between George Robinson and the Tasmanians. After the 'Black Drive' in 1830, Robinson was responsible for persuading the last handful of Tasmanians to surrender in 1835. (Courtesy of the Power Collection, Museum of Contemporary Art, Sydney)

an intellectual frame which is truly objectifying — for Woolley was employing a style of presentation that in his day would have been called 'anthropological'[10]. So soon to *disappear*, the subjects were already reduced to *types*; racial types. Yet this typing is partially cancelled in the portrait of Trucanini in which her accusatory stare challenges the camera's objectifying gaze (Plate 144). It is this plane of meaning that Marcia Langton, a contemporary Aboriginal anthropologist, seized upon when she captioned this photograph 'The past haunted us', in a recent exhibition (Langton 1983:14), thus contributing a uniquely privileged 'beholder's share' (Gombrich 1982:125) to the interpretation of this photograph.[11] In Geoff Parr's *The National Picture 1985* (Plate 23) Trucanini's portrait is the pivotal syntactic unit. Her expression, which is the classic one of anger, represents the past that must be confronted; her image is held as both a mask and an icon by a present-day Aborigine whose other

hand is grasped by the artist; other figures hold the survey staffs — the instruments of alienation of Aboriginal land. The confrontation between Trucanini and the photographer has been projected into the present.[12]

By way of contrast with Woolley's portraits, there is another series of some seventeen photographs of Tasmanians from Bishop Nixon's collection which, although they are reasonably well known, are seldom found in collections of anthropological photographs. They were taken at Oyster Cove near Hobart, in 1858, and the way in which the sitters have been regrouped in the different photographs, in a variety of relaxed poses, conveys a sense of the Tasmanians' individuality and something of their human predicament (Plate 143). Again it is the cumulative effect of the series that consolidates this impression. That they are not to be found in the collection of the Institute

24. A shop with porter, Velikorusskiye (Greater Russia). Exhibited in the Eastern Slav section of the *Moscow Ethnographic Exhibition*, 1867. (RAI 27138)

reflects the scientific as opposed to humanitarian stance adopted by the emerging anthropology.[13] This view is strengthened when one notes the absence from the collection of other photographs which in later decades were used to ventilate matters of humanitarian concern, such as the photographs of the 'Congo Atrocities' (see Vansina, this volume) that are still in the collection of the Aboriginal Protection Society but not in that of the RAI.[14] By contrast an anthropometric gaze was frequently turned on prisoners and other captive sections of society such as pauper schools and the army, as in the Anthropometric Survey of 1875–83.

The Nixon photographs were first exhibited at the Intercolonial Exhibition, London, 1862,[15] and the photographic representation of *other* provides an interesting counterpoint to the popular presentation of modelled figures of *other* within the self-defining frame of the nineteenth-century exhibitions of industry and achievement. Held both in metropolitan Europe and America, and in colonial capitals, these exhibitions projected variant national views of Man's social evolution in which the displays offered a reflection on Man's great variety within an imperially imposed order.

An oblique commentary on this sociocultural phenomenon is provided by another set of photographs, also predating the Institute, that are to be considered here — the 'Russkaya Fotografiya'.[16] These are of displays of modelled figures of the peoples of Imperial Russia at the Moscow Ethnographic Exhibition of 1867, organized by the Société Impériale des Amis de la Nature. They include 'non-Russian races' such as the Samoyed, as well as 'classes' of people, such as the Russian porter (Plate 24). The exhibit-

25.   A Croat couple from the valley of Serezan near Zagreb. Exhibited in the Western and Southern Slav section of the *Moscow Ethnographic Exhibition*, 1867. (RAI 27139)

48

ion also addressed the idea of pan-Slavic unity; the southern Slavs were represented by an impeccably costumed Croat couple from Serezan valley near Zagreb, who stood in a 'meadow' carpeted with authentic local flora (Plate 25).[17] Several photographs show an overview of some of the grouped displays within the great vault of the Moscow Riding School in a way that mirrors the imperial frame. But in most cases each group has been photographed so as to exclude all others from view, and the effect of this copy of a copy lends a spurious air of reality to the figures that elucidates the Russians' view that 'the exposition . . . has produced for us a series of new anthropological facts . . .'.[18] Facts that could be packaged as photographic (arte) facts and proffered as evidence — both physical and cultural — to a fraternal society, the Anthropological Society of London, along with four casts of skulls.[19]

Meanwhile, members of the Ethnological Society[20] were striving to formulate the structures for dealing with similar, garnered 'isolated facts' (*EJ* 1869:2) and, on a proposal of A. Lane Fox, they formed a Classification Committee 'for the purpose of examining and registering all branches of ethnological evidence' under the primary divisions of Race; Languages; Religions; Folklore and Superstitions; Laws, Customs and Institutions; Work, Art and Industry (ibid.). The stated *raison d'être* was that classification provided 'insights' into 'the natural growth and order of development of all branches of human culture' but the tentative language of the report suggests that they were also struggling to formulate a methodology of anthropological discourse: the 'evidence' could not be left to 'limited and partial judgement'; the quantity of data required 'a division of labour'; and 'truth' is arrived at by 'a balance of opinions'. It is against this background that a major event in the Society's calendar for that year must be considered (ibid.:3).[21]

Commencing in March 1869, the society devoted six ordinary meetings to a series of lectures that Huxley, in his opening speech, set within an ethnological frame.[22] They covered three broad areas of the world: India, North America and Polynesia, and photographs from *People of India* were used to illustrate the first of these (ibid.:ix, x, 89–90). One is tempted to write: Consider yourself set back in time, in the lecture theatre of the School of Mines, with the People of India 'disposed' around the room, while the assembled gentlemen — and ladies — listen attentively to G. Campbell's dissertation on *The Races of India as traced in Existing Tribes and Castes* (ibid.:128).

Although the accounts of the meetings provide no direct clues as to the interplay between text and image, or even which of the hundreds of photographs were displayed, the lectures, particularly Campbell's, do provide a context for consideration of the part played by the photographs. Campbell's thesis is implicit in his title; he dealt not only with physical form but also with 'racial character'; he categorized the black Aboriginal tribes as wild and the 'Chumars' as a 'helot race', all of whom were low in the scale compared to the 'handsome' Aryans — who, of course, could not be compared with the 'alloyed', therefore stronger, Aryans of Europe (Pinney 1990 and this volume).

Turning to the photographs: in its original conception *People of India* was initiated by Lord Canning to provide a 'memory of the peculiarities of Indian life', but after 'the pacification of India had been accomplished' (Forbes Watson:1868) it was transformed into an official undertaking of the Indian colonial service. Executed over ten years by a number of different officers, many of whom had learnt photography for the purpose, this photographic survey was published in eight volumes between 1868 and 1875,[23] and is among the earliest to make sustained use of tipped-in photographs. An examination of the artistic conventions adopted by the photographers suggests that to Victorians the photographs would have provided a satisfying affirmation of Campbell's thesis. In Volume 1, which also presents images of Aboriginal tribal people and lower castes, the majority of the photographs are of head and upper torso (Plate 26). The subjects are identified mainly through costume and ornament, but also by tools of trade and weaponry, and these last two items frequently reveal their status as signs because of the way in which they are held deliberately — and awkwardly — within the frame.

The encoded social-evolutionary message of these constructed images must have been quickly absorbed by contemporary eyes. Yet the great detail of cultural information also contained within the photographs probably generated a visual *noise* that worked against attempts to structure anthropological discourse at the lectures, for it was decided that, in future, it was 'desirable to give a more scientific character' to the meetings (*EJ* 1869:x).[24] An indicator of what was meant by this is the presence in the same volume of the journal of a tipped-in photograph of a naked man posed in front of a grid (Plate 61), by way of illustrating Lamprey's *Method of Measuring the Human Form* (1869:84). It is the first use of a photographic illustration in the journals, and although one would expect a photographic technique to be illustrated in the same medium, it is significant that this subject took precedence over photographs displayed at the lectures. Although retrospectively it can be seen that the same objectifying and systematizing process underlies both

DOOANEEAH.

MIXED RACE.

ASSAM.

(34)

26. *Dooaneeah*. Plate 36 in *People of India*, vol. 1, 1868. The accompanying letterpress is a lengthy quote from *Sketch of Assam*, (London, 1846), in which these tribesmen from the Burmese Assam frontier are described thus: 'Without the aid of the Dooaneeahs, no military attachment could move to many parts of the frontier, for none are so expert as pioneers'. But their addiction to opium made them unreliable as soldiers in an emergency. (RAI Library Collection, Museum of Mankind)

People of India and Lamprey's method of surveying and registering man's physical body, it is the latter technique that, in the period, denotes a shift from interest to intention in anthropological use of photographs that can be identified with the close focus on the body as an expression of anthropology's subject: Man.[25]

Another way of isolating the 'anthropological fact' for inspection was by the presentaion of living people at the great exhibitions (Mitchell 1989; Pinney, 1990; Street this volume.) An early variation on this idea was George Catlin's proposal for a floating museum of living mankind aboard the *Great Britain*, which could be added to as they travelled about (Catlin 1850). For the Calcutta exhibition of 1869, it was proposed not only to gather together representatives of tribes of India, Asia, Polynesia and Australasia but also to invite the European anthropological fraternity 'to examine, compare and photograph this curious assemblage' (*AR&J* 1867:5). These grand schemes — mostly unfulfilled — lent an air of scientific respectability to a well-established practice of exhibiting individuals and groups of 'out-of-the-way types of humanity' (anon 1884) in places of popular entertainment along with freaks, contortionists and other 'marvels'. Although the Matabele Princess, the Aztec children, and others who were similarly traumatized and robbed of their dignity, aroused compassion in some onlookers, for the majority these shows appeared to confirm the performers' lowly place in the scale of humanity. Whereas Catlin had regretted that, in the advance of civilization, 'the first enemy that must fall is *man*' (ibid.), the response of Charles Dickens on seeing the Pygmy Earthman was to write: 'I call him a savage, and I call a savage something highly desirable to be civilised off the face of the earth' (Dickens 1853:337).

By the 1880s science was enlisted by the showmen to lend credence to these popular displays. The 'Great Farini' at the Royal Aquarium, Westminster, billed Krao, the hairy girl, as 'The Missing Link' and advertised the Bushmen's performance as an 'anthropological levee' (anon 1884). For their part, the anthropologists took advantage of the availability of these touring groups to measure and examine them. The new Science of Man and these expressions of popular culture became inextricably tangled in the racial stereotyping of the period. The anthropological photographer Prince Roland Bonaparte welcomed the presence of '*indigenous and "mixed race" groups*' from Surinam at the Amsterdam Colonial Exhibition in 1883, because it allowed observation without the inconvenience of travel (Plate 27, Bonaparte 1884); he also photographed three Australian Aborigines for the Société d'Anthropologie de Paris who were being exhibited at the *Folies Bergère* at the end of 1885 (Mondière 1886:513) (Plates 28i–iii). These were the

27. Title-page of *Les Habitants de Suriname* by Prince Roland Bonaparte, Paris, 1884, depicting three groups: Aborigines, 'Maroons' or 'Bush Negroes' and Suriname Creoles at the Colonial Exhibition, Amsterdam, 1883. (RAI Library Collection, Museum of Mankind)

last survivors of a group of nine Aborigines who had been removed from Australia by the showman, R.A. Cunningham — in spite of an attempt by two of them to escape, and in spite of public protest. He had toured them 'during the tenting season of 1883 . . . and in all the principal museums of America with unbounded success' (Plate 29), except that only seven of these 'Australian Boomerang throwers' survived to entertain the British public (Cunningham 1884:4). At the time of their examination by the Société d'Anthropologie de Bruxelles, in May 1884, all showed signs of tuberculosis; a year later in Frankfurt only five remained. When Topinard and his colleagues examined them in Paris in November 1885, only Jenny, little Toby, and Billy were still alive. About the time they were being photographed Toby, Jenny's

28i–ii. i (*facing page*) Billy, Jenny and Little Toby, photographed by Prince Roland Bonaparte in Paris at the end of 1885, were survivors of a group of nine Aborigines removed from Queensland by R.A. Cunningham early in 1883 and toured for public exhibition. Jenny and the boy were mother and son, but Billy was from a different tribe, though they spoke languages from the same Dyirbal language family. (RAI 2100). ii (*left*) Billy. According to the Belgian account, which is the most detailed and informative, he was Warutchsenben from Hinchinbrook Island. (Houzé and Jacques, 1884. RAI 2101). iii (*below left*) Jenny, or Yarembera (Yerberi), was probably from Palm Islands, the home of her husband Toby or Wangong, who died in a Paris hospital. She was said to speak a different language but it was probably an 'avoidance vocabulary'. (RAI 2097)

29. The back cover of R.A. Cunningham's pamphlet (1884) advertised his show in similar language to that used on handbills to describe other toured groups of colonised people. Already reduced from nine to seven, like other groups, his 'captive band' was expendable. (Courtesy of the British Library)

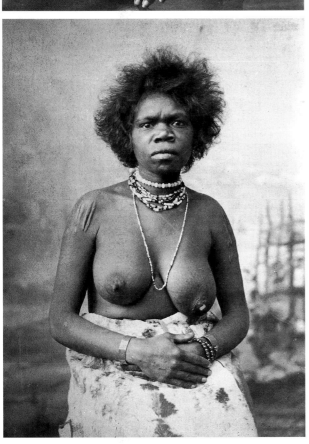

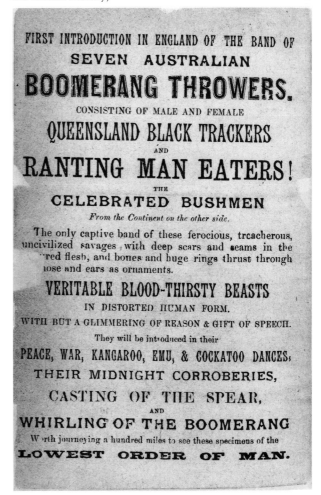

husband and the father of the boy, died in a Paris hospital. Topinard reported that he had tried — but failed — to acquire his body for Broca's laboratory. With astonishing insensitivity he attributed Jenny's air of being 'distanced from anything happening around her' to 'stupidity'. The Frenchmen also noted that Jenny and Billy were from different tribes, spoke different languages and 'hate each other' (Topinard 1885:683–99). Bonaparte's disturbing group portrait (Plate 28i) of them in their show clothes, with the stuffed dog as stage prop, while possessing some of the formal elements of the stereotyped image of the savage, catches something of their predicament and is an eloquent comment on their social dislocation.

In the first instance Billy's people had been driven from Hinchinbrook Island, off the Queensland coast, by a line of white settlers 'beating' the bush (Dixon 1972:37), and he and his companions (some of whom were from nearby Palm Islands) may well have chosen to go with Cunningham as the only way of surviving. They had ceased to be hunter-gatherers and had become show-people. Although technically not slaves, they were tied to a master whom they feared (Houzé & Jacques 1884:99)[26].

Rendered invisible

The visual corollary to this physical and actual translation of Aboriginal bodies is provided by J.W. Lindt's studio portraits of Clarence River Aborigines taken on the north coast of New South Wales. Other commentators have noted that the Aborigines were denied a meaningful place in early settler landscapes (Smith 1960:158–76; Urry 1985:63; Edwards 1988) but in Lindt's photographs of the early 1870s the process is completed; their removal from the bush to the constructed studio set, which is dressed with authentic local plants,[27] parallels their actual displacement as the land's owners. With their weapons laid aside and their wildness neutralized by the studio ambiance, they have been transformed into specimens — like the plants around them. Although these are not anthropometric portraits, their intention is anthropological.[28]

However, in these photographs the Aborigines' displacement has been masked by an aesthetic composition that only partially dispels the pervasive air of lethargy. Some of the sitters even seem to enter into the charade. The fisherman stranded on dry land is a romantic image which hints at the sacrifice of innocence for the sake of progress. (Plate 30). Lindt's creed was: 'Truth — but Truth in a pleasant form'.[29] It is a portrait of 'natural man' that can be compared with Lindt's other genre studio portraits, the shearer and the miner (Lebovic 1989:103). His style struck a respon-

30. Australian Aborigine, Clarence River, north coast of New South Wales, photographed in his studio by J.W. Lindt, early 1870s. (RAI 670)

sive chord in the public; he exhibited and marketed his Aboriginal portraits; they won him prizes, made him money and are found in every collection. By contrast, about 1878, his contemporary Fred Kruger, who was also a German immigrant, photographed Aborigines at Coranderrk Aboriginal Station, Badger's Creek, Victoria. These are not photographs of the 'Passing Aborigine' but of surviving Aborigines, mainly in European clothes, hop-picking, playing cricket and fishing. This kind of early documentary record is seldom found in anthropological collections.[30]

There are similarities between Lindt's visual displacement of the Aborigines and the way in which *People of India* can be seen as a visual projection of the process of imposing order on a conquered people too vast in numbers to disappear.[31] The same dichotomous way of seeing is illustrated by an album of some 700 photographs of American Indians given to the Institute by F.V. Hayden, Director of the American Geological Survey of Territories (1868–78).[32] These are a selection from a larger collection assembled and catalogued by W.H. Jackson (1877), the official photographer of the Survey. The majority are portraits and, although the intention implicit in their decontextualization is typological, they still contain a wealth of cultural information — and the histories of many of the subjects are recoverable (see Scherer, this volume).

Both 'ethnological' photography and topographical views were an important part of these North American surveys — geological, boundary and railway — that facilitated the opening up of the West and although both categories of photographs were often produced by the same photographers, they are seldom found together. The great views[33] — literally so, because frequently made on 20 × 24-inch glass plates — by men such as C.E. Watkins and W.H. Jackson, are expressions of an encompassing, appropriating gaze in which the Indian population is rendered near invisible. Jackson's Yellowstone landscapes underwrote the campaign for the establishment of a National Park.[34] And this containment of nature's spectacles and wildnesses can be seen as part of a consolidation of an American Nation after the Indian and Civil Wars. The photographs in both the 'Hayden Album' and *People of India* were specially taken and exemplify the complex interlocking of colonial process and anthropological purpose in which photography was the visual mesh.

An Atlas of 'types'

There were alternative sources of photographs of *other*, mainly in the form of the inexpensive carte-de-visite,[35] produced by those who set up their studios in commercial centres and ports of call throughout the world (Darragh 1981), which were disseminated widely. The complementary process by which these collected photographs were regarded in themselves as data is manifested in the practice of the German photographer C. Dammann, who, it seems, initially took photographs of visiting seamen and touring circus performers of other 'races' for the Berliner Gesellschaft für Anthropologie. He went on to assemble — and sometimes copy — the photographs of others, some of which were made available by the Society which, in turn, had received them from corresponding members abroad. Dammann's *Anthropologisch-Ethnologisches*, published as a partwork between 1873 and 1876, therefore also reflects the Society's interest in the use of photographs to encode a typology of race (Edwards 1982:259). Although it was never completed, and each issue of five sheets covered more than one geographical area, the scale and complexity of Dammann's intention is plain.[36] Tylor, in his review of it in *Nature* (1876:184), thought that it demonstrated the power of visual evidence over written 'to check rash generalisations as to race . . . by impressing on the minds of students the real intricate

blending of mankind from variety to variety'. Nevertheless it is in the concise English edition, *Ethnological Photographic Gallery of the Various Races of Man*, by C. & F.W. Dammann, 'produced in a binding suitable for a drawing room book' (ibid.), that the social evolutionism implicit in Dammann's approach is seen to serve an ideological function (Stocking 1987:232–7, 262). In spite of a mixture of genres from the anthropometric to the romantic, the layout of an average of eight cartes-de-visite to a sheet mirrored the systematizing intention of the work, and the arrangement of the sheets implied a hierarchy of race beginning with the 'Germanic & Teutonic type', of which David Livingstone provided the British example, and ending with the Australian Aborigines. The captions, which gave verbal expression to this hierarchy, began with named individuals (who were often either persons of rank, e.g. Bismarck, or iconic poses, e.g. an Italian Madonna); gradually they changed to denoting types such as 'Arab' or 'Kaffir', or used tribal group names such as 'Watschandi' (Australia). This gradation is paralleled visually by a transition from dressed to undressed; a line of descent from manufactured clothing via traditional or ceremonial costumes to natural native garb of fibre and skin.

Tylor's *Primitive Culture* had been published in 1871 and the sub-text to his *Nature* review is that he was aware from frustrating first-hand experience how difficult it was to distinguish between negative non-existent evidence and positive non-recorded evidence. He was a prime mover in the formulation of *Notes and Queries on Anthropology* (1874:5), a manual designed to assist the collection of ethnographic data by 'Travellers and Residents in Uncivilised Lands' and, because Tylor was convinced that 'the science of anthropology owes not a little to the art of photography' (1876:184), it is not surprising to find a section on photography was intended (but not produced in time). Although material of a generalized nature, including photographs, was being collected from 'remote tribes', there was no direct response to *Notes and Queries* until 1882, when E.H. Man presented to the Institute his report on the Andaman Islanders. Many of Man's photographs, for instance 'Shooting, dancing, sleeping, greeting' (Plate 67), are constructed with anthropological intention; they are visual responses to questions posed in *Notes and Queries*. It was not just the uses of photography but the whole methodological frame of *Notes and Queries* that was to be found wanting in the next two decades. Edwards in this volume looks at the ways in which Man exemplifies an attempt to integrate photography within anthropological practice in the field. My parallel concern is to look at the way in which, during the 1870s and 1880s, some of the

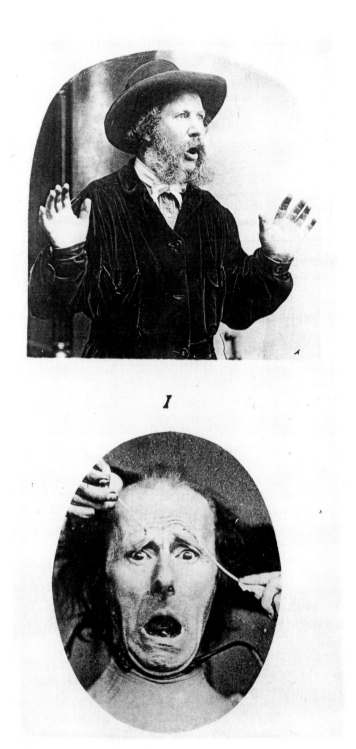

I

31i–ii. Darwin wrote: 'I have endeavoured to describe the diversified expressions of fear, in its gradations from mere attention to a stare of surprise, into extreme terror or horror.' (*The Expression of the Emotions in Man and Animals*, 1872: 307). He illustrates them in Plate VII thus: i (*top*) 'Astonishment: this gesture is represented by Mr Rejlander.' (RAI 35822) ii (*bottom*) When Darwin showed this one of a pair of photographs taken by Duchenne to fifteen persons, twelve read the expression as terror and three read it as agony or great suffering. (RAI 35822)

problems relating to the uses of photography within anthropology were being probed nearer home.

Photographs as 'anecdotal' evidence

A specific example of the controlled use of photography is provided by Darwin's *The Expression of the Emotions in Man and Animals*, 1872.[37] Darwin considered that the main 'sources of error' in observing facial expression derived from its 'fleeting nature', the interference resulting from the observer's own reaction to the emotion displayed, and the likelihood that because of 'the circumstances' of the occasion the observer sees what he expects to see (Darwin 1872a:8). Although not explicitly stated, it is evident from the way in which Darwin presented his case that he used photography to freeze the transient expressions, to distance himself from his subject, and to provide a representation that could be used to elicit comments from others. It was his application of this last use that has led recent investigators of expressions (Ekman 1973) to acknowledge that he was a methodological innovator. In order to test his own observations of the muscular movements that underlay particular emotional expressions, he selected photographs by his French colleague Duchenne of patients in which certain facial muscles had been 'galvanized' (Plate 31ii) and showed them to others for 'judgement' (Darwin 1872a figs. 20–1). He did not, however, extend this approach cross-culturally, by sending photographs to his contacts abroad to test his hypothesis concerning the universality of human expression (Ekman 1973:174).[38] As can be seen from an album (Darwin 1872b) of some 160 carte-de-visite prints she assembled, as well as selecting photographs of clinical experiments he collected those taken of both spontaneous and simulated expressions. Almost half of the prints in the album were supplied by the professional photographer Oscar Rejlander. What began as Darwin's search for the photographer of a portrait of a sad boy seen in a shop window (ibid.:182), developed into a collaboration in which Rejlander supplied photographs not only of involuntary emotional reactions like that of the Snarling Lady (ibid.:250) (Plate 32) but also of simulated emotions in which he often played the part himself — 'with some success' (ibid.:258) (Plate 31i).[39] In a way Darwin's use of photographs can be seen as an extension of his anecdotal method, which, in spite of its weaknesses, modern commentators consider he applied with some skill.

Although tangential to the main developments in anthropology, Darwin's book provides insights into the late-nineteenth-century nexus of face, body, photograph and anthropology. His concern was

32. Sneering, Defiance: 'I scorn the imputation'. 'Mr Rejlander . . . has photographed for me (Plate IV fig. 1) a lady, who sometimes unintentionally displays the canine to one side and who can do so involuntarily with unusual distinction.' In the album this print is annotated: 'Please keep this one carefully for Mr Darwin.' *The Expression of the Emotions in Man and Animals*, Charles Darwin, 1872. (RAI Library Collection, Museum of Mankind, RAI 35821)

with the 'language of emotions' rather than the physiognomy in the sense of 'the permanent form of the features', although he did consider that the latter could be affected by the frequent use of particular facial expressions (Ekman 1973:259) The sale of 6,200 copies of *Expressions* in the first week (*Nature* 7:35), however, indicates that the public acclaim derived less from the quality of the scientific exposition than from popular notions about the human face. This is confirmed by the anonymous reviewer in the *JAI* who compared the work unfavourably with Lavater's *Essays on Physiognomy*, which by then had reached its seventeenth edition in English. That the body became legible in the nineteenth century has been attributed (Shortland 1985) largely to the way in which Lavater developed a 'science' of physiognomy that involved the specification, ordering and definition of the exterior traits — 'the correspondences' between appearances and inner constitution (Lavater 1775–8:19–20). It involved both a close scrutiny of significant parts of the body such as the nose, forehead and chin, and a synthesizing gaze (Lavater's 'optic power') that

eliminated extraneous messages.[40] This physiognomic observation was practised in the streets and drawing-rooms of the metropolis, and the rules of physiognomy were applied in art (Cowling 1989). The notion of a comparative physiognomy that embraced class and race gained currency partly through Schadow's *National-Physiognomieen*, 1835, in which he extended his method of basing graphic representation on careful measurement of bodily features and underlying skeletal structures from different physical types to a range of national/racial types.[41] Like Prichard in *Natural History of Man*, 1843, he based his racial types on the published engravings (not original drawings) of the artists of the voyages of Cook, Baudin, Kotzebue and others — although he also drew from life.

Thus, for Tylor, Dammann's work demonstrated the authenticity of photographs as 'race-portraits' as compared with engravings. When he wrote, 'The skill of the collector lies in choosing the right individuals as representatives of their nations' (1876:184), two assumptions interlocked. These were: the underlying, all-pervasive idea of the period that there was a physiognomic code to be read in physical form, and that this operated within an evolutionary paradigm; and the view that there was a 'skill' involved in the reading — an observational technique that could be applied to photographs, which, after all, were the real thing. That this was so partly derived from the shared Victorian experience of being photographed in a carte-de-visite studio, where bodies were adjusted to the camera by seats that could be raised or lowered, heads were clamped in position, and persons were exposed for a fraction of time, against defining backgrounds such as 'the library', 'the outdoors', the 'drawing-room'. This quasi-mechanical procedure, dictated by the economics of the industry, produced uniform products; carte-de-visite portraits that appeared to be the ready-made constituents of a scientific narrative waiting to be pieced together. The extension of control over bodies implicit in anthropometric photography was but a short step to take.

'Skeleton features . . . living subjects'

The attempt to forge a methodology of 'comparative physiognomy' involving the close scrutiny of photographs was made primarily in an investigation that, in the 1870s, marked a shift of interest in British anthropology from the savage tribes to British origins. In the mid nineteenth century intellectual excitement had been generated by Max Müller's philological arguments for the common origins of 'Germanic' and 'Celtic' European languages in a parent Indo-European or 'Aryan' language, and a supposed language–race link was for a time made a priority in the speculative reconstructions of European racial migrations. It was only gradually, as an increased time-depth for man's history was established, that a possible model for sociocultural evolutionary reconstruction of British origins was based on attempts to correlate data from skeletal remains with the results of investigations into the physical characteristics of living populations. The struggle to achieve the procedural framework for this process is discernible in the activities of a series of BAAS committees, adjuncts to the Anthropometric Committee, and established between 1875 and 1883, that were known collectively as the 'Racial Committee'.

The reports of these committees provide the context for three albums in the collection. Untitled on the outside, each is labelled Type A, B or C on the inside and identified as belonging to the Racial Committee. At first glance the leather bindings, the decorated pages and the contents of the ubiquitous carte-de-visite and occasional cabinet-format photograph, appear to locate the volumes within the social frame of a Victorian family album.[42] On closer inspection a note at the end of Volume 3 indicates that the albums contain altogether 557 portraits — selected from a total of 844. Most of the subjects are named and their localities given. In the top-right corner of most pages there is a discreetly pencilled 'J.P.H.', indicating that J. Park Harrison[43] was responsible for the selection, and there is occasional reference to Mr Beddoe's or some other Committee member's special contribution or approval. A number of the annotations are directed particularly at establishing the person's 'pure descent' or 'long settled' status, either anecdotally as in the case of 'Murdoch Mcrae, "who never had trousers on but once . . ."' (Plate 33) or because they are genre photographs like that of a Newhaven fishwife from *Macara's Series of Scotch Photos* (Plate 34). There is a group of Cornish tin miners, men and boys (Plate 35), militia volunteers and the United South cricket team (Plate 36); and representatives of the new urban classes such as the seamstress (Plate 37) and the young dandy from Sussex. Although the albums present an impression of variety within overall homogeneity, a more complex narrative concerning the racial composition of the British seems to link the subjects.

The first of the committees to which the albums relate was given a broad brief to systematically examine human beings in the British Empire (their height, weight etc.) and to publish photographs of 'typical Races of the Empire' (BAAS 1876:liv). They chose to restrict the anthropometric part of the programme to Britain, refining their techniques of sampling and measurement and the form of their schedule of instruc-

tions to volunteers. The issues raised by the second part of the programme were not tackled until 1878, when a sub-committee set up for the purpose also limited this enquiry to 'the investigation, by means of photographs, of the national or local types of race prevailing in different parts of the United Kingdom' (BAAS 1878:155). This was not a division of labour but a separation of concerns; Lane Fox, Brabrook, and leading physical anthropologists such as Beddoe, Galton and Roberts served on the committee throughout its term.

'That characteristic differences of countenance [did] exist in different parts of the country' (*JAI* 1877:393) and were thought to be visible traces of earlier races, particularly in isolated parts of the Kingdom, (BAAS 1882:270) derived from a view, current in both popular and scholarly circles, of the racial make-up of the British as being a product of a series of invasions in which the Ancient Britons (Celts, Iberians and other tribes) had been pushed into the hinterlands by the Anglo-Saxons, who formed the English nation and were in turn conquered by the Normans. But the Anglo-Saxon core was thought to have reasserted its ascendancy over the Norman element, and this dominant racial character was identified by some in Victorian times as 'Teuton' (Urry 1984:83–5).

For Lane Fox, however, even the probability of the prevalence of a distinct type in a particular district was difficult to test because of 'the impossibility of establishing any recognizable standard of comparison of features'. He saw the problem as a methodological one. Either a vast number of photographs, supported by anthropometric documentation, had to be collected 'regardless of type' from different districts, or several 'independent observers . . . in the same district' had each to select first the physical type, and then the photographic examples of it. The committee could then judge if 'any agreement might be traced between them'. Either way 'the results would have to be treated with the utmost caution' (*JAI* 1877:393). The committee's decision was a compromise of the second option, the only control being the choice of persons whose 'pedigrees' established them as long settled in an isolated district.[44] A set of standardized anthropometric portraits were tabled as 'specimens of the way . . . the work should be done' (BAAS 1878:155). The one certitude was Lane Fox's prediction that there would be 'some little difference of opinion on the part of the committee' at arriving at a consensus (*JAI* 1877:393).

In the event, most of the collecting was done or initiated by the committee members themselves and few of the photographs were specially taken because of lack of funds. By 1880 over 400 photographs had been

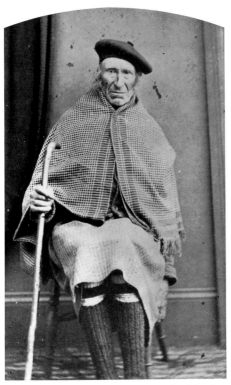

33. 'Murdoch McRae, a pure highlander living at Fort Augustus; native of Kintail, west coast of Ross-shire, "never had trousers on but once . . ."'. Carte-de-visite, photographed by MacFarlane. *c*.1878. Type 'B', vol. 2, no. 24. Selected by Dr Beddoe. BAAS 'Racial Committee' Albums. (RAI 2987)

34. 'A Fishwife from Newhaven, near Edinburgh.' Carte-de-visite photographed by Macara, *c*.1878. Accompanied by letter-press, *Macara's Series of Scottish Photos.* Type 'C', vol. 3, no. 41. Selected by J.P.H. BAAS 'Racial Committee' Albums. (RAI 2987)

35. 'A group of miners taken at Dolcoath tin mine a half mile from Camborne, Cornwall.' Cabinet format, photographed by Burrow. *c*.1878. Type 'A', vol. 1, no. 44. BAAS 'Racial Committee' Albums. (RAI 2799)

36. 'United South cricket team including Lillywhite, Gilbert, Cotterill, Humphry, Filling, I. Phillips, Charlwood, Wicock, W.G. Grace, Lillywhite, Poley, Southern, H. Phillips, Jupp and G.G. Grace.' Cabinet format, photographed by Russell & Sons, *c*.1878. Type 'C', vol. 3, no. 34. Selected by J.P.H. Not in BAAS 'Racial Committee' Albums. (RAI 3039)

37. The Seamstress, 'Neighbourhood of Bangor'. Carte-de-visite, photographed by Williams. Type 'C'. Selected by J.P.H. Not in BAAS 'Racial Committee' Albums but mounted on separate card 187. (RAI 2082)

38. 'W. Snare, Flint worker of Brandon, Suffolk.' Carte-de-visite, photographed by Boughen, *c*.1878. Type 'A', vol. 1, no. 32. Selected by J.P. Harrison. BAAS 'Racial Committee' Albums. (RAI 2788)

collected, mainly from Wales, Cornwall and remoter regions of England and Scotland, and arranged on cards for the purposes of comparison. Although it was acknowledged that 'few consequently of those obtained are of value for strict scientific examination', Mr Harrison's 'Welsh photographs' of 'the darker type' were thought to assist recognition of the type in the population of other parts of the country (Plate 38). For his part, 'Major General A.L. Fox Pitt Rivers' (in mid metamorphosis) insisted that the photographs were of no statistical value because 'the study of physiognomy was not yet reduced to a system' (BAAS 1880:159).

From the report of 1882[45] it is evident that the methodology had been dramatically restructured. Having conceded to the systematizers that 'photographic portraits do not, as a fact, assist materially in the definition of racial characteristics', the committee set about identifying the principal racial types by another method. Using what they termed 'comparative physiognomy' of selected physical features (Plate 39), they reorganized the photographs on cards according to shared features, irrespective of district. Meanwhile the three main types of 'skeletal profiles' from *Crania Britannica* (Davis & Thurnam 1856) were superimposed to produce a scale of profiles, and then these were compared with measurements the energetic committee had made of a large number of skulls from many parts of the country. It was then 'easy to compare' skeletal profiles with profiles of living subjects from the same area — by means of photographs — and a number which were believed to represent 'varieties

of the type' and 'crosses' were placed on cards. The three types were designated A, B or C, and the following year a table was produced that linked the external features with the underlying cranial characteristics[46] (BAAS 1882:270–4; 1883:307).

Although the arrangement of the photographs into three albums is similarly structured, when or why the albums were compiled is not clear — at one point publication was part of the brief. Ostensibly they were meant to demonstrate that three main strands in British racial make-up were still discernible in spite of the overall homogeneity. But it is in the third volume, covering Type C, designated as Schadow's pure Teutonic type, that the presentation has the force of an ideological statement. Given the structure of a typical family album, it opens with an idealized cabinet portrait of a Teutonic lady, followed by a same-scale portrait of the philologist Max Müller, coupled with French and German relations of the Teutonic type, then English and Scottish examples from a number of different counties. The total effect is of Teutomania superimposed on Cartomania to provide a composite view of a supposed highest plane of Victorian society. Whether the inclusion of Müller is by way of being the ironic comment of a physical anthropologist, a bow to a founding father of anthropology, or an acknowledgement of the reappraisal of the place of language and other 'social facts' in the comparative study of race, is a matter for each beholder to decide.[47]

The assembly of a 'variety of types' did not, however, constitute a representative portrait of a type. When Beddoe produced his definitive *The Races of Britain*, 1885, at least a quarter of his typical faces of Britons were based on photographs from the albums, but he used engravings to fix the types. As early as 1877 Galton had demonstrated a possible method of fixing the type; he produced a composite portrait of a criminal type by aligning in register eight photographs of different criminals. Galton made it clear that the process depended not only on the use of standardized portraits of the same scale and aspect, but also on an intensive preliminary selection of physiognomical characteristics (1877:99–100). To the committee, however, the resultant image did not appear to be a 'natural fact'; indeed the criminal type seemed to be eliminated and the 'natural man' emerged instead (*JAI* 1878:132–6). Despite this, at the BAAS meeting in Montreal in 1884, Tylor, still in search of the portrait of a type, advocated that the composite should be given 'a thorough trial' by the production of a 'galtonized' set of American Indian races (1884:903).

Galton's only use of the method to produce a portrait of a racial type was in 1885 with his much publicized and acclaimed composite of Britain's resi-

39. 'Table in which typical features of the Three principal races in the British Isles are compared.' BAAS, Report 1883. Only one column is mounted in any album — 'type C' in vol. 3. Photographs of the representative skulls are mounted in vols. 1 and 2.

	Features	A	B	C
a	Forehead	Vertical, square	Receding	Vertical, rounded
b	Supra-orbital ridges	Oblique¹	Prominent, continuous across brows	Smooth
c	Cheeks	Tapering to chin	Long	Wide, full
d	Nose	Straight, long	High-bridged, projecting	Short, bulbed
e	Mouth	Lips thick, unformed	Lips thin, straight, long	Lips well-formed
f	Chin	Small, fine	Pointed, projecting	Heavy, rounded
g	Ears	Rounded, lobed	Pear-shaped, channelled lobules	Oval, with full lobes
h	Jaw	Narrow	Large, square	Heavy, wide
i	Eyes	Dark	Blue-grey, sunk	Blue, prominent
j	Hair	Very dark, crisp, curling	Light-brown, slightly waved	Light, limp
	Skull	Dolichocephalic	Sub-Brachycephalic	Sub-Dolichocephalic
	Average height	5 feet 3 inches (m. 1·600)	5 feet 9 inches (m. 1·753)	5 feet 7 inches (m. 1·702)
	Habit	Slight	Bony, muscular	Stout, well-covered

dent other, 'the Jewish type'.[48] Within professional circles, however, the case for the composite was not proven in that its constituent elements had not been selected systematically.[49] It was not considered a substitute for the standardized anthropometric photograph that was being achieved by more precise attention to uniformity of pose, scale, illumination, background and so on (see Spencer, this volume). In fact photography had already been subsumed as only one of the techniques of anthropometric measurement that were being applied to an increasing range of bodily features and physiological functions. This increased specialization was part of the professionalizing process whereby physical anthropology was transformed into a sub-discipline.

'Facts about which there can be no question'

In several ways 1884 had marked anthropology's coming of age. It was the year in which it achieved full status among the other sciences with the formation of its own Section, H, within the British Association, and Tylor, who the same year was granted the first university appointment in anthropology, at Oxford, became president of the section. It was also the first year in which the Association met abroad — a move that can be seen in part as a process of consolidating the hegemony of British science within a colonial domain. For anthropology it also meant the location of its meeting within an important field of its study. It saw the initiation of a survey of the *North-western Tribes of the Dominion of Canada* (BAAS 1884) which continued until 1892. This style of broad ethnographic survey of a geographical–cultural area, in which the assistance of informed local residents such as government officials and missionaries was enlisted to collect data that would be formulated later by the professionals as a report, was to be a prevailing mode of anthropological practice, both at home and abroad, until the end of the century. In all these surveys the role of the camera as an observational tool became well established, and some of the material entered the collection.[50]

In Britain in the 1890s the attempt both to utilize this untrained input, and to gain mastery over the anthropological fact within the evolutionary paradigm, found expression in the ambitious programme outlined by the *Ethnographic Survey of the United Kingdom*. The aim was to bring together data from investigations into physical features, folklore, linguistics, ancient monuments and archaeological sites, in some 260 selected localities regarded as unaffected by the Industrial Age. The survey was organized by a BAAS committee drawn from the relevant societies, who prepared the instructions and coordinated the

investigations. The folklorists, who saw their study as starting where physical anthropology left off (Folklore 1896:41), considered themselves to be the prime movers of the survey. A number of anthropologists, particularly Haddon, were active in both societies; Haddon had made the original proposal and his survey of Aran, for which he made anthropometric, but nonetheless sympathetic, portraits had been tabled as a model (Haddon & Browne 1891–3). Through his lecture 'Photography and Folklore', in which the illustrations ranged from the descendant of a seal woman to stone circles, he demonstrated the worth of the photographic record (1895:222).

While at one level voluntary participation in the survey can be seen as operating within the framework of a *Notes and Queries* methodology, at another it must be looked at within the context of the general photographic surveys of the counties, beginning with Warwickshire in 1890, and paralleled by a number of similar surveys in Europe and America. From the contemporary utilitarian perspective the aim of these was to harness 'the horse-power running to waste . . . in the domain of photography' (Gower 1916:6). The BAAS report of 1895 made clear that the participating societies not only aimed to marshal their own memberships but also planned to tap into the work of the photographic surveys then under way. The scientific aspirations of the planners of the ethnographic survey, however, exceeded the local investigators' capacities; the level of technical competence expected of them in almost every department, but particularly in linguistics and physical anthropology, was too high, and these expectations ultimately undermined the project. The results were judged to be meagre and the programme was discontinued (Urry 1984:83–105).[51] The effects are visible in the collection, which holds a number of photographs that appear to be from the survey. These photographs are of archaeological sites, ancient monuments and artefacts that are difficult to place; they appear to be paragraphs and chapters in a collection of short stories rather than to form a coherent narrative.

The same social-evolutionism that underpinned the BAAS survey provided the ideological drive for Sir Benjamin Stone's vast National Photographic Record initiated in 1897, and found expression in the visual summation of late-Victorian society he constructed in his published selection of photographs (Stone 1905).[52] By contrast the earlier survey had aspired to recover the scientific 'truth' about the nation's past — a holistic vision that proved to be a chimera.

It was not only the failure of the survey that raised doubts about anthropological theory and practice. In the preface to the new ethnographic section of the

40. New Georgians, Solomon Islands. Photographed by Lieutenant H.B.T. Somerville, 1893–4. Described by Somerville in his lantern slide lecture of 1928, *Surveying the South Seas*, as: 'Here he is again [see plate 22], the left hand one of these two heads, which were taken to show the effect of an ear without, and an ear with an earring inserted respectively . . . The other man's head merely shows an ear lying fallow, as you might say, keeping rested for the next smart occasion.' (RAI 1782)

second (1892) and third (1899) editions of the recast *Notes and Queries*,[53] the editor, C. Read, urged that as much time as possible should be devoted to 'the photographic camera . . . for by these means the traveller is dealing with facts about which there can be no question, and the record thus obtained may be elucidated by subsequent inquirers . . .' (1899:87). His elevation of the photographed fact suggests that dependence on the untrained observer was beginning to falter. For him photography not only produced a filable fact but also seemed to offer the solution to the problem of the faulty interpreter and the recalcitrant informant — 'the savage' who, because of 'the limited range of his vocabulary and ideas . . . timidity . . . desire to please . . . will give the answer he thinks is wanted' (ibid.:87). (See also Pinney, this volume.)

Insight into the other side of the story — the attempt to integrate photographic practice into the investigatory frame of *Notes and Queries* — is provided by Somerville, whose published notes (1896) explicitly state that he followed the 'various heads' given in that manual. Although he made a series of competent

anthropometric measurements of the New Georgians (1893–4), he took no supporting anthropometric photographs, except for one of a sailor and a local side by side to show comparative build. Again, although his detailed notes reflect his interest in crafts such as the manufacture of shell armlets, the only processes he recorded, such as the making of fire, or activities such as playing the flute, were covered in single shots. Their inadequacy as explications of techniques cannot be attributed solely to the limitations of the equipment he was using because, in the New Hebrides, he responded to the stimulus of a ceremonial occasion — the *maki* — by attempting to break the bounds of technical limitations to make an *instantaneous* record. Rather, there seems to be a conflict between the strictures imposed by the *Notes and Queries* formula, and Somerville's personal response to the New Georgians. Consequently what appears to be a sensitive portrait of two men is, if his lecture notes are to be taken at face value, a record of ears with and without earplugs (Plate 40). As in the case of the New Georgian youths (Plates 22i–ii), there seems to have been an element of self-

41. Lieutenant H. Boyle Townsend Somerville with his surveying instruments, New Georgia, Solomon Islands, 1893–4. (RAI 27028)

presentation involved. Whether the conflict is between what he thought he was doing and a beholder's view is speculative, but this, taken together with his self-portrait (Plate 41) and others of the naval encampment, reveals an underlying current of encounter that links the whole series.

Facts too difficult to classify

Müller saw his appointment as president of Section H in 1891 as denoting a shift from an anthropology that 'treated only of the human body' to one that embraced Man's customs, laws, traditions, religions and so on (1891:791). Within the specific context of *Anthropological Uses of the Camera* im Thurn raised doubts about the value of anthropometric portraits, which he regarded as difficult, if not impossible, to obtain in the field, and of no value, being 'merely pictures of lifeless bodies' (1893:184–283). He supported his case for a more positive use of the camera — that of photographing 'living beings' — with examples from his own work among the people of 'Guiana' (Tayler, Pinney, this volume). However, the contextualization he provided in his article for his own photographs is perhaps of more interest than his tentative dialectic.

Müller notwithstanding, throughout the 1890s the physical anthropologists continued to play a dominant role within the institutional formations of anthropology. What seems to be the first strong realization that the reality of the image was challengeable — even at the denotative level — came from the criminal anthropologists, who for a time formed a separate department in Section H, and who were concerned to apply the greatest control over the photograph's production and classification. It was in the course of reviewing Bertillon's system of classification of the bodily measurements and photographs of criminals, that Professor Flower observed, 'Photographic portraits of even one's best friends . . .' were not always recognizable, and therefore it was not surprising that criminals with a determination to deceive were able to do so. He went on to declare that although 'photographs are extremely valuable as aids to identification', they have been found wanting 'as a primary method' (i.e. unsupported by measurements) owing to 'the difficulty, if not impossibility, of classifying them' (1894:769–70).[54]

For Portman, however, as a self-declared 'practical anthropological photographer of some experience', photographic/anthropological facts were still facts. He wrote that 'almost every act of the life of a primitive people can be photographed'. His instructions were expressed in the language of control: the subjects of anthropometric portraits should be 'stark naked'; 'bad sitters' should be sent away; and so on (Pinney, this volume). He was equally precise about selection and use of photographic equipment and darkroom apparatus: 'Keep a notebook . . . Number all negatives and prints . . . [File them] systematically . . .' and 'lock up all your apparatus from savages and others.' Finally he defined the subject as finite — there would soon be 'no more aborigines'. Therefore what was left to be recorded should be apportioned and 'the collections and photographs should be deposited, say, in the British Museum' (1896:75–7).

The same assumption that it was possible to contain the anthropological photograph is implicit in the 1906 BAAS committee's scheme for 'the collection, preservation and systematic registration of photographs of anthropological interest'. Similar schemes were being initiated in other sections, such as Geology, but the anthropological artefact proved more recalcitrant. The next year it was decided that sources of photographs such as missionary societies would be listed without having to lodge a permanent copy of the print. Although by 1908 a high proportion of the numbers allocated had been registered, two years later the scheme was abandoned, and the collection of photographs was passed to the Institute (BAAS

1906, 1907, 1908, 1910). The comparative impetus was passing; the collecting of photographs whose evidential value was beginning to be doubted was becoming an irrelevance to the new directions in anthropology.

As Professor Flower had observed in 1894, the Institute had remained a 'Society' in all but name. Attempts to strengthen its institutional role had failed and efforts to establish an Imperial or Colonial Bureau of Ethnography/Anthropology in the 1890s and early 1900s also foundered.[55] Ultimately the forces at work were centripetal and it was in the colonies that centres for anthropological research linked with administration were set up. At home the new formations that emerged both determined and were determined by the way in which anthropology became institutionalized. The nexus formed by the Institute, BAAS Section H, and the newly established university departments — at Oxford, Cambridge, and then London — was a characteristically English style of networking in which the Section H meetings served as centres of discourse — and as shock absorbers between factions. Increasingly, research projects, such as the Cambridge Expedition to the Torres Straits 1898–9, ceased to be coordinated or funded by the BAAS.

Photographs as curios

Professor Flower's doubts about the possibility of classifying photographs had narrowed the field of view in order to focus on a particular area of anthropological practice, but it also signalled a larger methodological problem. It was becoming increasingly evident that the avalanche of ethnographic facts could no longer be accommodated within the theoretical frame of the discipline. In 1878 Huxley had referred to the loci of disturbances that formed as scientific knowledge expanded, first in geology and biology — and by extension in anthropology (1878:573). By the turn of the century, the tremors that were disturbing the crust of anthropological thought and practice presaged a major shift of direction. A.C. Haddon gave expression to this change in South Africa in 1905 when, as president of Section H, he called for an 'œcological' framework for more intensive studies.

I would like to emphasise the fact that very careful and detailed studies of definite or limited areas are urgently needed, rather than a general description of a number of peoples which does not exhaust any one of them — in a word, what we now need is thoroughness. (Haddon 1905:512)

He was speaking with the experience of the Torres Straits Expedition behind him. Although this took the form of a survey it is regarded as the beginning of a new, more extensive field-based approach. There were other British field anthropologists, notably Baldwin Spencer in Australia, and both he and the Torres Straits team used still and movie cameras to specific purpose. In accord with the new institutional pattern their photographs were lodged with their own universities. Two of the Torres Straits team, W.H. Rivers (among the Todas) and C.G. Seligman (among the Veddas), pioneered the new approach. As Pinney has demonstrated (this volume) their attempts to integrate photography in fieldwork were closely entwined with their efforts to redefine the field of study. In time, the way in which photographs of *other* were firmly positioned within the travel genre, documentary and photojournalism was seen to compromise the discipline's use of photography with anthropological intention.

The new theoretical orientation was towards an ahistorical structural-functionalism (Stocking 1984), and for A. Radcliffe-Brown, founder of one of its schools, the visualization of this process was not photography and anthropology. Whereas Radcliffe-is space to deal only with that aspect of the development which has bearing on the relationship between photography and anthropology. Whereas A. Radcliffe-Brown's use of photography in the Andamans, 1906–8, conformed with the broadly evolutionary approach of his textual presentation (Radcliffe-Brown 1922; Stocking 1984), in Western Australia in 1910–11 he appears not to have used a camera at all. A review of the various locations where he collected the data on which his most important theoretical writings were based has been made elsewhere, mainly in the discourse about the mutual disillusionment between himself and Daisy Bates (Langham 1981; Needham 1974:155; White 1981; Grant Watson 1946:110). Relevant here is that he chose to spend six continuous months on Bernier Island, where there was a 'lock' hospital for Aboriginal men suffering and dying from venereal disease. These became his principal informants. Yet for a real picture of this place one must turn not to his ethnography but to fiction. For part of his stay Brown was accompanied by a young Cambridge biologist, E.L. Grant Watson, who afterwards wrote a novel, *Where Bonds are Loosed*, in which he described the new arrivals:

The natives were indeed in a miserable condition. They had been on board all night, and as most of them had never seen the sea before, they were very much frightened. Of necessity they were chained together by light chains that went round their necks. (1914:21)[56]

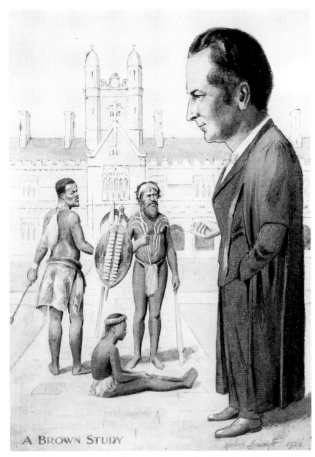

42. The Brown Study, 1929. Wash drawing by Herbert Beecroft. Radcliffe Brown in the Sydney University Quadrangle. (Courtesy of the Institute of Social Anthropology, University of Oxford)

Thus a photograph that would situate the anthropologist in his field would be one of the several extant of Aborigines in neck-chains (Langton 1988:61). The absence of a Radcliffe-Brown establishing field shot, in the Malinowskian manner, must be read in conjunction with the opening paragraphs of the former's 1931 monograph on social organization. One is led at least to speculate about the possible effect a different field experience would have had — not of course on the development of anthropological theory, but on Radcliffe-Brown's perspective (Plate 42).

Malinowski's criticism in *Argonauts* of works 'with the scientific hall-mark upon them' that fail to inform about the 'actual experiences' in the field, reads like a comment on the other man's methods (1978 edn.:3). The archetypal self-representation of Malinowski, the interpreter (creator) of cultures, is a beholder's view; it is the retrospectively selected one of a dark silhouette projected against the screen of 'chaotic' Trobriands life (Stocking, 1983:101). In *Argonauts* his own choice of establishing shots encompasses a progression from the

beach to the *heart* of Trobriands life in two paired photographs. In plate 1 his tent stands side by side with the huts of Nu'agasi and in plate 2 it is almost hidden in the 'restricted central area of Omarakana' (1978 edn.:17). In his self-flagellating review in *Errors of Omission and Commission in Coral Gardens* Malinowski listed his failure to make use of photography as a 'capital blot'. He considered that he had 'put photography on the same level as collecting curios . . .' — that is, in the fact-gathering style of the old anthropology (1966 edn.:461). From his list of the occasions on which he should have used it, it is evident that for him photography belonged on the ground between 'the brute material of information' and the ethnographer's 'final version' (1978:3–4). He wrote in explicit terms:

> In writing up my material on gardens I find that the control of my field notes by means of photographs has led me to reformulate my statements on innumerable points. (1966:461)

This *internalization* of photography, both as a technique of fieldwork and within the analytic process, typifies the way in which some anthropologists who used photography began to integrate it in their practice. For others it remained no more than a way of recording the ethnographic detail and of providing a visual dimension to the presentation of their work. Yet, as time went on, for later anthropologists the anchorage of text in an anthropological present filled the whole presentational frame. The photograph not only became redundant but was, in its immediacy, essentially in opposition to the objectifying intentions of the monograph. The publication of photographs of informants and places exposed the anthropologist's privileged field of view. (See Pinney, this volume, for another view.)

To some extent the divergence between academic anthropology's reservations about photography and a more generalized and popular anthropology's use of it is reflected in the physical locations of collections. For instance, Malinowski's is in the archives of the London School of Economics. Many of the donors of photographs to the Institute's collection in the early twentieth century, however, were figures marginal to anthropology: missionaries such as Grubb (South America) and Dauncey (New Guinea), government anthropologists such as Northcott Thomas (Nigeria) or administrators such as Barton (New Guinea). Some continued to produce images that reflected comparative concerns; all were directly involved with savage tribes as a subject people. Whatever anthropological intention they aspired to, the *aboutness* of the images articulated colonial power structures. Though the

MOUNTED CONSTABLES WILLSHIRE AND WORMBRAND WITH NATIVE POLICE
IN CENTRAL AUSTRALIA, MAY 20TH, 1887.

43.   'Mounted Constables Willshire and Wormbrand with Native Police in Central Australia, May 20th, 1887' provides an example of a constructed visual narrative typical of a settler society (see Peterson (1989) for analysis). (RAI 35530)

details of the events portrayed are often obscure, when they can be recontextualised they may extend the documentation of changing communities and assist the recovering of histories (Salmond, Binney, Edwards, this volume).

Other photographs that belong on the ground of popular anthropology were often produced in the settler societies like South Africa, Australia and New Zealand. Produced within a vernacular framework, they were published in books and newspapers and were widely disseminated as postcards. Those in the latter format neutralized 'wildness', as in representations of 'Our Maoris' or 'Dinkum Aussies', others were visual narratives in which the story of the frontier encounter was constructed (Plate 43). Some, such as Curtis and Reinhart in North America, produced the romantic, nostalgic images of 'natural man' restored to the landscape. All were images of appropriation. Considering the output, it is not surprising that examples of these genres, often found in travellers' albums, entered the RAI archives. Within the discipline these images, together with the earlier Victorian photographs once regarded as of anthropological interest, came in due course to be dismissed as curios.

Since the resurrection of the collection by Brownlee Kirkpatrick in the early 1970s much new material has been attracted to it from successive generations of anthropologists such as Richards and Gluckman, but the way in which these more recent scholars have integrated the photograph within their anthropological practice is the substance for a new chapter in an ongoing narrative.

ACKNOWLEDGEMENTS

All those who use the RAI Collection owe thanks to Brownlee Kirkpatrick for her thoughtful stewardship of it until 1976. I wish to thank Elizabeth Edwards, Christopher Pinney and Jonathan Benthall for their comments, support and encouragement, without in any way involving any of them in my follies of condensation or failures in analysis. Thanks are due to: the Mitchell Library, Sydney; the State Library of Victoria; Jenny Boddington, past curator of photography, National Gallery of Victoria; the State Library of Tasmania; the RAI staff; and the staff of the libraries of the Museum of Mankind, the Pitt Rivers Museum, and the University of Cambridge. The assistance of H. Persaud and the permission of the Museum of Mankind (British Museum) to rephotograph items now in the Museum of Mankind library is much appreciated.

NOTES

1   For instance, the cover of *RAIN* July/August 1974, and, with the cracks exaggerated, in the catalogue cover and poster for *Fremden-Bilder* (Brauen 1982), the exhibition of RAI's *Observers of Man*, in Zurich, 1982.

2   The plate may have been cracked as early as 1897 (*JAI* 1898). Somerville remained an active photographer; he did not need to print from the cracked plate.

3   Somerville lists the ways in which the society had been shattered: headhunting made more lethal by the gun, blackbirding, the influence of traders, the punitive raid on Rubiana by HMS *Royalist* in 1891. Somerville's reasoning was that the 'incurable laziness — the heritage of all Pacific races' made the Solomon Islanders expendable because their lands could be made more productive in the hands of 'more energetic and industrious people'. (1896:411)

4   This is the first edition of *Notes and Queries on Anthropology, For the use of Travellers and Residents in Uncivilized Lands*, drawn up by a BAAS committee; this paper is also concerned with the second edition, 1892, and the third, 1899. See Urry 1972 for the use of anthropological questionnaires predating *Notes and Queries* and for the *Notes* themselves.

5   For example a number of the large-format, paired (full-face and profile) anthropometric portraits of the Lapps, taken by Prince Roland Bonaparte in 1884 were split apart and used in other systems of classification now lost. See Bonaparte, H.H. Prince R. *Notes on the Lapps of Finmark (Norway)*, 1886, *JAI* 15:211–13.

6   Stocking's authoritative historiographic corpus precludes the necessity of detailing the way in which the principal strands — epistemological, institutional and social — that make up the history of anthropology in the nineteenth century intertwine.

7   The struggle between factions took the form of rival claims for the locus of the subject within the two sections of BAAS, Geography and Biology. For details see Stocking 1971, 1987.

8   Markers of the acceptance of anthropology within BAAS, in spite of dissension within its own ranks, during the crucial years are: 1870: Sir John Lubbock gave the evening lecture 'Savages' (also the year of the publication of his *Origin of Civilization*).
1871: E.B. Tylor gave the evening lecture 'The Relation of Primitive to Modern Civilization'.
1872: Sir John Lubbock in his capacity as president of the section built his address round Darwin's *Origin of Species*.

9   Col. A. Lane Fox (Vice President of the anthropological department of BAAS, Section D) hoped that 'Anthropology will be fairly admitted into the brotherhood of the established sciences...' (1872:157).

10 It might also have been called ethnological — it belongs to the physiognomic — typological approach to physical features, predating the anthropometric (Spencer, this volume).

11 See discussion on Darwin's *The Expression of Emotions in Man and Animals* below and see Ekman's *Darwin and Facial Expression*, also discussed below. By pursuit of only one plane of meaning, the 'framing', one can mask other content of evidential value. I am trying to abstract the range of meanings attaching to the signifier, Woolley, the Victorian photographer, and to the signified, the Tasmanians, including

the element of self-projection. Gombrich's discussion about the nature of the 'perception of physiognomic constancies' and 'the global impression of the face', particularly his interpretive strategy of separating out 'the permanent (p) and mobile (m)' aspects of the latter have contributed to this analysis (Gombrich 1982:125).

12 For a representation of Duterreau's painting see Stocking 1987: 274, where he uses as a chapter opening a reproduction of an engraving based on the painting from James Bonwick, *The Last Tasmanians...*, 1870, opp. 210.

13 Some of the series, however, are to be found in the Pitt Rivers Museum, Oxford. Collected by E.B. Tylor, they reflect his special interest in photography. The definitive set is seventeen prints in: MS. Dr Mitchell's Album, Mitchell Library, Sydney.

14 I do not mean to imply that the early societies were entirely without concern for humanitarian matters — e.g. see *Popular Anthropology* Vol. 1 1866:10, where 'the wilful extinction of Aboriginal tribes i.e. Aboriginal in the sense of indigenous in New Zealand, Africa and Australia' was condemned, and more specifically p. 12: 'In Queensland... white colonists are destroying the natives of whole tribes; and the government sanctions the system by a policy of non-intervention...'. There are a number of other examples in subsequent years.

15 Private communication from State Library of Tasmania. The British Library copy of the catalogue was destroyed during the war and I have not located it in another library.

16 Bogdanov, V.V. (compiler), *Catalogue to the Russkaya Etnograficheskaya Vystavka, Moscow, in the Manezh (Riding School)*, April 23–June 19, 1867. Organized by Obshchestvo Lyubiteleyei Yestestvoznaniya (The Society of Amateurs of the Natural Sciences, elsewhere in Russian correspondence called Les Amis de la Nature.) Those discussed here: No. 20 'The Samoyed from the Kanin Tundra'; Nos. 41 and 42 'Serezan man & woman'; No. 62 'The

Yardman [porter] Velikorusskiye [Greater Russia]'. Translation by S. MacKay, gratefully acknowledged.

17 That these accessories were provided by the good offices of a priest at the Russian embassy in Vienna who acquired them from an Ethnographic Committee in Zagreb, is an indication of the widespread interest in anthropology — as well as pan-Slavism.

18 Fedtschenko, Alexis, Oct. 4, 1867 (Moscow). A letter as read at meeting, Dec. 31, 1867. See *JAS* 1868:6:1

19 RAI Archive A.4. Minutes of meeting, Feb. 4, 1868: 'A letter was read from Prof. Bogdanov of Moscow, and a series of skulls presented by him . . . also a large series of photographs forming an Anthropological Album . . .'. The printed version in the journal establishes that there were two sets of photographs, those of the exposition and another of 'the natives of greater Russia'. Both sets are in the RAI collection. See *Anthropological Review and Journal* 1868. The *Journal* report of the meeting refers to four casts of skulls. It may or may not be the same gift.

20 It is important to recall that some of the 'players' were members of both societies, for instance Lane Fox and Tylor, but it was within the Ethnological Society that the more scientific approach was cultivated.

21 At the same time as Lane Fox was a prime mover in the establishment of the Classification Committee to assist the *interpretation* of anthropological facts he was also concerned with the formulation of guidelines to assist the *collection* of anthropological facts in the field that was finally produced in the form of *Notes and Queries* — not published until 1874.

22 I have used *published* sources rather than archival — the *reports* and *notes* — to provide contemporary context for the photographs under consideration here, in an attempt to articulate what 'they' thought they were doing with the photographs. I am aware that archival sources may provide more depth and/or mediate the argument, but others who have looked for photographic references in archival sources will know how rare they are.

23 The first three volumes were published in 1868.

24 Throughout the last three decades of the century the journal is peppered with references to the exhibition at meetings of many different kinds of photographs such as those of Peruvian antiquities, a tailed boy of Saigon, composite portraits of Sandwich Islanders' skulls and the Ainus of Japan, mainly to illustrate specific anthropological detail presented in an accompanying paper. This is the only example so far that I have found of an attempt to structure the presentation of visual and textual anthropological evidence within an interpretive methodological frame — difficult though it is to render the case entirely visible. The problem was compounded by the scarcity of journal illustrations.

25 There were economic and technological constraints on the use of photographic illustrations in the journals. The tipping-in of real photos had problems relating to permanence and consistency. The early photomechanical processes such as the Woodburytype and the carbon print (1860s), and the variations on the collotype process, such as the heliotype (1870s) were permanent processes but sometimes lacked the tonal range of the original. All were expensive, not only in the production but also in the binding. Engravings, often based on photographs, continued to be the most usual mode of illustration until, from the 1880s, they were gradually superseded by the halftone block, a reproductive technique that was at first no more than a coarse rendering of the original. The first heliotype illustrations are Dobson's photographs of the Andaman Islanders, *JAI*:4, 1874 (see Edwards, this volume). There are several illustrations in a collotype process in *JAI*:6, 1877, and in *JAI*:12, 1883, there are five of Man's photographs of the Andaman Islanders. In *JAI*: 10, 1881, there is a carbon-print frontispiece tipped-in portrait of Broca.

26 These photographs were recorded as a gift to the 'Library' from Prince Roland Bonaparte on December 8, 1885 (*JAI* 1886:422) and their acquisition was referred to again in the record of the meeting of April 26, 1887 at which Jenny, Little Toby and Billy were examined at the Anthropological Institute (*JAI* 1888:83). It is not possible within the scope of this paper to explore further the unholy alliance between the physical anthropologists and the promoters of popular shows of people. A reconstruction of the Aborigines' personal story is being attempted in a work in progress by the present writer. Thanks are due to Dr Peter Mesenhöller, Dr Paul Turnbull and Fiona Stewart for directing my attention to several of the sources.

27 Notes to Lindt's photographs in the RAI collection supplied by Isobel McBryde.

28 Lindt retained his interest in anthropological subjects and went on to cast himself in the role of official expeditionary photographer to Scratchley in New Guinea in 1885, afterwards publishing *Picturesque New Guinea* in which his photographs were reproduced as autotypes — an early mechanical printing process. Later in the 1890s he jeopardized his photographic business in Melbourne by making photographic field trips to Fiji and the New Hebrides; he failed to find a publisher and these photographs exist only in photographic folios and are not well known. His New Guinea photographs include 'field' photographs of people in their surroundings — and in the landscape, and are taken at an early stage of contact.

29 Lindt produced several self-advertising pamphlets that provide insight into his aesthetics and methods. For instance: *A Few Results of Modern Photography*, 1886, Melbourne, in which he included a Preface dated 1883 which opens 'My motto . . .': 3 (Copy Melbourne Public Library).

30 To date only several albums of Kruger's work exist in Victoria State Institution (see Boddington 1979). Personal communication from E. Edwards: there are thirteen prints in the Pitt Rivers Museum, collected by Tylor, that have been identified as Kruger's

by Sandra Smith, Aboriginal Liaison officer, Victoria Aboriginal Cultural Heritage Unit, who also supplied the date of the commission by the mission. Although these are all non-studio, sympathetic portraits, the album held by the National Gallery of Victoria contains a number of groups and activities. There is a scattering of other sympathetic portraits of surviving Aborigines from the same period, plus 'news' portraits such as those of the members of an Aboriginal cricket team, 1868, by Jennings Bakla & Co. (Lebovic 1989:49–51).

31 Some of the same photographers who were involved in *People of India* had studios which produced the picturesque views of India and its monuments; the landscapes incorporating colonial achievements such as the railways; activities such as the tiger hunt; exotic nature — bamboo and banyan — and, in Sri Lanka, portraits of young women in Oriental mode; in short all those constructed images of desire collected while abroad. Through the assembly of prints — particularly carte-de-visite — in personal albums, and through the stereograph these were a part of popular culture. Sometimes images of 'other' categorized as village views or native types — particularly if they exhibited signs of exoticism such as bare breasts or tattooing — were included. The dynamic and control of the production of this genre lay in the commercial domain, therefore it is not easy to discern how these exotic and romanticized images functioned when they entered the collection; usually they seem to have been classified as 'types'. The exploration of this aspect and the investigation of its development cannot be undertaken within the limitations of this essay.

32 Hayden's gift of the album to the Institute was on February 6, 1877, *JAI* 7:1, 1878. The Hayden Album contains many of the same photographs as in W. Blackmore's collection, used to illustrate the second series of lectures on North America at the Ethnological Society in 1869.

33 R. Krauss's discussion (Krauss 1985) of the discursive spaces of the flat landscape print and the stereographic view does much to restore these photographs to their status as topographical views. But I do not think it nullifies the point of view advanced here concerning the near-exclusive categories of views and ethnographic subjects. Both view and stereo cameras were used in the field. Not only views were photographed stereoscopically — for instance, the Treaty of Laramie was photographed by the same technique. See also Darragh for an assessment of the number of stereo photographs taken of 'Indians' (1964:85).

34 A selection of nine views was given to each member of Congress (Gernsheim 1969:289). An album of eighty-one photographs, *Views of Yellowstone* (Dept. of the Interior, USGS), 1871, was also given to Congress.

35 The carte-de-visite was first introduced and popularized by Disdéri, Paris, *c.*1855. Cameras with more than one lens and moving backs etc. were used, that could take up to twelve photographs of one person or of different people on the same negative.

36 My particular thanks are due to E. Edwards, who directed my attention to one of the most complete copies of *Anthropologisch-Ethnologisches Album von Dammann in Hamburg* in the British Library, and also for her generously imparted information from her in-depth documentation on Dammann work, particularly the holding of it in the Pitt Rivers Museum; both tempered my conclusions. (See Edwards 1990.) C. Dammann died in 1874 and the publication was continued by his brother Frederick. The British Library copy has bound into two volumes the fifty folio-size sheets referred to by Tylor in his *Nature* review. There are some 600, mainly carte-de-visite format, photographs from areas of Africa, America (North and South), Asia, Australasia, and areas of Europe such as Poland, Rumania, Lappland and Finland but not western Europe as in the more popular edition. Both the RAI copies of Dammann's albums, referred to by Tylor in his review, are now in the Museum of Mankind library. The German edition is incomplete; there are loose Dammann photographs in the RAI collection which may have come from this copy. There are some 158 photographs (about twenty of which are larger format than carte-de-visite) on twenty-three sheets, in the 'educational atlas in English'. Could this be the first coffee-table book?

37 The RAI's copy, inscribed 'from the author', is now in the Museum of Mankind library. It is illustrated by eighteen engravings and seven plates (each containing several photographs) of heliotypes — an early photomechanical process that facilitated the production of long runs of photographically illustrated books; a commercial proposition only for a bestseller.

38 From 1867 Darwin circulated *Queries about expression* to contacts throughout the world (Freeman & Gautrey 1975). He received thirty-six replies (Darwin 1872a:8). By modern standards this is too small a sample and the questions he framed often pre-empted the replies (Ekman 1973). I attribute more significance to Darwin's use of photographs than Ekman does (ibid.:261).

39 It is not entirely paradoxical that the innovative Darwin's chosen simulator was a photographic innovator in his own right. For in 1859 Rejlander had been the creator of a composite photograph, made from thirty different negatives, of a *tableau vivant* enacting the allegorical theme: *The Two Ways of Life*, by way of a personal affirmation of photography as art.

40 I am grateful to Pinney for directing my attention to Shortland's analysis of Lavater.

41 Schadow's work follows Blumenbach's (the skull as an index of race) 1775, Camper's (the application of a facial angle) 1794 (see Spencer, this volume) and Gall's (the disposition of men and animals by the configuration of the brain and head) 1835. Although there were many physiognomic popularizers in the nineteenth century his work seems to have been a primary influence because of his demonstration of a technique.

42 By the 1870s the popularity of this style of presentation amounted

to a 'Cartomania' (Gernsheim 1969:294). Victorians constructed their own carte-de-visite narratives in album form. A typical album opened with a portrait of the Queen and/or the Royal Family, followed by Men of Rank (the choice providing clues as to the political affiliations of the owner) and then came the family, arranged genealogically. If the family had a history of overseas service there would probably have been a thematic view of home — and there would be portraits of ayahs and other dark-skinned servants in attendance.

43 J. Park Harrison is an interesting minor figure in the anthropological scene for the two decades of the 1870s and 1880s. He seemed much concerned with the surface of the body: he contributed the notes on tattooing to the first edition of *Notes and Queries* and notes to the journal on hypertrichosis and another on the length of the second toe. He became convener of the Racial Committee.

44 The matter was urgent. As with 'remote tribes', they felt their subject was vanishing, owing to the spread of railways and related social factors.

45 It was now designated an independent committee, 'appointed for the purpose of obtaining Photographs of the Typical Races of the British Isles' (BAAS 1882:270) but with the same membership.

46 Type A: Dolichocephalic Dark (with the slight suggestion that these were akin to 'Iberians'); Type B: the Brachicephalic Fair, that includes 'Belgic, Cymric, and Danish varieties' with possibility of future differentiation of 'Anglian', 'Jutish' and 'Frisian' types; and Type C: the Sub-Dolichocephalic Fair, the true Saxon type that accords with 'Schadow's pure German (Teutonic) type'. The committee asked to be reappointed to tackle the next stage, the 'defining of the facial characteristics of the races and principal crosses of the British Isles and obtaining Illustrative Photographs' (BAAS 1883:306). But they had not developed a workable methodology for the correlation of physiognomic observations with the results of anthropometric and craniometric

studies and the programme was wound up in 1884.

47 When Park Harrison gave an Institute lecture, 'On the survival of certain racial features in the population of British Isles', in 1883 (*JAI* 12:243–56) the photographs apparently were still on cards; as they must have been for his earlier lecture, 'On the Collection of racial photographs' (BAAS 1881:693). His final appearance seems to have been a BAAS lecture, 'Definition of a Nation', in which he put forward the proposition that it was independent of Race and Language.

48 First published in *Photographic News*, April 17 and 24, 1885 with articles by Galton and Joseph Jacobs: 249. See also Frontispiece, *JAI* 1886:15. Galton's main interest in the composite and its place within the socio-economics of the period are beyond the scope of this essay. See Green 1985.

49 At the same time as this technical cul-de-sac was being explored, Jacob Riis was beginning (1887) to press the technical frontiers of photography (with flash) in the tenement slums of Mulberry Bend, New York, in the cause of social reform — an early stage in the development of the sociological/documentary approach.

50 As Tylor indicated at Montreal, part of the inspiration came from the work the US Bureau of Ethnology was undertaking in the field. Horatio Hale was appointed coordinator of the survey and, after 1886, Franz Boas was employed as anthropologist in the field (see Jacknis, this volume). Apart from the highly specialized anthropometric surveys, other surveys in which photography played a considerable part were as various as Prehistoric Remains in Mashonaland (Zimbabwe) and The Habits, Customs, Physical Characteristics and Religions of the Natives of India (both reported in BAAS Vol. 62 1892) and the Ethnographical Survey of Canada 1896–1904. It was not until 1899, in association with this survey, that Dr G.M. Dawson's Photographs of the Haida Villages of Queen Charlotte Islands, made for the earlier Canadian Geological Survey of 1878–9,

entered the collection (see Blackman, this volume).

51 At one point a folklorist department within Section H had been mooted. One casualty of the inter-societal strains was the proposed merger of the folklorists and anthropologists.

52 *Sir Benjamin Stone's Pictures* appeared in two volumes. The emblematic images of the one visualize the anatomy of power, while the other pictures the governance of the people by the process of fixing an imagined/invented traditional past in a ritualized present. The opening plate of the second volume, 'Welcome to our Fair', shows a cross-section of English village society, and the last plate, 'The Crier collecting the Pennies', is a visualization of the servant of the State collecting 'tax' from the governed. Together they visually enclose the argument.

53 There seems to have been always a time-lag in the content of the early *Notes and Queries* guidelines. Hence they illuminate immediate past practice. It was not until the 1899 edition appeared that much detailed advice was given about photography. Much emphasis was placed on practical and technical matters. Garson outlined how the precisions of anthropometric portraiture could be achieved in the field and Haddon called for photographs of ethnographic detail, including the 'common actions of daily life'.

54 Briefly, Bertillon had a bank of 100,000 'mug shots' of criminals, taken over a decade, with which to experiment. He devised a system of exact measurement of every suspect (between certain fixed points of the bony framework of the body); and these particulars were recorded on cards which were classified by filing them according to type in a series of sectioned drawers. When they were combined with photographs and notes of other distinctive features, identification was declared to be a matter of certainty. The upshot was that a resolution of Section H was passed, and endorsed by the Association's Council in 1892. It urged the Government to adopt Bertillon's method of identification, supplemented by Galton's fingerprinting

system (which was based on a method devised by Herschel). This was done. In 1893 Mr Asquith set up a committee and the procedure was adopted in June 1894. Was this the first achievement of a practical anthropology?

55 See particularly BAAS reports 1895 (Haddon), 1894 (Flower), 1909 (Myers) and 1913 (Temple).

56 In his autobiography, *But to What Purpose?*, Grant Watson detailed: 'The method of collecting the patients was not either humane or scientific. A man unqualified except by ruthlessness and daring, helped by one or two kindred spirits, toured the countryside, raided the native camps, and there, by brute force, "examined" the natives. Any that were obviously diseased or were suspected of disease were seized upon. These, since their hands were so small as to slip through any pair of handcuffs, were chained together by their necks, and were marched through the bush . . . When a sufficient number were judged to be collected, the chained prisoners were marched to the coast, and there embarked on an ancient lugger to make the last sad stage of their journey' (1946:112).

REFERENCES

AR & J: Anthropological Review and Journal
BAAS: *British Association for the Advancement of Science*
EJ: Ethnological Journal
JAI: Journal of the Anthropological Institute
Anon. 1884. 'African "Earthmen" and the Westminster Aquarium'. Newspaper cutting, Sept. 20, 1884. John Johnson Ephemera Collection, Bodleian Library, Oxford.
AR & J. 1867. *Manchester Anthropological Society Notes: Proposed Anthropological Congress in Calcutta in 1869.* 5:5.
— 1868. Minutes of a meeting, 4.2.68. Bogdanov letter. 6:xcvi. BAAS.
— 1874. *Notes and Queries on Anthropology.* London: Edward Stanford.
— 1892; 1899. London: Harrison.
— 1876. *[Appointment of] the Committee for Collection of Observations on the Systematic Examination of Heights, Weights etc. of Human Beings in the British Empire and the publication of photographs of typical races of the Empire.* Lane-Fox. Secretary.

46:liv.
— 1877. *Report of the Anthropometric Committee.* 47:231-2.
— 1878. *Report of sub-committee [of Anthropometric Committee] to deal with that portion of the reference to them that relates to publication of photographs of typical races of empire.* 48:155-6.
— 1879. *Report of the Anthropometric Committee . . .* 49:175-209.
— 1880. *Report of the Anthropometric Committee . . .* 50:120-59. On *Photographs.* 158-9.
— 1881. Galton, F. *On the Application of Composite Portraiture to Anthropological Purposes.* 51:690-1.
— 1881. *Report of the Anthropometric Committee . . .* 51:225-72.
— 1882. *Report of the Committee appointed for the purpose of obtaining Photographs of the Typical Races in the British Isles.* 52:270-4.
— 1883. *Report of the Committee appointed for the purpose of Defining the Facial Characteristics of the Races and Principal Crosses in the British Isles, and obtaining Illustrative Photographs.* 53:306-8.
— *c.1883. Racial Committee Albums: 1-3.* Annotated MS. RAI Phot. Coll.
— 1884. *Report of the Committee . . . and obtaining Illustrative Photographs with a view to their publication.* 54:294.
— 1884-92. *Reports on the physical characteristics, languages, and industrial and social conditions of the North-western Tribes of the Dominion of Canada.* 54-62.
— 1892-99. *Ethnographic Survey of the United Kingdom reports.* 62-9.
— 1906, 1907, 1908, 1909, 1910. *Anthropological Photographs — Report of the Committee appointed for the Collection, Preservation, and Systematic Registration of Photographs of Anthropological Interest.* 76-80.
Barthes, R. 1977. *Image Music Text.* Essays selected and translated by Stephen Heath. London: Fontana.
Beddoe, J. 1885 (reprint 1971). *The Races of Britain, A contribution to the anthropology of Western Europe.* London: Hutchinson.
Boddington, J. 1979. Fred Kruger (1831-88). *Art Bulletin of Victoria* 20:51-7.
Bogdanov, V.V. (compiler) 1867. *Catalogue to the Russkaya Etnograficheskaya Vystavka, Manezh (Riding School).* Moscow.
Bonaparte, HRH Prince Roland 1884. *Les Habitants de Suriname: Notes Recueillies à l'Exposition Coloniale*

d'Amsterdam en 1883. Paris: Imprimerie de A. Quantin.
— 1886. *Notes on the Lapps of Finmark (Norway). JAI* 15:211-13.
Brauen, M. (ed.) 1982. *Fremden-Bilder, Frühe ethnographische Fotografie, Fotografien vom Royal Anthropological Institute London.* Zurich: Ethnologische Schriften Zurich, Volkerkundemuseum der Universität.
Burrow, J.W. 1966. *Evolution and Society: A Study in Victorian Social Theory.* Cambridge: University Press.
Campbell, G. On the Races of India as Traced in Existing Tribes and Castes. *EJ* (NS) 1:128-40.
Careless, V.A.S. 1974. *The Ethnological Society of London.* Unpublished thesis, University of British Columbia, Canada.
Catlin, G. 1850. Proposal. Museum of Mankind. 3 pages. Catlin. Ephemera Collection, City of Westminster Libraries.
Cowling, M. 1989. The *Artist as Anthropologist, The representation of type and character in Victorian art.* Cambridge: University Press.
Cunningham, R.A. 1884. *A History of R.A. Cunningham's Australian Aborigines, Tattooed Cannibals, Black trackers and Boomerang Throwers.* London: Elliot.
Dammann, C. 1873-6. *Anthropologisch-Ethnologisches Album in Photographien . . . Herausgegeben mit Unterstützung aus den Sammlungen der Berliner Gesellschaft für Anthropologie, Ethnologie und Urgeschichte.* Berlin: Verlag von Wiegandt & Hempel.
Dammann, C. & Dammann, F.W. 1876. *Ethnological Photographic Gallery of the Various Races of Man.* Huddersfield, London: Trubner & Co.
Darrah, W.C. 1981. *Carte-de-visite in Nineteenth Century Photography.* Gettysburg: William C. Darrah.
— 1964. *A History of Stereographs and their Collection.* Gettysburg: Times & News Publishing Co.
Darwin, C. 1872a. *The Expression of the Emotions in Man and Animals.* London: John Murray.
Darwin Family Deposit. 1872b. MS 53[1] C 27. *The Album.* Cambridge University Library.
Davis, J.B. & Thurnam J. 1856. *Crania Britannica.* 2 vols. London: Printed for the subscribers.
Dickens, C. (ed.) 1853. The noble Savage. *Household Words.* June 11,

1853:7:168:337. London.

Dixon, R.M.V. 1972. *The Dyirbal language of North Queensland.* Cambridge: University Press.

Edwards, E. 1982. Some poblems with Photographic Archives: The Case of C.W. Dammann. *Journal of Anthropological Society of Oxford* 13(3):257–61.

— 1988. 'Representation and reality: Science and the Visual Image'. In Morphy, H. & Edwards, E. (eds.) *Australia in Oxford*: 27–45. Oxford: Pitt Rivers Museum.

— 1990 'Photographic Types: The Pursuit of Method'. *Visual Anthropology* 3(2–3):239–58.

EJ. 1869. *Notes on Classification Committee, Feb. 23.* (NS) 1:3 (Bound in following p. 332)

— 1869. *Minutes of Ordinary meeting, chaired by Huxley. March 9.* (NS) 1:ix–x, 89–93.

Ekman, P. (ed.) 1973. *Darwin and facial expression. A century of research in review.* New York and London: Academic Press.

Fedtschenko, A. Oct. 4, 1867. Letter. *JAS* 6:1.

Folklore 1896. *Report of the BAAS Ethnological Survey of United Kingdom.* 6:41.

Flower, Sir W.H. 1894. Presidential Address to Section H, Anthropology. BAAS *Transactions* 64. 762–74.

Freeman, R.B. & Gautrey, P.J. 1975. Charles Darwin's *Queries about Expression. Journal Society Bibliography Natural History*, 7(3):259–63.

Galton, F. 1877. Presidential Address to Anthropology Dept. BAAS *Transactions* 47:94–100.

Gernsheim, H. & Gernsheim, A. 1969. *The History of Photography.* London: Thames and Hudson.

Gombrich, E.H. 1982. *The Image and the Eye. Further studies in the psychology of pictorial representation.* Oxford: Phaidon.

Gower, H.D., Jast, L.S. & Topley, W.W. 1916. *Notes on the Camera as Historian.* London: Marston and Co.

Green, D. 1985. Veins of Resemblance: Photography and Eugenics. *The Oxford Art Journal.* 7(2):3–16.

Haddon, A.C. & Browne, C.R. 1891–93. The Ethnography of the Aran Islands, County Galway. *Proceedings of the Royal Irish Academy* 2. 3rd Series:452–505.

Haddon, A.C. 1895. Photography and Folklore. *Folklore* 6:222–4.

— 1905. Presidential address to

Section H. BAAS *Transactions* 75. 511–26.

Hayden, F.V. *c.*1877. *Photographic Portraits of the Indians of the United States of North America, representing 70 of the principal tribes.* Undated. MS Album. RAI Phot. Coll.

Howarth, O.J.R. 1931. *The British Association for the Advancement of Science . . . A Retrospect 1831–1931.* London: BAAS.

Houzé, E. & Jacques, V. 1884. Communication de MM. Houzé et Jacques sur les Australiens du Musée du Nord. Séance du 28 Mai, 1884. *Bulletin de la Société d'Anthropologie de Bruxelles.* III–IV:53–153, plates I–IV.

Huxley, T. 1878. Address of Chairman of Dept of Anthropology. BAAS *Transactions* 48:573–8.

im Thurn, E.F. 1893. Anthropological Uses of the Camera. *JAI* 22: 184–203.

Intercolonial Exhibition, Melbourne, 1866. Official catalogue.

Jackson, W.H. 1877. *Descriptive Catalogue of Photographs of North American Indians.* Washington: US Dept. Interior Misc. Publ. no. 9.

JAI. 1872. Review of Darwin's *Expressions. Anthropological Miscellanea* 2:444–6.

— 1877. 'Photographic Portraits of the Indians . . .' (The Hayden Album) received Feb. 6, 1877. *For the Library* 7:1.

— 1877. Report of the Anthropometric Committee BAAS by Col. A. Lane Fox. 7:391–3.

— 1879. Notes on Galton's Composite Portraits, made by combining those of many different persons into a single resultant figure. Meeting, April 30, 1877. 8:132–44.

— 1886. From Prince Roland Bonaparte a Collection of Photographs of New Caledonian and Australian Natives (Queensland). Dec. 8 1885. *For the Library* 1885. 15:422.

— 1886. Jacobs. J. *On Racial Characteristics of Modern Jews*, 1885. 15:23–62.

— 1888. *Exhibition of Natives of Queensland . . .* April 26, 1887. 17:83.

— 1898. Collection of Photographs and Lantern Slides. *Anthropological Miscellanea and New Books,* (Portman, im Thurn, Somerville), 1897. 28:346.

Krauss, R.F. 1985. 'Photography's discursive spaces'. In *The Originality of the Avant-Garde and Other*

Modernist Myths: 131–50. Cambridge, Mass. and London: MIT Press.

Lamprey, J.H. 1869. On a Method of Measuring the Human Form. *Journal of the Ethnological Society.* (NS) 1:84–5.

Lane Fox. Col. A. 1872. Vicepresidential Address to Dept. of Anthropology, BAAS *Transactions* 42:157–72.

Langham, I. 1981. *The building of British social anthropology: W.H.R. Rivers and his Cambridge disciples in the development kinship studies.* Dordrecht: D. Reidel (*Studies His. Mod. Sci.* 8.)

Langton, M. 1988. *After the Tent Embassy. Images of Aboriginal history in black and white photographs.* Sydney: Valadon Publishing.

Lavater, J.C. 1775–78. *Physiognomische Fragmente.* 4 vols. Leipzig and Winterthur.

— 1789. *Essays on Physiognomy, for the promotion of knowledge and the love of mankind.* 3 vols. 1st English edn., trans. Thomas Holcroft. London: G.G.J. & J. Robinson.

Lebovic, J. & Cahill, J. (ed.) 1989. *Masterpieces of Australian Photography.* Catalogue to an exhibition, June 24–July 22, 1989. Sydney: Josef Lebovic Gallery.

Lindt, J.W. 1886. *A Few Results of Modern Photography.* Melbourne. M'Carron, Bird & Co.

— 1887. *Picturesque New Guinea.* London: Longman.

Malinowski, B. 1966. (ed.) *Coral gardens and their magic.* 2 vols. London: George Allen & Unwin.

— 1978. (ed.) *Argonauts of the western Pacific.* London: Routledge & Kegan Paul.

Man E.H. 1883. On the Aboriginal Inhabitants of the Andaman Islands. *JAI* 12:69–175, 327–434.

Mitchell, D. n.d. MS Dr Mitchell's Album of F.R. Nixon photographs of Tasmanian Aborigines. Mitchell Library, Sydney.

Mitchell, T. 1988. *Colonising Egypt.* Cambridge: University Press.

Mondière, A.T. 1886. Les Australiens Exhibés à Paris. *Revue d'Anthropologie.* Series III:I:313–17.

Morrell, J. & Thakeray, A. 1981. *Gentlemen of Science: Early years of B.A.A.S.* Oxford: Clarendon Press.

Müller, M. 1891. Presidential Address to Section H, BAAS *Transactions* 61. 784–95.

Needham, R. 1974. 'Surmise, Discovery, and Rhetoric'. In *Remarks and inventions: Skeptical Essays about kinship*: 109–72. London: Tavistock.

Nature. Nov. 14, 1872. *Notes* 7:35.

Peterson, N. 1989. A colonial image: penetrating the reality of the image. *Australian Aboriginal Studies*: 1989(2):59–62.

Pinney, C. 1990. 'Colonial Anthropology in the "Laboratory of Mankind"'. In Bayley, C.A. (ed.) *The Raj: India and the British 1600–1947*. London: National Portrait Gallery.

Portman, M.V. 1896. Photography for Anthropologists. *JAI* 25:75–87.

Prichard, J.C. 1843. *Natural History of Man*. London: H. Baillière.

Radcliffe-Brown, A.R. 1922. *The Andaman Islanders*. Cambridge: University Press.

— 1931. The Social organization of Australian tribes. *Oceania Monograph*: 1. London: Macmillan & Co.

RAI Archives. 1868. A.4. *Minutes of meeting of Anthropological Society of London, 4.2.1868.*

Riis, J.A. 1971. *How the other half lives: Studies Among the Tenements of New York.* (Unabridged republication of text of 1901 edition (1st edn. 1890) in which original illustrations redrawn from photographs have been replaced by prints of original photographs.) New York: Dover Publications Inc.

Rivers, W.H.R. 1906. *The Todas.* London: Macmillan.

Schadow, G. 1835. *National-Physiognomieen*. 1 vol. text. 2 vols illustrations. Berlin: no pub.

Seligman, C.G. & Seligman, B.Z. 1911. *The Veddas.* Cambridge: University Press.

Shortland, M. 1985. Skin deep: Barthes, Lavater and the legible body. *Economy and Society*: 14(3):273–311.

Smith, B. 1960. *European Vision and the South Pacific 1768–1850.* Oxford: University Press.

Somerville, H.B.T. 1896. Ethnological Notes on New Georgia, Solomon Islands. *JAI* 26:357–413.

— Nov. 8, 1928. *Surveying in the South Seas.* Annotated typescript of lantern-slide lecture notes. RAI Phot. Coll.: 1–17.

Stocking, Jr., G.W. 1971. What's in a name? The origins of the Royal Anthropological Institute: 1837–1871. *Man* 6:369–90.

— 1973. 'From Chronology to Ethnology'. In reprint Prichard, J.C. 1813. *Researches into the Physical History of Mankind*: 9–110. Chicago and London: University of Chicago Press.

— 1983. 'The Ethnographer's Magic: Fieldwork in British Anthropology from Tylor to Malinowski'. In Stocking, Jr., G.W. (ed.) *Observers observed. Essays on ethnographic fieldwork. History of Anthropology.* 1:70–120. Wisconsin: University Press.

— 1984. 'Radcliffe-Brown and British Social Anthropology'. In Stocking, Jr., G.W. (ed.) *Functionalism Historicized. Essays on British Anthropology. History of Anthropology*, vol. 2:106–91. Wisconsin: University Press.

— 1987. *Victorian Anthropology.* London: Collier Macmillan.

Stone, Sir B. 1905. *Sir Benjamin Stone's Pictures. Records of National Life and History.* 2 vols. London: Cassell & Co.

Tagg, J. 1984. A Democracy of the Image: Photographic Portraiture and Commodity Production. *Ten-8*: 13:21–9.

Topinard, P. 1885. Présentation de trois Australiens vivants. Séance du 19 Novembre 1885. *Bulletin de la Société d'Anthropologie de Paris.* Series 3:683–99.

Tylor, E.B. 1876. Dammann's Race-portraits. *Nature* Jan. 6:184–5.

— 1884. Presidential Address to Section H. BAAS *Transactions* 54:899–910.

Urry. J. 1972. *Notes and Queries on Anthropology* and The Development of Field Methods in British Anthropology, 1870–1920. *Proceedings of the RAI.*

— 1984. 'Englishmen, Celts, and Iberians. The Ethnographic Survey of the United Kingdom 1892–1899'. In Stocking, Jr. G.W. (ed.) *Functionalism Historicized. Essays on British Anthropology. History of Anthropology*, vol. 2:83–105. Wisconsin: University Press.

— 1985. 'Savage Sportsmen'. In Donaldson I. & T. (eds.) *Seeing the First Australians*: 51–67. Sydney: Allen & Unwin Australia.

Watson, E.L. Grant. 1914. *Where Bonds are Loosed.* London: Duckworth.

— 1946. *But to What Purpose?* London: Cresset Press.

Watson, J. Forbes & Kaye, J.W. 1868–75. *The People of India, A series of Photographic Illustrations with Descriptive Letterpress.* 8 vols. London: India Museum.

White, I. 1981. Mrs Bates and Mr Brown: An examination of Rodney Needham's allegations. *Oceania* 51:193–210.

The Parallel Histories of Anthropology and Photography

Christopher Pinney

THAT THE HISTORIES OF ANTHROPOLOGY as we would recognize it today and of photography have followed parallel courses is a simple proposition to demonstrate. That they also appear to derive their representational power through nearly identical semiotic procedures requires, perhaps, a slightly more elaborate case to be made. It is with the establishment of these two related propositions that this essay is, in the first instance, concerned.

What the essay also seeks to do is sketch two apparently alternative interpretations of the histories of anthropology and photography which make rather different sense of their narratives. In the first interpretation, photography appears as the final culmination of a Western quest for visibility and scrutiny. It stands at the technological, semiotic and perceptual apex of 'vision', which itself serves as the emulative metaphor for all other ways of knowing (see Rorty 1980; Tyler 1984; Salmond 1982).[1] As truth, representation and commodity it is in an unrivalled class of its own. Those who accept this rendering of history include those who, like its early adherents, evaluate it positively (it was described as 'an angel copier; a God-like machine of which light and sunshine is the animating Promethean fire', *Journal of the Photographic Society* 1859:144), and also some of its more recent detractors, who reveal in their critiques a fear of its power.[2]

The second possible history stresses that photography, although often acclaimed as the apotheosis (either good or evil) of a Western civilization grounded in ocularism has always suffered 'moments of unease' (Jacqueline Rose, cited by Jay 1988:3–4). Such unease can be conceptualized in a number of ways ranging from a recurrent tension between photography's 'iconic' and 'indexical' status[3] (Jay n.d.), between 'art' and 'verisimilitude', or a stress on the deconstructive lines of fracture which both underpin and undermine photography's single-voiced authority.[4]

In seeking at this stage to establish the parallel histories of anthropology and photography, we do not digress from the above matter since in anthropology too we are likely to find the same disputed narratives and ostensibly closed meanings. Rather, recording the coincidence of the establishment of the Aborigines Protection Society in 1837 and that of the Ethnological Society of London in 1843 (Stocking 1971:369–72) with the development of the first successful daguerreotype in 1837 and the public announcement of Fox Talbot's 'photogenic drawing' in 1839[5] is intended to establish a coterminous framework in which we might see these two related practices performing the same disputed and undecided movements and routines.

74

The first history

Let us first examine the triumphalist version of photographic and anthropological history, which conceals supporters and detractors who both agree ultimately on the persuasiveness and certainty of its power.

Thus Paul Virilio, who is without doubt a detractor, sees in photography and film a technical manifestation of the process of knowing through visibility and the threatening penetration of light. This is akin to the process of military subjection through illumination, what Virilio calls the 'war of light' from the first use of the searchlight in the 1904 Russo-Japanese war to 'the bloody Hiroshima flash which literally photographed the shadow cast by beings and things, so that every surface immediately became war's *recording surface*, its *film*' (1989:68; original emphasis). In the atomic age, Virilio bleakly observes, we are all 'human negatives' waiting to be processed (1989:47).

Susan Sontag has espoused a particularly influential negative interpretation of photography which stresses its fatal attractions.[6] She sees the camera's popular incarnation as a predatory weapon which is 'loaded', 'aimed' and 'shot'. The camera is a 'sublimation of the gun' and 'to photograph people is to violate them . . .' (1979:14). It is a medium whose certainty and specificity can change lives — her own life, she observes, is divided by her 'first encounter with the photographic inventory of ultimate horror', photographs of Bergen-Belsen and Dachau glimpsed in a bookshop when she was twelve (1979:19). This was a 'negative epiphany' created by the power of photography: 'it seems plausible to me to divide my life into two parts, before I saw those photographs . . . and after'.

Such negative testimonies to the power of photography[7] also find succour from some interpretations of the work of Michel Foucault, although they place this power at one remove, as primarily a function of the requirements of a disciplining state, rather than of 'light'. Although he did not concern himself with photography *per se* (he was writing about the role of vision and visibility in the growth of the modern prison and the clinic), many writers have been forcibly struck by the remarkable parallels between the eye of surveillance that lay at the centre of the panopticon prison or traversed the disciplinarian spaces of the examination and the eye of the Western photographer who documented the other peoples of the world and

44. Cabinet card *c*.1880 by Hudson's Gallery, Tama, Iowa. Inscribed on the reverse: 'Winter houses of woven "slough" grass and cowskins, spoiled by the white man in the foreground'. Haddon Collection, draw 150/3. (Courtesy of Museum of Archaeology and Anthropology, University of Cambridge)

the strange inhabitants of his own domestic *terra incognita*, the expanding industrial city. Photography fitted perfectly into such a framework and can be substituted for the idea of discipline/surveillance in almost all of Foucault's writing. Simon Watney observes for instance:

> *Foucault might well have been talking about photography when he described the exercise of discipline as 'an apparatus in which the techniques that make it possible to see induce the effects of power, and in which conversely, the means of coercion make those on whom they are applied clearly visible'.* (Watney, no pagination; citing Foucault 1979:170–71)

The objects of photography can be easily and repeatedly substituted for the objects of discipline:

> *Disciplinary power . . . is exercised through its invisibility; at the same time it imposes on those whom it subjects a principle of compulsory visibility. In discipline, it is the subjects who have to be seen. Their visibility assumes the hold of the power that is experienced over them. It is the fact of being constantly seen, of being able always to be seen, that maintains the disciplined individual in his subjection.* (Foucault 1979: 87; see also Sontag 1979: 14 for a similar statement)[8]

Discipline and photography seem here to coalesce in a common language of success dependent on the assumed transparency of the medium (Sekula 1982:86). In photography, as with 'discipline', the photographer is invisible behind his camera, while what he sees is rendered completely visible (cf. Berger 1972:54 for comments on the absence of the 'principle protagonist' in painting). Photography's mimetic effect reduces the reader to the pure consumer of a sign in which the signifier appears to have collapsed with the signified (Tagg 1980:53). When photography is operated in conjunction with anthropology the necessity of stressing *re-production*, and repressing *production* (Burgin 1982) involves the effacement of any marks of the presence of the photographer's culture. At this point the recurrent anthropological quest for Otherness coincides exactly with the trick that photography enacts in pursuit of its 'reality effect'. Just as the anthropologist is often concerned with the polluting effect of his presence on those he studies (see for example Lévi-Strauss on the corrupting effect of the 'introduction' of writing among the Nambikwara — 1976:322–416, and Derrida's critique of this — 1976:107–40)[9]), so the anthropological photographer strives to preserve the purity of the cultural other that he represents. Thus the remark 'spoiled by white man in the foreground' in the Hudson's Gallery, Iowa, cabinet-card study of 'winter houses of woven "slough" grass and cowskins' (Plate 44) locates the

45. 'August Shower'. Photograph by E. Evans-Pritchard. (Courtesy of Pitt Rivers Museum. University of Oxford. PRM EP. N. I. 43)

European figure as a sort of scratch on the negative, a blemish which betrays the presence of the photographer and his culture.[10]

Such a line of argument might also point to an illustration in *The Nuer* (Plate 45) which depicts in the main an August shower in full pelt, but betrays through the peripheral presence of tent flaps the presence of the photographer (Evans-Pritchard) behind the camera. Precipitation has here precipitated the exposure of the photographer's presence and perhaps it is not too far-fetched to see this mirroring of the viewers' own culture in the tent pole and flap as modern anthropology's *Las Meninas* (Fernandez 1985; Foucault 1970).[11]

But photography's power does not reside only in the longed-for invisibility of its producer, but also in the apparent self-presence of its surface. While on the one hand the surface is invisible, a transparent window on to a slice of reality, the surface of the print maps a quantitative grid over the Cartesian depths which lie within the image (see Jay 1988:13 for painterly parallels). The influence of Johan Casper Lavater's physiognomy (Shortland 1985) among other factors had helped dispel the earlier 'noise' of the body to the extent that nineteenth-century anthropology was able to call on fully legible bodies for inspection.[12] These demanded formalized systems of reading and one of the most influential was produced by J.H. Lamprey in 1869.[13] In a paper in the *Journal of the Ethnological*

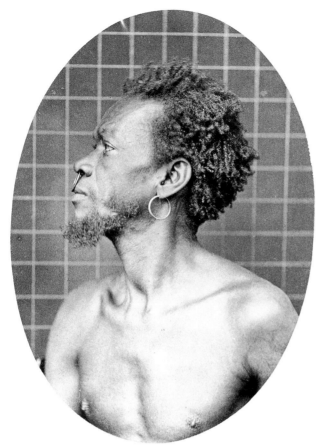

46. Anthropometric study, *c.*1870. Photograph by J. Lamprey. (RAI 35892)

Society of London he advocated the use of a wooden frame with silk threads hung so as to form two-inch squares (see Spencer, this volume). This provided a 'normalising' grid within which 'the anatomical structure of a good academy figure or model of six feet in height can be compared with a Malay of four feet eight in height' (1869:85).

Michel de Certeau has noted that normalization utilized a cellular grid that 'transforms space itself into an instrument that can be used to discipline' (1986:186) and Lamprey provided a disciplinary grid stripped of all metaphoricity. The grid made explicit the transcription of space on the very surface area of the photographic image (Plate 46). In the case of a study, probably by W.H.R. Rivers, of the 'reaction-time of Dog to sight of falling body (biscuit)' (Plate 47), the surface of the image literally becomes a rule, a precise marker.[14] The photograph depicts objects not only within a precise Cartesian perspectival depth, but also contains in the very material reality of its space another plane of 'truth'. Such things we take for granted. When such certainty and precision is attempted by the material surface of the written text (as in Plate 48) the effect is altogether alien.

Among those who argue for what I am describing here as the first history of photography, there is a consensus that the reason we are able to take this photographic verisimilitude for granted is that photography as well as being iconic (its images resemble, look like, its referents) is also indexical. By this is meant, following C.S. Peirce, its embodiment within its own iconic resemblance of a physical trace of the material world (see Wright, this volume). The dried skeleton of a leaf and the imprint of light on chemicals on the surface of the albumen print of the 'Lucknow immigrant' (Plate 49) are in Peircean terms the same.[15] The photograph, like the desiccated skeleton, is:

> *a trace, something directly stencilled off the real; like a footprint or a death mask . . . a material vestige of its subject.* (Sontag 1979:154)

> *a photochemically processed trace . . . parallel to . . . fingerprints or footprints or the rings of water that cold glasses leave on tables.* (Krauss, cited by Prochaska 1990:404)

Photography arrived with a peculiar ability to construct a photochemical index of the play of light over the surfaces of distant objects in the form of the photograph itself. The sensitivity of film emulsion as the recording surface of those objects passed before the lens has fulfilled in science (Green 1985; Sekula 1986) and the public (Bourdieu 1965; but see also Krauss 1984) the desire for what Tagg characterizes dismissively as a 'pre-linguistic certainty' (1988:4), for a signified that exists prior to attempts to represent it. As Sekula notes:

> *Nothing could be more natural than . . . a man pulling a snapshot from his wallet and saying, 'This is my dog'.* (1982:86)

47. 'Reaction-time of Dog to sight of falling body (biscuit).' Photograph probably by W.H.R. Rivers, 1890s. (Courtesy of Museum of Archaeology and Anthropology, University of Cambridge)

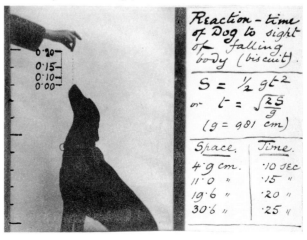

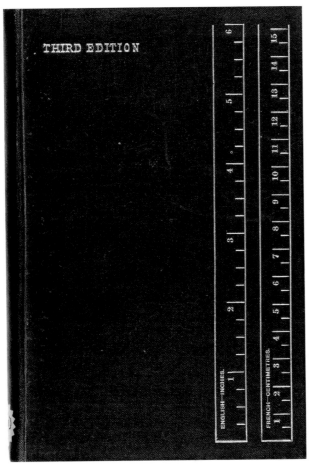

48. Measure on the cover of *Notes and Queries on Anthropology* 3rd edn, 1899. (Courtesy of the Balfour Library, Pitt Rivers Museum, University of Oxford)

its 'perfect analogon', 'a message without a code' (1983:196), and at the end of his life, following the death of his mother, he finally lights on an image of her which 'collected all the possible predicates from which my mother's being was constituted' and which, though phenomenologically an 'ordinary' object, achieved for Barthes, in his grief, 'utopically, *the impossible science of the unique being*' (1984:70–71; original emphasis). In his final manifestation, at least, Barthes plays an important role in the first history of photography. Let us at this point pursue some of the possibilities and implications of this first version of photographic history in which a fledgling anthropology, with pretensions to science, calls on this new and superior medium in its quest to re-present areas of darkness under the revealing light of investigation. The history of this relationship, which is dealt with in greater depth by Poignant (this volume), can for the purpose of this essay be broken into two movements. The first of these, running from anthropology's and photography's inception to the turn of the century, marks a productive union between two practices intent on 'de-Platonizing' the world, and sharing a common language of the penetration of light and the transcription of temporal disjunctions (Wright 1987). The second of these, becoming more manifest from the turn of the century onwards, saw the gradual displacement on to an invisible internalized world of meaning in re-Platonizing anthropological strategies such as a concern with 'social structure'. Although these have rightly been criticized for their synchronic nature and cumbersome geometrical and mechanical metaphorization, the 'social facts' they mobilized were not thought a suitable object for photography.

Crucial to the shift between these two movements was the emergence of the fieldworker as the central validator of the anthropological enterprise which, with its form that was semiotically identical to the 'ritual of photography' (Tomas 1982; 1988), was able to invoke and displace the earlier codes of truth.

Photography's 'de-Platonizing' tendency found a willing victim in early anthropology. When in 1893 Everard im Thurn in his advocacy of a new role for the camera in anthropology (one which, in theory at least, marked an important step towards documentary field photography) complained that until that date the objects of photography might just as well have been dead as alive, he was not condemning the unspoken desires of anthropology to control mute objects in its macabre museum of vanishing races and little-known facts. Rather, he was coolly suggesting the abandonment of what had been a quite clearly articulated anthropological privileging of the still and the silent over the quick and living. This may be seen in part as

Within four years of the announcement of photography, Feuerbach was bemoaning that 'our era . . . prefers the image to the thing, the copy to the original, the representation to the reality, appearance to being' (*The Essence of Christianity*, cited by Sontag 1979:153). Ever since, photography's power to institute an image world which supersedes its referents has continued to preoccupy theorists (see Boorstin 1963; Baudrillard 1983; Krauss 1981) and is encountered at every point in our daily lives (see Greenblatt's discussion (1987:10–11) of the photograph of the Nevada Falls etched into aluminium so that a sceptical public can compare it with the reality before them).

Some of the texts[16] of Roland Barthes, even, present photography as uniquely privileged, although as we shall see later he provides as many arguments for the undecidable and polysemic nature of the medium. Photography, he wrote at one point, involved no transformation or 'relay' between object and photographic image. The image was not reality, but it was

49.　Albumen print inscribed 'Lucknow Immigrant' pasted on the same sheet as skeleton of a leaf, *c.*1860s. (Courtesy of the Trustees of the British Museum)

one consequence of the medical training of many nineteenth-century anthropologists and the more general adoption by all investigations of which man was the object of a mode of enquiry whose origin was medical:

> *That which hides and envelops, the curtain of night over truth, is paradoxically, life; and death, on the contrary, opens up to the light of day the black coffer of the body: obscure life, limpid death, the oldest imaginary values of the Western world are crossed here in a strange misconstruction that is the very meaning of pathological anatomy . . . Nineteenth-century medicine was haunted by that absolute eye that cadaverizes life and rediscovers in the corpse the frail, broken nervure of life.* (Foucault 1976:166; cited by Jay 1986:21)

The autopsy — literally (mine) 'own eye' (Hartog 1988:xix) — stood at the apex of this visual examination contingent on death, the cessation of time which Barthes (1977:44) continually stressed and which in Christian Metz's view makes the still photograph a powerful fetish (Metz 1985). In photography's 'spatial immediacy and temporal anteriority' (Barthes: ibid) we may perhaps see the inverted precursor of 'the ethnographic present' of the post-Malinowskian monograph. Thus, in enacting this specific thanatographic metaphor, photography also colludes with anthropology in the temporal distantiation of its object (Fabian 1983; Thomas 1990). In photography's case the fractional moment of exposure necessarily produces an immediate *memento mori*, while in anthropology's case this temporal displacement in the form of the 'ethnographic present' can be seen to serve specific power interests.[17]

The non-photographic index in the nineteenth-century practice of anthropometry served to transform the living into the quiet, the subject into the object — indeed in this transformation lay the very definition of science and objectivity. Thus in 1890 Denzil Ibbetson, the President of the Anthropological Society of Bombay, argued for the indexical reliability of anthropometry in a talk on *The Study of Anthropology in India*:

> *First and in some respects most valuable of all, because most trustworthy, we have the actual physical confirmation of the individuals comprising any tribal or caste unit(. . .) No one who has not made the attempt can well realise how difficult it is to secure a full and accurate statement on any given point by verbal enquiry from Orientals and still more, from semi savages(. . .) Cranial measurements, on the other hand, are probably almost absolutely free from the personal equation of the observer.* (Journal of the Anthropological Society of Bombay 1890:121)

A similar distinction between dialogue and observation is made by Tylor, who cautioned enquirers against asking 'un-called for questions' and advocated instead the observation of 'religious rites actually performed' (Stocking 1983:72).

Perhaps the most elaborate use of the photographic and other indices is Portman and Molesworth's photographic and statistical survey of the Andamans completed in 1894. M.V. Portman made eleven volumes of photographs which depicted Andamanese in front of chequered screens (a later elaboration on Lamprey's grid — see Desmond 1982:55 for two examples), full-face and profile studies, and long narrative sequences which illustrated the procedures for making artefacts such as adzes and bows. There were additionally four volumes of statistics composed of printed schedules (Plate 50ii) headed *Observations on External Characters*. These elicited fifty-four items of information and tracings of each subject's right hand and left foot were appended (Plate 50i). A final blank page left room for more detailed observations, including, in some cases, an assessment of the subject's temperament (in the case of Riwa, vol. 14, 'nervo-sanguine').

Portman and Molesworth's great industry was directed towards the generation of statistical norms — they give figures in their preface for average height, pulse beats per minute, rates of abdominal breathing, rate of respiration, temperature and weight of males of the North Andamans. But this battery of data can also be seen as an embodiment of a superior Western knowledge underpinned by vision, and in this case photography. The possibility that the North Andamanese had more searching vision than their rulers is clearly something that Portman and Molesworth are eager to discount:

> *Allowing for the accurateness gained by practice and necessity, their sight does not appear to be superior to that of any ordinary European; who if passed through the same training would see as well as they do.*
>
> *I have heard astonishment expressed at the way in which they will accurately name other Andamanese who may be at a considerable distance but it should be remembered that they distinguish by gait, etc., as we do, and moreover they know whom they expect to see in that particular place, and therefore are on the lookout. I have seen them, when not thus prepared make many mistakes, while a European standing by them gave the accurate name of the person seen.* (Preface to *Measurements and Medical Details: Male Series: North Andaman Group of Tribes*, 1894:2)

Where vision stood as the paradigm of privileged knowledge, it could not but be so. Within the margin of this passage lies a further demonstration of the alliance of Western knowledge of the 'Other' and

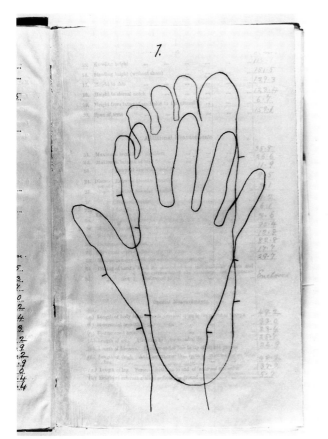
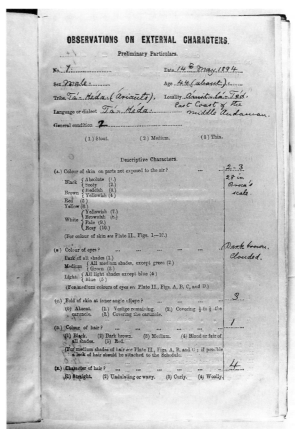

50i–ii. Tracings of Andamanese hands and feet and schedule of 'Preliminary Particulars' in M.V. Portman and W. Molesworth's *Observations on External Characters*, 1894. (Courtesy of the Trustees of the British Museum)

vision, for the possibility that the Andamanese have superior powers is received aurally (and is consequently incorrect), whereas verification of their inferior vision is reported visually ('I have heard' versus 'I have seen' — 'mere hearsay' versus the testimony of the 'eyewitness').

The matrix, photography–vision–Western knowledge–power, has I hope by now been sufficiently demonstrated in this hastily drawn sketch of the first history of photography. In this version, in the context of colonialism, the 'divine' power of photography comes to reflect a Western technological and epistemological prowess:

> the pagan nations of antiquity worshipped the sun . . . but we have learned a wiser lesson, we have scientifically utilised the object of pagan worship and made his golden rays subservient to the purposes of an artificial life. (introductory address in *The Photographic News* 1858, cited by Wright 1987:ii)

But, writing in 1962, Luc de Heusch noted the absence of photographs in monographs. Sometimes, he wrote, 'an ethnographer goes so far as to publish pictures of men he has known and liked, but does so

with considerable reluctance as if the emotive power of the picture, being foreign to his purpose embarrasses him' (1987:107). This may well explain the discomfiture created by portraits, but leaves unresolved the question of the increasing disappearance of the non-portrait photographic image. This fading away occurred first in the pages of learned journals and then in the ethnographic monograph, the norm increasingly becoming dense pages of unbroken written text.

One explanation for the partial elimination of the photographic image (as indexical proof of 'being there') in the postwar period might lie in the triumph of fieldwork and the fact that anthropology has so profoundly and subliminally absorbed the idiom of photography within the production of its texts that it has become invisible, like a drop of oil expanding over the surface of clear water. I have already hinted at the re-Platonizing trend of twentieth-century anthropology, and one further explanation may lie in the discipline's continuing attempt to distance itself from other imaginary genres such as travel photography and the emerging 'photo-text' (see Pratt 1986 for a parallel argument). But, is it possible that photography and a metaphorization of its technical and ritual procedures have so informed the determination of the squiggles and marks on the surface of the pages of the ethnographic monograph that it has ensured its own redundancy to the point where the photographic recording surface can be justified within anthropology only when allied with some other drive such as 'narrative' which allows it to be constituted as 'film'?

How could this be so? One line of poetic speculation might propose the following: the new heroic fieldworking anthropologist/ethnographer located the 'afar' which Rousseau had long before identified as essential for the study of 'Man' as a definite place ('the field') to which the anthropologist had to be indexically exposed for a recognized period (about two years in the Malinowskian model). A combination of the Durkheimian stress on the importance of distantiation as a guarantee of 'social facts' and anthropologists' position as members of imperial and colonial metropoles meant that nearly always 'the field' was a place characterized as 'remote' (Ardener 1987) — the inverse of the ethnographer's own society, a foreign periphery. The anthropologist's exposure to data thus occurred during a period of inversion from his normal reality, a stage which is formally analogous to the production of the photographic negative when the all-important rays of light which guarantee the indexical truth of the image are allowed to fall on the negative's emulsion (this analogy was first suggested by David Tomas — personal communication).[18]

Photography is thus revealed to be much less and much more important than we had thought. The anthropologist has taken on to his own person the functions of a plate of glass, or strip of film[19] which, having been prepared to receive and record messages in negative form during a moment of exposure in 'the field', is able, after suitable processing, to present them in a 'positive' state in the ethnographic monograph.

The other history of photography and anthropology

The second history of photography (one which has been slower to emerge) argues by reference to both a chronological narrative and the analysis of images that not only has photography *not* been able to validate its claims to truth, but that it has always betrayed, in its unconscious gestures, a lack of confidence in itself at every turn:

> Nothing could be more natural than . . . a man pulling a snapshot from his wallet and saying, 'This is my dog'. (Sekula 1982:86; emphasis added)

I have already suggested that Malinowski's mythologization marks the critical displacement of the indexical language of photography on to an area of 'culture' and its analogues which was precisely that terrain which for earlier figures such as Ibbetson had lain beyond the possibilities of indexicality. Whereas once it had been the camera which had recorded the refraction of light off objects, now the fieldworker-anthropologist came into what was articulated as an unmediated relationship with the people he studied. Participant observation transcribed in monographic text now captured the soul of a people.

This second history argues, first, that 'certainty' is the effect of other non-photographic structures, and, second, that this certainty, howsoever derived, was always very fragile.

Jean La Fontaine recently commenced her definition of what social anthropology *is* in terms of what it *is not* (La Fontaine 1985:1), commenting that such a strategy of identity grounded in negative differentiation is an innovative expediency for a burgeoning discipline which once *was* precisely sure about what its 'is' was. Mary Louise Pratt, by contrast, has argued that a textual fieldwork based on anthropology has always defined itself as a genre in a negative strategy. She shows, through an analysis of the ethnographic pioneers of monographic verisimilitude, that anthropology has always shown itself to be a 'not-something' rather than a 'thing-in-itself'. Its identity has always been constructed through superiority and difference, its authority was greater *than* that of the casual visitor whose naïve presence and presumptions were frequently conjured up in anthropology's rhetoric of truth (Pratt 1986:27), and it has always been something *other than* what would fall into the genre of travel writing.

The Malinowskian science of anthropology and its stigmatized rivals existed in the same 'logocentric' relationship of hierarchical oppositional dependence that pertains between speech and writing (Derrida 1976), and of more interest to us here, between photography and painting.[20] The temporal anteriority of the photograph may well suit an anthropology grounded in the temporal displacement of its object (Fabian 1983). However, photography's role as a form of speech (Benjamin noted that it had the quickness of speech) predisposes it in a more positive sense to record those cultures which, according to one anthropological paradigm at least, exist before the corrupting effects of writing (I have in mind Lévi-Strauss's discussion of the Nambikwara in *Tristes Tropiques* — 1976:322–416). There appears an affinity here between the natural presence of the photograph and the natural presence of the primitive, although both these ideas are equally questionable.

In 1883 that photographer of Australian Aborigines in reconstructed settings, J.W. Lindt, declared that:

MOUNTAIN TRIBES OF NEW GUINEA.

*The First Photograph taken of the Mountain Tribes of South Eastern
New Guinea.*

Photographed at an altitude of 8,000 feet on Mount Musgrave, part of the highest unexplored Oven Stanley Range,
by A. P. GOODWIN, May 29th, 1889, at the Special Request of H. E. SIR WILLIAM MC GREGOR, K.C.M.G.,
the Leader of the Expedition.

51. 'The First Photograph taken of the Mountain Tribes of South Eastern New Guinea.' Photograph by A.P. Goodwin, 1889. Albumen print on board with letterpress. (Courtesy of Museum of Archaeology and Anthropology, University of Cambridge)

I have always paid the greatest attention to the production of negatives as nearly as possible perfect in expression, lighting, and pose; and it is on such negatives that the work of the retoucher shows to the greatest advantage, while at the same time the quality of the negative enables him to keep the likeness (the vital part of the photographic portrait) intact. (1883, preface to Lindt 1886; emphasis added)

Similarly, Gregory Bateson was eager to distance the images in *Balinese Character: a photographic analysis* from the active threat of non-indexical visuals:

In a large number of cases, some shading was done in the process of enlarging the photographs, but this adds no drawing to the photograph, *only making it possible for the paper to give a more complete rendering of what is present in the negative.* (1942:41)

In both Lindt's and Bateson's cases, indexical truth is guaranteed by its depth in the negative, and its threatening pollutants are located on the surface. Just

as archaeology relies on the objective truths of the buried fragments of 'material culture' concealed from the surface pollution of the present by depth, so photography relies on a spatialization of its temporal anteriority within the negative. To be buried deep in the negative is to be true, just as to be 'first', to be 'before' the others (as in Plate 51, A.P. Goodwin's 'First Photograph Taken of the Mountain Tribes of South Eastern New Guinea' (1889)) locates its reliability in its priority.

But this indicates something of significance, for 'truth' here appears to be in retreat — hiding from a surface present, desperate to establish that *its* record comes before all subsequent (false?) imaging. One might ask how can this be so if photography is that all-powerful, good and evil, thing which we have described in the first history of the medium? Why, if from the date of its inception painting was dead, as was claimed, did photography (at least in the West) beat a retreat into the heart of the negative from this frightening interference with its surface?[21] Perhaps some clues to the answer may arise from an examination of the uncertain use made of photography by W.H.R. Rivers and C.G. Seligman, two veterans of the second Torres Straits Expedition (1898–9), which has come to symbolize a start of a new, recognizably modern, age in the use of the camera by the anthropologist. In their experience we can perhaps see further evidence of what the other history of photography might identify as the perpetual unravelling of photographic authority, a line of deconstructive fracture which runs underneath it and through which the literal always reveals itself in tropic figures, the indexical becomes iconic and symbolic, and photography becomes nothing more and nothing less than a kind of painting. How, in other words, the 'authority' of photography came to look as uncertain as that of painting.

The Todas, among whom Rivers (and for a short time Thurston) started fieldwork in 1901, had long been the subject of scholarly interest. For a time it was suggested that they might be one of the lost tribes of Israel. In 1832 Harkness illustrated his *A Description of a Singular Aboriginal Race Inhabiting the Summit of the Neilgherry Hills* with a frontispiece depicting a Toda group in 'a manner suggestive of a Jewish patriarchal family' (Rooksby 1971:113) and concluded that the traveller will be left wondering 'WHO CAN THEY BE?' (Plate 52). Such early representations, as John Falconer has pointed out (1984), give ample substance to complaints of the time concerning the 'Europeanization' of non-Western peoples in prephotographic media.[22] But from Rivers's perspective at the beginning of the twentieth century, photography had brought about little change in depictions of the Todas and in his publication of 1906 we can see clearly his faltering attempts to define an anthropological photography capable of representing the Todas without aestheticization. At this time the Todas were photographically defined largely through the views of studios such as Bourne and Shepherd who photographed them in family groups around their homes. *The Living Races of Mankind*, an early exercise in 'para-ethnography' reproduced one of these views as a full-page plate and remarked that Toda countenances were 'such as we are accustomed to associate with the ancient Roman' and that they inhabit 'a sort of tropical Switzerland [where] draped in a sort of toga, with one arm and thigh covered, they have quite the grand air' (Hutchinson et al. *c.*1900:188).

For Rivers, as for other anthropologists since, proof of methodological rigour lay in dis-enchantment. The earlier texts play the role of the 'mere travellers' or 'casual observers' which, as Pratt argues, substantialize the previous and inferior discourse against which

52. 'A Tuda family.' Frontispiece to *A Description of a Singular Aboriginal Race Inhabiting the Summit of the Neilgherry Hills, or Blue Mountains of Coimbatoor in the Southern Peninsula of India* by Captain James Harkness, 1832. (Courtesy of the Balfour Library, Pitt Rivers Museum, University of Oxford)

anthropology struggled to define itself. We can see here Jean La Fontaine's science of the 'not-something' struggling into life. Rivers's textual criticism of earlier romanticisms is, as the second history of photography would lead us to suspect, unsustainable in his imagery. A few of his photographic illustrations are reproductions from Breeks (1873), but the majority are either technically poor photographs from Rivers's own hand or artful and picturesque studies from the studio of Wiele and Klein.[23] Rivers's own photographs strive for a documentary functionalism; those by Wiele and Klein present a pastoral vision of a leafy arcadia (see Hockings, this volume). At every point Rivers's attempt to present the Todas as structured by 'the practical necessities of their daily life' (1906:26) is subverted by Wiele and Klein's images, in which they are once again dignified Roman senators with a marked 'grand air' (see Rivers 1906: plates 1–2).

The Veddas, among whom Seligman worked in 1907–8, were likewise the subject of a massive photo-

53. 'Bendiagalge — group' by C.G. Seligman, detail of which is reproduced in Seligman (1911: plate III) as 'Group of Veddas of Henebedda and Bingoda.' (RAI 4625)

graphic output. This work from studios such as W.H.L. Skeen, Scowen, Plâté and the Colombo Apothecaries Company stereotyped them as the 'wild men' of Ceylon. The photographs suggested that they spent all of their time in the jungle clutching hunting weapons. Seligman's fieldwork, however, revealed that:

> With all my efforts I was able to meet only four families, and hear of two more, who, I believe had never practised cultivation . . . [the Danigala who practised cultivation had] assumed the role of professional primitive men . . . they are commonly fetched to be interviewed by travellers at the nearest rest house, where they appear clad only in the traditional scanty Vedda garment, whereas, when not on show they dress very much as the neighbouring peasant Sinhalese. (Seligman 1911:vii)

Seligman's indexical exposure to the Veddas during fieldwork had allowed him to see behind the earlier iconic and symbolic 'truths' of travellers (the Veddas had 'looked like', and 'said they were' hunter-gatherers). Having thus discovered that surface effect could be deceptive, Seligman is then faced with a

problem in his use of a series of photographic illustrations on which clarificatory details have been painted. Retouching was a routine procedure in publishing at this time and Seligman explains that poor light in the 'depth of the jungle' necessitated underexposure in spite of the use of rapid plates (Seligman 1911:viii). Seligman advised his readers that the images had been 'more or less faked' and lest anyone confuse them with *real* photographs they are all marked with an asterisk at the end of the caption (see for example the series of dances, plates XXVI–LIV).

Part of Seligman's strategy here is certainly the demarcation of an area of anthropological truth from an area of para-ethnographic deception by means of a strategic retreat in which, because some of his photographs are acknowledged to be 'false', the majority are deemed to be 'true'.[24] This was doubly necessary because formally many of Seligman's 'true' photographs 'look like' the products of early commercial studios. Thus Seligman's image of Henebedda and Bingoda (Plate 53) has an affinity with a large albumen print (Plate 54) from the 1880s produced by W.H.L.

54. 'Group of Veddahs.' Albumen print by W.H.L. Skeen and Co., *c*.1880. (RAI 5118)

Skeen and Co. Both show a group in a forest setting carrying bows and axes and looking directly at the camera. The privileged nature of the anthropological representation is by no means clear here (or indeed anywhere). In the necessary process of 'defining itself by contrast to adjacent and antecedent discourses' (Pratt 1986:27) the quixotic God of Truth in anthropological photography demanded the sacrifice of victims whose death is marked by an asterisk (Pinney 1990). The tenets of the first history of photography do not lead us to expect that such a high price would be necessary.

By way of a conclusion, let us examine, for the third and final time, Sekula's observation that:

> Nothing could be more natural than . . . a man pulling a snapshot from his wallet and saying, 'This is my dog'. (1982:86)

We might note at this stage that nothing appears more natural than that this statement of the obvious should require to be spoken, a fact testified to by the dog's owner in the spoken caption 'This is my dog'. This validation of the indexical photograph by the merely symbolic vagaries of language, the triumph of 'mere hearsay' over the clarity of vision, bears closer scrutiny, for it signals a general retroversion by photography towards other orders of the sign. Just as Leslie Woodhead 'explains' his photograph of the Mursi watching part of a *Disappearing World* film about themselves by reference to a painting by Magritte,[25] so the truth of photographs often appears to be 'anchored', in Barthes' term, to a symbolic textual sign[26] which acts as a 'counter-taboo' (Barthes 1971:43; cited by Baker 1985:170). The act of exposing the film's emulsion to the light bounced off objects suddenly looks less important as the 'motivated' visual sign starts to take second place to the arbitrary identity of language:

> *The image freezes an endless number of possibilities; words determine a single certainty . . . that is why all news photographs are captioned.* (Barthes 1983:13; cited by Baker ibid.)

The possibilities of misspelling and misreading images, particularly photographic images, seem to be limited at a very basic level by what Barthes called their 'denotative' message. Thus the illustration of Kajji chiefs (Plate 55) from Major A.J.N. Tremearne's 1912 work *The Tailed Headhunters of Nigeria* is, Barthes might have argued, denotatively and indisputably a photograph of five people. It is not, for instance, a picture of the *Titanic* leaving the dock on its inaugural voyage. Writers such as Bryson and Bertin have argued that there is a certain level of visual primacy which enables us to identify with certainty particular forms of images. Thus according to Bryson it would be 'simply wrong to identify . . . a *Pietà* as an old woman with a corpse' (Baker 1985:164). Likewise, Bertin has argued that under certain 'monosemic' systems (such as maps) 'all the participants agree on certain meanings and agree to discuss them no further' (Baker ibid.).

It was the faith in such a denotative power of photography which underpinned the views outlined in the first history of photography. Photography, as the 'pencil of nature', denoted nature — along the straight line of transcription from nature to culture (from referent to photograph) there was no room for connotation. But, for our purpose here, it is difficult to define any area of, or context for, denotation in which we could commonly agree on anything other than the crude distinction between Kajji Chiefs and the *Titanic*.

Let us develop this argument further. We might say that part of the signification of the illustration from *The Tailed Headhunters of Nigeria* is of five subjected individuals who stand at the antipodes of the civilizational order which Major Tremearne is dedicated to upholding. We might hypothesize, in Foucauldian fashion, that the photograph is caught in a nexus of oppressive vision whose function is the disciplining of these five individuals. But might we not say the same thing of Plate 56? Whatever our personal and private responses to these photographs (and it is part of this argument that it is these responses which matter), we might perhaps all agree that our interpretation of these two images changes when we read them with the assistance of their captions:

1. 'Kajji Chiefs. *The man on the left is a dwarf: his beard is tied with grass, which is prolonged and hangs down upon his chest. This was probably copied from*

Kagoma, *the neighbouring tribe to the south. The next man was a very troublesome person being always "against the Government". Note the cowrie strings of the loin-covering of the right-hand man*' (Tremearne 1912:plate opp. 104)

2. 'North Texas. Sunday Morning June 1937. *All displaced tenant farmers. The oldest is 33. All native Americans, none able to vote because of Texas tax poll (sic). All on WPA. They support an average of 4 persons each on $22.80 a month. "Where we gonna go? How we gonna get there? What we gonna do? Who we gonna fight? If we fight what we gotta whip?"'* (photograph by Dorothea Lange, from her *American Exodus*, 1939 cited in Jeffrey 1981:166)[27]

However, the effect of language, what Barthes called the 'certainty of the word', can also be achieved through insertion within a language composed purely of images, through its placement within a visual syntagmatic chain.

Adopting Saussure's distinction between a lateral plane of language, the *syntagm*, a chain of meaning into which words are sequentially and contextually locked, and a vertical plane, the *paradigm*, enables us to see better how this operates.[28] The syntagm is constituted by a principle of addition, whereas the paradigmatic plane operates on the principle of substitution. This paradigmatic axis allows, as Jakobsen noted, for metaphorical association, whereas along the plane of the syntagm a metonymic contiguity prevails (Burgin 1982:56). Many photographs have the potential to enter primarily into paradigmatic (metaphorical and vertical) relationship with other photographs, such as in the two Samoan photographs from the Walker Collection[29] (Plate 57), but signifying force is largely the consequence of a horizontal narrative contextualizing plane, which Eco called (with reference to cinematic narrative) 'syntagmatic concatenation imbued with argumentative capacity' (1982:38).

Thus, when we view the image of the Kajji chiefs in the context of another image from the same work which shows (Plate 58) seven almost naked women from behind (it is captioned 'Kagoro women of Tuku Tozo', but at this point at least, my argument does not depend on any knowledge of any contextualizations other than the contiguity of visual images), once we become aware that 'Kajji Chiefs' is a subset of a discourse which also includes Kagoro women, it immediately becomes inconceivable that such an image could function as positive propaganda of the Dorothea Lange 'North Texas . . .' kind. The only question that arises from the retro-perspective of our knowledge of the visual language of *Tailed Headhunters . . .* is how we managed to constitute such a question as a possibility in the first place, how at an

55. 'Kajji chiefs' from Major A.J.N. Tremearne's *The Tailed Headhunters of Nigeria*, 1912: opp. p. 104.

56. 'North Texas, Sunday morning. June 1937.' Photograph by Dorothea Lange. Published in Lange and Taylor (1939) with the caption 'All displaced tenant farmers. The oldest 33.' (Courtesy of the Library of Congress)

57. Single sheet with two photographs of Samoa, *c.*1880. 'Lieut. Gaunt R.N. force of Samoans during the war' (sic); 'Heaps of Coconuts'. (RAI 35427, 35426)

58. 'Kagoro Women of Tuku Tozu' from Tremearne, 1912: opp. p. 92 (see caption to plate 55).

earlier stage we had hypothesized a similarity between Tremearne's and Lange's intentions.

The proliferation of images, the 'syntagmatic concatenation', here produces a momentary closure of finitude of meaning, the same closure of meaning which the first history of photography had led us to suppose was in the very substance of the single image or negative as a thing-in-itself. In Christian Metz's terminology (taken from the Danish semiotician Hjelmslev) the photographic unit of reading, or 'lexis', is in the process of enlargement towards the lexis of film. It is of course precisely the context and closure provided by syntagmatic concatenation which is the great rationale for ethnographic film as opposed to the truncated and castrated 'fetish' of the photographic 'look'.[30] Film thus incarnated plays Malinowski to still photography's Frazer (Strathern 1987).

There are several collections of still photographs in the RAI Collection which seem to prefigure and yearn after the status of moving film. Thus M.V. Portman made long narrative sequences of bow and adze manufacture among the Andaman Islanders, and Seligman himself in his long sequences of curing rituals among the Veddas seems to achieve a cinematic syntagmatic encompassment. Perhaps it was the subliminal acceptance of the indeterminacy of the image that inclined Victorians to photograph in prisons where photographic identity was buttressed by other, less transgressable, forces. It appears that all we can ever say is that *the what is* of photography, like that of anthropology, lies in its *what it is not*, its con-text (cf. Hobart 1985:41; Faris, this volume).

But such indeterminacy need not be the cause of dejection. Rather, it suggests two very useful conclusions. First, it reveals the function of the archive (for instance, an archive such as that called 'The Royal Anthropological Institute Photographic Collection') as concerned with the disciplining of its images within a language-based political view of the world and its peoples. The archive functions as a vast linguistic grid enmeshing otherwise volatile images within what it hopes is a structuring certainty. Imprisoned within the archival grid, images (thanks to the teleology of the archive) become self-evident things-in-themselves. The language of the archive, having filled in the blank space of the photograph, erases the undecidable nature of the image. This is one reason why the first history of photography outlined in this essay has been so powerfully persuasive.

It is *not* a paradox that anthropology is discovering the 'worth', the 'information value', of its archival images precisely at the moment that these images are decaying into invisibility, the honest statement of their own insignificance,[31] since they signify nothing but:

The loss of what has never taken place, of a self-presence which has never been given but only dreamed of and always already split, repeated, incapable of appearing to itself except in its own disappearance. (Derrida 1976:112)

If, as seems possible, the same image of a young Jewish boy alighting from a train at Auschwitz can serve as both a certification of the power of the Reich (when enmeshed in the language of the Nazi archive), *or* as an injunction to counter bigotry and its genocidal impulses (when used in a contemporary anti-racist campaign) it becomes everything and yet nothing. If this is so, then the study of anthropology and the camera is transformed from a relationship of simple production in which the camera is a mere 'tool' or 'conduit'[32] to the study of the determination (at a first and provisional level) of that 'what is' (the 'what it is not') which lies in the photograph, through a study of the significatory frameworks whereby these images are endowed and closed with meaning (Tagg 1988).

Photography is now being rephotographed. By this I refer not chiefly to the conservation process by which the decaying archival image is reproduced for another generation, but rather the manner in which dark recesses of photographic archives are coming under scrutiny and images of an imagined past brought from darkness to light by projects which stress the recuperative and forensic possibilities (medical metaphors again!) of this excavated material culture of the colonial and imperial heritage of anthropology.

I have suggested that once these objects — photographs, images — are brought to the surface it is we as viewers and interpreters who determine their meaning. Darkness and depth, like the creative absence of light in the photographer's darkroom, are vital metaphors which introduce a plane of presence distinct from the surface fractures of the present, which is the time in which we always read photographs:

There is a crack there. Construction and deconstruction are breached/broached there. The line of disintegration, which is not straight or continuous or regular . . . (Derrida 1987:133)

Secondly, if even syntagmatic concatenation is ultimately no guarantee of a fixed contextual meaning since context is a question of training, of establishing the context of the context, the syntagm of the syntagm, the appealing possibility of completely usurping any attempt to achieve this suggests itself — the heterotopia suggested by Foucault in which units of reading set free by a radical rupture of 'traditional' context align themselves in surreal disjunctions (cf. Harkness 1983:4).

The prospects of such heterotopic couplings are

encouraging and stem from the increasing conjunction of anthropology and photography as their old certainties and former histories collapse. The parallel first histories of photography and anthropology have been easy to demonstrate. What is also emerging is that both anthropology and photography are simultaneously discovering their own uncertainty and impossibility. Just as anthropology is discovering its status as *anthropo-graphy*,[33] a rhetorical 'visualism' (Fabian 1983:106), so photography is in the process of discovering that it is a language-based *photo-logy* or, more correctly, *photo-grammar*. As the traces of their trajectories approach each other, there is, for the first time, a possibility of a creative convergence.

ACKNOWLEDGEMENTS

I have filched acknowledged and unacknowledged ideas in this essay from Martin Jay, Chris Wright, James C. Faris, Peter Hoffenberg, Timothy Yates, David Tomas. The idiocies are wholly my own.

NOTES

1 Tyler argues that the hegemony of 'things' 'entails the hegemony of the visual as a means of knowing/thinking. Seeing is a privileged sensorial mode and key metaphor in (Standard Average European language and thought)' (1984:23). He proceeds to reverse some habitual privilegings in order to demonstrate this tacit prioritization ('I just wanted to taste what it looked like').

2 As Martin Jay notes: 'whether we focus on the "mirror of nature" metaphor in philosophy with Richard Rorty or emphasize the prevalence of surveillance with Michel Foucault or bemoan the society of the spectacle with Guy Debord, we confront again and again the ubiquity of vision as the master sense of the modern era' (1988:3).

3 See below, pages 26–7 for explication of these terms.

4 See Pinney (this volume) for a development of such an argument with reference to the photographing of India.

5 These dates do not merely record the moment of intervention by an accidental and unpredictable socially uncontextualized 'discovery' — photography.

Rather, there was what has been called a 'culture of need'.

6 See also Philippe Dubois's description of photography as 'thanatography' (Metz 1985:83).

7 The argument developed in this paper under the heading of the 'second history of photography' has many points of similarity with the heavily Foucauldian approach of John Tagg, to which it owes a great deal. However, we are also justified, I believe, in including a certain reading of it here in the 'first history' of photography, inasmuch as it stresses certainty within specific contexts. Tagg (1988) argues that photography was semiotically more or less neutral and was endowed with power because it suited the needs of an expanding state. He argues

against the idea that photographs can embody a 'pre-linguistic certainty' (1988:4), suggesting instead that they embody a language of political and disciplinary power which is determined outside of the technical processes of photography. The photographic image itself is a 'paltry paper sign' (1984:12) on to which society and history inscribes its truth (see also Green 1984 and 1985 for a parallel argument). When Tagg suggests that 'you ask yourself, and not just rhetorically, under what conditions would a photograph of the Loch Ness Monster (of which there are many) be acceptable' (1988:5), his argument places him centrally within the second disputed history of photography, a history which he has done much to delineate.

But in other areas of Tagg's project, although photographic truth is a consequence of a societal 'will to truth', ultimately, however, the truth 'effect' of the image is as great as Susan Sontag would have us believe although its source is 'power' rather than 'light'. Despite Tagg's denials that the 'reality effect' is the fully successful result of a conspiracy to impose a 'regime of truth' (1982:132) as we 'dream in the ideological space of the photograph' (1982:141), he continues to stress the closure of the whole process: '"currency" and "value" arise in certain distinct and historically specific social practices *and are ultimately a function of the state*' (1982:122; emphasis added). A general assessment of Foucault's critique of vision, placing it within a French literary tradition, has been given by Jay (1986). Foucault's critique of vision, on which later writers have based their statements on photography, follows very much the Heideggerian critique of Cartesian spectatorial subjectivism as a source of Western knowledge and power.

8   Part of the 'capillary' manifestation of power involved self-surveillance:

He who is subjected to a field of visibility, and who knows it, assumes responsibility for the constraints of power; he makes them play spontaneously upon himself, he inscribes himself in power rela-

tions in which he simultaneously plays both roles; he becomes the principle of his own subjection. (Foucault 1979:202–3)

One striking instance of this is the initiative of a young Irishman from Peckham Rye who wrote to A.C. Haddon in 1905:

You will perhaps recall speaking before a lecture at the University College on some Tuesday evening to a very dark-foreign-primitive Irishman.

I have endeavoured to measure with as much accuracy as possible and I make the length of the head 9.55 inches and the breadth 6.85 inches. This I take to give a long headed type as you surmised. I also enclose a photo of my brother whose head was even longer than mine as the photo would seem to indicate. (Haddon Photo. Coll. box 145/2)

9   See Woodhead 1987 for a recent filmic analysis of this concern.

10   This finds an anthropological idiom in the quest for an unblemished primitivism such as that pursued by a tourist group travelling from Kathmandu to Lhasa who encountered a group of Tibetan nomads:

the photographer among us, who had an interest in ethnic minorities . . . insisted on removing the huge multicoloured Chinese thermos flask which was displayed at the entrance to the main tent (before taking any photos). (Phillips 1989)

Tom Phillips notes that 'life was censored in favour of the ethnic dream . . . in the form of a Tibet without telegraph wires and trucks' (1986). See also Clifford (1988) for a discussion of this issue.

Such dreams of purity are a concomitant of a particular form of realism which attempts to efface all signs of the manufacturer of the image and lies at the opposite pole to 'modernist art' as defined by Clement Greenberg as a practice of self-reference which made 'no gesture to anything beyond its own boundaries' (Burgin 1982:11).

11   Velázquez's *Las Meninas* has emerged as a painterly metaphor for a kind of reflexive proto-modernism (which, as Strathern (1987) observes, looks rather like post-modernism). It was used as a

frontispiece to Foucault's *Order of Things* and has inspired much comment.

12   See Ginzburg (1983) for a discussion of the role of 'detection' and 'abduction' in reading bodily signs.

13   There were many other competing systems such as that advocated by Bonomi (1873).

14   Before his conversion to anthropology following his participation in the second Torres Straits Expedition of 1898–9, Rivers was a psychologist lecturing in the Cambridge Medical School on the physiology of the senses (Quiggin 1942:96). This image was found with his later Toda studies in the Haddon Collection, University of Cambridge.

15   Peirce distinguished three forms of the sign. *Symbols* (for instance, language) have an arbitrary relation to their referent. An *icon* bears a relation of resemblance to its referent. An *index* by contrast has a very direct relation with its referent being causally connected. Smoke is an index of fire. Peirce argued that photographs were both icons (there was a resemblance — although in the case of 'vortograms' and some experimental film-making this is harder to establish) and indexes (by virtue of the effect of light on the film emulsion).

16   To point out that there is a 'contradiction' between the Barthes who argues that photos are 'messages without a code' and the Barthes who argued that the polysemic photograph is determined by the univocal caption — 'the certainty of the word' — is to rather miss the point concerning this 'unworried inconsistency' (MacCabe 1985:1). As MacCabe further notes: 'Barthes's refusal of a canonical meaning for his own texts and the consequent ethic of a fundamental discontinuity of meaning and self appeared as a threat . . .' (ibid.). Throughout his texts (and this is probably also true of Bourdieu's writing on photography) the focus oscillates imperceptibly between assessments concerning 'popular' and personal perceptions of photography and statements concerning its ontology.

17   Fabian argues that 'Anthropology emerged and established itself as

an allochronic discourse; it is a science of other men in another Time. It is a discourse whose referent has been removed from the present of the speaking/writing subject' (1983:143).

18 A literal filmic representation of this occurs in the first film version of *Dracula*, F.W. Murnau's *Nosferatu* (1923), in which a scene occurring after the central character crosses a bridge on his way to Dracula's castle is printed in negative, 'suggesting the dialectical encounter with otherness in terms of a turning upside down of values' (Richardson 1991:20).

19 For a related argument couched in terms of 'subjective experience' see Clifford (1988:37).

20 Photography has an authority very similar to that of the spoken word within what Derrida has called 'phonocentrism' — the privileging of speech over writing. For Derrida, Plato's *Phaedrus*, which attacks writing as a pollution of the self-present meaning of *logos*, exemplifies a Western tradition of logocentrism and also demonstrates at the same time the violence within this written text that upholds in its inscriptions the primacy of speech. Speech is privileged because in entering into a relation with it one is necessarily brought into proximity with the speaker and the hearer can interrogate the speaker as to his intentions and desired meanings. Oral speech has a privileged proximity to the communicating presence which can adjudicate as to the intended meaning of any utterance (see Derrida 1976; Burgin 1982:54). In this respect the relationship might be described as indexical, like the photograph. The effect of light on chemicals is directly analogous to the confirmable intentions of the speaker. Writing, on the other hand, is like painting since what we consume as readers is severed from the source or its veracity. As a reader I can interpret any piece of writing in any way I please just as a painting (defined as 'art') is used to evoke certain open-ended indeterminate responses. In written texts, as with painting, the meaning is constantly deferred and displaced, and presence is never attainable as the reader experiences the pleasure of its plurality.

21 I am arguing here that, just as Derrida argues that speech ineluctably reveals itself (through its auto-deconstruction) to be a form of writing, so photography unavoidably reveals itself to be a form of painting/writing.

21 Other cultural traditions have never attempted to pursue this purity of the photographic image (see Sprague 1978; Gutman 1982).

22 See Falconer 1984, and W.T. Blandford's criticisms of Hooker's *Himalayan Journals* in *Bengal Asiatic Society Journal* 1871:393.

23 I have attributed photographs variously to Rivers himself or to Wiele and Klein on the basis of format. The images in the RAI Collection are a mixture of small, amateur images, presumed to be by Rivers, and larger technically competent studies, presumed to be the work of Wiele and Klein.

24 Seligman's tactic may have been partly responsible for Malinowski's declaration in *The Sexual Life of Savages in North-Western Melanesia* that:

> One gap, regrettable but hardly to be remedied, is the small number of illustrations bearing directly on erotic life. Since this, however, takes place in deep shadow, literally as well as figuratively, photographs could only be faked, or at best, posed — and faked or posed passion (or sentiment) is worthless. (1929:xxii)

25 Woodhead first suggests a parallel in 'the final chapter of some Agatha Christie novel', but then suggests a painting parallel: 'The television set brought to the forest clearing something of the surreal dislocations of a Magritte painting' (1987:7). He presumably had in mind the *Human Condition* series painted from 1934 onwards.

26 On captions in photographs see Baker 1985, Hutcheon 1988, Hunter 1988; in anthropological photographs, Faris, this volume; in film, Bollag 1988; in painting, Gombrich 1985.

27 *American Exodus* (1939) was one of the products of the Farm Security Administration documentation project and is an interesting early example of what has now become an ethnographic filmmaking orthodoxy — a collaboration between a photographer (Dorothea Lange) and a sociologist/anthro-

pologist (Paul S. Taylor) which used the direct speech of those photographed as captions, or narrative. Lange and Taylor note in their introduction that 'quotations which accompany photographs report what persons photographed said, not what we think might be their unspoken thoughts'.

28 This can, appropriately, be more easily grasped in diagrammatic form:

syntagm → (metonymy, contiguity)
↓
paradigm/system
(metaphor)

29 The combination of these two images is technically a simile since both terms of the comparison are present.

30 Thus Asen Balikci notes that 'the final effect (of the visual experience of ethnographic film) is to facilitate in the viewer perception of an original whole' (1988:42). Metz notes that whereas film 'lets us believe in more things, photography lets us believe more in one thing' (1985:88).

31 See Wright 1987:12.

32 Technological elaboration (which usually means 'progress') is a favourite means of organizing histories of the relationship between anthropology and the camera. Thus the recent Peabody exhibition 'From Site to Sight' progresses from the single perspective of Fox Talbot to the encompassment of 'Computerized Axial Tomography' (Banta & Hinsley 1986).

33 Ros Poignant has pointed out to me that 'anthropography' was used at the turn of the century to denote a particular system of anthropometric reading. Here I use it in a quite different sense to suggest the visual suppositions which underpin what had previously been thought of as a discipline of words. This parallels Derrida's programme of 'the *pictorialization* of writing and *grammatization* of the image' (Brunette & Wills 1989:100).

REFERENCES

Ardener, Edwin 1987. '"Remote Areas": some theoretical considerations'. In A. Jackson (ed.) *Anthropology at Home*, ASA 25. London: Tavistock.

Balikci, Asen 1988. 'Anthropologists and Ethnographic Filmmaking'. In J.R. Rollwagen (ed.) *Anthropological Filmmaking*. Chur: Harwood Academic.

Banta, Melissa & Hinsley, Curtis 1986. *From Site to Sight: Anthropology, Photography and the Power of Imagery*. Cambridge, Mass.: Peabody Museum Press.

Baker, Steve 1985. The Hell of Connotation. *Word and Image* 1(2):164–75.

Barthes, Roland 1977. *Image Music Text*. Trans. S. Heath. London: Fontana.

— 1984 (1980). *Camera Lucida: Reflections on Photography*. Trans. R. Howard. London: Fontana.

— 1983. 'The Photographic Message'. In S. Sontag (ed.) *Barthes: Selected Writings* 194–210. London: Fontana.

Bateson, Gregory & Mead, Margaret 1942. *Balinese Character: a photographic analysis*. New York: New York Academy of Sciences.

Baudrillard, Jean 1983 (1981). *Simulacra and Simulations*. New York: Semiotext(e).

Berger, John 1972. *Ways of Seeing*. Harmondsworth: Penguin.

Bollag, Brenda 1988. Words on the screen: The problem of the linguistic sign in the cinema. *Semiotica* 72 1/2:71–90.

Bonomi, Joseph 1873. A New Instrument for Measuring the Proportions of the Human Body. *Journal of the Anthropological Institute* 2:180–3.

Boorstein, Daniel J. 1963 (1962) *The Image or What Happened to the American Dream*. Harmondsworth: Penguin.

Bourdieu, Pierre 1965. *Un art moyen. Essai sur les usages sociaux de la Photographie*. Paris: Editions de Minuit.

Breeks, J.W. 1873. *An Account of the Primitive Tribes and Monuments of the Nilagiris*. London: India Museum.

Brunette, Peter & Wills, David 1989. *Screen/Play: Derrida and Film Theory*. Princeton: Princeton University Press.

Burgin, Victor 1982. 'Photographic Practice and Art Theory'. In V. Burgin (ed.) *Thinking Photography*. London: Macmillan.

Clifford, James 1983. On Ethnographic Authority. *Representations* 1(2):118–46.

— 1988. *The Predicament of Culture*. Harvard: University Press.

De Certeau, Michel 1986. *Heterologies: Discourse on the Other*. Manchester: Manchester University Press.

De Heusch, Luc 1987. The Cinema and Social Science: A Survey of Ethnographic and Sociological Films. *Visual Anthropology* 1(2): 99–156.

Derrida, J. 1976. *On Grammatology*. Baltimore: Johns Hopkins University Press.

— 1987. *The Truth in Painting*. Chicago: University of Chicago Press.

Desmond, R. 1982. *Victorian India in Focus*. London: HMSO.

Fabian, Johannes 1983. *Time and the Other: How Anthropology Makes Its Object*. New York: Columbia University Press.

Falconer, John 1984. Ethnographical Photography in India: 1850–1900. *The Photographic Collector* 5(1): 16–46.

Fernandez, James 1985. *Persuasions and Performances: the play of tropes in culture*. Bloomington: Indiana University Press.

Foucault, Michel 1970. *The Order of Things*. London: Tavistock.

— 1976. The Birth of the Clinic: An Archaeology of Medical Perception. London: Tavistock.

— 1979. *Discipline and Punish: the Birth of the Prison*. Harmondsworth: Penguin.

— 1983. *This is not a Pipe*. Berkeley: University of California Press.

Ginzburg, Carlo 1983. 'Clues: Morelli, Freud and Sherlock Holmes'. In U. Eco & T.A. Sebeok (eds.) *The Sign of Three: Dupin, Holmes, Peirce*. Bloomington: Indiana University Press.

Gombrich, Ernst 1985. Image and Word in Twentieth Century Art. *Word and Image* 1(30):213–41.

Green, David 1984. Classified Subjects — Photography and Anthropology: the Technology of Power. *Ten-8* 14:3–37.

— 1985. Veins of Resemblance: Photography and Eugenics. *Oxford Art Journal* 7(2):3–16.

Greenblatt, Stephen 1987. Towards a Poetics of Culture. *Southern Review* 20:3–15.

Gutman, Judith Mara 1982. *Through Indian Eyes: 19th and early 20th century photography from India*. New York: Oxford University Press/International Center of Photography.

Harkness, James 1983. 'Translator's Introduction'. In M. Foucault *This is Not a Pipe*. Berkeley: University of California Press.

Hartog, Françoise 1988. *The Mirror of Herodotus: The Representation of the Other in the Writing of History*. Berkeley: University of California Press.

Hobart, Mark 1985. 'Texte est un con'. In R.H. Barnes, D. de Coppet & R.J. Parkin (eds.) *Contexts and Levels. Anthropological Essays on Hierarchy*. JASO Occasional Paper 4. Oxford: JASO.

Hunter, Jefferson 1988. *Image and Text*. Harvard: University Press.

Hutcheon, Linda 1988. Fringe Interference: Postmodern Border Tensions. *Style* 22(2):299–323.

Hutchinson, H.M., Gregory, J.W. & Lydekker, R. n.d. *The Living Races of Mankind: A popular illustrated account of the customs, habits, pursuits, feasts, and ceremonies of the races of mankind throughout the world*. London: Hutchinson.

Ibbetson, D. 1890. The Study of Anthropology in India. *Journal of the Anthropological Society of Bombay* 2:117–46.

Jay, Martin 1986. 'In the Empire of the Gaze: Foucault and the denigration of vision in twentieth century French thought'. In *Postmodernism* (ICA Documents 4). London: ICA.

— 1988. 'Scopic Regimes of Modernity'. In H. Foster (ed.) *Vision and Visuality*. Seattle: Bay Press/Dia Art Foundation.

— n.d. 'Photo-unrealism: the Contribution of the Camera to the Crisis of Ocularcentrism'. Unpublished MS.

Jeffrey, Ian 1981. *Photography: A Concise History*. London: Thames and Hudson.

Krauss, Rosalind 1981. A Note on Photography and the Simulacral. *October* 31.

— 1985. 'Photography's Discursive Spaces'. In R. Krauss (ed.) *The Originality of the Avant-Garde and Other Modernist Myths*. Cambridge, Mass.: MIT Press.

La Fontaine, Jean 1985. *What is Social Anthropology?* London: Edward Arnold.

Lamprey, J. 1869. On a method of measuring the human form for the use of students of ethnology. *Journal of the Ethnological Society of London* 1:84–5.

Lange, Dorothea & Taylor, Paul S. 1939. *An American Exodus*. New York: Reynal & Hitchcock.

Lévi-Strauss, Claude 1976. *Tristes Tropiques*. Harmondsworth:

Penguin.

Lindt, J.W. 1886. *A Few Results of Modern Photography*. Melbourne: M'Carron, Bird & Co.

Malinowski, Bronislaw 1922. *Argonauts of the Western Pacific*. London: Routledge & Kegan Paul.

— 1929. *The Sexual Life of Savages in North-Western Melanesia*. London: Routledge & Kegan Paul.

MacCabe Colin 1985. *Theoretical Essays: film, linguistics, literature*. Manchester: University Press.

Metz, Christian 1985. Photography and Fetish. *October* 34:81–90.

Phillips, Tom 1986. Finding Objects of Desire. *Times Literary Supplement* January 24:89.

Pinney, C. 1990. Classification and Fantasy in the Photographic Construction of Caste and Tribe. *Visual Anthropology* 3(2–3):259–88.

Portman, M.V. 1894. *Measurements and Medical Details: Male Series, North Andaman Group of Tribes*. Manuscript, Museum of Mankind.

Pratt, Mary Louise 1986. 'Fieldwork in Commonplaces'. In J. Clifford & G.E. Marcus (eds.) *Writing Culture: the poetics and politics of ethnography*. Berkeley: University of California Press.

Prochaska, David 1990. The Archive of Algérie Imaginaire. *History and Anthropology* 4(2):373–420.

Quiggin, A. Hingston 1942. *Haddon the Head Hunter: a short sketch of the life of A.C. Haddon*. Cambridge: University Press.

Richardson, Michael 1991. *The Crisis of Objectivity in Anthropology: A consideration through Romanticism and Surrealism*. Unpublished Ph.D. thesis, School of Oriental and African Studies, University of London.

Rivers, W.H.R. 1906. *The Todas*. London: Macmillan.

Rooksby, R.L. 1971. W.H.R. Rivers and the Todas. *South Asia* 1: 109–22.

Rorty, Richard 1980. *Philosophy and the Mirror of Nature*. Oxford: Basil Blackwell.

Salmond, Anne 1982. 'Theoretical landscapes: on cross cultural conceptions of knowledge'. In D. Parkin (ed.) *Semantic Anthropology*. London: Academic Press.

Sekula, Allan 1982. 'On the Invention of Photographic Meaning'. In V. Burgin (ed.) *Thinking Photography*. London: Macmillan.

— 1986. The Body and the Archive. *October* 39:3–64.

Seligman, C.G. & Seligman, B.Z. 1911. *The Veddas*. Cambridge: University Press.

Shortland, Michael 1985. Skin Deep: Barthes, Lavater and the Legible Body. *Economy and Society* 14(30): 273–311.

Sontag, Susan 1979. *On Photography*. Harmondsworth: Penguin.

Sprague, S.F. 1978. Yoruba Photography: how the Yoruba see themselves. *African Arts* 12:52–9, 107.

Stocking, George W. 1971. What's in a Name? The Origins of the Royal Anthropological Institute (1837–71). *Man* 6:369–90.

— 1983. 'The Ethnographer's Magic: Fieldwork in British Anthropology from Tylor to Malinowski'. In G. Stocking (ed.) *Observers Observed: Essays on Ethnographic Fieldwork*. (*History of Anthropology* 1). Wisconsin: University of Wisconsin Press.

Strathern, Marilyn 1987. Out of Context: the persuasive fictions of Anthropology. *Current Anthropology* 28(3):251–81.

Tagg, John 1982. 'The Currency of the Photograph'. In V. Burgin (ed.) *Thinking Photography* 110–41. London: Macmillan.

— 1984. The Burden of Representation. *Ten-8* 14:10–12.

— 1988. *The Burden of Representation: Essays on Photographies and Histories*. London: Macmillan.

Thomas, Nicholas 1990. *Out of Time: History and Evolution in Anthropological Discourse*. Cambridge: University Press.

Tomas, David 1982. The Ritual of Photography. *Semiotica* 40 1/2: 1–25.

— 1988. Toward an anthropology of sight: Ritual performance and the photographic process. *Semiotica* 68 3/4:245–70.

Tremearne, A.J.N. 1912. *The Tailed Headhunters of Nigeria*. London: Seeley, Service & Co.

Tyler, Stephen 1984. The Vision Quest in the West or What the Mind's Eye Sees. *Journal of Anthropological Research* 40(1):23–40.

Virilio, Paul 1989. *War and Cinema: the logistics of perception*. London: Verso.

Watney, Simon 1987. 'The Image of the Body'. In *Figures*. Cambridge: Cambridge Darkroom.

Woodhead, Leslie 1987. *A Box Full of Spirits: Adventures of a film-maker in Africa*. London: Heinemann.

Woodhead, Leslie & Singer, André 1988. *Disappearing World: Television and Anthropology*. London: Boxtree.

Wright, Chris 1987. *Visible Bodies: anthropology and photography, 1850–1900*. Unpublished MA thesis, School of Oriental and African Studies, University of London.

Case-studies

Some Notes on the Attempt to Apply Photography to Anthropometry[1] during the Second Half of the Nineteenth Century

Frank Spencer

ONE OF THE EARLIEST REFERENCES to the utility of the photographic process in anthropology is to be found in the *Manual of Ethnological Inquiry* published by the British Association for the Advancement of Science in 1852 (BAAS 1854:195). While the potential of this new process for apprehending an 'accurate record of individual likenesses' was clearly recognized, photography at this juncture was still a cumbersome process that did not readily lend itself to operations in the field. However, during the next decade some of the inherent technical restrictions of daguerreotyping and calotyping were removed by the introduction of the wet-collodion method. This development marked not only a major turning point in the general popularity of photography but also in its application to the ethnographic enterprise.

Where previously the photographic process had been seen as no more than a convenient device by which to enhance the objectivity of an ethnological narrative, there was now a definite movement to transcend the boundaries of mere illustration and anthology, and to employ the photographic image as a 'measurable' scientific datum. To a large extent this nascent movement was prompted by the pervasive fear among anthropologists of the period 'that many of the [human] races were slowly being annihilated with the spread of [Western] civilization' (Urry 1971). Photography provided, so it seemed at the time, a convenient means by which to salvage this rapidly vanishing resource (cf. Edwards 1990). The problem was how to transform the ethnological photograph into a document that would permit the recovery of reliable comparative morphometric data.

During the second half of the nineteenth century a number of abortive attempts were made to develop standardized photometric methods, all of which, in one way or another, are seen as modified versions of two systems devised in the late 1860s by Thomas Henry Huxley and John Lamprey respectively.

Evidently Huxley's scheme was drawn up and submitted to the Colonial Office with the specific intention of securing 'the formation of a systematic series of photographs of the various races of men comprehended within the British Empire' (Huxley Papers [1869] 30:75; cf. Edwards 1990; for specific details on Huxley's anthropological agenda, see Gregorio 1984:168–80). According to Huxley:

> [While] great numbers of ethnological photographs already exist . . . they lose much of their value from not being taken upon a uniform and well considered plan. The result is that they are rarely either measurable or comparable with one another and that they fail to give that precise information respecting the proportions and the conformation of the body, which . . . [is of paramount]

99

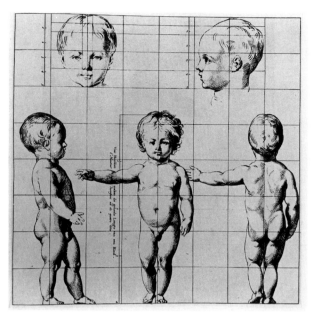

59. 'Infantile Proportions' from Jacob de Wit's *Teekenboek der proportien*, 1747.

worth to the ethnologist. (Huxley to Lord Granville, Dec. 8, 1869/HM-ICA:30.75–8)

In an effort to produce a photographic document that would permit the subsequent recovery of reliable comparative and morphometric data, Huxley recommended that all subjects be photographed naked, according to established anthropometric poses (Plate 59), and that each view be accompanied by a plainly marked measuring scale placed in the same plane as the subject. To further ensure constant scale it was recommended that the subject be placed at a fixed distance from the camera (Plates 60i–iv). Specifically, this system called for the production of two full-length photographs of each subject: one frontal and the other in profile. In the former position, the subject was required to stand upright with 'heels together' and with the 'the right arm . . . out-stretched horizontally, [and] the palm of the hand [turned] towards the camera'; while in the latter, the subject was positioned so that the left side of the body was presented to the camera with the arm bent in a manner that did not interrupt the contours of the trunk. In particular Huxley noted the desirability that the arm in female subjects should be 'so disposed as not to interfere with the contour of the breast which is very characteristic in some races' (Huxley to Lord Granville, ibid.). Huxley also recommended the supplementation of these photographs with full-face and profile portraits of the subject's head.

In recommending the above somatic and cephalic poses Huxley was optimistic about being able to retrieve from these photographs several specific somatic statistics then considered useful in making racial comparisons, particularly those of stature and arm-span (plus various dimensions of the head and face). However, contrary to his expectation, the ability to extract such data from a photograph was fraught with many overt and hidden technical difficulties, as exemplified by the seemingly simplest of procedures: the determination of stature. In order to achieve a satisfactory measure of stature, a subject's buttocks and shoulders should be firmly pressed against a vertical surface to which a measuring rod (anthropometer) is affixed. Huxley's instructions do not stipulate this; in fact he recommended (evidently to ensure that it would be positioned in the same plane as the subject) that the 'measuring rod [be placed] . . . against the back of the [outstretched] arm . . . [and] fastened there with a bit of thread or thin string . . .'. While these instructions might achieve stability they did not necessarily guarantee the verticality of the anthropometer. In the case of Plates 60i–ii, the verticality of the anthropometer has been achieved, whereas in Plate 60iii it appears to be leaning (unfastened) against the subject's forearm, and in Plate 60iv it is being handheld. Since Huxley did not provide definitive instructions in this regard, one is left wondering how much time was spent checking the alignment of the anthropometer and correcting the subject's position before taking the photograph. To say the least, Huxley's scheme would have been an exacting experience in technical terms for both the photographer and subject.

Aside from these criticisms, other crucial elements in the determination of stature involve the positioning of the subject's head and arms. In the case of the head, it should be held so that the visual as well as the biauricular axis are horizontal (which seems to be the case in Plate 60iii), whereas the subject's arm should not be held up (as Huxley demands) but rather allowed to hang down in a natural position. Finally, under normal experimental conditions the height of the vertex is determined by means of a square which is applied to the head horizontally to facilitate a correct reading. And this presents another problem. Since the thickness of the subject's hair is unknown, the vertex can only be roughly estimated from Plates 60iii–iv. To overcome this problem the head would need to be shaved! Although this prerequisite had been recognized by other investigators (cf. Anonymous 1862), it was one that was not easily put into practice. And evidently Huxley thought so too, since this requirement does not appear in his instructions. The acquisition of head length and breadth (required to calculate the cranial index) from Plates 60i–ii would also be, at best, rough estimates. These latter measures depend

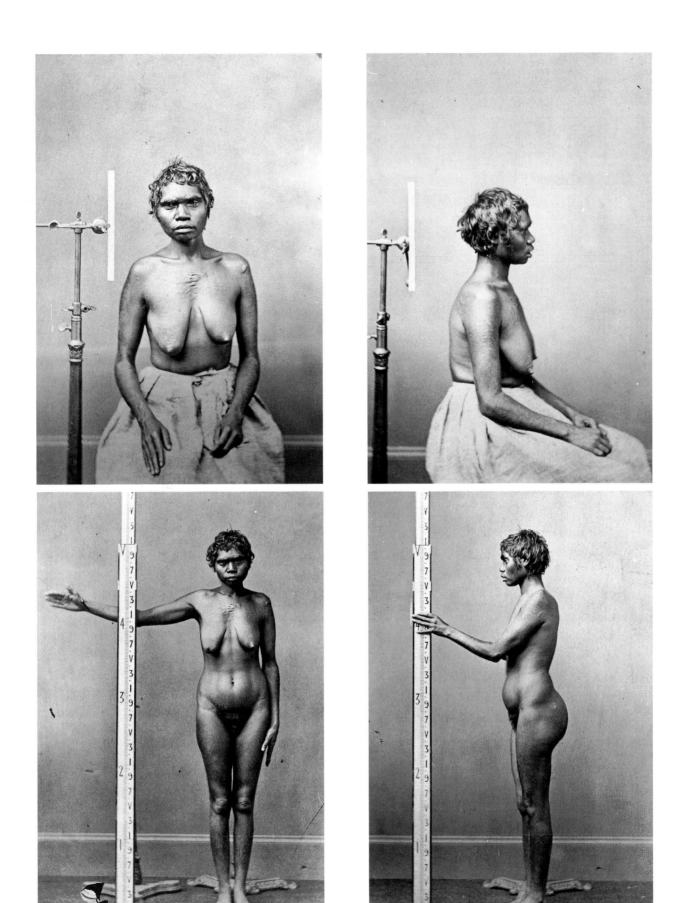

60i–iv.   i (*top left*); ii (*top right*); iii (*bottom left*); iv (*bottom right*)   Four views of a South Australian aboriginal female ('Ellen' aged twenty-two), photographed *c*.1870 according to Huxley's 'photometric instructions', photographer unknown. (RAI 2116, 2117)

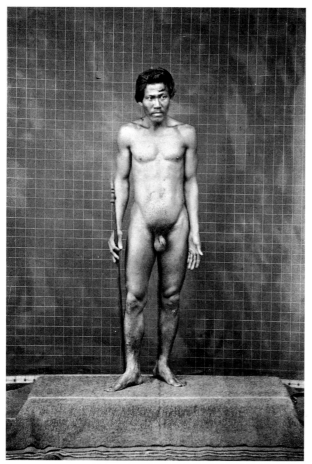

61. Front and profile views of a Malayan male, photographed by J. Lamprey, c.1868–9. (RAI 2116, 2117)

on the detection of anatomical landmarks which are essentially invisible to the eye and only revealed by the maximum determinable extension of the branches of a spreading caliper.[2] Indeed, the same may be said of a large number of somatic measurements whose determination (and accuracy) depend on the palpation of specific osteological landmarks, for example the upper border of the symphysis pubis, or the superior and external border of the acromion process. In addition to this it should also be noted that circumference measurements such as diameters of the chest are also impossible to determine from a photograph. Compounding these various technical limitations with the prevailing lack of consensus among workers regarding how and what measurements should be employed,[3] it is not surprising that Huxley's and similarly orchestrated photometric schemes were ultimately seen as a failure.

More enduring, however, was Lamprey's system, unveiled before the Ethnological Society of London in 1869. Expressly, Lamprey suggested that a simple way of enabling a comparison of photographs was to employ the metrological grid system which had long been used by artists (as well as some of the early anthropometrists such as Johann Bergmüller (*Anthropometria*, 1723) and Jacob de Wit (*Teekenboek der proportien*, 1747; cf. Plate 59) faced with the problem of accurately depicting body proportions. Adapting this methodology to the needs of the anthropologist, Lamprey proposed that the nude human subject be photographed standing in front of a cross-sectional mesh constructed from 'threads' stretched 2 inches apart, both horizontally and vertically on a 3 × 7 ft frame. He further recommended the subject be photographed full-length, both front and profile. 'By means of such photographs [cf. Plate 61]', Lamprey declared:

the anatomical structure of a good academy figure or model of six feet can be compared with a Malay of four feet eight in height; and study of all those peculiarities of contour which are so distinctly observable, in each group, [is] greatly helped by this system of perpendicular [and horizontal] lines, and they serve as good guides to their definition, which no verbal description can convey, and but few artists could delineate . . . (Lamprey 1869:84–5)

While the resulting images photographed in this manner were constrained by the same technical limitations manifest in the Huxley system (i.e. it was not possible to recover directly from the photograph reliable morphometric data), they did provide a convenient and relatively accurate way of comparing general and regional body morphology. As a consequence variations on Lamprey's grid system were widely adopted and the principle continued to find application among workers interested in somatomorphology well into the twentieth century (cf. Dupertuis & Tanner 1950; Abbie & Adey 1955).

At the same time that investigators were exploring the possible application of photography to the comparative study of the living human races, others were attempting to adapt the photographic process to the specific needs of craniology. In contrast to the ethnologists, however, it would seem the craniologists were by and large highly critical of the new process, and doubted if the photograph could serve to replace the utility of an accurate drawing. For as one commentator noted in a presentation on this subject before the Anthropological Society of London:

Many skull photographs are rendered almost useless in consequence of the operator being seldom an artist, and still more rarely a scientific man. The mistakes about position, elevation, etc . . . [though] common to many drawings, are even of more frequent occurrence in photographs of the skull. Too great attention cannot be paid to the lighting of the photographs, since in a photograph, as in nature, there is no outline. Everything is defined by the shading, so that if the lighting be injudiciously managed, the object cannot be correctly represented. By the arrangement of the light alone parts may be suppressed, and insignificant details be brought into undue prominence . . . (Wesley 1866:193)

As this commentary reflects, photography was not an entirely unmediated and objective operation on reality, as generally supposed. Indeed, as Eadweard Muybridge's photographs later revealed, there was a remarkable difference between what the eye perceived and what the camera recorded (see Wright, this volume). Furthermore, where a drawing could be readily produced to secure the transmission of discriminating information, the photograph did not seem to have the same flexibility. To reveal one particular feature often meant the sacrifice of others, and to overcome this impediment required not one but several different photographs of the same object under varying conditions of lighting and orientation.

Implicit to these reservations was the long-standing debate over the relative merits of geometric versus perspective drawings in anatomical subjects. According to some craniologists a perspective drawing of a skull as a supplement to metric data provided invaluable morphological insights (particularly with regard to any resident idiosyncrasies) that could not be revealed in a straightforward geometric illustration. Anti-perspectivists (Geometricists), however, contended that the introduction of perspective into a drawing precluded all possibility of measurement and comparison, which they felt were the primary targets of craniology. Adherents to this latter school also argued that perspective drawings were prone to subjective inaccuracies, and as such were advocates of the *camera lucida* for the preparation of all anatomical drawings. Thus for these reasons alone the Geometricists tended to regard the photographic process as merely an alternative route to perspectivism and all that it implied.

Among those craniologists who briefly flirted with photography in the 1850s was Joseph Bernard Davis. Plates 62 and 63 are from a collection made by him and serve to underscore the contemporary criticisms levelled at these photographic efforts. First, neither of the depicted skulls is orientated according to any immediately recognizable convention; though they are seen to approximate the horizontals used by Petrus Camper and Jules Cloquet (cf. Plate 64). Before 1882, when the Frankfort Horizontal was established by international agreement (cf. Garson 1885),[4] a number of horizontal planes were operative (cf. Jacquart 1856 and Plate 64), which, by contrast, not only placed the skull in a non-realistic attitude but were more often than not defined by unreliable topographical landmarks. Second, none of the Davis photographs is accompanied by a scale, which renders any metric comparison of the respective skulls impossible. But it is unclear if this had been Davis's original intention. It is conjectured that they might well be experiments. The differences between the photographs in Plates 62 and 63 are quite marked. In Plate 63 (all views appear to be life-size) Davis seems concerned primarily with the problem of depicting the cranial profile more than anything else. Profile studies provided a means by which to compare and qualify specific structural differences in the conformation of racial crania. During the 1860s and 1870s a number of methods had been developed to this end (cf. Huxley 1863, 1867; Broca 1862, 1865), and it is conjectured that Davis may well have been experimenting with a photographic tracing method. The contrast between the subject and the light foreground and dark background has yielded a well-defined profile of the cranial vault, which would

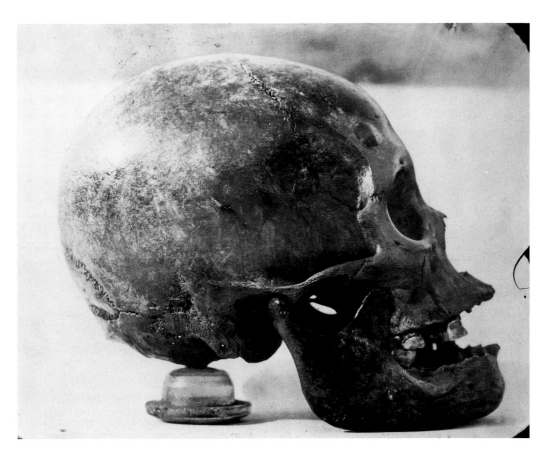

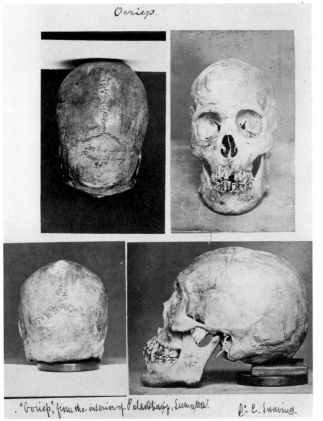

Oeriep.

"Oeriep", from the interior of Palambang, Sumatra.   *Dr. C. Swaving.*

62. (*above*) Skull no. 1051; a male negrito from the Island of Panay, Philippines. Photograph from the Joseph B. Davis collection. (RAI 35592)

63. (*left*) Four views of a male skull from Sumatra. From the Joseph B. Davis collection. (RAI 35591)

64. (*below*) Some examples of the various conventions employed before the establishment of the Frankfort Horizontal (F–H) in 1882. J–C: horizontal plane proposed by Jules Cloquet (1821); P–CA: horizontal plane advocated by Petrus Camper (1786); and G–SH: the plane used by Geoffrey St Hilaire (1795). For further details see Jacquart (1856).

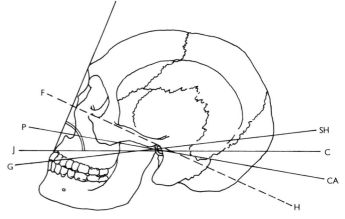

65. Broca's stereograph. (RAI Library Collection, Museum of Mankind)

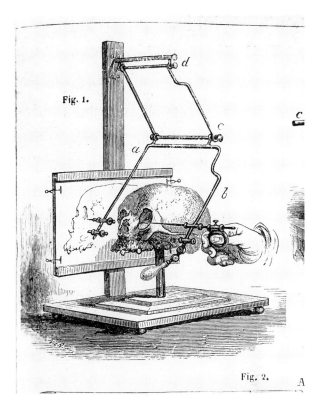

66i–ii. Two examples of the 'composite' photograph of John S. Billings: i (*below left*) 'Composite photograph of eight male *Ponca Indian Skulls* (adult) side view: nos. 836, 837, 835, 834, 831, 487, 877, Section IV, a.m.m. Beebe's gelatin dry plate, exposure 3 seconds'. ii (*below right*) 'Composite photograph of seven adult male *Sandwich Islanders Skulls*, side view; nos. 425, 444, 442, 445, 446, 438, 286, Section IV, a.m.m. Wet process, exposure 70 seconds'. (RAI 36689, 35590)

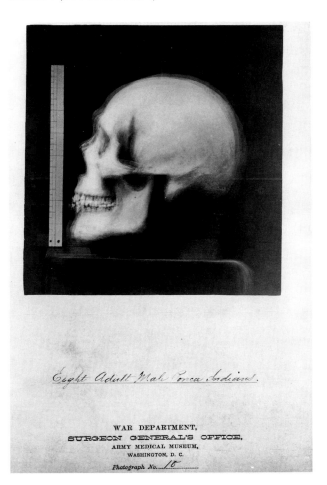

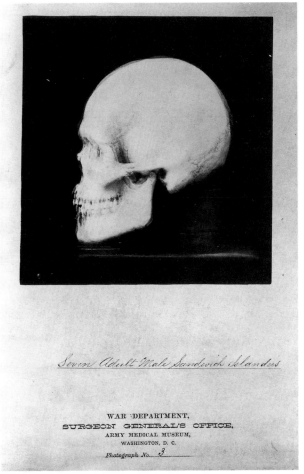

have allowed him to trace and compare it with silhouettes produced from similar photographs — but whether this had been the *raison d'être* of this photographic genre in the Davis collection is pure speculation. If it had been so, he may have abandoned it with the introduction of Paul Broca's stereograph in 1868 (Plate 65). The development of this simple device, however, does not seem to have kept others, such as the American physician John S. Billing at the US Army Medical Museum in Washington, DC, from experimenting with the photographic process in an effort to compare cranial profiles (Plates 66i–ii). Apparently Billings had undertaken this investigation according to the method suggested by Francis Galton, in 1878 (1879). Specifically, Billings's study involved the development of an apparatus for producing multi-exposure images or 'composite photographs' (1885), but which, despite subsequent improvement (1887), failed to match both the convenience and proficiency of Broca's stereographic technique.

As for Bernard Davis's photographs depicted in Plate 63, they are far more conventional, and evidently here the primary objective, indicated by both the change in lighting arrangement and background, was to provide maximum information on both general and regional morphology. However, the utility of such a photograph as a source of metric data would have been restricted, not so much by the absence of a scale reference as by other technical problems such as loss of dimensional accuracy and definition due to enlargement (and vice versa); all of which conspired against the assembly of a reliable body of statistics.

Although the photographic camera ultimately became a standard piece of equipment in the physical anthropologist's arsenal for record keeping, its limitations were, as indicated, quickly recognized. And since the late nineteenth century it has been employed in varying degrees to supplement traditional analytical methods and for illustrative purposes.

NOTES

1 The term *anthropometry* was coined by the German physician Johann Sigismund Elsholtz (1623–88) to describe a system of measurement he had devised to investigate the old Hippocratic proposition that there was an intrinsic relationship between body proportions and various diseases. During the late eighteenth and early nineteenth centuries, however, this term acquired a more inclusive meaning. According to this new definition, 'anthropometry' was seen to be primarily a system of measurement of the living human body to determine its respective proportions not only 'at different ages, in order to learn the law of relative growth of the [body's] parts' but also 'in the [human] races, so as to distinguish them and establish their relations to each other . . .' (Topinard 1881:212). Although this term could technically be used to cover systems of measuring the human skull and skeleton, more often than not investigators in the nineteenth century tended to characterize such studies employing the specific terms *craniometry* and *osteometry* respectively. Occasionally the term *cephalometry* is encountered in the nineteenth-century literature which refers specifically to the study of the animate human head. During the late nineteenth and early twentieth centuries, the terms *somatology* and *somatometric* also enjoyed some popularity and can be regarded as synonyms of anthropometry and anthropometric respectively.

2 Maximum head length (glabello-occipital diameter of vault) measures the distance between the most prominent point of the glabella (anterior) and occiput (posterior); whereas maximum head breadth is the greatest horizontal and transverse diameter determined solely by the maximum breadth of the head above the supramastoid and zygomatic crests.

3 It was not until the early 1890s that any serious attempt was made to adopt standard methods of measuring the living body (cf. Collignon 1892) — a movement which led to the Monaco Agreement of 1906 (cf. Papillault 1906; Marett 1913).

4 The Frankfort Horizontal is an imaginary line drawn between two easily identified landmarks: the *orbitale*, the lowest point in the margin of the orbit, and the *porion*, the uppermost point in the margin of the auditory meatus.

REFERENCES

JAI: Journal of the Anthropological Institute.
JESL: Journal of the Ethnological Society of London.
RAI: Royal Anthropological Institute of Great Britain and Ireland.

Abbie, A.A. & Adey, W.R. 1955. The nonmetrical characters of a Central Australian tribe. *Oceania* 25: 198–207.

Anonymous. 1862. Photography Applied to Ethnological Science. *British Journal of Photography* 9:49.

Billings. J.S. 1885. (Photographic study of cranial series). *JAI* 14:287.

— 1887. (Improvements on composite technique). *JAI* 16:96–8.

British Association for the Advancement of Science 1854 (1852). A Manual of Ethnological Enquiry. Reprinted in *JESL* 3:193–208.

Broca, P. 1862. Les projections de la tête et sur un nouveau procédé de céphalometrie. *Bulletin, Société d'anthropologie de Paris* 3:534–44.

— 1865. Procédé géométrique pour mesurer l'angle sphénoidal sans ouvrir le crâne. *Bulletin, Société d'anthropologie de Paris* 6:564–72.

— 1868. Sur le stéréographe, nouvel instrument craniographique destiné dessiner tous les détails du relief des corps solides. *Mémoires, Société*

d'anthropologie de Paris 3(NS):99–126.

Collignon, R. 1892. Projet d'entente international au sujet des recherches anthropométriques dans les conseils de révision. *Bulletin, Société d'anthropologie de Paris* 13:186–8.

Dupertuis, C.W. & Tanner, J.M. 1950. The pose of the subject for photogrammetric anthropometry, with special reference to somatotyping. *American Journal of Physical Anthropology* 8:27–42.

Edwards, E. 1990. 'Photograph Types': The Pursuit of Method. *Visual Anthropology* 3(2–3):235–58.

Galton, F. 1879. Notes on Galton's Composite Portraits, made by combining those of many different persons into a single resultant figure. *JAI* 8:132–44.

Garson, J.G. 1885. The Frankfort craniometric agreement, with critical remarks thereon. *JAI* 14:64–83.

Gregorio, M.A. di 1984 *T.H. Huxley's place in natural science.* London: Yale University Press.

Huxley, T.H. 1863. *Evidence as to man's place in nature.* London: Williams & Norgate.

— 1867. On two widely contrasted forms of the human cranium. *Journal of Anatomy and Physiology* 1:60–77.

— 1869. The Huxley manuscripts

(HM). Imperial College of Science and Technology, London.

Jacquart, H. 1856. Mémoire sur la mesuration de l'angle facial, les goniomètres faciaux, et un nouveau goniométrie facial inventé par l'auteur. *Mémoire, Société de Biologie* 57. Paris.

Lamprey J.H. 1869. On a method of measuring the human form for the use of students of ethnology. *JESL* 1:84–5.

Marett, R.R. 1913. Report of an international conference on the unification of craniometric and cephalometric measurements. *Proceedings of the 18th International Congress of Americanists.* London.

Papillault, G. 1906. Report on the international agreement for the unification of craniometric and cephalometric measurements. *L'Anthropologie* 17:559–72.

Topinard, P. 1881. Observations upon the methods and processes of anthropometry. *JAI* 10:212.

Urry, J. 1972. *Notes and Queries on Anthropology* and the development of anthropological field methods in British anthropology, 1870–1920. *Proceedings of the RAI* 1972:45–57.

Wesley, W.H. 1866. On the Iconography of the Skull. *Memoirs of the Anthropological Society of London* 2:189–194.

Science Visualized: E.H. Man in the Andaman Islands

Elizabeth Edwards

IN 1858 THE BRITISH established a permanent settlement at Port Blair on the Andaman Islands, an event which had devastating consequences for the native population. At the same time it subjected them to intense anthropological attention and exposure for a short while and therafter secured them a place in the annals of anthropological historiography. Before 1858 very little was known about the Andamanese, despite the fact that the islands and their inhabitants had long been a focus of European fascination and dread. A certain amount of information of mixed accuracy had been gathered during an abortive settlement in 1786–94, from marine-survey ships and from a few subsequent observers. However, it was the popular view which pertained — that the Andamanese were cannibals, barbarously cruel and 'the least civilized, perhaps in the world, being nearer to a state of nature than any other people' (Colebrook 1794, cited in Portman 1899 (1):68).[1]

That the Andamanese were indeed hostile to strangers was not in doubt. It was this which made the British, in 1856, begin seriously to consider settlement of the islands. The Andaman Islands are situated near the lucrative shipping routes between India and east and south-east Asia and Australia. In British eyes the implacable hostility of the Andamanese to strangers constituted an intolerable threat to shipping. The most viable solution, economically, was to revive the late-eighteenth-century plan for a penal settlement, a scheme which was precipitated by the need for a secure penal colony following the Great Mutiny of 1857. The ensuing development in relations between the British and the Andamanese, and the growing knowledge of Andaman culture form the background to the nineteenth and early-twentieth-century record of the Andaman Islands of which the photographic record was an integral part. The success of British policy depended not merely on tolerant coexistence of two cultures but on the active cooperation of the native population, who opposed the intrusion on their land in a series of violent incidents. The Andamanese had to be persuaded not only to assist rather than massacre shipwrecks, but also to desist from attacking convict lines and the settlement, and to assist with the recapture of escaped convicts. Without their cooperation, British policy was largely inoperable, so in essence the Andamanese were being asked to participate in the colonization of their own islands.

For future policy to succeed it was appreciated that an understanding of native culture was essential. From the beginning the British had adopted a conciliatory policy towards the Andamanese. The slow process of contact was established through the leaving of presents at Andaman camps and by the capture of Andamanese, who were favourably treated, exposed to the wonders of technical superiority and then released to spread good reports of British intentions and power. The main instrument of British influence became the 'Andaman Homes', the first of which was established near Port Blair in 1863, 'erected by Government with a view to establishing cordial relations between the aborigines and ourselves and reclaiming them, if possible, to some degree of civilization' (Man 1932:ix). The Andamanese were encouraged to visit the Homes, to abandon their nomadic hunting and gathering life and become economically productive in European terms. By the late 1870s the Homes were fulfilling this purpose admirably to an increasing number of Andaman groups, dispensing food, medicines, and tobacco and other luxuries. The system was used to demonstrate to the Andamanese not only the good intentions of the British but their power to punish non-cooperation, for the benefits of civilization were the reward for meeting the expectations imposed on them by British policy.

The attitude to the Andamanese as a race was of crucial importance both to the development of relations and to the growing record, both written and visual. The study of the Andamanese, physically and culturally, was given impetus by the evolutionary concerns of contemporary anthropologists. The apparently lowly position of the Andamanese in the evolutionary scale elevated them to great scientific importance. They were perceived as a pure, un-contacted race, living in very primitive conditions with very primitive beliefs. Thus to nineteenth-century thinking they represented culturally an early stage in the 'childhood of mankind' and racially 'an infantile, undeveloped or primitive form of the type from which the African Negroes... and the Melanesians... may have sprung' (Flower 1880:132).

By the late 1870s and 1880s there was added urgency in the recording, for it became apparent that the Andamanese were a dying race. The cause was, as in so many other instances, contact with Europeans, who brought in disease and undermined a finely balanced traditional culture, so debilitating the native population. By 1880 there had been serious epidemics of ophthalmia (1876) and measles (1877); syphilis (including hereditary syphilis) was well established, and as large tracts of forest were cleared by the settlers, malaria and pulmonary diseases increased. There was also a drastic fall in the birthrate and high infant mortality. A population of at least 5,000 in 1858 had dropped below 2,000 in 1901, the greatest decline being among those groups with long association with the settlers.

There were thus three interrelated forces underlying the recording of the Andamanese: the necessity of understanding their culture to establish peaceable relations permitting the furtherance of British policy; the recording of data for the scientific study of the Andamanese within the overall evolutionary structure; and finally, through anthropological observation, the recording and collecting of a culture which was threatened with extinction through contact with a powerful colonizing culture.

It appears that E.H. Man became interested in anthropology soon after his arrival in the Andaman Islands in 1869 as a colonial officer. He joined his father, Colonel H. Man, who in 1858 reclaimed the islands for the British in the name of the East India Company (surely one of its very last acts) (Man 1932:xx). By 1873 E.H. Man had developed his own system for anthropological recording and had started to collect material culture. In 1875 he was appointed Officer in Charge of the Andaman Homes. It seems likely that his appointment must have confronted him with a conflict of interests as he enforced the official policy of 'taming' the Andamanese, both morally and physically. The meticulous recording of their traditional culture was perhaps an attempt by Man to come to terms with this insoluble dilemma and his way of accepting the moral responsibility he felt to recompense the Andamanese for their sad fate. In the course of thirty years' contact with the Andamanese, Man made a definitive contribution to the knowledge of their culture. He collected a large vocabulary and spoke the language of the Aka-bea-da tribe, wrote copiously on Andamanese culture and made large collections of objects for a number of major European museums. At another level the appropriation of the Andamanese by anthropology was merely an extension of the political appropriation, both being centred on the Homes (Tomas 1987:272). Andamanese culture became contained within the anthropological frame and, as we shall see, the photographic frame, both literally and metaphorically.

The main instrument of representation was *Notes and Queries*. In 1876 Man abandoned his own recording system on receiving a copy of this volume: 'the value of such systematic guidance... can only be appreciated by those who have endeavoured to collect information from savages.... possessing interest to ethnologists' (1932:x); 'I have worked almost entirely upon the guidelines therein laid down' (1882:69). Man adopted this new method of enquiry with enthusiasm. Information was gathered in such a way that it could be compared, quantified and classified according to the demands of contemporary method.[2] Man's photography was a visual response to *Notes and Queries*, a carefully posed and constructed image to complement his observations. Culture is expressed in quasi-

67. 'Andamanese Shooting, Dancing, Sleeping and Greeting', c.1880. Photograph by E.H. Man. (RAI Library Collection, Museum of Mankind)

quantifiable terms, for example his photograph of Andamanese sleeping, greeting, dancing and shooting all on one image (Plate 67), where every limb is positioned precisely to illustrate Man's answers to *Notes and Queries* (Edwards 1989:73–4); or people presented as generalized 'physical types' (Plate 68). Here the underlying view was the same whether in a strictly anatomical format or merely a group, measuring pole in their midst, giving clear scientific reference (Plate 69). These latter photographs have little of the scientific rigour envisaged by Lamprey or Huxley (see Spencer, this volume) but nonetheless they are a mode of representation which was a direct response to the expectations of observable 'science'.

Against this should be balanced perhaps the idea that Man appears to have been no more than a technically competent photographer and that his 'scientific photography' was precisely that: a clearly defined technical record in which a self-conscious aesthetic had little place. The dominating aesthetic, if it can be called such, was the disciplinary statement of *Notes and*

Queries. Despite improvements in photographic technology the act of photographing was still by no means a simple procedure, and thus it is perhaps to Man's credit that he attempted to express 'culture' in visual terms at all. Nonetheless Man's visual expression of the Andamanese never really developed beyond this early disciplinary prescription. As late as 1901, immediately before his retirement, Man was still photographing formal groups in a way which suggests scientific reference, directly related to his photography of some thirty years earlier. Subjects are carefully posed to show aspects of material culture, for example his photograph of the stamping board (Plate 70). This shows us exactly how the instrument was played, and even allowing for contemporary technical constraints, it is a visual scientific description recording none of the essential spirit of music making which was so important to the Andamanese.

However, there is another side to Man's photography which reveals a more spontaneous response to the islands themselves and the immediate environment

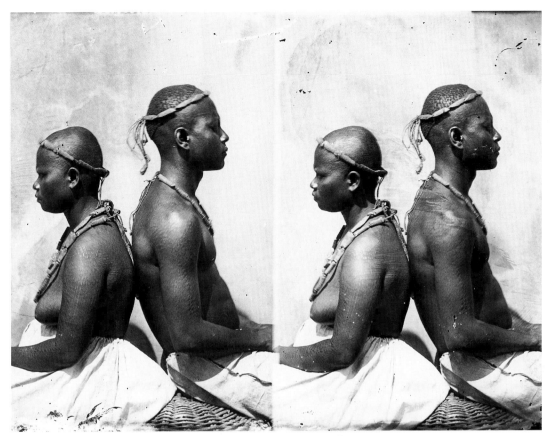

68. 'Andamanese Man and Woman showing profiles', stereo-photograph, *c*.1800. Photograph by E.H. Man. (RAI 34463)

69. Andamanese group with measuring rod, *c*.1876. Photograph by E.H. Man. (RAI 183)

70.   Andamanese demonstrating the sound board and the vocal accompaniment. The man on the right is Nicobarese. Photograph by E.H. Man. (RAI GN12)

such as the convict settlement (Plate 71), jungle Home or creeks and inlets. Some of these photographs have an almost picturesque quality, bearing out remarks made by writers, including Man, who described the luxuriant foliage and dramatic mountainsides in terms which betray a conventional European aesthetic response to the majesty of nature. That this clear divide exists suggests that Man saw the Andamanese as something apart, an object of study, and his visual response to them was likewise contained within the dictates of a disciplinary structure. This categorization maintained the impression of cultural 'purity' of the anthropological object, decontextualized in a double temporal dislocation: that created by the camera and that created by the perception of anthropological object which denied historical circumstance. This view is supported by the fact that, with the exception of one photograph of a boat, none of Man's more 'spontaneous' responses was used in his academic papers in his lifetime.

Man had an undoubted affection for the Andamanese. However, he was in many ways conventional in his attitudes. His affection was paternal-istic and at times condescending, for his view of the Andamanese as 'wayward but attractive children' (Prain 1932:21) corresponds with the view of primitive races as representing the childhood of mankind. Despite his interest and understanding, Man believed firmly in the necessity of redeeming them yet regretted the detrimental effect of civilization on his noble savage — 'it is delicious to come across a true junglee, one I mean, who has never had anything to do with us, and find how ignorant he seems in the art of lying and prevarication' (Man, cited in Lane Fox 1878:453).

It was inevitable that anthropological observation was limited to those groups already under some degree of European influence — indeed anthropological observation was part of that relationship — although Man stresses the verification of his observation through reference to those groups *outside* this sphere of influence (in other words, culturally or anthropologi-cally pure) (Man 1932:x). Throughout the 1870s and 1880s an increasing number of Andaman groups were contacted by the British and the differences in culture and language became more widely observed. However, Man's anthropological work was largely restricted to the Aka-bea-da and Puckikwar groups around the Homes and thus dependent on the European presence. This restriction is apparent in Man's photography. For, although scientific in content, these highly constructed images were themselves constructed in what was, for the Andamanese, an unnatural environment and thus far removed from them as a people.

Man's collection of data in both the Andaman Islands and the neighbouring Nicobar Islands appears to have been obsessive. Moseley[3] described him as 'the sort of man who might well send four or five entire Nicobar villages with all the inhabitants inside' (Pitt Rivers Museum, Tylor Papers M3). His meticulous and somewhat pedantic recording of native culture appears to have fulfilled some sort of need within him. It was, on the one hand, perhaps the need for recognition and approval from the academic and colonial establishment. This is suggested by his extreme sensitivity to criticism of either his science or his data, as is illustrated by the comment made by M.V. Portman to E.B. Tylor[4] in 1899 that

Man is very much hurt by the way he thinks I have criticised him . . . I adhere to my opinion that much of the Notes on their [the Andamanese] Anthropology is incorrect . . . His work is chiefly written on the information of a few boys of different tribes and two convict Jemadars. This is not my idea of accurate scientific research and the results, though good for 1881 will not do for 1899. (Pitt Rivers Museum, Tylor Papers M10)

On the other hand, he clearly needed a sense of power over, affection and deference from and obligation towards the Andamanese in what was, after all, a lonely station. It was also perhaps a response to the predicament in which he found himself as a primary agent in the orchestrated destruction of a culture about which he felt deeply. However, little of this feeling comes across in much of his photography, which is highly structured, clinical and void of the sympathy he is known to have had. Nevertheless, it was this 'scientific' image which was widely disseminated and despite all its shortcomings provided the visual foundation for the anthropological representation of the Andamanese.

The record of other photographers reveals a remarkable difference in style and approach, throwing a sharp light on Man's images and stressing the precise way in which he used photography. G. Dobson photographed the Andamanese on only one occasion, May 4, 1872. Although a zoologist, clearly his interests did not include scientific anthropology. His recording is unstructured and his resulting paper (1875) was precisely the kind of quasi-anthropological observation which *Notes and Queries* was intended to remedy as it tried to define the boundaries of disciplinary observation. Not taken within a strictly 'scientific' framework, Dobson's photographs have a much more relaxed tenor than Man's images. They do not portray the Andamanese as specimens but nonetheless suggest a different if interrelated set of assump-

71.   The Convict Workshops, Phoenix Bay, Andaman Islands, 1901. Photograph by E.H. Man. (RAI 27350)

114

72i–ii. (*facing page and above*) Maia Biala, the Chief of Rutland Island and his wife. May 4 1872. Photograph by G.E. Dobson (courtesy of Pitt Rivers Museum, University of Oxford, PRM. B30.Misc.Ic; RAI 5758). iii (*right*) The photograph as published in *JAI* 1875. (RAI Library Collection, Museum of Mankind)

tions about primitive man, for they have an exotic and voyeuristic tone, reflecting the attitudes implied in Dobson's paper. Yet in many ways, photographed at the Home near Port Blair, seated on the steps of a hut, chewing on clay pipes, Dobson's subjects portray more of the reality of Andamanese experience at the time (Tomas 1987:307).

Dobson's photographs also operate as expressions of colonial reality at another level. The relaxed atmosphere of these images well illustrates the changes in relationships which were taking place as British policy began to succeed, first with the Aka-bea-da, who lived around Port Blair, and then with other tribes of Middle and South Andaman. Maia Biala, Chief of Rutland Island, and his wife (Plate 72i), as photographed by Dobson, exemplify the success of British policy, Maia Biala having 'distinguished himself in catching runaways and in assisting some fishermen who were in distress' (Portman 1899 (2):586). Dobson reports on the Andamanese's lethargy, implied in his comment 'Very soon after arrival I commenced to erect my photographic tent; but although this is a very remarkable object when

erected, the natives scarcely took the trouble to look at it, and none expressed any surprise' (1875:464). His photographs catch something of this subdued nature. Indeed, by the 1870s writers had begun to add the words 'lazy' and 'indolent' to the traditionally violent list of adjectives applied to the Andamanese. For the Andamanese continued to be reluctant to espouse the European ethic of 'usefulness' and the increasing influence of the Homes undermined traditional modes of existence and the physical and mental health of the native population. Questions of exoticism, appropriation and interpretation mesh in subsequent printings of this famous image, the Chief of Rutland Island undergoing some interesting transformations. In addition to a print from the whole plate, there is a further version in the Royal Anthropological Institute's collection which encloses the subject within a European aesthetic convention, softly framed in a misty vignette; the noble savage fades out both literally and metaphorically (Plate 72ii). In the published version in the *Journal of the Anthropological Institute* in 1875 (Plate 72iii) the image has been reversed and the genitals carefully obliterated by bunches of grass scratched

73. Europeans with a group of Onges, Little Andaman, 1880s. (RAI GN34532)

strategically on to the plate (in order to avoid censorship). The Chief of Rutland Island becomes appropriated by science in the pages of a learned journal, so his image and that of his culture becomes reversed and symbolically emasculated.[5]

There were two groups which persistently resisted all attempts at contact and thus anthropological investigation, the Onges on Little Andaman and the Jarawa of the interior of South Andaman. In 1880 the British adopted a more vigorous policy towards the Onges, using the usual methods of contact. Despite some success, relations remained volatile for some years although friendly contact did increase during the early 1880s. Man was actively involved with this policy and his photograph of four Europeans with a group of Onges in many ways encapsulates the whole process (Plate 73). Although not perceived as 'scientific' by Man, this photograph tells us more in a truly modern documentary sense than those photographs he intended to stand as documents. Being outside Man's perception of the anthropological, it admits the colonial presence. The Europeans hover somewhat uneasily behind the Onges, a paternalistic and controlling hand on a shoulder, as if cementing the con-

tact. There is a tension in the photograph which is heightened by the photographic object itself, in that one is somehow aware of the dynamic of the situation contained within the frame. It is a photograph of a peaceful if uneasy relationship which typifies this stage of Onges–British relations, a sense of the impact of European contact coming through in a way which is denied in Man's 'scientific' work.

It was, however, Man's scientific work which provided the visual groundwork on which others with anthropological interests built. M.V. Portman, who was in charge of the Homes for almost twenty years from 1879, produced in the early 1890s a meticulous series of photographs 'collecting' technologies of the Andamanese (Plate 74).[6] In these he extends Man's technique of the posed scientific study, the photograph being central to the accumulation of data. Again *Notes and Queries* was the guiding hand: 'Properly taken photographs, with the *additional* explanatory letter-press will be found the most satisfactory answers to most of the questions in "Notes and Queries on Anthropology"' (Portman 1896:76; emphasis added). Thus subjects are photographed against a plain background in the then accepted ethnological mode, and

The end is then cut to the right length, and smoothed.

The back is then similarly trimmed, and chopped close in the same curved line as the handle.

74. Stages in the manufacture of an adze, *c*.1890–5. Photographs by M.V. Portman. (RAI 814, 815)

each stage of production, from gathering the raw materials to the finished article, is illustrated with an explanatory caption. Although he does not doubt the overall received view of the Andamanese, British policy or the ultimate objectification of the anthropological subject (indeed he was rigorous in the control of his photographic subjects (Portman 1896: 76–7)) Portman is nevertheless prepared to sympathize with the Andamanese viewpoint. His photographs have a directness, a concentrated observation. These qualities are enhanced by his chosen camera angle, which suggests that he extended to photography the advice in *Notes and Queries* to which he draws attention, that 'Savages will be found to answer more freely when the interrogator places himself on the same level as themselves, *i.e.* if they sit upon the ground he should do the same' (1896:77): in photographic terms it will be more revealing visually. His approach is directly descended from Man's scientific approach to observation. It is interesting that much of Radcliffe-Brown's photography in the Andaman Islands (1906–8) also derives from the anthropo-

logically accepted Man and Portman view of the Andamans, although developments in both photographic technology and anthropological method had broadened the possible scope of the record.[7]

However, to some of those photographing in the Andamans at the turn of the century, the Andamanese were merely a native group caught up in the inexorable advance of British rule. In a way not unreminiscent of Dobson's work some twenty-five years earlier, their photographs show the Andamanese in this relationship. The more 'spontaneous' nature of these photographs highlights the way in which the anthropological mode of observation constrained visual response. By 1900 the British had been firmly established in the islands for nearly fifty years and as more and more groups of Andamanese became acculturated, the colonialized picture is the truer. Particularly pertinent is Rogers's photograph of a Jarawa woman at Port Blair (Plate 75). It was probably taken in February 1902 after an expedition against the Jarawa to teach them that 'they cannot raid and murder with impunity' (Temple 1930:94). C.G. Rogers,

75. Captured Jarawa woman at Port Blair, 1902. Photograph by C. Rogers. (RAI 1517)

76. Onges' greeting ceremony, Little Andaman, 1911. Photograph by H. Seton-Karr. (RAI HWS–K)

77. Dancing at the King's Dinner. December 30 1902. Photograph by R. Boreham. (RAI 1504)

Deputy Conservator of Forests, had been on the expedition (on which a British officer had been killed) and appears to have had little sympathy with the Andamanese, seeing them rather as an irritation to be controlled. There is a poignancy to the image of an isolated figure, her child on her back, wearing an unfamiliar loincloth and staring uncertainly into the camera. She represents the result of concerted policy against the Jarawa which must ultimately be the instrument of their destruction. Although at first glance such an image is not dissimilar to some 'scientific' photographs of 'types', an examination of the context imbues it with a very different meaning, where overt control rather than the subtler structures of understanding was the overriding consideration and

the figure of the woman assumes a quietly symbolic character.

H. Seton-Karr's photograph of the Onges also reveals the progress of British policy (Plate 76). That the photograph could be taken on the 1911 Census Tour is significant. In 1901 relations with the Onges were such that the census party, which included Man, could only estimate their number, noting that 'the occasion being taken to show as much civility as possible to a party of Onges' (Temple 1903:2). By 1911 progress was such that the Census for the first time was able to attempt an enumeration of the Onges. Seton-Karr's photograph of the greeting ceremony (on which observers had commented from the earliest days) was probably taken on March 7 at

Chetamale. Its relaxed nature suggests a familiarity with and confidence in the British and possibly their photographic equipment, very different from the uncomfortable group of Onges photographed some twenty-five years earlier by Man and expressing visually the change in relationship between the two cultures.

Finally, Boreham's photograph of Andamanese dancing and music (Plate 77) also throws into contrast Man's image discussed above, for it captures something of the spirit of Andamanese music making. R. Boreham, a colonial officer, photographed at the 'King's Dinner' of December 30, 1902, a major imperialist expression to celebrate the declaration of Edward VII as Emperor of India. It is as decontextualized a view of the true Andamanese as Man's image but in a very different way. Some 300 Andamanese from all over the islands were present at the dinner: tribes which fifty years earlier had been in a state of constant aggression both towards each other and towards the outside world. All those present were given an enamelled mug decorated with the pictures of the King and Queen, surely symbolic of the final assimilation of the diminished Andamanese as good subjects of the Empire.

The photographic record of the Andaman Islands represents a microcosm of wider processes, distilled and concentrated through the geographical and cultural isolation of the islands, through the singularity of the colonial operation in the Andamans and through the intensity of the work of their major nineteenth-century recorder. Man's approach to his subject was exemplary in nineteenth-century anthropological terms and became a model for such studies in its day. However, his rigorous recording and meticulous attention to detail essentially distanced the Andamanese as a thing apart to be culturally dissected, and in the process the whole is lost, rendering Man's photographs decontextualized on two planes, cultural and intellectual. The reality of the effect of British policy finds no place in Man's 'scientific' photography as he defined his object of study. Yet it was his work above that of all others which laid the foundations of the understanding of Andaman culture and the consequent success of British policy. Without E.H. Man, Boreham's photograph of the 'King's Dinner' could never have been taken. This is the essential paradox which surely underlies all Man's anthropological photography and one with which he himself never fully came to terms.

ACKNOWLEDGEMENTS

I should like to thank Fiona Stewart, who first persuaded me to look at E.H. Man's work and fed me so much useful material, and David Tomas, some of whose ideas have been unconsciously absorbed here.

NOTES

1 The most notable example is Arthur Conan Doyle's *The Sign of the Four*.
2 General Pitt Rivers's (Lane Fox) use of Man's material is a classic example of the method. In a paper given to the Anthropological Institute in 1878 he discusses each item of Man's collection of material culture, finding parallels from other cultures and thus by implication classifying the Andamanese racially (Lane Fox 1878).
3 H. Moseley was Professor of Human Anatomy at the University of Oxford. He had considerable interest in anthropology, was a close colleague of E.B. Tylor and was instrumental in acquiring the Pitt Rivers collection of ethnographic objects for Oxford in 1884.
4 M.V. Portman was Officer in Charge of the Andaman Homes for a number of periods between 1879 and 1899. He did a considerable amount of work on Andamanese culture and the history of British involvement with them (Portman 1899). He built on the work on Man and in the course of doing so refuted some of Man's observations. E.B. Tylor was Reader in Anthropology at the University of Oxford, a post established as a condition of General Pitt Rivers's deed of gift when his collection of ethnographic material was donated to the university in 1884.
5 The latest manifestation of this image is on a calendar for 1990, *Images*, produced by the UK's Channel 4 to accompany a television series on photography of the same name. Here the Chief of Rutland Island (in vignetted mode) is sandwiched between photographs by Alfred Stieglitz and Clement Cooper.
6 This series was made for the British Museum (Read 1893:403; Portman 1896:77). The negatives and a set of prints are in the collections of the Museum of Mankind, London.
7 Radcliffe-Brown's album of Andaman photographs is at the Pitt Rivers Museum, University of Oxford.

REFERENCES

JAI: *Journal of the Anthropological Institute*
JME: *Journal of Museum Ethnography*

British Association for the Advancement of Science 1876. *Notes and Queries on Anthropology*. London: BAAS.

Conan Doyle, A. (1978). *The Sign of the Four*. In *The Complete Sherlock Holmes Long Stories*. 15th impr. London: John Murray.

Dobson, G.E. 1875. On the Andamans and Andamanese. *JAI* 4:457–67.

Edwards, E. 1989. Images of the Andamans: The Photography of E.H. Man. *JME* 1:71–8.

Flower, W.H. 1880. On the Osteology and Affinities of the Andaman Islands. *JAI* 9:108–33.

Lane Fox, A. 1878. Observations on Mr. Man's Collection of Andaman and Nicobarese Objects. *JAI* 7:434–70.

Man, E.H. 1882. On the Andamanese and Nicobarese Objects presented to Major-General Pitt Rivers. *JAI* 9:268–94.

— 1883. On the Aboriginal Inhabitants of the Andaman Islands. *JAI* 12:69–175, 327–434.

— 1932. *On the Aboriginal Inhabitants of the Andaman Islands*, repr. of 1885 repr. London: RAI.

Portman, M.V. 1896. Photography for Anthropologists. *JAI* 15:75–87.

— 1899. *History of our Relations with the Andamanese*. 2 vols. Calcutta: Government Printer.

Prain, D. 1932. 'Memoir of E.H. Man'. In E.H. Man *The Nicobar Islands and their People*. repr. Guildford: RAI.

R[ead], C.H. 1893. Mr. Portman's Photographs of Andamanese. *JAI* 12:401–3.

Temple, R.C. 1903. The Andaman and Nicobar Islands. *Report of the Census of India* 3. Calcutta: Government Printer.

— 1930. *Remarks on the Andaman Islanders and their country* (repr. from *The Indian Antiquary*). Bombay: British India Press.

Tomas, D. 1987. *An Ethnography of the Eye. Authority, Observation, and Photography in the Context of British Anthropology 1839–1990*. Unpublished Ph.D. Thesis, Dept. of Anthropology, McGill University.

Tylor, E.B. 1872–1907 Tylor Papers: Pitt Rivers Museum Archives, University of Oxford.

British Popular Anthropology: Exhibiting and Photographing the Other

Brian Street

FOR THE GENERAL PUBLIC at the turn of the century, images of other societies with their underlying associations of race, hierarchy and evolution, were most vividly experienced through exhibitions, photographs and postcards.[1] These ethnographic shows were seen not simply as 'entertainment' but as having educational value: through them British society learnt about the 'other' peoples of the earth. Members of 'savage' countries were taken to England and other European societies in remarkable numbers to be viewed as specimens or zoo-like exhibits, to satisfy curiosity and to reinforce the confidence of the public in their own 'progress'. In England, large exhibition halls such as Earls Court, Olympia and the White City had been opened in the late nineteenth century and the numbers attending ran into many millions.

Living members of other societies were frequently included among the exhibits, as in the case of the Ainu brought over for the Japan-British Exhibition at the White City in 1910, which was seen by eight million people. As Schneider (1977) points out, 'ethnographic exhibitions developed as a new medium of popular culture that played a powerful role in shaping European popular attitudes towards non-westerners'. At first the exotic peoples were asked simply to carry on their daily routines for the viewing public, but later the financial necessity of drawing large crowds led sponsors to emphasize the unusual or bizarre in response to the public's wish to be entertained. Similarly, 'natives' were brought over to perform at London theatres, as in the case of some Batwa pygmies seen at the Hippodrome in 1905. Eskimos, so-called 'Aztecs', members of Bantu races, Australian aboriginals, and Sioux Indians, as well as the Ainu from Japan and Batwa pygmies from the Congo were all variously brought to Europe to be exhibited to the general public, also incidentally providing anthropologists with a source of study that saved them the difficulty of procuring specimens themselves. Although the more sensational aspects of such exhibitions were modified in the early twentieth century as official bodies took them out of the hands of commercial impresarios, the early emphasis on the bizarre continued to run through even such supposedly sober trade fairs as the Japan-British Exhibition of 1910.

The exhibits at these public events were also photographed for popular postcards, some of which sold as many as a quarter of a million copies in the Edwardian period. According to Peterson, 866 million postcards were posted in the United Kingdom in 1909–10 (1985:166). Such photographic companies as that of William Downey, who became famous with his best-selling portraits of the royal family, turned amateur photography into a successful commercial venture and it was his company that was called on to provide the official record of the Batwa pygmies. Attempts to interpret the photographs of an earlier period are clearly fraught with the danger of giving them a 'modern' reading, so the main concern of this essay will be to examine the context in which popular media, such as exhibitions, photographs and postcards were viewed at the time in order to attempt some tentative insight into how the Edwardians themselves saw these images of other cultures. This requires attention to both the content of contemporary ideas about other cultures and to the conventions in which photographic form was interpreted. While the portrayals of 'native' visitors rest on deeper concepts and assumptions regarding race and empire, different genres of photography can be distinguished within this field which also affect how viewers saw the subjects. Downey's photographs of the Batwa, for instance, combine the genre of royal portraiture with the anthropological conventions associated with recording racial types. Sir Benjamin Stone's photographic record of the same visitors, on the other hand, derives from his concern to record customs and events for posterity, and so his photographs focus more on the situation in which the subjects are located than on their appearance alone.

In terms of the theoretical framework for interpreting photographs proposed by Kolodny (1978) and elaborated by Peterson (1985), Downey's studio shots are part of the 'romantic' ideology in which contradictory feelings towards other cultures are resolved by 'transforming them into aesthetic phenomena and in so doing decontextualising and distancing them', while Stone's images could be said to be 'documentary' in the sense of 'salvaging remnants of a changing world' (Peterson 1985:165). Both involve elements of the third 'type' of photographic ideology employed by these sources, namely 'realism': photography is directly associated with positivist science in which empirical enquiry is assumed not to transform the objects it records but simply to present them to our scrutiny. The photograph takes on 'the status of a pure trace, an indexical fragment' (Rischon 1985) that negates its character as a constructed image. In order to pursue such an analysis, however, we need first to know more about the context in which the subjects themselves were brought over and the ways in which they were displayed and photographed. I will examine two examples: the Ainu and the Batwa.

The Ainu

The Ainu peoples, who inhabit a group of islands north of Japan, had a flourishing culture from the tenth until the sixteenth century. Their victories over the neighbouring Okhotsk people were recorded in heroic epics that served as reminders of a lost glory to future generations who lived in very different conditions (Watanabe 1962:1–4). By the nineteenth century, when European travellers were taking considerable interest in the Ainu as exotic curiosities, with their long beards, bear ceremonies and 'primitive' living conditions, their culture and economy had been destroyed by Japanese domination. They had become, according to one source, 'a pitiful doomed people living in the most abject conditions of poverty, disease and degradation' (Philippi 1979:15). Thus the Ainu who were brought to England for the Japan-British Exhibition of 1910 were akin to the North American Indians in their relationship to those exhibiting them.[2] At the time of the exhibition, however, 'native' peoples were viewed within the dominant ideology as curios, remnants of a disappearing world, interesting for their superficial differences from 'us', such as in dress and 'ritual' behaviour: as in racial classification, these surface characteristics were read to signify deeper cultural and moral differences. Their appearance in the capitals of Europe served to reinforce belief in European moral and rational superiority, which was re-emphasized the more pathetic and lost the visitors appeared.

In addition to these European conceptions, the representation of Ainu in the Japan-British Exhibition is further mediated by the view that the Japanese themselves held of their subjugated neighbours. At the time, the Japanese government was encouraging Japanese settlers to take up farms and keep cattle in the lands formerly used for hunting and fishing by the Ainu and were allotting plots of land to them and offering some training in agriculture, thereby replacing their traditional economy and further displacing traditional social groupings. To the Japanese, the Ainu symbolized a 'primitive' and economically 'inefficient' past, by the standards being adopted by 'modern' Japanese, and it was this that their participation in the exhibition was intended to display. They wanted to demonstrate to Europe how they had 'lifted' their colonies in Formosa, Korea and Manchuria 'out of a long sleep' and the appearance of the Ainu with their simple thatched huts, hints of ritual sacrifice in the bear ceremonies on which much publicity focused and the 'Rip Van Winkle' beards of their menfolk, all served to reinforce the message of 'progress', 'modernisation' and 'civilisation' among the 'modern' Japanese (Fletcher & Brooks n.d.). The caption to an *Illustrated London News* photomontage on the Ainu, which includes pictures from the exhibition and drawings of 'real-life' ceremonies in the home

In the Ainu Home,
Japan-British Exhibition

Feast of the Bear, Ainu Home,
Japan-British Exhibition

124

78. Four postcards of Ainu people at the Japan–British Exhibition of 1910. (RAI 35824, 35826, 35825, 35823)

The Bear Killer, Ainu Home, Japan-British Exhibition.

In the Ainu Home, Japan-British Exhibition.

environment, carefully distinguishes all of this from the 'modern' Japanese: 'The Ainus, it should be noted, represent the primitive population of Japan and are of non-Japanese race and language' (*Illustrated London News* Aug. 23, 1910:601).

The meaning of the exhibition itself and of the photographic images and postcards that accompanied it, is to be understood within this construction of a modern, civilized self in contrast with a primitive 'Other'. The selection of items for exhibition and the photographic representations derive from this framework. The postcard of 'The Bear Killer' (Plate 78) incorporates many of the elements that contribute to this image. In typical 'romantic' terms, the subject is 'recontextualized' into a supposedly 'natural setting' and is represented as a general type, with no personal name: an old man with an unusual beard and exotic paraphernalia poses beside the head of a bear in front of a reconstructed 'native' hut. Accounts of the killing of bears (Munro 1962; Hitchcock 1890) suggest that it was an important social and public event accompanied by much dancing, drinking and ritual: the bear was killed by a carefully directed arrow fired most likely by a young archer and then ceremonially but reverentially strangled between two poles. Its head with the skin attached would be placed upon a *nusa*, a sacred fence consisting of *inau*, sticks with shavings attached that served as symbolic offerings to various spirits. The photograph depicts an inevitably simplified version of these complex events, with a single person only, a rather thin 'fence' with few of the usual ritual objects and nothing that would begin to provide a Western observer with any understanding of its meaning to the participants. The construction of the photograph and the old man's pose, for instance, suggest an association between him and the bear that is falsely reminiscent of European conceptions of the hunter and his trophy.

Similarly the postcard entitled 'Feast of the Bear' (Plate 78), depicting the Ainu at the exhibition supposedly acting out the situation of feasting associated with the bear ceremony, is quite misleading ethnographically, serving rather a more immediate ideological purpose. It portrays a group of Ainu sitting somewhat stiffly in a semicircle, dressed in their 'best', simply posing and framed against the reconstructed models of their houses in such a way as to provide the observer with a picturesque image of the exotic 'Other'. Ethnographic accounts of such a 'feast' suggest it would probably have been held indoors (Munro 1962:171) and would have been associated with 'hilarity and drunkenness' (Hitchcock 1890:482).

Correct detail, however, did not concern either the general public or the political and commercial interests involved, despite the appeal to scientific truth and method on which the legitimacy of such representations rested. Behind this rhetoric, the immediate ideological purpose was to present the 'primitive' peoples of the world as exotic and colourful contrasts to the 'real' business of scientific and commercial progress, with its hard new machinery and technology. Occasional glimpses of the quaintness, backwardness and irrationality of peoples such as the Ainu served to remind Europeans of how lucky they were to have escaped from a similar condition in their own past and provided a warning of what would happen if people took seriously the scepticism of romantic writers, Luddites and others who spoke out against 'progress'.

The imagery of the photographs is selected through this ideological grid. The convention is clearly 'romantic' in Kolodny and Peterson's sense, but presented as though it were 'realist', as though the photograph was 'capturing the native world as it is', thereby avoiding having to confront what that world was really like. By focusing on the surface detail and selection of exotic moments taken out of context, it deflected observers from having to confront the harder questions and contradictions of their own society's relationship with such peoples and, in the case of the Ainu, the harsh treatment being still meted out by the Japanese. The images were in any case generally treated as minor ones within the larger and more important context of the commercial purposes of the exhibition. The Japanese government seems to have invested considerable time and money in order to exhibit Japan's products and their commercial worthiness to Europe, for the first time on such a scale (Fletcher & Brooks n.d.), although British manufacturers are reported as not exhibiting for fear of having their wares imitated by the Japanese, who would then produce them more cheaply (*The Standard* July 20, 1910). In this context it is not surprising that newspaper references to the Ainu's part in the exhibition are relatively brief while advertisements are generally limited to one-liners such as 'Fair Japan', 'Japanese Wrestlers', 'Ainu Home', etc. The images of non-European peoples that we are considering here were, at this level, marginal to the central business concerns, although at a deeper level they were integral to the very conceptualization and reproduction of the ideology that underpinned those concerns. This can be seen too in the other photographs considered here, those of the Batwa pygmies.

The Batwa

In 1905 a group of Batwa pygmies from the Ituri forest region of the Congo were brought to England by an explorer and big-game hunter, Lt-Col. James J. Harrison. They appeared for a season at the Hippodrome theatre, along with such 'entertainments' as seventeen polar bears, a 'Rob Roy' show featuring Scottish dancers, and jugglers and circus acts. The Batwa appeared on the stage 'wearing only girdles of long grass fastened around their waists, and necklaces of beads', the males armed with miniature spears, or bows and arrows, and one with a tom-tom, against a 'scenic background representing their native village' (*The Globe* June 2, 1905). The audience were informed by a commentator that this 'represented a fairly exact picture of the pygmies' homes in the Ituri forest of Central Africa' (*The Era* June 10, 1905).

At first the Batwa were somewhat shy and reluctant to perform their 'native' dances for the audience, and a number of newspaper reports tell how their first attempts to do so were brought to a halt when the audience applauded and the pygmies 'retreated'. The reports emphasized their simpleness and indeed simple-mindedness, and repeated such details from the press handout as their tastes — teetotaller, Turkish tobacco —, their 'peculiar' hair — growing in tufts and mossy in texture — and their preference for straw and bare walls rather than carpeted houses. Most reports urged readers to attend the show on the grounds that they would rarely have the chance to see such unique specimens of the human race, 'savages untouched by European customs and just as in their primeval forests' (*Daily Telegraph* June 7, 1905). A number commented that the pygmies seemed happy enough and were well treated, though none went beyond this easy conscience-salving gesture to comment on the circumstances in which they were brought to England or to see it as an ethical issue.

The Batwa were clearly specimens, available to European curiosity both popular and scientific (Plate 79). As with the other peoples brought over during this period, such as the Ainu, these two viewpoints merge at the level of a common concern for the minutiae and empirical detail of 'native' dress, appearance and customs, which were seen as overt manifestations of cultural difference and inferiority. Although the anthropologists perhaps had more concern for accuracy, in neither case did European cultural assumptions and values promote much interest in analysis of the situation in which 'native' peoples now found themselves, whether at home or as spectacles in European capitals: indeed, the very attention to visual and surface detail militated against consideration of the role of European colonialism in their current condition. European cultural assumptions and values did not or could not allow such questioning.

The theoretical framework within which such people were described was again that of social evolution, hierarchy and race. That the pygmies were portrayed as childlike, for instance, was not simply a reference to their size but part of a larger conceptualization of the evolution of mankind, on the analogy of individual development from child to adult. The pygmies who came to London were dressed in children's sailor suits for their visit to the House of Commons and the photograph of them on the Terrace (Plate 80) clearly represents them as childlike in both external and internal features in contrast with the fatherly figures of the British MPs who encircle them. A contemporary commentary on the photograph brings this out explicitly: 'Surely extremes met when the little folk from the heart of the Ituri Forest in Central Africa, mixed with the Members on the Terrace of the House of Commons. They are supposed to be of the lowest type, mentally as well as the smallest, physically, of the human race. What did they think of the greatest Legislature of the world? What dim conception did they form of its purpose and its work?' (Stone 1905).[3]

Sir Benjamin Stone, who took the photograph, was himself interested in collections of 'curios' and had begun his photographic career by attempting to gather 'a deliberate record of people, places and things' (National Portrait Gallery 1974:6) with the object 'to show those who will follow us, not only our buildings, but our everyday life, our manners and customs' (*Cassell's Saturday Journal* Oct. 18, 1905, cited in National Portrait Gallery 1974:6). His photographs of the House of Commons, when he became an MP, were in the same vein, and his record of the Batwa pygmies is not so much to depict them in their own right as to record the kinds of events in which MPs were involved: they were of interest as part of the life and manners of the House. This is brought out by another photograph that Stone took of them, where they appear virtually naked, carrying bows and arrows and standing somewhat lost in a cul-de-sac somewhere in London, with a brick wall and dirt yard as background (Plate 81): the cursory, almost cynical nature of the construction suggests that all Stone was seeing was a caricature of 'savage' life, to the extent that the background did not require the careful attention to detail evident in the composition of his shot on the Terrace of the House. There he combines formal use of the pillars of the doorway to frame the scene, with careful placing of the MPs in a semicircle around the visitors, their 'mental' and political 'superiority' emphasized in their visual and physical encapsulation of the Batwa.

An element in the representation that is peculiar to the Batwa is the attempts to make sense of their size.

THE PYGMIES.

BOKANE (CHIEF).

KUARKE (PRINCESS).   MONGONGA.   MAFUTIMINGA.

MATUKA.

AMURIAPE.

ROTARY PHOTO, E.C.

79.   Studio portrait of Batwa pygmies. Photograph by W.N. Downey. (RAI 35827)

80. Group of Batwa pygmies with Members of Parliament on the terrace of the House of Commons, London, 1905. Photograph by Sir Benjamin Stone. (Courtesy of the National Portrait Gallery)

81. Group of Batwa pygmies, 1905. Photograph by Sir Benjamin Stone. (Courtesy of the National Portrait Gallery)

African Pygmies in London.   J. Benjamin Stone.
Aug 9th 1905

Popular accounts confuse them with dwarfs and with European stories of small peoples such as Gulliver's Lilliputians, while the scientific approach represented by the RAI attempted some imaginative explanations for the legends of little peoples across the world. Professor Macalister, in his presidential address to the RAI in 1895, had pointed out that there seemed to be more stories of dwarf peoples than of giants and he conjectured that it may be that pygmies once inhabited the whole world but were gradually exterminated by their larger neighbours, remaining only in folk legend. Students of folklore, he suggested, 'have sought the origins of these folk-tales in the half-forgotten traditional memories of race-conflicts with pygmy tribes' (1895:464). A lot of work still needed to be done, he argued, to analyze, in a 'scientific spirit, the scattered fragments of these archaic conditions which are embedded in language, traditions and literature' (1895:467). The arrival of the Batwa in England was likely to provide further such images, and for those who did not see them at the Hippodrome, the photographic record would help to give visual reality to such 'scientific' accounts that fed the folk memory. Again popular conceptions were closely connected with those of the scientific, anthropological community.

Similarly, while the anthropometric photograph by Downey (Plate 82) may seem at first sight to belong to a different genre from the others we have been considering, one more connected with the scientific than the popular imagination, there is again a common discourse underlying differences among the visual images themselves. Green, for instance, suggests that the nineteenth-century focus on the physical and visual features of cultural variety gave to photography a particular role in 'the formation of a particular discourse of race which was located in the conceptualisation of the body as the object of anthropological knowledge' (1984:31). Anthropological interpretation of the body was conceptualized through 'physiognomy' — the belief that the facial and bodily features indicate specific mental and moral characteristics. The photographs we have been considering — both popular and scientific — were at this level part of the same discourse and, as Cowling has demonstrated with regard to paintings and illustrations (Cowling 1989), were likely to have been 'read' through the same framework of anthropological knowledge.

Again, as in the written representations of non-European peoples, nineteenth-century European discourses on race and evolution continued to frame visual portrayals, even at a time when anthropologists

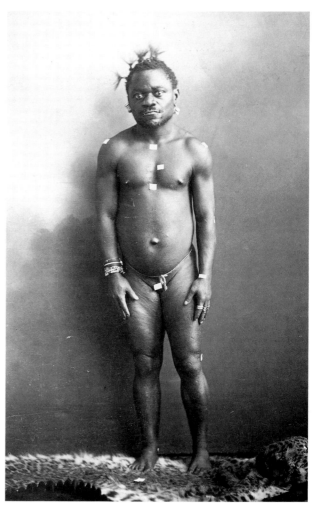

82.   Anthropometric study of Batwa man. Photograph by W.N. Downey. (RAI 1790)

themselves were beginning to move, via fieldwork methods, towards a more characteristically twentieth-century interest in how people might see themselves and towards a more relativist less physically based view of cultural difference. The interest in legends of little people, in little bodies as a sign of little minds, in 'savage' customs as a justification and rationale for 'scientific' and business 'progress', as in the exhibitions and photographs of the Batwa, Ainu and other 'natives' brought to England at the turn of the century, was still firmly rooted in a common framework of race, evolution and hierarchy. Both the form and the content of the representations we have been considering served to construct and perpetuate this conceptual framework, beyond its academic life, for larger portions of the public than could be influenced solely by the books and literature available on the subject at the time.

NOTES

1 The use of cartoons in the late nineteenth and early twentieth centuries to represent distinctive features of 'other' cultures or 'races' is clearly linked with the representations we are considering here, as Mary Cowling (1989) and L.P. Curtis (1968) have demonstrated. They document, for instance, how paintings and cartoons, such as those of the Irish in popular magazines such as *Punch*, legitimated political commentaries on Anglo–Irish relations with reference to the same biological and racial stereotypes prevalent in the photographs under consideration here.

2 More recently the Japanese government has come to view this fact with shame and attempts are being made to challenge it through the revival of indigenous ethnicity and culture among the few identifiable Ainu remaining (cf. Philippi 1979:16).

3 A present-day social anthropologist might respond that their conceptions of British politics were likely to be no more confused than were those of British travellers (such as Harrison himself) attempting to understand the complexities of Batwa legal and political life.

REFERENCES

JAI: *Journal of the Anthropological Institute*
Anthropological Insitute, 1873. Minutes of meeting, May 26. *JAI* 3:137–9.
Cowling, M. 1989. *The Artist as Anthropologist: the representation of type and character in Victorian art.* Cambridge: University Press.
Curtis, L.P. Jr. 1968. *Anglo-Saxons and Celts.* New York: University Press.
— 1905 *Daily Telegraph.* Report on Batwa trip. June 7.
— 1905 *The Era.* Report on show with Batwa at Hippodrome. June 10.
Fletcher, F. & Brooks, A. n.d. *British Exhibitions and their Postcards.* Part I 1900–1914. East Boldon: no pub.
— 1905 *The Globe and Traveller.* Report on bringing of Batwa to England. June 2.
Green, D. 1984. Classified Subjects: Photography and Anthropology — the technology of power. *Ten-8* 14:30–7.
Harrison, J. 1905. *Life Among the Pygmies.* London: Hutchinson and Co.
Hill, C.W. 1978. *Edwardian Entertainments: a picture postcard view.* Burton on Trent: MAB Publishing.
Hitchcock, R. 1890. *The Ainus of Yezo Japan.* Washington: Smithsonian Institution.
Holland, Lt. S.C. 1874. On the Ainus. *JAI* 3:233–44.
— 1905. *Illustrated London News.* Article and picture spread on Batwa. June 10.
— 1910. *Illustrated London News.* The Men of the Sacred Hair: and the Woman of the Tattooed Lips. 601. April 23.
Kodama, S. 1979. 'Historical Changes of the Designation of the Ainu Today'. In Kodama, S. *Ainu: Historical and anthropological studies.* Sapporo: Hokkaido University.
Kolodny, R. 1978. *Towards an Anthropology of Photography: Frameworks for Analysis*, MA thesis. Dept. of Anthropology, McGill University.
(n.d.) 'Africa Introductory: The Pygmy or Negrillo Races'. In *Living Races of Mankind.* 265–70. London: Hutchinson & Co.
(n.d.) 'The Hairy Ainu'. In *Living Races of Mankind* 152–9. London: Hutchinson & Co.
Macalister 1895. Presidential Address. *JAI* 463–6.
Munro, N. 1962. *Ainu Creed and Cult.* London: Routledge & Kegan Paul.
National Portrait Gallery 1974. *Benjamin Stone 1838–1914 and the National Photographic Record Association 1897–1910.* Text by Colin Ford. London: National Portrait Gallery.
Peterson, N. 1985. 'The Popular Image'. In Donaldson, I. & Donaldson, T. (eds.) *Seeing the First Australians* 164–80. Sydney: Allen & Unwin.
Philippi, D. 1979. *Songs of Gods, Song of Humans.* Princeton: University Press.
Proud, D. 1979. Royalty — on a Plate. *South Tyneside Gazette*, June 30.
Rischon, O. 1985. Representation: the harem and the despot. *Block* 10:34–44.
Schneider, W. 1977. Race and Empire: the rise of popular ethnography in the 19th century. *Journal of Popular Culture* 11(1):78–109.
— 1979 *South Tyneside Gazette.* Article on William Downey. June 30.
— 1905 *The Standard.* Report of the arrival of the Batwa. June 2.
— 1905 *The Standard.* Report of the Batwa show at the London Hippodrome. June 5.
— 1910 *The Standard.* Reports on the Ainu. May 12, July 20.
Starr, F. 1904. *The Ainu Group at the St Louis Exhibition.* Chicago: Open Court Publishing Co.
Stone, Sir J. Benjamin 1905. *Benjamin Stone's Pictures.* Records of National Life and History with descriptive notes by Michael MacDonagh. 2 vols. London: Cassell and Co.
Watanabe, Hitoshi 1962. Introduction to *Ainu Creed and Cult*, by Neil Munro. London: Routledge & Kegan Paul.

Representing the Other: The North American Indian

Brian W. Dippie

ON VIEWING A LATE-NINETEENTH-CENTURY photograph of two handsomely attired north-west American Indians, Paul Fussell was prompted to remark, 'If they've not read *Hiawatha*, the photographer has' (1982:37). Many Indian portraits from the period raise this suspicion: the photographer knew what a noble savage should look like, and did not hesitate to impose his vision on his subjects. It could be in the tilt of a head to reveal a Roman profile, hand clutching a tomahawk to chest, or in dramatic lighting to pick out craggy features and an air of stoic resignation.

Geronimo was not often the object of sympathy but he was often the subject of photography. The best-known likenesses show him during his negotiations with the US army and in captivity, scowling and defiant. Yet in subsequent representations he was tamed, placed out of context — in a watermelon patch, or at the wheel of a motor car, a top hat crowning his head, in one popular variation on the Indian novelty images that proliferated after the turn of the century. While they were meant to amuse, they had a serious point to make. In *Ancient Society* (1877) Lewis Henry Morgan had charted man's rise from savagery through barbarism to civilization, a glacially slow process that photographers encompassed within the frame of a single image. A traditionally costumed Indian and a car, a telephone, a bicycle or an aeroplane illustrated the great lesson of civilized progress: the past meeting a future in which it would play no part. Frank A. Rinehart's 1898 portrait of Geronimo (Plate 83) avoids such didacticism: nondescript in appearance, transformed by age and circumstance, Geronimo is still granted a measure of dignity, his expression pensive, almost wistful. He was an unlikely noble savage for a generation that only a few years before had thrilled with horror at the mention of his name. But the passing of the frontier had produced that detachment so conducive to sentimentality, and time had made this 'tiger in human form' the representative of a race, colourful, sad and doomed to disappear.[1]

Before the invention of photography, there were two distinct traditions in American Indian portraiture. One found the sitters posing in the artist's studio dressed in their ceremonial best, members perhaps of a delegation who had come to call on the Great White Father. Charles Bird King served as Washington's resident Indian painter from 1822 to 1842. His work, commissioned by the Indian Office, reflected the belief shared by most Americans that the Indians were a vanishing race, making a pictorial record of their principal leaders indispensable to posterity (Viola 1976). How much more desirable, then, a record of their likenesses and cultures made where they lived. This was the second tradition in Indian portraiture, the

83. Geronimo, 1898. Photograph by F.A. Rinehart. (RAI 5866)

1057 Navajo.   *Mariamie*

84. Mariamie. Photograph by W.H. Jackson. (RAI 1164)

work of artists who journeyed west to see the tribes in their own setting. It, too, was given to a fatalistic reading of Indian destiny. The *real* Indians, unspoiled by long contact and uncorrupted by white vices, were disappearing daily. Only the 'venturesome artist' (as the most celebrated of all, George Catlin, put it) could rescue them in paint so they might rise 'phoenix-like' from the canvas and 'stand forth for centuries yet to come, the living monuments of a noble race' (Catlin 1841, I:16).

Not surprisingly, photographic portraiture of the Indians in the nineteenth century represents a continuum and fits into these two traditions. By the early 1850s camera had replaced paintbrush in recording Indian visitors to Washington, and after the Civil War, photographers in increasing numbers transported their cumbersome apparatus into the field to record Indian camp life, supplementing the formal studio portraits that remained a staple in Indian photography with relatively candid shots equivalent to Catlin's quick field sketches (Fleming 1985; Fleming & Luskey 1986)[2]. Whether the photographer worked in a studio or outdoors, however, noble savagery and a belief in

the Indians' imminent disappearance shaped his vision as surely as the painter's.

Catlin, in creating his Indian Gallery of nearly 500 oils in the 1830s, had frequently shown his subjects in poses borrowed from classical statuary. Photographers adopted the same conventions. Standing figures draped in blankets resembled Roman orators in their togas. Some stepped forward on to a rock or mound, heirs to Chingachgook, who was not the last of the Mohicans after all; others reclined on a blanket or bearskin like the Turkish sultan in an orientalist's fantasy. Their poses conjured up romantic associations, though Mariamie, a Navajo photographed by William H. Jackson (Plate 84), appears unamused. Jackson's portrait of Petalasharo, a Pawnee, is as mannered as that of any Victorian gentleman (Plate 85). But Petalasharo is a gentleman of the Indian persuasion, as his head-dress, shirt and leggings attest; his left hand rests on a tomahawk, not an open book. The pose he strikes is classical, but also conforms to noble savage conventions. This, his costume tells us, is a nobleman of the forests and plains, and consequently a living anachronism, without a future in the new age of technological progress — and cameras. Could he, then, be civilized and saved? The image, after all, conveys the admiration reserved for certain progressive Indians — Washakie the Shoshone, Quanah Parker the Comanche, and Joseph the Nez Perce, for example — who were thought to have behaved admirably in recognizing the writing on the wall and accepting the new order. They established at least the possibility of Indian improvement.

Some photographers showed their Indian subjects with crucifixes, presidential medals and peace pipes, implying just such a saving progressive spirit. But most showed them bristling with bows and arrows, spears, pistols, rifles and, especially, tomahawks. A tomahawk was the favourite all-purpose prop. It verified the savage in the noble savage (even Petalasharo carried one), established the warlike qualities that made him a dangerous enemy and helped explain why the race — once so implacably resistant to civilization's overtures — had been doomed in America. Brandishing a tomahawk and bow, his face streaked with paint, a Sac and Fox man (Plate 86)

86.   Sac and Fox man. (RAI 1453)

85.   Petalasharo. Photograph by W.H. Jackson. (RAI 1230)

seems the incarnation of the 'red devil'. On closer examination his eyes and the set of his mouth express more apprehension than ferocity; the weapons he clutches are simply props. He is meant to look the fierce warrior, but beneath the paint and head-dress and the bear-claw necklace is a recognizable person: the photographic subject all dressed up for a formal portrait and uncomfortably self-conscious. If the resulting image is ambivalent, however, the photographer's intention is not. This is the bloody savage of frontier legend, a figure that haunted the American imagination and inspired fear rather than regret. He justified that exterminatory war civilization waged on savagery, and explained the vanishing race in terms that put the blame squarely on the Indian.

The opposite image in Indian portraiture, one identified with the boarding schools of the late nineteenth century, showed the subject as a white man with dark skin. This photograph of Komus, a Ute (Plate 87), his hair cut short and neatly parted, relatively relaxed in his formal attire, has a single point to make: he is just like us, from the placement of his hands (no tomahawk here) to the spotless starched collar. It is also an image faithful to the theory of the

87.   Komus. (RAI 1412)

88.   Pawnee Schoolchildren. Photograph by W.H. Jackson. (RAI 1247)

vanishing Indian as it had evolved after the Civil War, arguing not racial but cultural extinction. 'We accept the watch-word,' the founder of Carlisle Indian School was fond of saying. 'There *is* no good Indian but a dead Indian. Let us by education and patient effort *kill* the Indian in him, and save the *man*' (Richard H. Pratt, cited in Gates 1886:31). Carlisle as part of its promotion distributed sets of photographs showing incoming students in native costume and long hair wearing worried expressions, then the same students a few years later in school uniforms, the boys with short hair and the girls coiffured, looking more at ease in the now-familiar surroundings. Such images of transformation were intended to document the progress young Indians were making at a time when the US government was committed to a policy of assimilation. Komus in his natty attire was the model red progressive, a glimpse into the Indian future — and a comment on a vanished culture.

Photographers of the American Indian at the end of the nineteenth century worked both sides of the line. They recorded a picturesque yesterday, serving as memorialists of the once noble, vanishing Indian; and they recorded a hopeful, if less colourful, present, serving as propagandists for assimilation. A William Jackson photograph of Pawnee schoolchildren is especially evocative because it marries past and present (Plate 88). Boys posed against the brick schoolhouse wall still display bow and arrows and a tomahawk though their hair is cropped, while a long-haired man displays only a book. Other pupils sit on the window ledge above the group, what appear to be moccasined feet dangling, their informality undercutting the formality of the subject. The open windows admit the outdoors into stuffy rooms; they are also escape hatches, and the figures perched on the ledge seem literally suspended between two worlds. The old-time Indian would one day disappear, the photographers tell us, his war paint washed away, his feathers and beads and buckskins discarded, his tomahawk buried. Then he would exist only in the paintings of a King and a Catlin, or in the photographs made by men who had read their *Hiawatha*.

NOTES

1 For a fuller development of ideas in this essay see Dippie 1982.
2 See Paula Fleming, 'Studio Photographs of Indian Delegations Visiting 19th Century Washington, DC', unpublished paper, The Photograph and the North American Indian Conference, Princeton University, Princeton, NJ, September 1985; and Fleming & Luskey, *The North American Indians in Early Photographs* (1986). The Princeton conference also generated an extensive bibliography on its theme.

REFERENCES

Catlin, George 1841. *Letters and Notes on the Manners, Customs and Conditions of the North American Indian.* 2 vols. New York: Wiley and Putman.
Dippie, Brian 1982. *The Vanishing American: White Attitudes and U.S. Indian Policy.* Middletown, Conn.: Wesleyan University Press; repr. 1991, Lawrence: University of Kansas Press.
Fleming, Paula 1985. Studio Portraits of Indian Delegations Visiting 19th Century Washington, DC. Unpublished paper, The Photograph and the North American Indian Conference, Princeton University, Princeton, NJ, September 1985.
Fleming, Paula & Luskey, Judith 1986. *The North American Indians in Early Photographs.* New York: Harper and Row.
Fussell, Paul 1982. *The Boy Scout Handbook and Other Observations.* New York: Oxford University Press.
Gates, M.E. 1886. Land and Law as Agents in Educating Indians. *Journal of Social Science* 21.
Morgan, L.H. 1877. *Ancient Society.* New York: Henry Holt.
Viola, Herman 1976. *The Indian Legacy of Charles Bird King.* Washington, DC: Smithsonian Institution Press and New York: Doubleday & Co.

Of 'Peculiar Carvings and Architectural Devices': Photographic Ethnohistory and the Haida Indians

Margaret B. Blackman

THE MAGNIFICENT ARCHITECTURE and monumental art of the Haida Indians of British Columbia's north coast attracted numerous photographers in the late nineteenth century. Some came on official government business, some in search of saleable images, some as tourists, some as missionaries and some as ethnographic collectors. All, whether inadvertently or intentionally, documented fragments of Haida history, totalling at most a few hours of elapsed time, but representing a visual legacy that can be inspected, reassessed and reinterpreted repeatedly by later generations of scholars, native people and the interested public. A closer look at the village of Masset, on the northern end of the Queen Charlotte Islands, through two sets of images, one taken in 1878 and the other in 1890, is suggestive of the richness of the photographic record and the value of this record in the study of ethnohistory.

Photographs of the Haida may have been taken earlier but do not appear to have survived. For instance, George Robinson of Victoria, who came to Skidgate in 1865 to oversee the development of a coal mine, brought a camera with him, but none of his photographs — if he took any — have surfaced. Similarly, Charles Horestsky, who travelled to the northern Queen Charlottes in 1872 had a camera with him. Finally, in 1875, the official photographer on the US Revenue cutter *Wolcott* reportedly photographed several Haida who came on board.

The earliest surviving photographs of Haida villages were made by the geologist George Mercer Dawson in 1878 during an exploratory survey of the Queen Charlottes. During his two-and-a-half month excursion in the islands, Dawson took sixty-three photographs. Most of these reflected the geological and geographical purpose of his survey. Eighteen were ethnographic, taken at the Haida villages of Skidgate (three), Cumshewa (three), Skedans (four), Tanu (one), Masset (three), Yatza (two), Kung (one) and Dadens (one). Three important Haida villages were not documented by Dawson: Kuista and Yan in the north and Ninstints, the southernmost Haida village. Dawson took only three photographs of Masset, one of which was of the mission complex exclusively. Despite such slim representation of some individual villages, all of Dawson's photographs are the visual baseline against which the later ethnographic content of Haida villages must be assessed. At least ten photographers are known to have visited and photographed Masset between Dawson's visit of 1878 and the beginning of the twentieth century. They left behind a legacy of nearly 100 images of the village. The most detailed record was made by Robert Reford, scion of a Montreal shipping family, who journeyed to northern British Columbia on behalf of his family's shipping interests in 1890. Reford and his party stayed in Masset a few days, where he made twenty-two images of the village and its people.[1]

Just twelve years separate Dawson's and Reford's visits, but the changes in Haida culture documented by their photographs are striking. Comparison of the images also, not surprisingly, reveals differences between the photographers' approaches to their subject matter. Dawson used an 8 × 10-inch view camera and dry glass plate negatives. Like other scientific expedition photographers of the late nineteenth century, Dawson saw himself as a documentary image maker. His Haida images as well as the sketches he made in his journal reflect his fascination with Haida monumental architecture and carving. His perspective was that of a landscape photographer. Horizontal in orientation, his Haida village images reveal the same balance of foreground, middle distance, horizon and sky as the geological and 'picturesque interest' images he made (Huyda 1983:210). Only one of Dawson's photographs (taken at Kung) narrows its view to the individual house and pole. Dawson seemed intent on recording as much as possible of a village in a single image without sacrificing detail. Indeed, his photographs of Masset encompass in two images virtually the entire village.[2]

Although Dawson commented in his journal on some of the Haida people he met, he made few photographs of them. A photograph of Skedans shows the backsides of three individuals seated on a horizontal carving (MacDonald 1983:81), and the single photograph of Tanu has captured the preparations for a potlatch. Dwarfed by the totem poles and houses which were the focus of Dawson's camera are a group of potlatch guests and a carver putting the final touches on a frontal pole (MacDonald 1983:90–1). At another Haida village (Yatza) on August 23, 1878, just before a big potlatch, Dawson took a photograph of a group of people and two chiefs standing on the beach. Native response to his camera, as well as Dawson's overriding interest in what he saw as disappearing architecture and carving, surely contributed to his lack of photographs of people. He recorded in his journal for that day: 'Took photo of two chiefs and of as many of the rest of the people as would come. Most, however, disliked the idea, and especially the women, not one of whom appeared' (Dawson n.d.). Most of Robert Reford's images contain people, both Haida and fashionably attired members of his travelling party. He was in all likelihood more interested in people than in the architecture that so fascinated Dawson.

By 1890 Haida curiosity about the camera was apparent, and the new technology made candid shots possible and the act of photography itself less conspicuous.[3] Reford made a Kodak snapshot of several Haida men and boys clustered behind the black cloth of his view camera. Haida women were more reluctant than the men to be photographed as evidenced by their positions in the background of Reford's images and by the captions Reford gave to two Kodak shots: 'lady using bad language' (to the photographer apparently) and 'ladies frightened by Kodak'.

Overall, Reford's Haida images are inferior technically and aesthetically to Dawson's. Though he was much more the tourist-photographer, his photographs are nonetheless historically significant; in some ways Reford was the most experimental of the photographers of the Haida, making images with both a glass plate view camera (ten images) and with the new fixed-aperture and fixed-focus Kodak No. 2 (twelve images). Reford photographed single houses and totem poles in both the horizontal and vertical orientations, took two panoramic views of Masset, and made photographs of people both posed before his view camera and in candid Kodak shots. A few of his scenes and subjects were duplicated by his two cameras.

The two village panoramas made by Dawson and the two taken by Reford encompass in each instance a substantial portion of Masset. Both photographers missed some of the northern end of the village, and Reford omitted the southern extremity. Plate 89 by Dawson and Plate 90 by Reford show the same section of the village, albeit from different vantage points. Reford's is a straight-on view looking east and taken from a boat in front of the village: Dawson's was made on the shore and is oriented south-south-east. The Dawson photograph was taken just two years after the arrival of the Anglican mission on the Queen Charlottes, yet the overwhelming impression is one of a traditional Haida settlement.

Housing appears minimally influenced by Western culture and totem poles — a few fairly new in appearance — dominate the landscape. Though not readily apparent from the photograph, several houses in 1878 had rectangular doorways and pane glass windows set into their façades. The mission complex, sitting on a hill behind the central section of the village and recorded by Dawson in another photograph, is not visible from this angle. In the Reford photograph the number of poles has diminished substantially (from thirty-two in this section of the village in 1878 to twenty), and there are more white-style houses than Haida ones. The bell tower of the white-frame Anglican church is visible in the centre section of the photograph.

The Church was the force behind the architectural

89. Masset looking south–south–east. Photograph by George M. Dawson, August 10 1878. (RAI 2075)

90. Masset from the water. Photograph by Robert Reford, 1890. (Courtesy of the Public Archives of Canada)

and settlement pattern changes that occurred between 1878 and 1890. From the outset totem-pole raising was discouraged (though, in 1890, not completely quelled) by the missionaries and the people were encouraged to take down old poles. Totem poles were removed as they rotted, and between 1882 and 1902 ten poles from Masset were purchased by museums at the bargain rate of $1–2 per foot. MacDonald (1983:131–53) records the totem poles that ended up in museum collections. The earliest date a pole was removed from Masset was 1882 when a frontal pole was purchased by English photographer-tourist Bertram Buxton as a birthday present for his mother; Adrian Jacobsen acquired three poles in 1885 for the Museum für Völkerkunde in Berlin, and the remainder were purchased by C.F. Newcombe for various museums (Pitt Rivers Museum, Oxford, Philadelphia University Museum, National Museums of Canada, Royal British Columbia Museum). White housing was urged by the missionaries in an attempt to improve the standard of living and encourage habits of 'civilization'. The simple, stark box-like houses documented in Reford's photographs mimic the architecture of the mission station recorded by Dawson. Reford's photographs indicate that a few villagers held to the old ways: four native houses in good repair and obviously inhabited

contrast with the fifteen non-native houses. At least two of those holding out were important chiefs who, despite their conversion to Christianity, elected to live in the old-style houses or at least to maintain them for ceremonial purposes. One of these four houses was even erected between the time Dawson and Reford documented the village (Plate 91). Replete with milled siding, church-style windows and gingerbread trim, it nonetheless displayed only a superficial conformity to the white houses. Other photographs document its traditional interior, its thick plank sides, and the smokehole rising from the roof above its central fireplace. Its frontal pole, one of Masset's finest, can be seen today in the Pitt Rivers Museum. Photographs from the late 1890s document the abandonment and razing of this and the town chief's house (the large Haida-style house shown in the centre of Plate 90); by the early years of the twentieth century only one old-style house remained in the entire village.[4] Inspection of the Dawson and Reford images suggests that only the canoes on the beach and the forest rising behind the village remained unchanged.

Other photographs postdating Reford's (Plate 92) lead the viewer to the last totem pole raised in the village, to the construction of stores and streets more elaborate white-style houses with bay windows and

91. Chief Anetias' house, Masset. Constructed between 1881 and 1883. The frontal pole was sold to the Pitt Rivers Museum, Oxford. (Courtesy of the Public Archives of Canada)

92. Main street, Masset, c.1914. From the Indian Commission Reserve Album 1913–16. (Courtesy of the Provincial Archives of British Columbia, No. 94608)

fenced yards, and to the replacement of canoes with gasoline-powered fishing boats.

The entire body of historical photographs of the Haida has facilitated the construction of model Haida villages at museums (Smyley & Smyley 1973), has informed the architectural and art styles employed by the tribe (MacDonald 1983), as well as the organization of space and personnel within the late-nineteenth-century Haida house, the adoption of western material culture, the details of Haida settlement patterns and the adaptation of mortuary practices to Christianity and missionary demands (Blackman 1981). The great houses in many cases can be followed through later images as they give way to the frame buildings urged by the missionaries, and through sequences of historical photographs we can visualize the process of decay of other plank houses and poles as they were reclaimed by the ground from which they once rose. In many respects these kinds of changes are ones that have gone undescribed in Northwest Coast Indian ethnography and are thus accessible primarily through visual images.

Dawson had the foresight to see his ethnographic images as a lasting legacy when he commented, upon publication of the results of his Queen Charlotte Islands expedition: 'The peculiar carvings and architectural devices of the Haidas . . . had not before been photographed, and owing to the rapid progress of decay, it will be impossible to obtain satisfactory illustrations of them in a few years' time.' The images made by Dawson, Reford and others who journeyed to the Queen Charlotte Islands continue to serve, in ways their makers could not have envisioned, as a stimulus for studies of Haida art, architecture and cultural change.

NOTES

1 Two additional images of Masset may have been made by Reford, for they appear to have been taken at the same time as his others.
2 Dawson was limited in the number of glass plates he could transport, and this too may have contributed to his propensity for whole-village scenes.
3 Haida response to the camera is discussed in detail in Blackman 1982a.
4 This house was reported to the author by Florence Davidson (born 1896) who remembered, as a child, taking food to the elderly inhabitants (Blackman 1982b:88).

REFERENCES

Blackman, M. 1981. *Window on the Past: the Photographic Ethnohistory of the Northern and Kaigani Haida.* Mercury Series, Paper 74. Ottawa: National Museum of Man.
— 1982a. 'Copying People': Northwest Coast Native Response to Early Photography. *BC Studies* 52:86–112.
— 1982b. *During my time: Florence Edenshaw Davidson, a Haida Woman.* Seattle: University of Washington Press.
Dawson, G.M. 1880. *Report on the Queen Charlotte Islands.* Ottawa: Geological Survey of Canada. Report of Progress for 1878–9.
— (n.d.) *Queen Charlotte Islands Cruise 1878.* Microfilm. Montreal: McGill University Library.
Huyda, R. 1983. 'Photography and the Haida Villages of Queen Charlotte Islands: an Historical Perspective'. In MacDonald, G.F. *Haida Monumental Art* 207–14. Vancouver: University of British Columbia Press.
MacDonald, G.F. 1983. *Haida Monumental Art.* Vancouver: University of British Columbia Press.
Smyley, J. & Smyley, C. 1973. *Those Born at Koona.* Saanichton, BC: Hancock House.

George Hunt, Kwakiutl Photographer

Ira Jacknis

George Hunt (1854–1933) is remembered today as the Kwakiutl assistant to anthropologist Franz Boas, yet the scope of his career went far beyond that of mere 'assistant'. Though he has been the subject of recent research (Cannizzo 1983), his significance as a native ethnographer has yet to be fully explored. Not only was Hunt one of the earliest American Indians to turn to ethnography; he was perhaps the first to use the camera as an ethnographic instrument. This essay is devoted to his pioneering photographic work.

Born on February 14, 1854, George Hunt grew up in the interracial community of Fort Rupert, British Columbia. His English-born father, Robert Hunt, was a merchant for the Hudson's Bay Company, and his mother, Mary Ebbetts, was the daughter of a Tlingit chief. While not Kwakiutl by birth, Hunt was essentially raised as one, though he also spoke English from an early age. The Hudson's Bay Company at the time encouraged mixed marriage, and several of Hunt's siblings married whites, including his sister Annie, who took as a husband Stephen Allen Spencer, one of the first photographers in Victoria.[1] Around 1885 Spencer gave up his Victoria business to attend to the Alert Bay cannery he had founded in the early 1870s. Hunt himself married Kwakiutl women (his first wife died in 1908) and participated actively in Kwakiutl potlatches and ceremonialism.

George Hunt began his ethnographic career in 1879 as an interpreter for BC Indian Commissioner I.W. Powell on one of his inspection trips around the Province. In 1881–2 Hunt acted as interpreter and assistant for Johan Adrian Jacobsen on his collecting trip for the Royal Ethnographic Museum of Berlin. Hunt's meeting with Franz Boas in 1888 transformed his life. Boas chose him to make a collection for the World's Columbian Exposition (Chicago World's Fair), held in 1893, and to lead a party of Kwakiutl there. On the fair grounds Boas instructed Hunt in the orthographic symbols needed to write his language. When Boas next visited Fort Rupert, in the fall of 1894, Hunt again offered vital assistance. One of the most significant aspects of this trip was Boas's work with O.C. Hastings, a professional photographer from Victoria (Jacknis 1984).[2] While George Hunt performed a variety of jobs in his career (merchant, interpreter, hunter/trapper, guide, miner, constable, night watchman), the one closest to his heart and to which he devoted the most time and effort was ethnographic documentation for Franz Boas.

Fairly early on in his work for Boas, Hunt realized the value of the camera. As soon as Boas left Fort Rupert in 1894, Hunt set to work on his own gathering artefacts and legends to send to Boas in New York. As early as February 1896, after witnessing a

143

dramatic series of dances, Hunt exclaimed to his mentor: 'Oh if I Had your camera with me.'[3] In 1900, when sending along two photographs made for him by one of Spencer's sons, he repeated his request for a camera, arguing that 'I think it would show this things plain if we can get it taken in that way,' and '. . . for lots of this things is Done and I cant Explain it.'[4]

Exactly how Hunt obtained his first camera is unclear. In later letters Boas indicates that he gave Hunt a camera when the latter visited him in New York in early 1903, but Hunt wrote, in a 1901 letter enclosing some photos that he said he took, 'after I get use to my Kodak I can sent you lots of this kind of Plases [historical sites] . . .'.[5] From the surviving negatives and prints, we know that Hunt used cameras with both 4 × 5-inch and 5 × 7-inch glass plates, which he developed himself. We can assume that either Spencer or one of his sons taught Hunt the procedures, as Hunt wrote in 1900 that one of Spencer's sons agreed to teach him 'to print the potograph'.[6] Most of his surviving pictures were taken out of doors, and while a few document house interiors, there is no evidence that he used a flash apparatus. Although Boas may have instructed Hunt orally when they met in 1900 (in British Columbia) and 1903 (in New York), there are no indications in these early letters that he directed Hunt's photography. Apparently it was Hunt's idea to get a camera, and all his early use of it seems to be at his own initiative.

George Hunt's most important pictures were taken for the Jesup North Pacific Expedition (1897–1902), organized by Franz Boas for the American Museum of Natural History. From the summer of 1901, when he took his first photographs, to the summer of 1905, when Boas left the Museum, Hunt sent in about ninety photographs. The subjects were quite diverse. While generally corresponding to his work for Boas, they often capture other aspects of Kwakiutl life. Among the topics were scenery (villages, places of mythological occurrences), subsistence (women drying seaweed and halibut, stringing clams, roasting salmon), artefacts and technology (canoes and canoe-making, totem poles, potlatch figures, grave monuments), portraits (ritual leaders, his family), potlatches (repaying marriage debts, giving away blankets, buying coppers), and ceremonialism (costumed dancers, chiefs in regalia carrying coppers, shamans, men gambling). In 1904 Hunt exposed an important series of pictures to document the Nootkan whalers' shrine that he collected for the Museum with some difficulty.[7] Other than the Nootka set, most seem to have been taken in Fort Rupert and Alert Bay.[8] During this period Hunt also identified and annotated photographs of potlatch figures and other large carvings he had collected for the American Museum of Natural History.[9]

From 1906 until about 1911 Boas directed Hunt's camera work a bit more closely. During these years Boas was finishing his account of Kwakiutl material culture (1909) and its continuation (1921). From time to time Boas requested specific illustrations, but he often had to be patient. For instance, his first request for an image of a tree from which boards had been split off, in a letter of April 1906, did not seem to have been answered until the spring of 1909. There were a number of reasons for the delay. One was that most subsistence activities could be photographed only at a certain time of the year, and one would have to wait a whole year if one missed it for some reason. And Hunt had personal problems; there were times during these years when he was ill, and he was quite depressed over the death of his wife in 1908. One winter his plates froze as he was developing them, causing him to put off the task until the spring.[10]

In November 1907 Boas was able to get authorization from the Smithsonian's Bureau of American Ethnology for Hunt to be paid $2 per photograph, up to a total of fifty, to illustrate his account of Kwakiutl technology, especially food preparation (Boas 1921). As Boas made them realize, '. . . it is very difficult to understand some of the descriptions of the cutting without illustrations'.[11] And as he indicated in this letter, one of Boas's motivations in this commission was the procurement of extra income for Hunt.

Between 1906 and 1911 Hunt continued his collecting for George G. Heye, a wealthy New York collector who founded the Museum of the American Indian in 1916. In 1908 Hunt came across a rock covered with petroglyphs and offered to send a photo of it to Boas to see if Heye wanted to buy it, to which the answer was in the affirmative.[12] After some exasperating delays Heye remarked, 'It certainly is not easy to do business with an Indian at a distance of over 3,000 miles'.[13] Photography made long-distance collecting somewhat more efficient.

As Boas's direct relationship with museums and material culture began to taper off around 1910, Hunt's photography underwent a similar decline. Yet his camera projects were by no means over; Hunt was quite active as an assistant to a long line of visiting photographers. Beginning in 1912, he spent two years assisting famed Indian photographer Edward S. Curtis with his visual account of the Kwakiutl in stills (1915) and film (1914). Holm and Quimby summarize George Hunt's indispensable role in researching and composing the text, commissioning and gathering the sets, costumes and props, recruiting the actors and directing the filming. In addition to these tasks Hunt was active with a 5 × 7 camera, used, most likely, to obtain sample 'location' shots (1980:28, 57).

Despite his active cooperation, George Hunt was rather critical of Curtis's approach. For the image of his wife dressed as for her marriage, Hunt wrote to Boas, 'he Dont know what all the meaning and the story of it. for on that Picture you cant see the four carved Post under it.' Not only did Curtis not photograph the most important elements according to a Kwakiutl viewpoint, but, unlike Boas, he was interested principally in visual effect: '. . . about the photo of my wife there is story belong to it. But Mr Curtice did not take the story or did not care as long as he get the picture taken' (Jacknis 1984:47–8).[14] During these years Hunt also assisted Samuel Barrett with the photography on his 1915 collecting trip for the Milwaukee Public Museum.

George Hunt was crucial in the making of the first five films of the Kwakiutl. First, as mentioned, there was Curtis's 1914 film, *In the Land of the Head-Hunters*. In 1922 Pliny Goddard visited Fort Rupert on a collecting trip for the American Museum of Natural History. Although Goddard did some collecting, he spent most of his time filming Hunt and his wife demonstrating the use of tools and craft techniques. In the twenties Harlan I. Smith, a former Jesup Expedition colleague of Hunt's, made a series of films of British Columbia natives, including one of the Kwakiutl, for the Canadian National Museum. In 1930 George and Francine Hunt participated in two more films on traditional Kwakiutl culture. In each they demonstrated crafts as well as dances. The first was *Totemland*, made by J.B. Scott for Associated Screen News of Montreal. It was something of a newsreel, featuring the visit of a famed soprano to the Indians. Later in the year, Franz Boas arrived for his last field trip and for the first time used a movie camera as an ethnographic tool (Ruby 1980). Although crafts and games were included, Boas's prime interest was in motor pattern and gesture.[15]

Throughout the twenties there are references in Hunt's correspondence to miscellaneous photography projects. For his work for Pliny Goddard at the American Museum of Natural History, Hunt forwarded in 1924 a set of five pictures of Arthur Shaughnessy carving a set of four houseposts that Hunt had commissioned.[16] Hunt sent in a few more pictures as he and Boas returned to subsistence and material culture, subjects that they had tackled years before.[17]

In the twenties and thirties, as Boas and Hunt were ending more than four decades of ethnographic collaboration, they became acutely aware of the historical nature of photographs. On one level, beyond their

uses for scientific documentation, these images could serve as personal *souvenirs* or mementoes of past people and events. In 1921, thanking Hunt for a photo of him and his son, Boas acknowledged that it made him realize that 'we are both getting older'.[18] The following year, Hunt asked Boas for a copy of a book he had seen at the Provincial Museum, 'for I like to see the Photographs of my old friends who are all Daid now . . .'.[19] In 1933, when sending Hunt a photograph taken forty years earlier (of Tom Haima'selas at the Chicago World's Fair in 1893), Boas wrote, 'May be his widow would like to have it', to which Hunt replied: 'she was wel Pleased'.[20]

As with all ethnographic media, Boas was quite concerned about the archival function of photographs, and in 1930 wrote to Hunt about the preservation of his images:

From time to time in earlier years you sent me photographs which you had taken. Unfortunately all the prints which I have have faded completely so that they cannot be used. Would it be at all possible for you either to have new prints made of the films or to let me have the films so that I could have new prints made for you and for myself. I am writing out now much of the material that you have sent me and I should like very much to illustrate it, but what I have now will not do. Some of the photographs I have go back to the year 1895.[21]

After Boas's death in 1942, the American Museum of Natural History acquired his large photographic collection, including many of Hunt's faded prints, but it is unclear when these were made. For whatever reason, none of Boas's later publications contained photographs.

During his last decade, then, Hunt was no longer an active photographer, though pictures continued to be an important concern to him. Although he recovered from a stroke in 1931, he was ill for much of his last years. George Hunt kept at his writing for Boas until the evening before his death on September 5, 1933, at the age of seventy-nine.

George Hunt as a native photographer

George Hunt must be counted as perhaps the earliest and most important of Native American ethnographic photographers. Although there have never been many of them, their significance was in almost inverse proportion to their numbers. Scholars have recently reviewed the topics of native anthropologists (Liberty 1978; Mark 1982) and anthropological and American Indian photographers (Banta & Hinsley 1986; Fleming & Luskey 1986), but very little attention has been paid to the few who combined these roles.[22]

George Hunt, however, was not the only native photographer on the Northwest Coast (Blackman 1982:107–10). George Eastman, inventor of the Kodak camera and film, often stopped in Alert Bay on his travels to the region. Reportedly, he instructed the natives on how to operate a camera.[23] Hunt's Kwakiutl competitor in the field, Charles Nowell, asked his mentor, collector Charles F. Newcombe, for a camera, but there is no record that he ever received one. Yet Hunt's nearest analogue as a pioneering photo-ethnographer was Tlingit Louis Shotridge, who took approximately 178 pictures for the Museum at the University of Pennsylvania (Milburn 1986:65, 72, 74).

Like his teacher, Franz Boas, Hunt's preferred ethnographic medium was the native text, but he was sensitive to the uses of alternative media. Hunt was no stranger to mechanical recording devices. At the World's Columbian Exposition of 1893 he sang for the first recordings of Kwakiutl music (among the earliest made of non-Western music) for Boas and musicologist John C. Fillmore. Recognizing its potential for ethnographic recording, he requested an apparatus from Boas soon after returning to Fort Rupert.[24] Early in his career Hunt realized the vital role of the phonograph and camera in preserving what the written word could not ('for it will show you every thing Plainer then writing it alon').[25]

A proper analysis of George Hunt's photographs encounters several problems. Many seem to have been lost,[26] and others have become separated from their documentation. The American Museum of Natural History holds all the photographs currently attributed to Hunt, numbering about ninety unique images.[27] Few of Hunt's photographs were published in his lifetime. Boas illustrated four in his 1909 monograph on Kwakiutl material culture, but they were uncredited (Jacknis 1984:40). In 1905 John Swanton published Hunt's picture of the family totem pole at Fort Rupert — again unattributed (1905: opp. 85).

A review of the Hunt corpus indicates that he did possess a distinctive native approach to ethnographic photography. This can be found primarily in his choice of subject, but also in his visual style and documentation. Unlike photographs of the Haida studied by Blackman (1981:68), which emphasize houses and totem poles, Hunt's photographs deal overwhelmingly with human activity. From his annotations we know that Hunt exposed his relatively few shots of scenery, not for the sake of an attractive image, but to document places in which mythological encounters occurred. His several pictures of subsistence reveal that he was interested in and available when these mundane processes occurred. One unique image of daily life is his photograph of an old man 'who is killing lice or flees from his shirt By Biting his shirt, in the old ways'.[28] By contrast with the Boas–Hastings corpus, Hunt took no physical 'types,' the systematic portraits that were used for purposes of physical anthropology. His few portraits tend to feature individuals important in Kwakiutl ritual.

George Hunt's principal photographic subject was ceremonialism. While others did photograph Kwakiutl potlatches (though they are not that common: Blackman 1976; Jacknis 1984:26–8), Hunt was the only one to photograph shamanism (Plate 93).[29] Most of the few images of Northwest Coast shamans were posed in a studio (Wyatt 1989:68–9). A notable exception is the series of seven taken by Marius Barbeau in 1927 on the Nass River; they depict a Nishga shaman re-enacting a cure (Riley 1988:127–30). While Hunt's photographs may have been similarly staged, his special access was no doubt greatly facilitated by the fact that he himself was a shaman (Boas 1966:121–5). His two pictures are particularly rich in ethnographic content. One caption reads: 'Doctor Healing a sick man with the Basket and sharp Pointed stick to Drive the Evel spirit away and spruce tree for the same.' This detail is corroborated and explained in Boas's ethnography:

> A Nimpkish shaman places his patient in a house of spruce branches erected in the woods. Two open work baskets, through each of which are stuck four sticks sharpened at both ends, hang on each side of the entrance. These are called 'Quills to hurt the Woman-Doing-Evil.' Strips of cedar bark undyed and dyed red are hung up inside and both patient and house are covered with eagle down. (1966:133)

Kwakiutl shamanic seances vary somewhat in detail, but Hunt was certainly referring to this kind of cure. Here one can see the doctor, wearing a cedarbark ring, sucking the illness out of the patient's body. Beside him are the requisite new mat and bowl of water.

Technically and formally, Hunt was an adequate, not distinguished, photographer. For instance, many of his potlatch pictures (e.g. Plates 94–5) give as much space to the foreground and spectators as to the ritual action at the rear of the picture plane. Paradoxically, photographing the backs of people has the effect of drawing the viewer into the image, so that he strains to discern their point of interest. However, Hunt's native stance can be seen in his literal closeness to native people and activities; most other pictures of Kwakiutl potlatches were shot from a greater distance. Moreover, in both images illustrated here one can see clearly the Kwakiutl ordering of ceremonial space (Blackman 1976:56). In a marriage repayment the goods are

93. Kwakiutl shaman and patient, Fort Rupert?, British Columbia, *c.*1902. Hunt's caption: 'Doctor Healing sick man with a Basket and sharp Pointed stick to Drive the Evel spirit away and spruce tree for the same.' (Courtesy of the American Museum of Natural History. From copy negative, AMNH 22868)

typically laid out in a square or rectangle that represents a loaded canoe (Boas 1966:74). The guests sit around it, arrayed according to their kinship relations. In addition to the horizontal extension, Hunt's pictures reveal the vertical elevation of flags, piles of blankets and the poles strung with frontlets, hats, silver bracelets and dance aprons. The filling of both dimensions increases the impression of abundant wealth.

Hunt's sensitivity to native categories and distinctions can be seen from his frequent series, such as the paired images of a *hamatsa* (cannibal-dancer) initiate upon returning from ritual seclusion. In the first image (Plate 96) the wild and possessed dancer wears hemlock boughs, while in the second (Plate 97) his cedar-bark rings indicate that he has been partially tamed. Of the several major photographers of the Kwakiutl potlatch (O.C. Hastings, H.I. Smith,

C.F. Newcombe, W.M. Halliday, S.A. Barrett), he was the only one to record the same kind of event (in this case, the wife's father repaying a marriage debt to his son-in-law) in more than one place and time (Plates 94–5). As a local resident, Hunt clearly had opportunities denied to more transient photographers.

Finally, Hunt's native perspective can be seen in his detailed annotations. He usually identifies the kind of ceremony, its stages and action (e.g. the number of blankets given away), participants, and the place (though never the date). In these, as in most of his pictures, Hunt gives a native, Kwakwala, gloss for the action. For instance, for the father-in-law's repayment of the bride-price debt, he uses the Kwakwala term *kotexa* (or *qotexa*), not *potlatch*, derived from the regional, Chinook jargon term. Many of the preceding attributes, taken alone, also characterize the work of

94. Potlach, Alert Bay, British Columbia, 1902–5. Hunt's caption: 'Kotexa or Marriage Debt Paid by the Womans father' (to his son-in-law). (Courtesy of the American Museum of Natural History. From original negative AMNH 104463)

95. Potlach, Fort Rupert, British Columbia, 1902–5. Hunt's caption: 'Kotexa or Marreg Debt Paid by the Woman father'. (Courtesy of the American Museum of Natural History. From original negative AMNH 104473)

96. Hamatsa initiate returning from ritual seclusion in the woods, British Columbia, *c.*1902. Hunt's caption: 'Hamats!a just caught from the Bush Dressed in Hemlock Branch, Nak!waxdox tribe'. (Courtesy of the American Museum of Natural History. From copy negative AMNH 22866)

97. Hamatsa initiate being restrained by his attendants, British Columbia, *c.*1902. (Courtesy of the American Museum of Natural History. From copy negative AMNH 22858)

non-natives. It is only when considered together that they firmly stamp Hunt as a Kwakiutl photographer.

George Hunt's lifelong goal was the recording of Kwakiutl cultural history. Acutely aware of the great changes he was witnessing, he was engaged in a kind of remembrance of things past. In first urging Boas to send a camera, Hunt wrote excitedly: 'oh Mr Boas, What I have seen over there I will never see again for the Dances was showed in the Really old ways . . .' In sending his first prints, he commented: 'I think we ought to Done [it] long ago,' for it would 'make our work correct'.[30]

NOTES

This essay, a part of my ongoing research on the problem of ethnographic representation in Boasian anthropology, is an excerpt from a longer study on the Boas–Hunt relationship (cf. Jacknis 1991, 1992). It incorporates passages from the section on Hunt in my essay 'Franz Boas and Photography' (1984:8).

As far as is known, the sole repository for original George Hunt negatives is the photographic collection in the American Museum of Natural History, Dept. of Library Services, whose permission to reproduce these images is gratefully acknowledged. Unless otherwise noted, all the references are from the Franz Boas Professional Papers, held by the American Philosophical Society (APS). Letters from the American Museum of Natural History (AMNH) are in the Dept. of Anthropology.

1 S.A. Spencer was born in 1829 in New London, Connecticut, and died in 1911 in Victoria. For studio information, see Mattison 1985.
2 Perhaps not accidentally, Hastings was a former partner of S.A. Spencer and took over the studio after his retirement.
3 G. Hunt to F. Boas, February 15, 1896.
4 G. Hunt to F. Boas, March 27, 1900; G. Hunt to F. Boas, February 5, 1900, MS. no. 1927, part 3, APS.
5 F. Boas to G. Hunt, December 22, 1908, F. Boas to G.T. Emmons, January 11, 1904,

AMNH; G. Hunt to F. Boas, August 12, 1901.
6 G. Hunt to F. Boas, January 9, 1900.
7 Cf. Cole 1985:161–2. As part of their forthcoming monograph on the Nootka whalers' shrine, Richard Inglis and Aldona Jonaitis have analyzed these photos in depth. I would like to thank both of them for sharing with me their research on Hunt's photos of the shrine.
8 Other locations were the Kwakiutl sites of Xumtaspi (Hope Island), Meemkumlees (Village Island), Kolokwis (Turnour Island), Nimpkish River, as well as several unknown places.
9 F. Boas to G. Hunt, May 12, 1901. These pictures are in the Boas photograph collection, Dept. of Anthropology, AMNH.
10 G. Hunt to F. Boas, March 10, 1908.
11 F. Boas to G. Hunt, November 22, 1907.
12 G. Hunt to F. Boas, January 6, March 10, 1908.
13 G. Heye to F. Boas, December 18, 1907.
14 G. Hunt to F. Boas, May 4 and June 7, 1920.
15 Unfortunately neither the Smith nor the Goddard film survives. The Anthropological Collections Section, Royal Museum of British Columbia, has a copy of Totemland, and the Boas film is available from Audio-Visual Services, University of Washington.
16 Acc. 1924–78, AMNH.
17 G. Hunt to F. Boas, October 12,

1922, May 25, 1926, November 9, 1928.
18 F. Boas to G. Hunt, May 4, 1921.
19 G. Hunt to F. Boas, October 12, 1922.
20 F. Boas to G. Hunt, February 20, 1933; G. Hunt to F. Boas, April 6, 1933.
21 F. Boas to G. Hunt, January 13, 1930.
22 One of the best volumes on photography by Native Americans is Masayesva & Younger (1983) on the Hopi.
23 A.M. Wastell, 1955, 'Alert Bay and Vicinity, 1870–1954,' typescript, p. 20, Vancouver City Archives.
24 There is no evidence that Hunt ever got his phonograph. The thirty-seven original cylinders from the Fair were transferred from the American Museum of Natural History, where Boas had deposited them, to the Archives of Traditional Music at Indiana University.
25 G. Hunt to F. Boas, December 3, 1907.
26 For instance, still missing are Hunt's pictures of subsistence taken to illustrate Boas's BAE report. When it appeared in 1921 there were no pictures (though there were line drawings). Nor have the Hunt photos for Curtis been located.
27 The negatives and prints are in the Photographic Collection of the Department of Library Services; the original prints in the Department of Anthropology. These were attributed and documented

by a combination of sources: Hunt's negative lists in the accession files (1904-13, 1904-38, 1905-40), his handwriting on the backs of the original prints, references in Hunt's letters, notations on the backs of file prints and contextual knowledge of his subjects.

28 From the original print, Dept. of Anthropology, AMNH.

29 G. Hunt to F. Boas, April 8, 1902, AMNH Acc. 1902–46.

30 G. Hunt to F. Boas, February 15, 1896; August 12, 1901.

REFERENCES

Banta, Melissa & Hinsley, Curtis M. 1986. *From Site to Sight: Anthropology, Photography, and the Power of Imagery*. Cambridge, Mass.: Peabody Museum Press.

Blackman, Margaret B. 1976. Blankets, Bracelets, and Boas: The Potlatch in Photographs. *Anthropological Papers of the University of Alaska* 18(2):53–67.

— 1981. *Window on the Past: The Photographic Ethnohistory of the Northern and Kaigani Haida*. Canadian Ethnology Service, Mercury Series, Paper 74. Ottawa: National Museum of Man.

— 1982. 'Copying People': Northwest Coast Native Response to Early Photography. *BC Studies* 52:86–112.

Boas, Franz 1909. The Kwakiutl of Vancouver Island. *Publications of the Jesup North Pacific Expedition* 5(2): 301–522. Memoirs, American Museum of Natural History.

— 1921. Ethnology of the Kwakiutl. *35th Annual Report of the Bureau of American Ethnology*. Washington, DC.

— 1966. *Kwakiutl Ethnography*. Edited and abridged, with an introduction by Helen Codere. Chicago: University of Chicago Press.

Cannizzo, Jeanne 1983. George Hunt and the Invention of Kwakiutl Culture. *Canadian Review of Sociology and Anthropology* 20(1): 44–58.

Curtis, Edward S. 1915. The Kwakiutl. *The North American Indian*. Vol. 10. Norwood, Conn.

Fleming, Paula Richardson & Luskey, Judith 1986. *The North American Indians in Early Photographs*. New York: Harper and Row.

Holm, Bill & Quimby, George Irving 1980. *Edward S. Curtis in the Land of the War Canoes: A Pioneer Cinematographer in the Pacific Northwest*. Seattle: University of Washington Press.

Jacknis, Ira 1984. Franz Boas and Photography. *Studies in Visual Communication* 10(1):2–60.

— 1991. 'George Hunt, Collector of Indian Specimens'. In Aldona Jonaitis (ed.) *Chiefly Feasts: The Enduring Kwakiutl Potlatch*. New York: American Museum of Natural History; Seattle: University of Washington Press.

— 1992. *The Storage Box of Tradition: Museums, Anthropologists, and Kwakiutl Art, 1881–1981*. Washington, DC: Smithsonian Institution Press.

Liberty, Margot 1978. American Indians and American Anthropology. In Margot Liberty (ed.) *American Indian Intellectuals* 1–13. *1976 Proceedings of the American Ethnological Society*. St Paul: West Publishing Co.

Mark, Joan 1982. Francis La Flesche: The American Indian as Anthropologist. *Isis* 73:497–510.

Masayesva, Victor, Jr. & Younger, Erin 1983. *Hopi Photographers/Hopi Images*. Sun Tracks. Vol. 8. Tucson: University of Arizona Press.

Mattison, David 1985. *Camera Workers: The British Columbia Photographers Directory, 1858–1900*. Victoria: Camera Workers Press.

Milburn, Maureen 1986. 'Louis Shotridge and the Objects of Everlasting Esteem'. In Susan A. Kaplan and Kristin J. Barsness et al. *Raven's Journey: The World of Alaska's Native People* 54–77. Philadelphia: The University Museum, University of Pennsylvania.

Riley, Linda. (ed.) 1988. *Marius Barbeau's Photographic Collection: The Nass River*. Canadian Ethnology Service, Mercury Series, Paper 109. Hull, Quebec: Canadian Museum of Civilization.

Rohner, Ronald P. (ed.) 1969. *The Ethnography of Franz Boas: Letters and Diaries of Franz Boas Written on the Northwest Coast from 1886 to 1931*. Chicago: University of Chicago Press.

Ruby, Jay 1980. Franz Boas and Early Camera Study of Behavior. *The Kinesis Report* 3(1):6–11, 16.

Swanton, John R. 1905. Explanation of the Seattle Totem Pole. *Journal of American Folklore* 18(69):108–10.

Wyatt, Victoria. 1989. *Images from the Inside Passage: An Alaskan Portrait by Winter & Pond*. Seattle: University of Washington Press, in association with the Alaska State Library, Juneau.

The Fading of Appearances: Anthropological Observations on a Nineteenth-Century Photograph

H.L. Seneviratne

THIS PHOTOGRAPH (Plate 98) appears to depict a religiously homogeneous scene where a social group is wrapped together in common worship. Underneath this apparent unity, the beholder soon discovers a mild insurrection, the little group of three monks in the top-right corner. Thus the picture, while exhibiting a primary level of unity, also depicts underneath, a tension between a 'centre' (centre of the picture) and a 'periphery' (top-right corner). As I shall try to show, the dominant or the truly 'central' group is the one that is located peripherally in the picture. Even at first glance, significant clues present themselves. The three (peripheral) monks occupy a higher location in relation to the apparently central group. And, as if in conscious non-conformity with the central figures, they are not in worshipping posture. In the historical context the photograph depicts, the dissidents on the picture's periphery are in fact central to the territory and the monastic hierarchy of Sri Lanka. They are the establishment, and the conformists of the picture the rebels.

The scene depicted is at the Dalada Maligava, 'the Palace of the Tooth Relic' or the Temple of the Tooth, in Kandy, Sri Lanka (hereafter referred to as the Palace). Most of those squatting in the foreground are Burmese laymen. Exceptions are, first, the third person squatting from left, who is a Sinhalese peasant, identifiable by his hair style and the absence of head and upper body wear and, second, the three monks in the middle centre. The two figures standing on the left and right are clearly identifiable by their dress as Burmese laymen. All others in the picture are monks. It is difficult to distinguish whether all of them are Burmese. Many appear to be so on physiognomical criteria. A few Sinhalese monks may have joined the Burmese visitors, who were probably their guests. If so it is probable that they came from the south-western seaboard of the island which had ecclesiastical relations with Burma from about the eighteenth century. The scene depicted here also appears in J. Ferguson's *Ceylon in 1903* (1903: opp. 134) where the camera faces the south. In this picture the focus is on the south-east. One monk, possibly Burmese, slightly left of centre and at the left edge of the table, is seated apparently on a stool, and about six Burmese monks are seated on the flight of steps leading to the elevation to the right, which is the northern portion of a narrow outer corridor that surrounds the Lower Floor of the Palace. The partially framed kneeling figure in white, with a string of beads hanging from clasped palms, is indistinct in this picture, but on the basis of Ferguson's, appears to be a Burmese layman. Three monks stand on the elevated corridor, at the top of the steps, almost exactly in front of the northern door, hidden from view, of the Lower Floor. These monks

98.   Dalada Maligava — The Palace of the Tooth Relic. Photograph by C.T. Scowen? (RAI 5880)

could possibly be the three monks in attendance at daily ritual at the Palace, two at the Upper Floor and one at the Lower Floor, and who are recruited each year alternatively from Asgiriya and Malvatta, the two great monastic centres in Kandy located on either side (north and south) of the Palace. In Ferguson's picture, four more monks are standing on this elevation.

Kandy was the last seat of government of the Sinhalese monarchy, which has a history of some 2,200 years and ceased to exist with the British conquest of the Kandyan Kingdom in 1815. Within the next few decades British political and administrative dominance was consolidated and, conditions being favourable to agricultural enterprise, British entrepreneurs were attracted to open up the island for the cultivation of coffee and later, tea. Along with factual information about the possibilities for investment in the island, near-legendary ideas about the island as an exotic and fabulous place seem to have spread to Europe. Subsidiary enterprises such as facilities for tourism seem to have sprung up to cater to both the resident British population and visitors, particularly in the second half of the nineteenth century. Simultaneously, a publishing industry developed, which produced a variety of books, pamphlets and other literature describing the island. Typically, this literature provided comprehensive information on location, climate, flora and fauna, natural and man-made resources, sites of interest and so on. Photographs formed an important part of this information. The photograph discussed here is tentatively dated 1870–1900 and was sold through the Colombo Apothecaries Company, a general store which also housed a photographic studio. It seems likely that the photograph was taken by Charles T. Scowen. The Apothecaries bought up Scowen's stock in the 1890s and subsequently sold it under their own name. However, it is possible that this picture is by an Apothecaries photographer, but if it is indeed Scowen's its date is conceivably closer to 1870 than to 1900, a conjecture supported by the fact that the print is on albumen paper.

The Tooth Relic itself was held in great veneration throughout history: it was the palladium of the

Sinhalese kings and as it was considered mystically powerful its proper custody and care was considered an indispensable duty of the state. One manifestation of this was the extreme security that surrounded the Relic and the rarity of its public exposition. The security measures at the Palace and the reluctance to expose the Relic to frequent public view found a parallel in the spatial arrangements of the Palace: it was housed in the least accessible and innermost chamber of the Upper Floor, and a series of reliquaries of decreasing size constituted its dwelling. The arrangements and ritual that attended public expositions of the Relic further expressed these concerns.

Such expositions were very rare. They were held, perhaps at intervals of some years, out of a sense of public duty, to enable the accumulation of merit by ordinary people, or when considered necessary, such as during a period of prolonged drought. There were also special expositions occasioned by the visit of a distinguished guest, typically royalty, such as the 1875 visit of the Prince of Wales (*The Graphic*, 1876:27). The preference for special expositions for the benefit of visiting royalty was no accident. It is in keeping with the immemorial associations of the Relic with sovereign power.

Expositions were not alone in being attended by considerable ritual and ceremonial. In fact all relations with the Relic are marked by formal behaviour as the daily ritual illustrates. Although it is commonly believed that the Relic is borne in procession during the Äsala (June-July) pageant, what is in fact taken is only a substitute reliquary which probably contains some other relics. This further illustrates the solemnity with which the Tooth Relic is treated and the great reluctance to move it out of its Sanctum. During an exposition, under all normal circumstances, the Relic is moved no further than just across its ante-room to an area that opens out into the public space of the Upper Floor.

We can now focus more closely on our photograph, because it appears to depict an exposition of the Relic. On the table we see the characteristic view of the Relic during an exposition, resting a few inches over a lotus blossom, in all likelihood made of precious metal, held by a thread-like precious-metal support. On either side are reliquaries, the one on the left smaller than the one on the right, which therefore must be the outer of the two. (The Relic is believed to be enshrined in the seventh of a series of reliquaries of decreasing size, each bigger one enclosing the one immediately smaller.) The central figures in the picture strike a piously worshipful posture characteristic of devotees in the presence of the Tooth Relic. Despite these

appearances, however, there are several features both present and absent in the picture which make it doubtful that it depicts an exposition of the genuine Tooth Relic.

First, as already noted, great solemnity is observed in the form of customary observances in any matter relating to the Tooth Relic. This is so even in the daily ritual when there is no need to move the Relic from its dwelling. When it is pretended that the Relic is moved (during the Äsala pageant) there is greater than usual ritual attendance on even the substitute reliquary. It hardly needs to be emphasized that when the Relic is in fact moved and taken out of its sevenfold abode, and exposed to the gaze, though reverent, of diverse strata, ritual and ceremonial attendance would be considered indispensable. In this picture we see no evidence of even a trace of such ritual—no drummers, singers, minstrels, torch bearers, lay custodians or monks in attendance.

Second, the table on which the objects are placed in this picture is bare of all but one piece of white (embroidered?) cloth that serves as a table cloth. In a genuine exposition, more elaborate material must distinguish the surface on which the Relic is placed and several layers of costly and colourful cloth, cushions and so on enhance the appropriateness of that surface to accommodate so sacred an occupant. Trayfuls of flowers, heaps of loose flowers (typically the culturally valued and symbolic jasmines, lotuses and the like) crowd the surface of the table in a genuine exposition, and attending monks can sometimes be seen reverently and gently throwing flowers towards the Relic. This picture is denuded of all these.

Third, as we know, during an exposition the Relic is not moved beyond the public area of the Upper Floor. The present scene, however, takes place on the Lower Floor. 'Upper' and 'Lower' in Kandyan categories have symbolic meanings. For example, the Upper Floor of the Palace is served only by the ritually pure upper-caste functionaries. The Relic is never brought down to the Lower Floor for a public exposition (what is taken out in the pageant is not the Tooth Relic but a substitute reliquary). Moreover, the location depicted in this picture is not even the Lower Floor, but the roofless Inner Courtyard of the Temple. It is inconceivable that the Tooth Relic should be ceremonially conducted outside to an unroofed area without elaborate canopies being held over it, none of which we see in this picture. In the nineteenth century, when expositions were held in the Great Courtyard in front of the Palace, such canopies formed part of the temporary structures built to house the ceremonial, and even today, when the substitute reliquary is taken out in the Äsala pageant, the canopy over it constitutes an invariable item of the proceedings.

Fourth, the picture shows three Sri Lankan monks who, as already suggested, are possibly the three attending monks. During all times when monks are in formal attendance or in formal ritual performance, they are dressed in the full formal attire of an ordained monk. This consists of three robes (the 'single fold robe', the 'double fold robe' and the 'wearing robe') and a 'belt', which is a broad piece of cloth (a sash) worn high above the waist over the main outer robe. The three monks in the picture are not at all in such attire and actually look quite casually dressed. Their expression is also one of casualness verging on amusement or inquisitiveness and it appears as if they are present only out of a courteous condescension at an occasion they rather would not attend. This is in sharp contrast to the rapt devotion of the worshippers below. Moreover, as already observed, these three monks are standing on an elevation. This violates the upper/lower rule which would scarcely be unobserved in the presence of the real Tooth Relic. Indeed it is tempting to see a resemblance between the relative positions occupied by these monks and the worshippers in the courtyard, and the ritual closing of the Palace for the night when the three monks stand on a similar elevation on the west side of the outer corridor with lay functionaries occupying lower elevations. In that posture the monks are daily expressing their status superiority over the lay functionaries. Thus it appears that in this occupancy of a higher elevation by the Sri Lankan (Kandyan) monks, there is a shadow of superiority.

On further reflection it appears that the monks are a group apart, relatively passive participants who play no integral part in the activity taking place in the centre of the picture. Neither the position the three monks occupy nor their expression would be acceptable had the Relic shown here been the genuine Tooth Relic. One could say that in a purely formal sense, the Relic shown here is unattended just as it is unattended by the material and ritual accoutrements that usually surround the public presence of the Relic. For this reason we can further doubt the genuineness of the Relic shown here, for the real Tooth Relic is always attended when it is in social relation with the outside.

The reader might wonder why the worshippers around the Relic are not considered here as being in attendance. This is precisely because they are worshippers. The Tooth Relic is worshipped in two ways. First, there is the official worship instituted by the king and paid for by the state. Worshippers who perform acts of worship in this category are employees of the state who consider what they do to be 'work' and not 'worship'. They are religious functionaries who are performing a function they are contractually obliged to perform, namely functions in the daily and cyclical rituals. Their functions alone constitute formal attendance on the Relic. The second type of worshipper is quite different. They are true worshippers who worship the Relic out of devotion and for the gaining of merit. Such devotees are not part of an organized cult but are individual worshippers moved by religiosity. The worshippers in this picture are of this second type and therefore not in attendance. The genuine Tooth Relic, in its societal relation, is never unattended. Thus the Relic shown here, despite the presence of about forty people, is formally alone, and therefore is unlikely to be the genuine Tooth Relic.

What, then, could this photograph possibly represent? For an answer we might consider some relevant aspects of Buddhism in the island at the time. In particular we might focus on the Sangha, the monastic order. In keeping with a practice of religious exchange that had developed between the three Theravade countries, Burma, Thailand and Sri Lanka, since about the twelfth century, each had been borrowing monks, doctrine, and ordination from one or both of the others to restore or revitalize the religion perceived as being in decline. The last of such borrowings under state patronage in Sri Lanka was the importing of ordination during the reign of Kirti Sri Rajasingha (1747–82). As the British government was non-Buddhist, any exchanges after 1815 had to be done on private initiative. The monastic revival that followed Kirti Sri Rajasingha's attempts overflowed the boundaries of the Kandyan Kingdom and exerted considerable influence on the southern maritime provinces which were under Dutch control. However, the monks in these provinces, dissatisfied with the caste-exclusive ordination policies of the Kandyan monastic hierarchy, entered into a series of ordinational relations with several monastic centres in Burma. Thus Burma looms large in the religious history of nineteenth-century Sri Lanka. With the greater availability of overseas travel facilitated by the European commercial presence in the south Asian seas, it is possible that prosperous Buddhists travelled to other Buddhist lands for religious and quasi-religious purposes. Travels of this type are an old tradition as exemplified by such travellers as Fa-Hien and Hiuen Tsiang. It is possible that such religious travellers took with them symbols of their religiosity as gifts to persons, groups or the state in the country visited. Typically, such gifts were representations of the Three Jewels of Buddhism — the Buddha, Dhamma (Doctrine) and Sangha. Thus the guests from Thailand who brought ordination to Sri Lanka during the reign of Kirti Sri Rajasingha brought along with them a golden Buddha statue and sacred books.

A particularly suitable and diplomatic gift that visitors to Sri Lanka from another Buddhist land could bring would be a replica of the Tooth Relic — a symbol of the esteem in which their own country held the Relic. This is possibly what the Burmese visitors shown here have done. The fact that the larger reliquary in the picture is stylistically more Burmese than Sri Lankan lends support to this hypothesis. It might also be mentioned that in the 1950s a Chinese Tooth Relic was brought to Sri Lanka on a temporary sojourn, which confers on the practice of bringing replicas a measure of conventionality and continuity.[1]

Visual records are an unusually valuable ethnographic resource, and all the more so when they show the people or items in question during periods of rapid social change. In this sense this picture is of more than mere antiquarian interest. While the main building visible in the picture in its right is the oldest part of the present Palace, the picture gives us a glimpse of the surrounding building (the white structure in the background), which has since been replaced by a new building. It must be said that pictorial documentation of this part of the Palace, which no longer exists, is found in other sources too, such as the various guide books published at the time. But this fact does not detract from the value of the present documentation. One might note in passing that the Palace lights at the time the picture was taken were the glass lamps that are seen hanging from the ceiling. Pictures that can be dated a few years later do not show these lamps and possibly signify the advent of electricity.

Clearly the picture was available for purchase by tourists and other foreigners. But it is unlikely that it was made for this purpose. Whether it was taken by Scowen or another photographer, we can only make suggestions as to who commissioned the photograph. Did the photographer just happen to be at the Palace when the Burmese visitors arrived? Or was the event known beforehand and a professional photographer sought to 'cover' it? As the picture shows singular lack of enthusiasm on the part of the Palace authorities, lay as well as monastic, it is unlikely that they were informed beforehand by the photographer, or he asked their permission. In fact, since the focus is on the Burmese visitors, it is likely that someone may have been interested in them and their mission. That interested party may have been an individual such as the photographer or a group such as the photographer's employers, or more likely, a group of Buddhists known to or associated with the Burmese visitors. Or the Burmese on their own may have been interested in a photograph for purposes of record and distribution among devotees and friends, or even in the service of furthering a sectarian cause. Alter-natively, the photographer, the Burmese and possibly local Buddhists may all have had a common interest in taking the photograph. For the photographer it is likely that the scene was yet another exotic one suitable for largely European consumption. The occasion of the picture thus represents a variety of possibilities, the more so for want of precise information.[2]

One among these possibilities can be selected for brief yet special comment, considering the background of religious and social history of the period. Broadly, this background consists of the significance of Kandy to the southern maritime provinces. As already mentioned, owing to the religious revival of Kirti Sri Rajasingha, there was a renaissance of religion and culture outside the Kandyan Kingdom and in particular in those provinces. But, because of the caste exclusiveness of the Kandyan monastic hierarchy, the southern monks also harboured a hostility to Kandy. On the secular scene there were analogous developments. Kandyan élites considered themselves superior to their more dynamic and often wealthier counterparts of the south. For their part the latter considered themselves more advanced while secretly admiring the glamour of Kandyan institutions among which the Palace was one of the foremost. Consequently they sometimes tried to establish affinities with Kandy, a process that goes on even in modern politics. Thus against a background of mutual ambivalence on the part of Kandy and the maritime south, the latter has also been attempting to rub shoulders with the former and establish links, which were often rebuffed. The present photograph seems to fit rather well into this pattern of relations. In seeking ordination from Burma in defiance of Kandyan monastic authority the monks of the southern seaboard made a break with the Kandyan establishment. But to the monks of the maritime south, as to the laity of that region, Kandy still represented the continuity of ancient tradition, and therefore constituted a source of envy. What remains of the last palace of the Sinhalese kings is located in Kandy and in it linger the memories of the union between Sangha and king idealized in the chronicles composed in its cloisters. Above all the Palace was the contemporary representation of that union, with the monks and modern lay authorities (survivors of the king) jointly holding in trust the custody of the Relic. Since the Burmese visitors most likely had some connection with one or other of the southern monastic groups established on the basis of Burmese ordination, it is possible that this photograph represents one more attempt on the part of the southern monks and their powerful lay supporters to establish a connection, however vicarious or symbolic, with Kandy, and with the Palace.

From such a perspective, the apparent anomalies of the present picture appear in a more understandable light. The Burmese monks and their local allies are admitted to the Palace premises, but allocated space outside the strictly respectable boundaries. The absence of any high-status Kandyan lay official enhances this left-handed treatment, because as a rule foreign dignitaries with credentials acceptable to the Kandyan authorities are never welcomed to the Palace without considerable fanfare. It is striking that in this picture some monks are squatting and others seated on steps, two sedentary postures entirely unacceptable, especially on a ceremonial occasion, to Sri Lankan ideas of monastic decorum. It is even more striking that the monk at the left edge of the table is sitting on a stool. The fact that he is sitting probably signifies that he is a senior monk, if not the most senior, among the visitors. But the fact that his seat is a stool, and that other apparently senior monks are standing, are indignities for in Kandyan custom even junior monks are on all ceremonial occasions made to sit decorously on chairs or cushions, covered with freshly laundered white cloth. In this instance none of these courtesies is observed and a good reason is that, from the point of view of the Kandyan monastic hierarchy, the Burmese are the allies of their caste inferiors. Ideologically,

however, visiting monks, especially those from another Theravade country, must be shown a minimum of formal courtesy. Hence the apparent participation of the Kandyan monks in the ceremony.

When we consider the possibility of a dissonance of this sort the postures struck by the monks on the elevation make sense too, as do other anomalies already discussed. For, as already mentioned, the three monks in the picture seem uninvolved and unconcerned with the devotion that is in abundance in front of their eyes. The monk on the right is leaning against a pillar, a casual if not disrespectful posture, totally unsuited to a ceremonial occasion. Though indistinct, the second figure from left appears inquisitive, surprised or amused and the third from left, perhaps the most senior, appears to exhibit a detached tolerance. They are not even expressing the most elementary gesture of worship — clasping of palms. In Ferguson's picture with four additional monks, all appear to be more decorous but give the distinct impression of being aloof and detached. They just stand there, like a phenomenon *sui generis*. Their posture seems to yoke together a cooperation they cannot deny and a patronization they cannot withhold. Clearly something is wrong, and at present we can only make the kind of guess outlined above.

I wish to thank Michael Carrithers, Elizabeth Nissan and Elizabeth Edwards for their valuable comments. Fiona Stewart provided historical and other background information and made perceptive suggestions at every stage of the essay's progress. Without her assistance it would have been much poorer and I am deeply grateful to her. I wish to thank also Dr Nissanka Wijeratne, Diyavadana Nilame of the Palace of the Tooth Relic, for his courteous and useful response to Fiona Stewart's initial enquiry.

NOTES

1 With better access to sources than I have in Charlottesville, Virginia, this hypothesis can be verified. Ample records exist for this period — newspapers, books, letters, official records and so on — in Sri Lanka and, one would suppose, in some quantity in England too. Since recruitment to ritual service at the Palace is exclusively made from the Asgiriya and Malvatta monasteries, and since these monasteries have good records of their scholastic ancestry which often include photographs, it is likely that the Sri Lankan monks in this picture are identifiable. It is equally likely that the present-day monks who are the pupillary successors of these monks, and other contemporary monks as well who are acquainted with the relevant 'ordination lineages', could provide information leading to more precise identification of the picture.

2 Comparison of the detail in this with that in Ferguson's *Ceylon in 1903* suggests that the pilgrims were photographed twice, either in the same session or on two different but similar occasions, or that the two pictures show two sets of pilgrims visiting within a fairly short time of one another. A number of figures appear in both photographs, notably the monks, who strike remarkably similar attitudes. But this is more than a straightforward shift in camera angle. The axis of the whole group is different and the table with the religious objects is likewise at a different angle (in both photographs they are on a plane parallel with the camera). This conundrum is, on presently available evidence, insoluble, but nevertheless both photographic occasions occurred within a framework of religiosity, and even an element of positioning or reconstruction by the photographer (possibly in response to technical demands) does not necessarily remove the picture from the realm of the religious for the worshippers themselves.

REFERENCES

Ferguson, John 1903. *Ceylon in 1903 . . . with useful statistical information; a map of the island, and upwards of one hundred illustrations*. Colombo: A.M. and J. Ferguson.
The Graphic, January 8, 1876. London.

Focal Length as an Analogue of Cultural Distance[1]

Martha Macintyre and
Maureen MacKenzie

MANY OF THE BRITISH who recorded their first encounter with Papuan people remarked on their strange and uncivilized customs of greeting. British sensibilities were often affronted as a Papuan grasped the visitor's nostrils and probed his navel (Moresby 1875:166–7). Not one reciprocated this salute, nor did any enquire as to its meaning. The Papuans were asserting their recognition of the stranger as a fellow human being, one who breathed the same air and was born in the same way as themselves. In their own way British observers were intrigued by the humanity of the indigenous peoples of Papua and New Guinea, but their interest was in difference, and they maintained an appropriately civil distance from the subjects of their enquiry. In many respects the use of the camera, imposed as it is between the British observer and Papuan subject, epitomizes the social and cultural distance, and similarly the range of photographic genres, from observational panorama through to the intimacy of close-up portraiture, reflects much of the relations between photographer and subject.

The Europeans who went to Papua and British New Guinea in the early twentieth century were mainly administrators, missionaries, traders and miners. The region was not considered desirable as a place for settlement and the European expatriate community was small by comparison with other colonies. Those who went were usually educated middle-class men, inspired not only by the ideals of Empire and evangelism but also by an intellectual curiosity that was fuelled by contemporary academic preoccupations. Anthropologists followed the tracks cleared by these men and confined their studies to those regions that had some mission influence or colonial presence (Young 1984:7).[2] In the period up to 1920 these were the coastal and insular regions of Papua.[3]

Eminent photographers such as Captain Frank Hurley, J.W. Lindt and G. Landtman produced volumes of their work in Papua (Hurley 1924; Lindt 1887; Landtman 1927). But almost all Europeans used the camera as one of their tools to describe, document and inform the public at home about the life and customs in this remote part of the world. They selected their photographic subjects with the disciplined eclecticism of contemporary ethnologists. All facets of life fell within their purview, and yet a glance through any substantial photographic collection reveals their adherence to ethnological taxonomic classifications that divided their worlds by human physical type, technology, material culture, clothing and body decoration, architecture, weaponry, rituals and recreations.

While similarities of theme and subject abound, the pictures of Papuan life presented by different

99.   Guests dancing into the village enclosure at a funeral feast, Amala, 1910. Photograph by R.M. Williamson. (RAI 24861)

photographers reveal considerable variation in intention, aesthetic vision and technical competence. R.M. Williamson was a traveller and amateur anthropologist who went to Papua to fulfil a lifelong ambition to 'see something of savage life' (1922:xvii). His visit to Papua was brief, from April to July 1910, but in that time he travelled west of Port Moresby, along the coast and hinterland, in the adventurous style of those colonial explorers he so admired. He approached the Mekeo, Kuni and Mafulu (now Goilala) people as a detached, rather than a participant, observer concerned to document their vanishing customs. For him the camera became a scientific instrument, encapsulating vistas, preserving events and providing a detailed record of people and place. His visual overview captured the excitement and spectacle of first encounter. Committed to an ideal of scientific veracity, he eschewed the use of backdrops or the relocation of subjects in striking surroundings, portraying people always in the context of their social and physical environment. He did not encourage or elicit performance in any way, but set himself apart from and outside of the action to record events as they occurred. In the service of scientific enquiry he sought to record the truth of Papuan existence in the actuality observed

and preserved through his lens. Williamson employed only the skilled use of photographic technology, his choice of camera angle and focal length, to shape the moment, while his sole conscious intervention in the creation of the image was to stop the action for the length of his time exposure.

Williamson's photograph (Plate 99) of guests dancing into the Amala village enclosure, inaugurating a funeral feast, epitomizes the aspect of his 'observational'[4] approach to photographic documentation that might be described as the grand sweep. Viewed through his remote and still lens, the village vistas convey his sense of wonder but also his lack of social relations with the subjects. The panoramic scope created by his distant and unobtrusive vantage point emphasizes the emptiness and openness of the Amala enclosure, abandoned by its residents for this stage of the mortuary rite. Thus the composition of his picture creates an air of expectancy, inviting the observer to anticipate the progress of events as the dancers sweep down the length of the village towards the focus of their procession, and his lens, the grave.

As external observers we are the spectators, but not in the same sense as the indigenous spectators, the hosts, who sit on the raised platform of the men's house watching the entire performance from the top and centre of the village clearing. We are able, by Williamson's technical competency in achieving an extended depth of field, to look inwards, up the length of the village. The physical distance from the participants becomes a direct analogue of the other cultural gap between photographer and subject. For, as in all his photographs concerned with the representation of an event, there is no recognition of the photographer's presence. The distance between participant and observer is apparently unmediated.

The large cultural distance that existed between many colonial photographers and their Papuan subjects is integral to the genre of panoramic photography that Williamson favoured. His distal viewpoint, combined with his stopping down the aperture to ensure sharp focus throughout, his sensitive framing and his appropriate selection of the dramatic moment, enabled him to control the aesthetic of the grand sweep. In these panoramic images Williamson attained a narrative quality, managing to create the implication of further action within a medium which ordinarily simply arrests time.

Williamson approached social action, human subjects and material culture in the same mode, so that all were re-presented through his lens as exotic artefacts. When he set the tripod closer his effect is less successful, for in the genre of portraiture his lack of rapport with the people restricted his control over the elements captured in the image. In his close-ups we are confronted by Papuan awareness of his outsider status. A young man glowers or a child gapes as if intimidated or frightened by the stranger behind the camera. His subjects' expressions of discomfort and suspicion are at odds with what we expect from late-nineteenth-century portraiture, with its emphasis on the pleasing image of composure and dignity. Viewed from the vantage point of modern modes of portraiture and the concern for reflexivity in ethnographic representations, Williamson's portraits speak to modern preoccupations with 'otherness'. For now those same truculent stares and baffled sidelong glances are being purposely captured by photographers concerned to raise questions about the whole history of culture contact.[5] The expressions of anger or mistrust become pictorial analogues of the aggression between cultures, and the resentment of colonized subject to anthropological scrutiny. The confrontational gaze of Williamson's reluctant subjects mirrors the cultural gap between them and this fleeting visitor. Williamson's photographs are the stranger's view of the unfamiliar.

Reverend Harold Dauncey (1863–1919), a missionary with the London Missionary Society, worked among Motuan people in Delena from 1897 to 1907. He too exploited photography as a means of accurately recording the alien world of Papua, but for a different audience. While a few of his photographs were published (Dauncey 1913; Seligman 1910), most were aimed at depicting the changing way of life at Delena. Pictures of beplumed and decorated people were implicitly contrasted with those of mission converts in calico. Whereas Williamson's scientific aims led him into a romantic representational style with the untouched savage dynamic traditional events as its theme, Dauncey's snapshot approach had a subtly moral purpose and captured ideas extraneous to the image itself. Dauncey with his assumed superiority wanted to transform his savages into Christians, to document the process of conversion, not the process of traditional life. His pictures, many of which were made into postcards for fund-raising, reveal both the task ahead and the victories won. However, unlike many of his fellow missionaries, Dauncey refrained from making the melodramatic criticisms that are explicit in the work of fundamentalist evangelists such as Bromilow (1927). While Dauncey's overall choice of subject-matter creates a moral distance discernible within the entirety of his work, there is a warmth in the construction of each individual depiction of village life that conveys his empathic and physical proximity.

Dauncey's familiarity with the Delena people allowed him to enter a village unobtrusively and to photograph at close range without disturbing his subjects. A potter could continue to coil her clay, a man mend his nets and children remain engrossed in their games as he moved on the narrow pathways between houses, capturing their activities on photographic plates. He worked within a framework of shared space and shared humanity. The familiarity engenders an intimacy of the ethnographic situation which is implicit in the engaging gaze of the people of Delena.

Dauncey's photograph of two young women grooming portrays one such moment of intimacy (Plate 100). This candid image of camaraderie as one woman delouses another epitomizes the snapshot quality of his work. Dauncey shows little concern for the aesthetic framing of shots, and a shadow obtrudes across the foreground as he focuses on the two women. Nor does he control background detail. Rather, the legs of a third woman ascending the steps to her home serve to stress the quotidian nature of the scene.

Dauncey's 'behind the scenes' photographs document the customs and habits of aspects of Papuan life that could have been readily perceived by the audiences of nineteenth-century England as savage and

100. Two women grooming, Delena. Photograph by Revd H. Dauncey. (RAI 34348)

101. Two women grooming, Hanuabada? Photograph by F.W. Barton. (RAI 20311)

uncivilized. His observational approach emphasizes the disparity between the cultures of the observer and the observed. In striking contrast to this naturalism of Dauncey, the photographic eye of Captain F.R. Barton (1865–1945) manipulates the same ethnographic subject, transforming two Papuan women sitting in the dust into exotic maidens secluded in an idyllic setting (Plate 101). Barton creates an inviting vignette by importing particular conventions of female representation from the Western aesthetic tradition to re-present the scene. Freshly decorated for Barton's camera, with frangipanis in their hair, aromatic native mint in their armlets and crisp, clean grass skirts, the delouser becomes a coiffeuse while her companion sits coyly aware of her centrality. As an ethnographic text Barton's photograph, with its soft-focus background marginalizing context, is less informative than Dauncey's. Barton's ethnographic focus is the detail of facial tattoo, carefully highlighted by the angled and uplifted position of the girl's head. No moralizing attends Barton's image. What is implied is the slightly titillated immorality of the voyeur. Barton's photographs reveal a response to the girls that Reverend Dauncey most certainly would not have shared.

Barton was a colonial administrator, educated in the Victorian and Classical high-art traditions, who had a passion for photography as an art form, and a peripheral anthropological interest. Based in Port Moresby, he was a familiar figure in the satellite village of Hanuabada where he staged many of his photographs. In contrast to Williamson, the itinerant traveller, and Dauncey, the missionary, Barton, a government administrator, was perhaps in a position to exert considerable control over the indigenous Papuans.[6] The full corpus of Barton's photographs show the many ways in which he manipulated and posed his subjects to convey his own idiosyncratic interpretations of their culture.

Barton used his social position as Governor in conjunction with aesthetic and technical skills to exploit the photographic medium, commanding images through careful control of lighting, depth of field, composition, posture and expression. Ignoring the recommendations of his contemporary Portman (1896:85) that flat, diffuse lighting is most appropriate for anthropological photography, he frequently employed side lighting for dramatic effect. Barton minimized extraneous visual elements, removing his subjects from naturalistic contexts and placing them in picturesque settings that enhance the lyrical mood. Rhythmic tangles of mangrove roots, dappled light on coral shores, or rippling reflections on shallow tidal flats provide the subtle settings for his pictures.

102. Motu girl paddling a canoe. Photograph by F.W. Barton. (RAI 20535)

His series of photographs illustrating tattooing in south-east Papua New Guinea reflect his 'directorial' approach. They are almost all of young women in staged tableaux. The tattooed area of the body is usually highlighted or centrally positioned, yet one is aware that Barton was exploring the medium to create aesthetic as well as scientific statements. Moving beyond the scientifically defined boundaries of anthropological study, Barton directed his compositions according to late-nineteenth-century high-art traditions. The girls become artist's models, choreographed by Barton to emulate the postures of Hellenic sculptures. Yet Barton's focus is not the pure contemplation of aesthetic form. His vision is a parody of Classicism, for his images conjure exotic sexuality and the tropical fantasy that was such a part of the Western and colonial vision. The young Papuans become Oriental odalisques, their sexual attractiveness being cloaked in the Edwardian high-art genre. The focus on tattooing enhances sexuality, both for the Western intruder and in the ethnographic reality. Tattooing for Motuan people was associated with feminine attraction, fertility and marriageability. The patterns that decorated a girl's thighs, buttocks and pudenda were on public view only during the initiation ceremony, and thereafter were seen exclusively by her husband. These tattoos were simultaneously the focal point of female sexuality and shame. The attitude to nudity that is an essential aspect of Barton's pictures would not merely have affronted Papuan propriety, but would have constituted an entirely alien ideal of beauty. Where nakedness is commonplace, adornment is the crucial expression of beauty. Barton exploited his young subjects' love of adornment to make them feel at ease, and to share, apparently with complicit enjoyment, his representations of the grooming, the water carrier and the reclining beauty.

In his explorations of the aesthetic fringe of the erotic postcard genre Barton did sometimes succeed in moving images beyond the sexual kitsch to work as an aesthetic expression in their own right. His photograph of the nubile canoe paddler (Plate 102) concentrates attention on the illuminated tattooed lower abdomen, mirroring its exotic texture in the dappled, still, tropical water, while echoing the patterning of both in the receding blurriness of the mangroves. Barton's presence is projected into every dimension of the image. The distance between the subject and himself is almost measurable as she gazes directly back into the central eye of the lens. Her stare denies the possibility of her being taken as a sexual object; she meets him and us on an equal footing. The capturing of this moment in combination with the carefully controlled setting allows Barton to express successfully an aesthetic vision of his idealized fantasy.

Some of Barton's photographs were obviously taken with the express purpose of illustrating his ethnographic texts. He stood people on boxes against backdrops to ensure a uniformly blank background; he arranged frontal and profile views within the same frame; he touched up tattoos with lampblack to exaggerate contrast and he directed tableaux in which displayed items of material culture are juxtaposed with staged social action. Yet the substance of his work reveals the preoccupation with photography *per se*, of using young people's body forms, which were synonymous with the contemporary pre-Realism notions of high art, to create pleasurable images. It is as though his anthropological interest was but a means for him to achieve his major goal — the creation of photographic artworks. When producing photographs within his published articles he frequently cropped the original image so as to exclude the lyrical elements (such as the source of diffuse lighting) and so shift focus to the ethnographic detail (Barton 1918). The clarity and perfection demanded by scientific reference are technical achievements embedded within his singular aesthetically dominated vision.

The difference in cultural distance between colonial photographer and Papuan subject discernible in the photographic image reflects both the range of photographic genres and the varying degrees of control exerted by those behind the lens. The experiences, the motivations and the social positions of the photographers are intrinsic to the images. Williamson had the technical skills to control panoramic shots, but could not achieve the subtle intimacy engendered by Dauncey's physical proximity. Only Barton, as administrator, chose to exercise authority and to direct shots, so that while Williamson and Dauncey excluded themselves from the scene to preserve the image of what was there at that moment, Barton actually created the world in which he directed his subjects.

As so many photographed the people of Papua and New Guinea during this period, it is impossible to claim these three as typical, or even representative. However, their photographs do provide a range of views from which we can discern both the extraordinary cultural diversity that they sought to represent and the variety of perspectives that derive from the culture of the colonial photographers.

NOTES

1 We wish to thank Dr Luke Taylor for his incisive comments on an earlier draft of this paper.

2 Young (1984) discusses the ways in which anthropologists selected fieldwork sites close by mission stations.

3 The preface to C.G. Seligman's *The Melanesians of British New Guinea* (1910) indicates not only his close association with missionaries and administrators but also his dependence on ethnographic, linguistic and photographic data that they had collected.

4 The term 'observational' is discussed at length by McDougall (1975:109–24).

5 For example in the portraits of Western Australian Aborigines by Nicholas Adler (1988).

6 Barton's influence over the Papuan villagers is evidenced in the correspondence between the missionary W.G. Lawes and Attlee Hunt, Secretary for External Affairs between 1897 and 1906. Lawes was affronted by the fact that while the mission at Votorata had managed to ban many Motuan customs because of their sexual connotations, Barton was organizing the restaging of ceremonies. 'An invitation from the Governor to the natives,' Lawes wrote, 'is looked upon as a command and treated accordingly.' (*LMS Correspondence*, Box 11, April 11, 1905).

REFERENCES

Adler, Nicholas 1988. *Portraits from an uninhabited land.* Sydney: Bantam Press.

Barton, F.R. 1918. Tattooing in South-Eastern New Guinea. *Journal of the Royal Anthropological Institute* 48:22–79.

Bromilow, William 1927. *Twenty Years among Primitive Papuans.* London: Epworth Press.

Dauncey, H.M. 1913. *Papuan Pictures.* London: London Missionary Society.

Hockings, Paul (ed.) 1975. *Principles of Visual Anthropology.* The Hague: Mouton.

Hurley, Frank 1924. *Pearls and Savages: adventures in the air on land and sea in New Guinea.* New York and London: G.P. Putman & Sons.

Landtman, G. 1927. *The Kiwai Papuans of British New Guinea: a native-born instance of Rousseau's ideal community with an introduction by A.C. Haddon.* London: Macmillan & Co.

Lindt, J.W. 1887. *Picturesque New Guinea, with an introduction and supplementary chapters on the manner and customs of Papuans.* London: Longmans Green & Co.

McDougall, D. 1975. 'Beyond Observational Cinema'. In Hockings, P. (ed.) *Principles of Visual Anthropology* 109–24. The Hague: Mouton.

Moresby, John 1875. Discoveries in Eastern New Guinea by Captain Moresby and the officers of H.M.S. Basilisk. *Journal of the Royal Geographical Society* 45:153–70.

Portman, M.V. 1896. Photography for Anthropologists. *Journal of the Anthropological Institute* 25:75–87.

Seligman, C.G. 1910. *The Melanesians of British New Guinea.* Cambridge: University Press.

Williamson, R.M. 1922. *The Mafulu Mountain People of British New Guinea.* London: Macmillan & Co.

Young, M.W. 1984. The intensive study of a restricted area, or why did Malinowski go to the Trobriand Islands? *Oceania,* 55(1): 1–26.

Underneath the Banyan Tree: William Crooke and Photographic Depictions of Caste

Christopher Pinney

THIS ESSAY CONCERNS A MOMENT in the photographing of the Indian Empire. If it is true, however, that most Western knowledge, and particularly anthropological knowledge, is predicated on the primacy of sight and its associated metaphors then the argument here has resonances beyond the history of photography in India alone.

The Algerian poet Malek Alloula has argued that colonialism could not tolerate invisibility. When the women of Algeria created a leucoma in the eye of the colonial photographer with their veils, this visual medium was harnessed to their stripping — the rendering visible of the colonized body in an orchestrated and public revelation played out across the surface of a million postcards (Alloula 1987:7).

A consideration of colonial photography in India from 1860 to 1890, however, casts a rather different light and suggests a different dynamic at work. In much of the archive created in India there is this apparent drive for visibility at every point, a process of unravelling which reasserts a desire to maintain distance and difference. In the example discussed here this consists of *making the potentially knowable dark at every turn*, a process which renders darkness increasingly visible and the object of colonial scrutiny correspondingly invisible.

Visibility and the ever-present possibility of its refusal by the objects of photography was, it is true, a vital component in the constitution of photographic truth. Thus the unwillingness of those depicted in photographs to be so pictured is often adduced as a proof of both its power and its objectivity (nothing could stop the logic and rightness of this vision). This emerged as a common theme in European and American prison photography. Resistance became the subject of genre photography in the United States, such as an 1880s image; 'Photographing a Female Crook', in which police struggle with the hideously contorted form of a felon who struggles through physiognomic distortion to elude the acquisitive and coercive power of the camera (Stange 1989:28, Fig. 1.17).

Photographic certainty involves the imposition of light over darkness, the triumph of statis over flux, of eternity over temporality, of presence over shifting webs of uncontrollable meanings, the penetration of the previously inscrutable, the readability of the previously illegible. This was, and continues to be, its mythic and ontological justification. However, as I have argued following Eco (1982) and Tagg (1988) (see Pinney, this volume), we might also see this certainty as an effect, a fleeting effect, produced by images by virtue of their membership within a wider corpus of images in which meaning is dependent on insertion within a network of other signifying practices, rather than on the formal properties of the individual image.

Here, in the context of photography in India, we can see that this meaning was unstable and subject to fracture, not only within photography as an institutional practice but also within single images, which always finally affirm a great deal less than they promise. In India in particular we may trace areas of blankness, sites of life-giving darkness which agitate dead museum exhibits and photographic objects in a manner that serves to place them beyond the explanatory powers of the dominant society.

Sergeant Wallace and William Crooke

The specific site on which we will trace this process in operation is a photograph of two Chamars by one Sergeant Wallace of the Royal Engineers. Within the RAI archive it exists as a large albumen print, grouped together with nine similar images. Within the published record of colonial India it exists as an illustration for the entry on 'Chamars' in William Crooke's *Tribes and Castes of the North-Western Provinces and Oudh*, published in four volumes in 1896. Other similar images by Wallace (about whom almost nothing is known) appear as illustrations to J.D. Anderson's *The Peoples of India* (1913), and a set of images printed to a similar size are in the Haddon photographic collection in the University of Cambridge Museum of Archaeology and Anthropology. Taken together, these images in archives and publications suggest that Wallace was attempting to document different tribal and caste groups in Mirzapur District, Oudh (now Uttar Pradesh). His photographic studies of representatives of groups ranging from Brahmans and Kayasthas to Chamars, Bhangis, Banjaras and Kols, are clearly part of a well-established colonial preoccupation with the systematic recording and arrangement of what became known as 'the peoples of India' who, by the 1880s and 1890s when these photographs were taken, had become recognized as 'types', instances in a hierarchy of groups which were by then enumerated by Censuses (Cohn 1987), measured by anthropometrists, sociologized by anthropologists, problematized by administrators and sanitized by hygienists.

The use of photography for 'anthropological' purposes was already well established by the time Wallace came to take his photographs. In the early 1850s the surgeon John McCosh was photographing 'types' in Burma and India (McKenzie 1987) and the compendious representations of castes and tribes and occupations, which had been produced on talc and mica since the early eighteenth century, were com-

103. 'Minstrel (called Langhans) Sind.' Albumen print by Houghton and Tanner, *c*.1861. (Courtesy of Asiatic Society, Bombay)

pletely taken over by photography. However, this technical and indexical medium was characterized by administrative and scientific drives which had been lacking in earlier modes. Officers of the Royal Engineers were trained in the use of the camera from 1858. This bore fruit in such surveys as a collection of studies of regional Hindu and Muslim castes and tribes from Sind (now Pakistan) compiled by a Captain Houghton and Lieutenant Tanner on the orders of the Commissioner of Sind in 1861 (Thomas 1980:48). Where possible groups are photographed with material artefacts associated with their occupations, occupations which in many cases were thought to be implied by a presumed biological identity. In Houghton and Tanner's Sind album 'Shikarees' (huntsmen) are shown with guns and dead birds, a fruit seller is shown with his fruit, a 'Mohana' or fisherman with his net, and as illustrated here, 'minstrels shown' with their instruments (Plate 103).

In the case of the minstrels, artefacts are here caught up in a system of *doing*, occupation as a practice, a lived reality of noise and rhythm. More commonly, however, especially with Hindu castes, objects were used to create 'museum' registers of material artefacts which ran parallel to the photographic record of 'types'. They constituted another sign of identity, together with physique, dress and sectarian insignia whereby the British could come to identify the diversity of the Indian population.

The People of India, published in eight volumes from 1868 to 1875, reproduced many of the Sind photographs. The accompanying letterpresses frequently comment on the nature of objects depicted in photographs as if seeking to substantialize and displace the identity of the living subject into a more controllable and more easily classifiable realm of the tangible and inanimate. *The People of India* marks a watershed in the 'anthropologizing' of India. It had been interrupted by the insurrection of 1857 and what had started as an informal request by the Governor General Canning to civilians and army officers to contribute to a souvenir of his time in India became an official catalogue of the subject peoples compiled under the supervision of the Political and Secret Department of the India Office. Forbes Watson noted in his preface to the first volume that the 'great convulsion' of 1857–8 had 'imparted a new interest to the . . . people who had been actors in these remarkable events' (1868: not paginated) and a concern with the administrative complications and dubious political loyalties is apparent throughout the work.

Debates about caste and the anthropological object world

Objects associated with caste occupation came to be nuanced in a specific way from the 1870s, when we can trace two competing views about caste — one economistic and the other biological. The first of these, espoused by Ibbetson, Nesfield and latterly William Crooke, argued that caste had an occupational basis.

The second view saw caste as a form of race. Its chief exponent was Herbert Risley, who was later to become Honorary Director of the Ethnological Survey of the Indian Empire (from 1901) and to hold important posts in the administration of India before finally becoming President of the Royal Anthropological Institute from 1909 to 1911. As a brief outline of his career suggests, Risley believed science and administration to be inseparable, and he makes this point repeatedly in his theoretical writings on caste.

In 1891 Risley published *The Tribes and Castes of Bengal*. Two volumes of this four-volume work, which was financed by the Government of Bengal, consist of anthropometric measurements of 6,000 heads representing eighty-nine different sections of the population. These statistics collected by Risley with the surgeon Dr James Wise led Risley to the conclusion that many castes shared specific physical characteristics which separated them from other genetically distinct castes. In this respect India differed from the nation-states of Europe where there were 'national types' and this was a conclusion which had obvious political ramifications for a British administration eager to assert the refractory and divided nature of Indian society. The anthropometric identification of discrete 'types' demonstrated, Risley argued, that there was 'no national type, and no nation in the ordinary sense of the word' (1909:288). Having stressed this fragmentation of identity on the basis of 'racial' idiosyncracy, Risley was able, through his device of the 'nasal index', to reunite the people of India within a hierarchical grid, a space in which positive and negative judgements could be made:

> *If we take a series of castes . . . and arrange them in order of the average nasal index, so that the caste with the finest nose shall be at the top, and that with the coarsest at the bottom of the list, it will be found that this order substantially corresponds with the accepted order of social procedure.* (1891:xxxiv)

By 'caste', Risley clearly refers here to *jati* — local endogamous groups — although he was later to advocate a theory that laid more stress on seven 'types' to be found throughout India.

The rendering of Indian society into lines, grids and hierarchies of types characterized the interaction of the West with India and it is within these linear patterns (be they military parades or lines of servants) that the administrative, academic and casual travellers' experiences of India as an explicable and ordered grid of castes and types intermesh and become mutually sustaining.

William Crooke was a great enthusiast for such order. The immensely detailed alphabetical ethnographic glossary in his 1896 work elaborated the structure used earlier by Sherring in an 1872 work on castes in Benares. Further he never doubted the usefulness of anthropometry as a 'true test of race'. However, he was in many important respects in profound opposition to Risley and the wider ideology of caste, the latter's views of which formed the officially sanctioned apex. Crooke (1848–1923) spent all his official life as a Magistrate and Collector in the United Provinces of Agra and Oudh, being in charge, successively, of Etah, Saharanpur, Gorakhpur and

Mirzapur. It was in his last posting that Crooke completed his *Tribes and Castes* in which Wallace's photographs appeared. Crooke was a prolific author and editor — he produced many other influential texts and edited the journal *Punjab Notes and Queries*. However, according to his old friend Richard Carnac Temple 'he could not win the promotion to which his unusual acquirements entitled him' (Temple 1926:576) because of his outspoken criticism of the Secretariat and the incurring of official disapproval. It is difficult to say what part his disagreements with Risley played in this.

In *The Tribes and Castes of the North-Western Provinces and Oudh* Crooke revived arguments which had been made earlier by Nesfield and Ibbetson to the effect that caste was the outcome of a 'community of function or occupation' (1896:cxxxix) rather than, as Risley argued, the result of the genetic isolation of groups combined with the marital strategies of invader societies. Using the detailed evidence collected by Surgeon-Captain Drake-Brockman, Crooke argued against Risley's anthropometric argument on its own terms, concluding that 'no evidence could be more convincing if anthropometry has any meaning' (1896:cxxxvii) and further concluding in agreement with Nesfield that a 'stranger walking through the classrooms of the Sanskrit College at Benares would never dream of supposing that the students seated before him were distinct in race and blood from the scavengers who swept the roads' (1896:cxxv).

Such scant details fill in at least some of the ideological context in which Sergeant Wallace's photographs were required to operate. All the photographs reproduced in *Tribes and Castes* portray individuals or small groups of various castes and are often posed before a cloth screen or a banyan tree (Plate 104). Most of the subjects appear full-length, holding some material sign of their caste occupation, and none are named as individuals (although Wallace does record the names of many on his original prints); only their 'caste' or 'tribe' is stated. The generally rigid full poses suggest that the chief interest in these subjects is as physical specimens of their 'type' and the objects they hold appear as subsidiary motifs. However, the objects refer to a dual identity which does not necessarily overlap and as such set up a tension within the images. In the case of the two Chamars (Plate 105) the erect posture seems to say 'we have the bodies of Chamars' (the Risley argument), but the quietly held pair of shoes in the hands of the elder figure seems to argue against this, saying 'but if we didn't hold these, could you really distinguish us from any other caste?'

In trying to explain what this image is about, what it 'says', we are already, even within the confines of a relatively bounded chain of images which is linked to a text of more deducible intentions, faced with a troubling level of indeterminacy. Thus we are forced into conjecturing fragile hypotheses. A formal reading of the individual image would certainly tell us nothing beyond a recognition of a denotative depiction of two figures, one older than the other. Knowledge of Crooke's stance in relation to Risley's hegemonic argument allows us perhaps to gesture towards Crooke's possible intention in using the image but ultimately even its insertion within a syntagmatic chain (all the other photographs in *Tribes and Castes*) reveals remarkably little 'argumentative effect' (Eco 1982:32). We might render matters even more indeterminate by observing that other photographs taken by Wallace, in many respects very similar to the ones discussed here, were also used in J.D. Anderson's *The Peoples of India* (1913), the product of a close follower of Risley who claimed that 'caste has undoubtedly tended . . . to perpetuate such differences between classes of men as we readily recognise between different breeds of horses or cattle' (1913:5).

Forest officers and banyan trees

So far I have argued that the presence and certainty in Wallace's image of two Chamars is rather difficult to capture and that we are hard put to situate it decisively within structures of anthropology and photography in nineteenth-century India. Here I wish to suggest another possible line of slippage.

Situating the image of the Chamars within the wider corpus of Wallace's work, or within the ideological framework of the publications in which it appeared, is concerned primarily to elicit a level of intentional meaning, a hypothesis about what the photographer and the user of the image might have *wished* the reader to conclude. An alternative approach is to suppose what meaning the reader might have constructed given the wider context of images within which Crooke's publication of 1896 was being consumed. One immediately striking feature of the image of the two Chamars is the use of a natural backdrop, of the gnarled trunk and roots of the banyan tree (*Ficus indica*).

Here I will briefly sketch a context, a syntagmatic tradition of image making involving the banyan, within which this single image might have been imbued with argumentative effect by the reader of 1896. Simply stated, the banyan tree may well have been read as a symbol of the sacred, of Hinduism itself, within which caste operated. Ron Inden has recently noted that throughout orientalist scholarship probably the commonest metaphor for Hinduism was that

104.   Photographs of different castes by Sergeant Wallace, including Banjaras, Bhangi, Mohana, Chamar, *c.*1890. (RAI 2722, 2725, 2726, 2729, 2730, 2731)

105. Two Chamars. Photograph by Sergeant Wallace, reproduced in Crooke, 1896. (RAI 2722)

of the jungle. This was clearly argued by Sir Charles Eliot (1862–1931) who claimed that 'the jungle is not a park or garden. Whatever can grow in it does grow. The Brahmans are not gardeners but forest officers' (1954:ii, 166, cited by Inden 1990:86). Of all the plants in the 'jungle' it was the banyan which became the most symbolically loaded. It came to signify an India of superstition, described by Ann Wilson, a Punjab civil servant's wife, as:

a branch of universal pathology which can be studied in no place better than in India . . . the old gnarled tree still flourishes in India; it still shoots out grotesque buds and branches, and there anyone can witness still their strange abortive birth. (cited by Wurgaft 1983:57)

All Asiatic botany provided a store of metaphors about the vastness of the East, but the banyan stressed difference as well as fecundity and complexity since, as Bernard Cohn has noted, 'it grew up, out and down at the same time' (1985:327). For this reason, Cohn suggests, it was unamenable to use in standard arboreal metaphors.

The idea of India and Hinduism as a jungle had, however, been visually established much earlier than Eliot. In the mid eighteenth century Picart (Plate 106) had elaborated Jean-Baptiste Tavernier's observation a century earlier of fakirs under a banyan tree near Surat (Cohn n.d.:10). This long pre-photographic tradition included the Daniells, D'Oyly, and James Fergusson, all of whom painted studies of the banyan, and it became sufficiently definitive for the Royal Asiatic Society to incorporate it in its library stamp. It was sufficiently denotative to be dropped without explanation or caption in the middle of text on caste in Robert Brown's *Peoples of the World* (1892) (Plate 107).

Photographers continued to make use of the motif. Studios such as Skeen (Plate 108) and Scowen in

GREAT BANYAN, OR SACRED TREE, OF INDIA (*Ficus indica*).

classes, between which hard and fast lines are drawn, and who, theoretically at least, follow from one generation to another the same pursuits, intermarry with each other, and, so far as commingling with each other is concerned, might almost be said to be distinct races. Though much has been written on the subject of caste, great misunderstanding still exists regarding its nature.

In the "Institutes of Menu," a work which lays down the earliest arrangements of Hindoo society, the rules of caste are very distinctly defined. In this code we find four castes defined as composing the nation, though the existence of mixed castes is also mentioned. These four main divisions are :—1, The Brahmin, or priest ; 2, The Kshatriya, Chuttree, or soldier ; 3, The Vaisya, or husbandman ; and 4, The Soodra, or servant, in which were

* Monier Williams: "Modern India" (1878); "Hinduism" (1877).
† *Caste*, or *cast*, is from the Spanish or Portuguese word *Casta*, signifying breed.

127

107. 'Great Banyan, or Sacred Tree' from *The Peoples of the World* by Robert Brown, 1892, p. 127.

106 (*below left*) 'Hindu fakirs practising their superstitutious Rites under the Banyan Tree.' Engraving by Bell after Picart (*c*.1739) from Gardner (n.d.).

108. Banyan tree. Photographed by W.H.L. Skeen, *c*.1870s. (Private collection)

109. 'Among the aerial roots of a single banyan tree'. Stereoscopic card by Underwood and Underwood. (Courtesy of Pitt Rivers Museum, University of Oxford. PRM. S.53)

Colombo produced images from the 1870s onwards which partly decontextualized and emphasized the swirling lateral growths of the roots as though to affirm that the 'East' was indeed a place where simple linear dendritic symbols could not apply. A turn of the century Underwood and Underwood stereoscope announced 'instead of showing the entire tree at a distance I have chosen to bring you among its wonderfully multiplied trunks' (Plate 109).

Perhaps then the reader of 1896 looking at this image of two Chamars might have glimpsed them emerging briefly from this jungle for a momentary illumination in front of Wallace's camera before returning to a world of mysterious 'superstition'. There is a brand of anti-orientalist critique which would see this as further affirmation of the power of orientalist discourse played out graphically in this instance. Thus perhaps this photograph is placing the Chamars as a caste in a tangled web of otherness, of spirituality, belief, and ultimately of the immaterial, the familiar realm of the 'Orient'. This may be so, but it seems equally convincing to turn this around and see it as an admission of defeat by colonial discourse rather than as proof of its extraordinary power to say completely opposite things which ultimately have the same meaning. Homi K. Bhabha has written of the autonomy which colonial discourse gave to the Hottentots by making them 'indescribable' and to the Chinese by rendering them 'inscrutable' (1986:173). This after all was what the prisoners with whom I started this paper were trying to do themselves in front of the police camera which sought to endow them with identities to which could then be affixed crimes, judgements and penalties. Perhaps we might add to Bhabha's list the example discussed here, the Hindus with their banyan tree, lost in the depths of the jungle, in a dark vegetation free of the deathly illumination and scrutiny of Western science.

REFERENCES

Alloula, Malek 1987. *The Colonial Harem*. Manchester: University Press.

Anderson, J.D. 1913. *The Peoples of India*. Cambridge: University Press.

Bhabha, Homi K. 1986. 'Signs Taken for Wonders: Questions of Ambivalence and Authority under a Tree Outside Delhi, May 1817'. In H.L. Gates Jr. (ed.) *'Race', Writing and Difference*. Chicago: University of Chicago Press.

Brown, Robert 1892. *The Peoples of the World — Being a Popular Description of the Characteristics, Condition, and Customs of the Human Family*. Volume iv. London: Cassell.

Cohn, Bernard S. 1985. 'The Language of Command and the Command of Language'. In R. Guha (ed.) *Subaltern Studies IV*. Delhi: Oxford University Press.

— 1987. 'The Census, Social Structure and Objectification'. In B. Cohn *An Anthropologist Among the Historians and Other Essays*. Delhi: Oxford University Press.

— n.d. 'The Past in the Present: India as Museum of Mankind', unpublished MS.

Crooke, William 1896. *The Tribes and Castes of the North-Western Provinces and Oudh*. 4 vols. Calcutta: Superintendent of Government Printing.

De Man, Paul 1971. *Blindness and Insight, Essays in the Rhetoric of Contemporary Criticism*. New York: Oxford University Press.

Derrida, Jacques 1976. *Of Grammatology*. Baltimore: Johns Hopkins University Press.

Eco, Umberto 1982. 'Critique of the Image'. In V. Burgin (ed.) *Thinking Photography*. London: Macmillan.

Eliot, Charles 1954 (1921). *Hinduism and Buddhism: An Historical Sketch*. 3 vols. New York: Barnes & Noble.

Foucault, Michel 1979. *Discipline and Punish: the Birth of the Prison*. Harmondsworth: Penguin.

Gardner, James n.d. *The Faiths of the World: A Dictionary of All Religions and of Religious Sects*. 2 vols. London: A. Fullarton and Co..

Ibbetson, Denzil 1916. *Panjab Castes: being a reprint of the chapter in 'The Races, Castes and Tribes of the People' in the Report on the Census of the Panjab published in 1883*. Lahore: Superintendent of Government Printing.

Inden, Ron 1990. *Imagining India*. Oxford: Basil Blackwell.

McKenzie, Ray 1987. 'The Laboratory of Mankind': John McCosh and the beginnings of photography in British India. *History of Photography* 11(2):109–18

Risley, Herbert H. 1891. *The Tribes and Castes of Bengal*. 4 vols. Calcutta: Bengal Secretariat Press.

— 1909. 'Ethnology and Caste'. In *The Imperial Gazetteer of India*. Oxford: Clarendon Press.

Sherring, M.A. 1872. *Hindu Tribes and Castes as Represented at Benares*. 3 vols. Calcutta.

Stange, Maren 1989. *Symbols of Ideal Life: Social Documentary Photography in America: 1890–1950*. Cambridge: University Press.

Temple, R.C. 1926. William Crooke 1848–1923. In *Proceedings of the British Academy*, 576–9.

Thomas, C. 1980. The Peccavi Photographs. *History of Photography* 4(1):46–52.

Watson, J. Forbes & J.W. Kaye 1868–75. *The People of India: A Series of Photographic Illustrations with Descriptive Letterpress of the Races and Tribes of Hindustan*. 8 vols. London: India Museum.

Wurgaft, Lewis D. 1983. *The Imperial Imagination: Magic and Myth in Kipling's India*. Middleton, Conn.: Wesleyan University Press.

Whose Pose is It? A Photo-ethnographic Conundrum from South India

Nicholas J. Bradford

IN THE EARLY YEARS of this century, a photograph (Plate 110) was taken under the direction of Edgar Thurston, Superintendent of the Madras Government Museum.[1] It was one of a large series taken specifically to illustrate the nature of the various social groups of south India. A companion photograph, taken at the same time, appears in Thurston's *Castes and Tribes of Southern India* (1909: opp. 257) over the caption 'Jangam' in a section entitled 'Lingayat'.[2] In fact the photograph discussed here and its companion are evidence that this is *not* a Lingayat Jangama (or 'ascetic of the priestly class', as Thurston puts it) but a *puravantaru*, a ritual exponent of the myths of Vīrabhadra, a fiery son or form of the Hindu god Śiva scarcely mentioned in religious texts but nevertheless prominent to this day in the rural pantheons and pilgrimage centres of Karnāṭaka.

A number of intriguing questions are raised by the hiatus between the photograph and the accompanying ethnographic description and classification of the subject (Thurston 1909, II:257–8). How and why are these two forms of ethnographic evidence contradictory? What does this tell us about the relationship between the ethnographer and the subject of his investigation? What light does this case-study shed on the modern history of Indian god-men such as we find here in Thurston's photograph? Does the camera help us answer such questions?

Whatever the subject may have wanted to call himself and in whatever way the ethnographer may have wanted to classify him, the camera reveals that this man is a *puravantaru*, a title not even mentioned in Thurston's commentary. *Puravantaru* perform mostly at night at special marriage rites (*guggala lagna*) reserved for the male first-born in families whose lineage deity is Vīrabhadra. They do not, as Thurston puts it, indulge in 'shouting' and 'dancing' but rather relate the heroic deeds of Vīrabhadra in an archaic, poetic language delivered in a dramatic, stylized manner. They are known in Karnāṭaka as the 'soldiers of Vīrabhadra', who is himself represented as a fearsome slayer of demons — hence the weapons carried by the *puravantaru*, and the trophy-heads of Daksa-Brahma (Śiva's father-in-law, whom Śiva, in a dispute between affines, sent his son Vīrabhadra to destroy).

The rather wild, aggressive appearance of Thurston's *puravantaru* with his weapons, unkempt hair, red-painted face and red shirt (called *kāśi* and worn by all *puravantaru*) is thus wholly in keeping with the conventional mythical representation of Vīrabhadra. Furthermore, the studied imitation of the icon of the deity in the *puravantaru*'s stance is sociologically astute, since unlike the Hindu ascetic, the *puravantaru* is indeed a mere representative and sub-

110. *Puravantaru*, *c*.1905. Photographed under the direction of E. Thurston. (RAI 6137)

111.   Jangama: the Rambhāpuri Pañvācārya Jagadguru in procession. Bangalore, 1972. Photograph by the author.

ordinate of the deity he serves. However, the photograph also expresses Thurston's fascination with the 'magpie' aspect of Hindu iconography: the *puravantaru*'s adornment and paraphernalia, in keeping with the iconography, are elaborate — so much so that one feels this man could do with as many arms as the deity whose image is strung from his neck!

Although Thurston gives a full ethnographic description of the accoutrements of his subject in the accompanying commentary, he nonetheless refers to them rather disparagingly as 'quaint ornaments'. He is also distracted by the voluminous detail of the *puravantaru*'s garb, while at the same time refusing, or not knowing how, to take it all seriously. A modern anthropologist, however, would have no difficulty in understanding, at a general level at least, the significance of, for example, the *puravantaru*'s mass of unkempt hair, his numerous bells (at the knees as well as from the waist), and the skins of wild animals (tiger and bear, according to Thurston). In the light of structuralists' observations that humans institutionalize ambiguity in ritual, the marginal, removable parts of the body, in this case hair, take on a particular significance (Leach 1958; Hallpike 1969; Hershman

1974; Obeyesekere 1981). While some Hindu ascetics keep their heads shaven, and through their restraint become god-like, other Hindu holy men, who become divine by virtue of being possessed by the gods, let their hair grow long and matted. According to mythology Vīrabhadra was born from Śiva's hair, at the precise moment when Śiva's wife undid his matted locks and shook them. Sometimes, as in the case of this *puravantaru*, a mane of hair is worn rather than grown. Such hairpieces are normally made from the hairs of wild water-buffalo. The half-animal, half-wild 'nature' of divine humans is reiterated here in the use of wild animal skins as clothing. Anthropologists have also noted the formal use of noise or 'percussion' in rites of transition (Needham 1967) — for example, the use of gunfire at moments of transition in weddings and funerals. In India the bell is prominent as an instrument of percussion in ritual.

There is evidence to suggest, mainly in the commentary but also in one intriguing detail of the photograph (which I identify below), that the *puravantaru* has used the occasion of the ethnographer's visit to the village in which he was carrying out his ritual services (but in which he was probably not a resident) to try to raise his social status: at the very least this *puravantaru* appears to be toying with the idea of redefining his official identity. The end result is that Thurston and his associates are led to believe, wrongly, that being a *puravantaru* is synonymous with being a Jaṅgama — that is, a member of the priest-guru caste of the Lingayat community. Most *puravantaru* are not even Lingayat, let along Jaṅgama. For example, although Vīrabhadra of Gōdachi (the principal seat and pilgrimage centre of this god in North Karnāṭaka) is a popular lineage deity amongst Lingayats, the chief *puravantaru* at Gōdachi are in fact Carpenter (Viśvakarma Badigēr) by caste. But even if this particular *puravantaru* were Lingayat Jaṅgama by caste, which is highly unlikely, such status is irrelevant in the definition of his ritual office as a *puravantaru*.

At the time when Thurston and Rangachari (his Brahmin assistant) were compiling their caste-tribe compendium the general social and political climate of India, together with the British rulers' desire for a tidy, legally watertight classification of Indian social groups and their customs, in effect caused Indians to become increasingly conscious of caste status. The rather perfunctory treatment of ritual institutions to be found in Thurston's commentary is symptomatic of the overriding official interest in social classification. The British census reports of 1891, 1901 and 1911 for the Lingayat heartland areas provide abundant evidence of widespread Lingayat concern about how their caste status should be defined for the purposes of official classification (Narasimmiyengar 1892:238–9; Enthoven 1902:197; *Mysore Chief Court Reports* 1899:96–7). The Jaṅgamas, being the gurus and literati of the sect, became the focus of attention in the search for a self-ascribed identity and the competition for high status — a process which was soon to develop into a bitter internecine conflict within the Lingayat community. Modern field research has confirmed something of which Thurston was demonstrably aware: that the concept and institution of 'Jaṅgama' are extremely complex matters (Bradford 1988). In its 'original' sense Jaṅgama refers to peripatetic, Śaivite renouncers who formed the vanguard of the twelfth-century Lingayat movement. More recently the term refers to the dual headpiece of the Lingayat sect: that is to say, on the one hand to cloistered, shaven-headed, Lingayat ascetics (called *virakta*) who theoretically need not be, but in fact usually are, born Jaṅgamas; on the other hand, to a caste (the purest amongst Lingayat castes) of householder priests organized into five

exogamous patri-clans, headed by five 'king-gurus' occupying five 'thrones'. A photograph of the former kind of Jaṅgama is to be found in Thurston's compendium (1909, iv: opp. 245) over the caption, appropriate in this case, of 'Jaṅgama'. The second photograph is of the latter kind of Jaṅgama, in particular of the present incumbent of one of the five king-guru thrones (that of the Rambhāpuri Śimhāsana) being processed through the streets of Bangalore, the State capital of Karnāṭaka in 1972 (Plate 111). Although quite elaborately adorned there is nothing 'wild' about this Jaṅgama.

'Jaṅgama', then, denotes high status, priesthood, and sometimes asceticism, and it is more than possible that Thurston was deliberately misled by a *puravantaru* intent on raising his social status rather than describing his ritual office. Such an intent could not, however, be so readily promoted in a photographic record. The man cannot alter or hide from the camera all the trappings of a *puravantaru*, especially since it is precisely these 'quaint ornaments' which have attracted Thurston's attention in the first place. However, there is one small but revealing detail in Thurston's photograph which suggests that the *puravantaru* himself is indeed intent on a rather different version of his identity than that conveyed by his appearance: the icon of his deity Vīrabhadra is pushed slightly to one side, just enough to reveal half of a massive liṅga-casket. Such a casket, containing a miniature liṅga representing Śiva, is often worn by all sorts of Śaivite god-men in Karnāṭaka, but it is also the prime marker of Lingayat, and thus high social status. Among the ordinary people of Karnāṭaka only the Lingayats wear such caskets. There is one tantalizingly unanswerable question: did the photo-ethnographer make the adjustment to the icon in order to reveal another bit of the magpie's collection, as it were, or did the *puravantaru* do this in order to confirm the title of Lingayat Jaṅgama which he had communicated verbally to Thurston? Could it be that this photograph captures a moment in the history of rather 'wild' and low-status god-men on the brink of becoming more 'tame', ascetic and socially respectable? Is the contradiction found in this case between general appearance and self-ascribed status indicative of the beginnings of the ascendancy of asceticism over the traditions of the *puravantaru*, a trend which has in modern times come to fruition with the rise in Karnāṭaka of popular renouncer-gurus and the 'taming' of aggressively Śaivite god-men?

NOTES

1 Thurston's photographs were actually taken, technically, by his assistant K. Rangachari (Thurston 1909, i:x).

2 'Lingayat' is the name of a populous, high-status sectarian community in Northern Karnāṭaka.

REFERENCES

Bradford, N.J. 1985. 'The Indian Renouncer: structure and transformation in the Lingayat Community'. In R. Burghart and A. Cantlie (eds.) *Indian Religion*. London: Curzon Press/New York: St Martin's Press.

Enthoven, R.E. 1902. Bombay Census. *Census of India 1901* 9. Bombay: Government Central Press.

Hallpike, C. 1969. Social Hair. *Man* (NS) 4:254–64.

Hershman, P. 1974. Hair, Sex and Dirt. *Man* 9(2):274–98.

Leach, E.R. 1958. Magical Hair. *Journal of the Royal Anthropological Institute* 88:147–64.

Mysore Chief Court Reports. 1899. Vol. 4. Bangalore: Government Press.

Narasimmiyengar, V.N. 1892. Mysore Census. *Census of India 1891* 25. Bangalore: Government Central Printing Office.

Needham, R. 1967. Percussion and Transition. *Man* (NS) 2(4):606–14.

Obeyesekere, G. 1981. *Medusa's Hair — An Essay on Personal Symbols and Religious Experience*. Chicago: University of Chicago Press.

Thurston, E. 1909. *Castes and Tribes of Southern India*. Vol. iv: K–M. Madras: Government Press.

The Yellow Bough: Rivers's Use of Photography in *The Todas*

Paul Hockings

At the very beginning of this century a model study of the Todas was completed by Dr W.H.R. Rivers, a British psychologist-turned-ethnologist. The Todas, a small tribe of buffalo pastoralists living on the Nilgiri Hills in southern India, were already known to scholars through two remarkable ethnographies by Breeks and Marshall, both published in 1873 and both including some of the earliest field photography ever to illustrate an anthropological work. Rivers did his field study in 1902 and published his lengthy book in 1906. He did not take his own pictures for the most part, employing instead a person from the well-known Madras company, Messrs Wiele & Klein, to work 'under my supervision'.[1]

At the time Rivers was working in India, James G. Frazer was the most prominent of all the Cambridge anthropologists. He had been an instigator of Rivers's first collaborative field venture, the Torres Straits Expedition of 1898, and was the greatest living popularizer of what that expedition's leader, Dr A.C. Haddon, then had to call 'our Cinderella science' (1903.22). Frazer's relationship with his somewhat younger colleague has never been examined in detail. It is known, however, that Frazer did lend Rivers a manuscript of his booklet on fieldwork questions (Frazer 1907) for comment, and an intellectual interaction between the two is clear from *The Golden Bough*. The second edition (Frazer 1900) of this immensely popular and influential work had appeared shortly before Rivers left for India: it made no mention whatever of the Todas. The much-expanded third edition of 1911–15, however, discussed them at twelve separate points, citing Breeks (1873), Marshall (1873) or Rivers (1906) in each instance. Frazer had evidently digested the ethnography.

In the earlier edition, when describing the temple at Nemi which was sacred to 'Diana of the Wood', where grew the Golden Bough, Frazer evoked

> . . . *the scene as it may have been witnessed by a belated wayfarer on one of those wild autumn nights when the dead leaves are falling thick, and the winds seem to sing the dirge of the dying year. It is a sombre picture, set to melancholy music — the background of forest showing black and jagged against a lowering and stormy sky, the sighing of the wind in the branches, the rustle of the withered leaves under foot, the lapping of the cold water on the shore, and in the foreground, pacing to and fro, now in twilight and now in gloom, a dark figure . . .* (Frazer 1900:I, 3)

And the crucial explanation:

> *Within the sanctuary at Nemi grew a certain tree of which no branch might be broken. Only a runaway slave was allowed to break off, if he could, one of its boughs. Success*

179

112.   The Dairy of Kiûdr with its Dairyman-Priest, Etamudri. (Rivers 1906: fig. 31) (RAI 6540)

113.   Dairyman-Priest of Kars, Kernpisi, standing beside his dairy. (Rivers 1906: fig. 23) (RAI 6534)

in the attempt entitled him to fight the priest in single combat, and if he slew him he reigned in his stead with the title King of the Wood . . . (idem I. 4)

What do these scenes from such a well-known writer have to do with Rivers's specialized Indian ethnography? Nemi was nowhere near India: Frazer was writing about classical, even pre-classical, Latium, sketching, as he later conjured it, 'an image of what Italy had been in far-off days when the land was still sparsely peopled with tribes of savage hunters or wandering herdsmen . . .' (Frazer 1911:I, 8; not in 1900 edn.). Yet certainly the scenes were familiar to Rivers, as they were to all British anthropologists of the period (e.g. Malinowski 1932: xviii; Rivers 1926:165, n.1; Westermarck 1932:191). I contend that the classic scene at Nemi prompted Rivers's staging of many of the Toda photographs, and that Frazer himself later recognized some sort of parallel between the priests of Nemi and those of the Todas, consequently adding to his text — *after* having seen these Toda scenes — this pictorial image:

> *Thus I put the mysterious priest of Nemi, so to say, in the forefront of the picture . . . because the picturesque natural surroundings of the priest of Nemi among the wooded hills of Italy, the very mystery which enshrouds him, and not least the haunting magic of Virgil's verse, all combine to shed a glamour on the tragic figure with the Golden Bough, which fits him to stand as the centre of a gloomy canvas.* (Frazer 1911:I, viii–ix)

Had it appeared in the 1900 edition, this image could well have served as a prescription for Rivers's photographer. Why do I suggest this connection? Because there are twenty plates in *The Todas* (figs. 5, 7, 8, 13, 14, 16, 19–21, 23, 24, 27, 28, 31, 42, 44, 59, 65, 70, 72) which seem to be illustrating this theme from Nemi. Each one has the same features (Plates 112–13): first, a more or less shadowy figure, usually a priest, standing guardedly in the middle distance, sometimes with a wand, and wearing a black loincloth or toga-like shawl; secondly, behind him a lactarium (dairy-temple) with rough drystone walls suggestive of great antiquity; thirdly, a grove of deciduous trees with spreading branches in the background; fourthly, the cameraman was usually looking *up* the slope towards this scene, its dominating aspect being further enhanced by a fairly empty expanse of grass in the foreground; and finally, as printed, the skies appear uniformly grey.

There is not just one example of this illustration (which we would dismiss as a slight coincidence): over a quarter of all the plates in the book suggest the one romantic theme. Nor is that theme entirely new with Rivers, for it was perhaps first suggested in

the exquisite frontispiece (drawn by Louis Haghe, 'lithographer to the King') in Capt. Harkness's book (1832), which shows 'A Tuda Family', which he suggested to be of Roman origin, posed and clad as for a classical *fête galante* — noble savages indeed (see Plate 52). And Harkness closed his book with the perpetual question, 'WHO CAN THEY BE?'.

Recently M.B. Emeneau recalled his own attempts at photographing Toda dairy officiants during the 1930s:

> *I found that when I attempted to take pictures of buffalo ceremonial and the dairyman in his more unapproachable moments, I was kept as far as possible from the officiant (e.g. when he was replacing the dairy implements in a rebuilt dairy). The result was a most mysterious picture with a dark figure dressed in a scanty loincloth streaking across the background of trees and shrubbery, at a considerable distance from the camera. None of these pictures turned out to be capable of reproduction. But the general effect may be what you are hinting at in your comparison of Rivers and Frazer.* (Emeneau, letter, Jan. 18, 1986)

Given that in all of his work Rivers was methodologically rigorous and eschewed Victorian romanticism, what possible motivation could he have had for peppering his book with priestly plates in the manner suggested above? It certainly seems inconsistent with his careful observations and unemotional, scientific tone of writing. But then, as Mandelbaum comments, 'he interspersed his meticulous field reports . . . with flightier speculations . . .' (1980:285). George Stocking's estimate is similar: 'he also possessed an uninhibited (Mauss said "intrepid") explanatory imagination . . ., and was quite capable of pursuing a pet hypothesis well beyond the limits to which rigorous method would carry him' (1983:85). So, stimulated by the style of the Haghe drawing and the institution of the priesthood, Rivers was, I think, struck by an analogy that his empirical stance would not allow him to express in words, for he could not substantiate it. If we may for brevity use a Lévi-Straussian equation the idea was this:

Teivali priest: Tarthar men: slave-become-priest at Nemi: devotees at Nemi

To elaborate: Rivers shows repeatedly (ch. XXIX) that although men of Teivali (i.e. *Töwfíly*) moiety serve as priests in the temples of Tarthar (i.e. *To·rθas*) clans, Teivali moiety is inferior in status to Tarthar, so that 'The dairyman [priest] is regarded by the Todas as a servant . . .' (Rivers 1906:62, 683). The Teivali priests alone handle the sacred bough called *tûdr* at a funeral for the other moiety, and 'the prominent position of the Teivaliol in this ceremony is evidently due to the use of this sacred substance' (*idem* 684). Hence the analogy I suggest with runaway slaves

THE TÛDE OR SACRED BUSH.

WEAPONS. BOW & ARROW, USED AT WEDDINGS & FUNERALS.

IMITATION BUFFALO HORNS.

114.   The Yellow Bough, *tûdr*, from Marshall, *A Phrenologist amongst the Todas*, used as an illustration by Rivers. (Courtesy of the Balfour Library, Pitt Rivers Museum, University of Oxford)

182

who alone could fight to become priest of the Nemi temple, and serve its many wealthy patrons. Among Todas the dairyman-priest (*palol*) must come from Teivali moiety and, should he stay in the office for eighteen years, he goes through a special ceremony after which he may have relations in the wood with a young woman of Tarthar moiety (*idem* 98, 103). It is true that the lowest grade of dairymen may have relations with Teivali women, but the next higher ranks, *kudrpalikartmokh*, *wursol*, and *palol* (i.e. *kuṛ poɭy xaṛp o'ɭ*, *wïs o'ɭ*, *poɭ o'ɭ*), can only have relations with women of the higher-status moiety, and the highest of all priests, *pohkartpol* (i.e. *po'w xaṛp o'ɭ*), though of that higher moiety himself, must remain quite celibate (*idem* 80, 236). In short, and reverting to Lévi-Straussian algebra:

Teivali priest : Tarthar woman :: Nemi priest : goddess Diana.

(It must be remembered that in the normal course of things Teivali men can only *marry* Teivali women.)

If Rivers was the first, he was not the only one to sense a parallel between the two cults: at one point Frazer too spelled out an analogy between Nemi and the Todas. After describing the cult of Diana he cites Rivers, saying 'when the Todas of Southern India desire to obtain more buffaloes, they offer silver images of these animals in the temples'; and he adds in a footnote which does not appear in the 1900 edition, 'The analogy of these offerings to the various votive figures found in the sanctuary of Diana at Nemi is obvious' (Frazer 1911:I, 56, n.3).

But is there a sacred bough in Toda ritual to complete the parallel? Indeed there is, and it is quite central. On numerous ceremonial occasions a Teivali priest (though sometimes men of Tarthar moiety too) uses as a purifying agent the bark, leaves or wood from the sacred *tûḏr* tree (i.e. *tïṛ*, *Meliosma simplicifolia pungens*; Rivers 1906:434, fig. 58; our Plate 114). The dark green leaves have a yellow underside; the bark has an orange–rust colour, and must be chipped from the tree with a stone (Fyson 1915:92). Suffice it to note here only that it is with a *tûḏr* bough that the priest annually sacrifices the calf (Rivers 1906:278–9; our Plate 115). The subsequent feast is reminiscent of the annual feast to Diana of the Wood at Nemi, in which a kid was eaten. Frazer would have agreed that the Todas were 'feasting on the totem'; indeed, by citing this unique Toda sacrifice as 'a sacrifice of the Egyptian type' (1912:314), Frazer may possibly have set Rivers on the road to the hyperdiffusionism of G. Elliot Smith and W.J. Perry.

But further, Nemi was sacred to the Latins because, so they believed, it was there the goddess Diana had once mated with Virbius, the first King of the Wood.

His successor priests were *all* husbands of the Huntress, to ensure her continuing fertility and that of the soil of Latium. Here then was a kind of serial monogamy not too much different in structure from Toda polyandry. Since Toda priests were not permanent appointments but often quite brief ones, but since too the higher-ranking priests were prohibited from sexual intercourse with their wives, the effect on the polyandrous marriages of priests was of a series of men cohabiting with their wife at different periods (Rivers 1906:68, 72, 80, 99, 103, 236). This was spelled out clearly in the case of the *palol*, a very high-ranking dairyman-priest: 'The *palol* must be celibate, and if married, he must leave his wife, who is in most cases also the wife of his brother or brothers' (*idem* 99).

At this point we might ask where Rivers's ideas about field photography came from. Had he learnt it all from Anthony Wilkin during the Torres Straits Expedition? Or from Haddon? — for in Rivers's book (1906) most photographs follow the prescriptions of *Notes and Queries on Anthropology* in two important respects: they document technical processes and record the complex details of ceremonial (Haddon 1899:240). However, I sense that Theodor Klein, Rivers's probable photographer, was not above ignoring Haddon's valuable advice in *Notes and Queries* where commercial possibilities beckoned. Haddon had commented there that 'it must never be forgotten that when a native is posed for photography he unconsciously becomes set and rigid, and the delicate "play" of the limbs is lost' (*idem* 239). The posed woodenness of which he warned was common in the work of ethnographic photographers at that time: witness the 'Toda hut', taken by Mr A.T.W. Penn, another local professional photographer, and published by Thurston & Rangachari (1909:VII, 129). Numerous stiff poses appear in *The Todas* too, especially when men are standing in front of dairy-temples.[2]

But in three other respects Rivers's use of photography was quite innovative. He tied the photographic record into his genealogical charts (which were equally innovative at that time): this was done through numbers in the captions; and he was the first of a small cohort of twentieth-century anthropologists actually to name the persons appearing in his photographs (a very useful feature for later anthropologists).

Secondly, he is one of a much larger cohort who scatter through their English, French or German texts a sizeable vocabulary of 'native' words, to the chagrin of most readers. But in Rivers's case, one must admit, these words refer to Toda roles, artefacts or practices that are really untranslatable. Many are illustrated through inclusion in his picture captions.

A third special use of photographs is in illustrating

115. Punatvan hits the calf's head with a *tûdr* club. (RAI 6590)

116. He then passes the *tûdr* club and leaves between its hind legs. (Rivers 1906, p. 279) (RAI 6591)

how particular rituals are performed, especially the supposedly secret calf sacrifice (Rivers 1906: figs. 37–41; our Plates 115–16), which some more recent Indian writers have claimed never occurred in this 'purely vegetarian' tribe. Although admittedly the photographs as published are not very clear because of the thick *shola* woodland under which they had to be exposed (*idem* 277, n.1), they are still just clear enough to show the essential stages in the sacrifice, butchery and roasting. The series constitutes the best evidence that this rite actually occurred (though it probably no longer does). However, it was somewhat surprising to see the original pictures for figs. 37–41 recently in the archives of the Royal Anthropological Institute, for they are definitely clearer than as published. A further surprise was to find that the series includes photographs which have never been published, among them one of the actual moment of sacrifice (Plate 115).

Why was it, one might ask, that these unavoidably obscure pictures in the book did not convince everyone that the Toda calf sacrifice really occurred? For they accompany Rivers's own detailed eyewitness description (*idem* 274–88); while much earlier Harkness (1832:139) and Muzzy (1844:363) had also left eyewitness accounts. I favour a simple explanation, one of yet another cultural reading. Most of the non-believers in this event have been Indians, mainly scholars who have talked with Todas. They have gladly accepted modern Toda protestations of a purely vegetarian diet.[3] Even Rivers had great difficulty in getting Todas to admit that sacrifice occurred, his informants 'denying at first all knowledge of any ceremony among the Todas in which a calf was killed or eaten. As soon as they found out that I knew positively of the existence of the ceremony, they acknowledged that they killed a calf, but said they could not tell me anything about it' (Rivers 1906:274).[4] The main ethnographers to have worked with the Todas, namely (in chronological order) Harkness, Breeks, Rivers, Thurston, Emeneau, Prince Peter, Mandelbaum, and Walker, have never denied that the sacrifice took place.[5] A census publication reported an annual sacrifice in the 1960s (Nambiar 1965:77); and the sacrifice is also referred to in eight Toda songs (Emeneau 1971:948).

To summarize, I am suggesting that while Rivers did try to follow the prescriptions of *Notes and Queries* for 'scientific' recording of technical processes and ceremonies (he was himself on the editorial board of the fourth edition and wrote part of it), he and his photographer still contrived to render the Todas in a heroic light that hinted at classical antiquity; and this would augment his very tentative final chapter (XXX) on 'The Origin and History of the Todas'. He even suppressed the crucial picture of the actual calf sacrifice, perhaps lest its evident cruelty detract from the image of classical nobility his plate selection was aiming for.

Leach's estimate of Rivers, which many today would share (e.g. Mandelbaum 1980:279), is germane to my argument. He wrote:

> By the standards of the time The Todas (1906) was an outstanding example of precise documentation, and for many years this book served British anthropologists as a model for ethnographic monographs. Like all his contemporaries, Rivers took it for granted that the objective of the anthropologist is to reconstruct the history of the primitive peoples whom he studies. (Leach 1968:527)

Through the disparate media of text and image, Rivers really achieved both aims — precise documentation and historical reconstruction — which on the surface may seem contradictory. Klein's or Penn's photographs evoke the sense of a lost mythic past, the search for which would have to be sacrificed to meet the tenets of a new scientific ethnography that was to be rooted in the present. So, through these photographs, Rivers was attempting what Frazer and Malinowski were also known to do:

> . . . undertake the work of convincing the readers by managing their imaginations in a way that would allow them to conceptualize in images what the text could not present in full. If the details of native life were 'imponderabilia', it is because they could only be constructed in the readers' imagination once the moment of experience was past. (Thornton 1985:8)

My interpretation of Rivers's aims in illustrating this book is certainly speculative. He was an empiricist in both psychology and ethnology, and as such would have been wary of a subconscious selection of photographs that lent credence to a very different kind of anthropology. Yet if this selection was indeed his first step backward into the realms of mythology and pseudohistorical cultural origins, it is an element in the history of British anthropology that has not previously been noted.[6]

NOTES

1 He also acknowledged having borrowed a few plates from the Breeks and Marshall studies. The photographer was most probably Theodor Klein, a frequent resident of Ootacamund. (I own his stereoscopic camera, which he left behind there.) While most of the Rivers photographs in the RAI collection are by a professional hand, some, including the calf sacrifice, are more amateurish and probably by Rivers himself.

2 I believe both Klein and Penn subsequently sold their Toda photographs to other writers and even as picture postcards, thus helping to fuel the tourist image of the Todas as a picturesque anachronism in modern India. Their pictures certainly appear in other publications. (Both men had shops in Ootacamund.)

3 Such protests have become increasingly common among tribes and low castes of modern India; they are part of a process of Sanskritization whereby the claim of a vegetarian diet may be used as a lever to higher social status.

4 Furthermore, copies of The Todas have long been almost unobtainable in India: few libraries there have one. I suspect all those denying the reality of the sacrifice are people unaware that photographs of it exist.

5 Marshall, on the other hand, asserted that 'no offerings to gods' were made (1873:188).

6 This paper has benefited greatly from the patient editing and many valuable suggestions of Fiona Stewart and Joanna Scherer.

REFERENCES

Breeks, James Wilkinson 1873. *An Account of the Primitive Tribes and Monuments of the Nilagiris*. Edited by his widow, Susan Maria Breeks. London: India Museum.

Emeneau, Murray Barnson 1971. *Toda Songs*. Oxford: Clarendon Press.

Frazer, James George 1900. *The Golden Bough, a Study in Magic and Religion . . .* 2nd edn. revised and enlarged. London: Macmillan & Co.

— 1907 *Questions on the Customs, Beliefs, and Languages of Savages*. Cambridge: University Press.

— 1911 *The Magic Art and the Evolution of Kings* (*The Golden Bough*, vol. I). 3rd edn. London: Macmillan & Co.

— 1912 *Spirits of the Corn and of the Wild* (*The Golden Bough*, Part V, vol. II). 3rd edn. London: Macmillan & Co.

Fyson, Philip Furley 1915. *The Flora of the Nilgiri and Pulney Hill-tops (above 6,500 Feet) Being the Wild and Commoner Introduced Flowering Plants round the Hill-Stations of Ootacamund, Kotagiri and Kodaikanal*. Vol. I. Madras: Superintendent Government Press.

Haddon, Alfred Cort 1899. No. LXXVII. — Photography. In Charles Hercules Read (ed.) *Notes and Queries on Anthropology*. Edited for the British Association for the Advancement of Science. 3rd edn. 235–40. London: The Anthropological Institute.

— 1903 'Anthropology: Its Position and Needs. Presidential Address'. *JAI* 33:11–23.

Harkness, Henry 1832. *A Description of a Singular Aboriginal Race Inhabiting the Summit of the Neilgherry Hills, or Blue Mountains of Coimbatoor, in the Southern Peninsula of India*. London: Smith, Elder, & Co.

Leach, Edmund Ronald 1968. Rivers, W.H.R. in David L. Sills (ed.) *International Encyclopaedia of the Social Sciences* 14:526–8. New York: The Macmillan Company & The Free Press.

Malinowski, Bronislaw Gaspar 1932. *Argonauts of the Western Pacific, an Account of Native Enterprise and Adventure in the Archipelagoes of Melanesian New Guinea*. London: George Routledge & Sons, Ltd.

Mandelbaum, David Goodman 1980. *The Todas* in Time Perspective. Reviews in *Anthropology* 7:279–302.

Marshall, William Elliot 1873. *A Phrenologist amongst the Todas or the Study of a Primitive Tribe in South India: History, Character, Customs, Religion, Infanticide, Polyandry, Language*. London: Longmans, Green, and Co.

Muzzy, C.F. 1844. Account of the Neilgherry Hill Tribes. *Christian Instructor and Missionary Record* 2:358–66.

Nambiar, P.K. 1965. *Census of India 1961*. Vol. IX, Madras, Part V-C, Todas. Delhi: Manager of Publications.

Rivers, William Halse Rivers 1906. *The Todas*. London: Macmillan & Co.

— 1926 *Social Organization*. London: Kegan Paul, Trench, Trubner & Co., Ltd.; New York: Alfred A. Knopf, Inc.

Stocking, George W., Jr. 1983. 'The Ethnographer's Magic: Fieldwork in British Anthropology from Tylor to Malinowski'. In George W. Stocking, Jr. (ed.) *Observers Observed* (*History of Anthropology*, vol. 1) 70–120. Madison: University of Wisconsin Press.

Thornton, Robert J. 1985. 'Imagine Yourself Set Down . . .': Mach, Frazer, Conrad, Malinowski and the Role of Imagination in Ethnography. *Anthropology Today* 1(5): 7–14.

Thurston, Edgar, and Rangachari, Kadamki 1909. *Castes and Tribes of Southern India*. Madras: Government Press.

Westermarck, Edvard Alexander 1932. 'The Study of Popular Sayings'. In Warren R. Dawson (ed.) *The Frazer Lectures 1922–1932 by Divers Hands* 190–211. London: Macmillan & Co.

'Very loveable human beings': The Photography of Everard im Thurn

Donald Tayler

Yet, at last, it seems that there are two morals to be drawn: one that a pleasure so great as to be conceivable only by experience is to be had, even in this world of growing commonplace, from travel in places where the way has not yet been smoothed; the other is that there still exist human beings — and very loveable and in their way admirable human beings — who, entirely without the spectacles of civilization, see life in very bright colours but from an entirely different standpoint from that on which we look at it. (im Thurn 1934:93)

SO WROTE EVERARD IM THURN in 1893, reflecting on a long journey of many weeks, by canoe and overland, in central British Guiana (now Guyana). Im Thurn was a botanist first. All his life he sent plant collections back to the Royal Botanic Gardens at Kew and, although he may have become a colonial administrator, an explorer and an anthropologist, it was botany that brought him into contact with the indigenous population of British Guiana. It was the collecting of plants which drew the Indians to him, and conversely created his fascination with them, not least because of their intrinsic knowledge of plants. An Oxford graduate, im Thurn was Curator of the British Guiana Museum, Georgetown (known then as the Museum of the Royal Agricultural and Commercial Society of British Guiana) appointed through the recommendation of the Director of Kew, Sir Joseph Hooker. He later became a district magistrate and administrator in the colony. Subsequently he became Governor of Fiji and High Commissioner of the Western Pacific and during his retirement a distinguished and active President of the Royal Anthropological Institute (1919–20). Although his scientific activities might be construed as part of the overall colonial structure, he was at the same time set apart in some ways[1] from his colonial administrative colleagues in his early years by his occupation as a botanist, and his first and lasting contact with the Indians bears little if any relation to the master-servant hierarchical necessities of colonialism. A gentle proselytizer, he constantly advocated 'better understanding of native ways' (1934:xxi) by the British people, and he frequently chided his lecture audiences to appreciate the 'Redman': 'if you knew him as I have been fortunate enough to see him, you would realize that he is naturally a fine fellow and a gentleman' (1934:170).

It was through his inexhaustible travelling in 1877–9 as a Curator, and as an administrator from 1881 to 1897, that im Thurn gained an extensive and intimate knowledge of the Indian peoples of Guiana. *Among the Indians of Guiana* (1883), an acknowledged anthropological classic of its day, was the outcome of these first two and a half years as explorer-curator and was followed over the years by numerous articles, a number of which were published in *Timehri*, a journal of which he himself was the founder and first editor. He wrote on many subjects. Those concerning the Indians ranged from games to the domestication of animals, and the descriptions of his journeys give us remarkable portraits of tribal life at that time. It is this intimacy with the native peoples, and not only the polyglot northern communities, but also the Indian tribes of the interior, when his duties could have confined him to a desk in Georgetown or later his house on the Pomeroon River, which seems now all the more remarkable. It undoubtedly gave him a most perceptive eye when he concentrated his photography on indigenous people during his second extended stay.

Im Thurn's interest, indeed passion, for photography does not appear to have been separate or distinct from his commitment to anthropology. He saw photography as an intrinsic, if aesthetic and humanizing part of the subject and did not forbear from criticism of some contemporary practice: 'Among the innumerable uses now made of the photographic camera, that which might be made of it by the anthropologist, and especially the travelling anthropologist, seems to be insufficiently appreciated and utilized' (1893:184). And of those who have the temerity to try, he is equally scathing, referring to the 'almost uniform badness of illustrations of living primitive folk in books of anthropology and travel' (1893:185). In many ways his article 'On the Anthropological Uses of the Camera', for which he is so well known, should, in relation to his own photography, be viewed as a retrospective rationalization rather than a manifesto.[2]

By the time im Thurn presented his paper he had, as far as we can ascertain, ceased his photography.[3] It was, in effect, a justification for his earlier dedication. First, it set his photographs, some taken more than a decade before the publication of his paper, within the framework of the current shift from evolutionary theory towards a more relativist cultural anthropology. Secondly, he used his paper as a means to attack the accepted stereotypes of anthropological photography, and replace them with a more spontaneous (or what he might term 'natural') approach which he regarded as being more relevant and informative to anthropology. His view of the 'natural' in its most straightforward sense meant taking pictures without imposition or arrangement, and his collection, or what little of it that we have, seems to demonstrate his vision. The intention of the present essay is to place im Thurn's photographic record of the British Guianan Indians in this context by considering the possibilities presented by three of his images, rather than explore his output in terms of broader and more theoretical orders or hierarchies, or indeed of complementary and binary oppositions (such as nature/culture) which have been discussed elsewhere (Tomas 1987).

During his first sojourn in Guiana, when he divided his time between curatorial duties and forays into the interior, im Thurn came into contact with many Indian tribes, including the Arawak and the Warrau peoples of the northern and coastal areas, and the Wapishana, Akawaio, Macusi and Arecuna of the interior. The knowledge and insights he gained from these early encounters meant that when subsequently he returned more fully equipped as a photographer he knew largely what he wanted to photograph.[4] On all his many journeys during this later period, journeys which included the first ascent of Roraima, the legendary mountain first reported by Robert Schomburgk and which later inspired Arthur Conan Doyle's *The Lost World*, familiarity with his subject resulted in remarkable photographs which bear the authority of foreknowledge and foresight. Moreover, their wide coverage of so many different tribal peoples was probably not rivalled as a collection until Theodor Koch-Grünberg's expeditions in the north-west Amazon and Orinoco some two decades later. All we have of this collection now, unless other photographs come to light, are those in the archives of the Royal Geographical Society, the Pitt Rivers Museum, Oxford, and the Royal Anthropological Institute.[5] This last collection and the most relevant to this paper, im Thurn presented to the Institute, apparently mindful, as with his earlier geographical landscape collection, of its scientific and historical worth. It amounted to some forty-nine photographs in all. Most, if not all of these, he used to illustrate his lecture on photography (1893).

Although the Royal Anthropological Institute material was ostensibly a lecture selection and may not reflect the range and content of im Thurn's work, it does give us a sense of his style — his mode of interpretation and the images *he* considered significant. With the exception of a few prints of family and village life and related activities, the bulk of the prints are concerned with various Indian games — particularly those of the Macusi and the Warrau, and a series to illustrate physical types — some upright and unadorned; others, with greater aesthetic emphasis, in languid pose; and some more clearly intended to demonstrate ornamentation and dress. Unlike the work of some of those contemporary photographers he criticized, they are all taken under natural conditions with the possible exception of four photographs for which he uses a pre-prepared section of palm-thatch roofing on the ground, on or in front of which his subjects are situated, in a manner reminiscent of studio photography. They involve no unnatural poses or contortions of the body, or anthropometric devices. Rather there are several prints of individuals or groups caught spontaneously without any trace of manipulation by the photographer, and we are presented with a vision of the 'reality' of the Indian existence. His photographs demonstrate a sympathy with his subject which is too often lacking in anthropological photography of the time. This apparent realism is realized in part through his sympathy with his subject, a sympathy which his images evoke in the viewer.

Im Thurn saw his work, in some ways, as the antithesis of traditional scientific anthropological photography, which dehumanized and objectified. That he was driven by a certain sense of mission in photographic interpretation of native peoples is apparent when after showing several slides of contemporary examples, he states:

> Just as the purely physiological photographs of the anthropometrists are merely pictures of lifeless bodies, so the ordinary photographs of uncharacteristically miserable natives. . . . seem comparable to the photographs which one occasionally sees of badly stuffed and distorted animals. (1893:186)

Im Thurn gives good advice on camera equipment which is suitable under the conditions in which he worked (1893:200–3). He himself used two cameras: one, which he termed a 'hand camera', worked on the modern principle of using film negative, the other was a large stand or plate camera. That he resorted to using both on occasion, and was sometimes equally unsuccessful with either, is evident from the following description of a Pomeroon (Akawaio) dance he witnessed.

> Meanwhile I had wedged myself with my small hand camera against the wall of the house in which the para-sheera were to drink, in the hope of obtaining some instantaneous photographs. Whether by accident or design, the long procession closed around me, yelling, shrieking, and roaring, and waving their dancing sticks so closely around my head that I had continually to duck to avoid them. Then it passed on round the house; and just as I made a rush for my larger camera, which I had before stationed in a position ready for another chance photograph, the procession, to my great disappointment, wended its way into the house. (1934:55)

Despite his failure on this occasion, this account does show im Thurn consciously trying to record a culture as he saw it in as objective a way as possible, spontaneous and without intervention. He makes fairly frequent allusion to the trials of photography which, it must be remembered, was still technically cumbersome. This is very unusual. If there were few anthropologists who used the camera in as integrated a fashion, despite the promotion of photographic recording in contemporary manuals of anthropological observation, there were even fewer who felt inclined to describe the technical and human problems involved. Watching his Indian companions attempting to ford the Ireng River he writes: 'I saw my most cherished possessions — photographic apparatus included — dragged relentlessly under water' (1934:76). He even describes his unsuccessful attempt to take his very first photograph of a 'Redman':

> My red-skinned subject was carefully posed [sic] high upon a mangrove root. He sat quite still while I focussed and drew the shutter. Then, as I took off the cap, with a moan he fell backwards off his perch on the soft sand below him. Nor could he by any means be persuaded to prepare himself once more to face the unknown terrors of the camera. (1893:188)

Of visiting an Akawaio village im Thurn records that 'I enticed several of the dancers out by presents of pipes and tobacco, but could hardly get them to stand to the camera, from which they always fled in terror' (1934:57). Elsewhere he writes that at the very moment when he had to withdraw and to replace the lens cap, the man he was photographing suddenly concealed his face in his hands. He explains this as the Indians' resistance to 'having their features put on paper and being thus submitted spiritually to the power of anyone possessing the picture' (1893:188).

Im Thurn's use of the word 'pose' in the previous quotation is interesting and perhaps requires some consideration. The modern meaning of the word suggests an active intervention in the creation of the image. Most tropical-forest Indians are, in my experience, extraordinarily graceful while still in the prime of life, both in movement and repose. Their attitudes in repose which im Thurn has caught might be considered as poses. They are, more correctly, naturally poised stances which suggest themselves in an intangible aestheticizing way as 'poses', a view perhaps reinforced by his not infrequent and ambivalent use of the word 'pose' to mean an arrangement for the camera that does not *necessarily* imply direct intervention. I shall be considering this question further in relation to one of the photographs.

It is interesting that im Thurn found it necessary to justify his own 'natural' approach to photography by denigrating the work of others — particularly the 'physiological photography' of the 'anthropometrists'. He alludes to their 'influence' over their subjects: of the difficulty of 'inducing' the subject to stand 'in exactly the *artificial* positions requisite for the purpose' (1893:188; emphasis added). Although he himself took a number of 'posed' photographs, he clearly felt that they were more natural, and involved no coercion or compulsion. His aesthetic inclinations were more in tune with the painter of American Indians, George Catlin, whom he admired, rather than with his contemporaries, despite all the positivist advantages offered by the mechanical realism of photography.

117. 'A father and his two sons whom we found in one of the houses,' *c.*1889–90. (RAI 610)

Im Thurn's naturally spontaneous approach to photography is apparent in his Warrau photographs. The difficulties of reaching these north-west coast swamp-dwellers would have deterred many. 'By wading through mud and climbing fallen trees', he writes, 'one penetrates to their [the Warrau's] actual homes, and if on arriving there one does not frighten them into a misery of shyness, one finds them happy and attractive enough' (1934:170). There is certainly no attempt to depict 'physical type' in the print described in his lecture notes (1893:199) as 'of a father and his two sons who we found in one of the houses . . .' (Plate 117). It is not the picture's composition which strikes one so much, rather its intimacy. The sense of intrusion on privacy is palpable in these haunted and wary faces — an indictment of the intrusive eye of the camera, so that one's sympathies are drawn to its subject, and equally perhaps one's awareness of the discomforture of being faced with that intrusion. And yet equally one cannot help but admire the artist who catches this fleeting imagery of the human face. It is a portrait in the true sense in that it transcends the anthropological and descriptive purpose, making a more universal statement. It is a remarkable picture.

The Rodinesque group of three Caribs (Plate 118) could easily be dismissed by the casual observer as posed in a structured sense. It was possibly its obvious appeal to a classical Western aesthetic tradition which made this particular scene 'photographable' to im Thurn, being sympathetic to his vision of these 'admirable human beings'. Im Thurn notes that this picture was taken under the most natural conditions and without their knowledge (1893:190). Again he finds it necessary to justify the picture, but anyone who has witnessed tropical forest Indians in their everyday circumstance would recognize their posture. Titled in the RAI collection 'Which way down the falls?', it shows an entirely typical stance for Indians pausing above a section of rapids to scrutinize a likely route for a canoe to navigate the rock outcrops and turbulent water or witness the progress of a craft. Thus it is an image which operates at two levels. First, it is an accurate representation of Indians 'as they are' in their environment. Second, it is an image which suggests certain aesthetic and representational conventions to the viewer (hence the possible assumption that the photograph was posed) which in their turn suggest a set of values and assumptions on the nature of the 'primitive' — the 'noble savage'. As has already

118. 'Which way down the falls?' *c*.1883–4. (RAI 639)

been suggested, it is difficult to determine how 'posed' some of im Thurn's photographs are, but this image does appear to be one in which his intervention could quite easily, but erroneously, be misread.

We know nothing about the individual Indians depicted in either of these two pictures: we can only extrapolate from the image we have in front of us and from the historical, intellectual and disciplinary structures which framed its making. In the first example we may interpret much from the attitude and features of these three men about the circumstance of that moment in time between the photographer and the photographed. In the second example we cannot even see faces, only the elegant and natural posture of these Caribs. We may interpret the hand on the shoulder as a mark of affection of one man for another, or as the purely physical need to balance on a slippery log. The photograph is, like the first, beautifully composed. Im Thurn was clearly moved by the natural aesthetic of Guianan Indians. It is apparent in his action pictures of games and in his physiological portraits. This suggests great respect for his subjects, an attitude confirmed in his writings.

Unlike the two previous pictures discussed here, we know precisely who the portrait in Plate 119 depicts. It is Lonk. In his paper on anthropological uses of the camera, im Thurn uses this picture as an illustration of the use of photography in depicting material objects in their natural ambience. He names the wearer of the necklace as Lonk, from whose shoulders he acquired it. He notes also:

> *And it may, in passing, be of interest to add that these necklaces, in the manufacture of which only the tusk teeth of the peccary are used so, that, in proportion to its size, each represents a very large number of animals, are most highly valued as heirlooms and as representing the accumulated prowess not only of the wearer for the time being, but also of his ancestors, for this property is handed down in the male line of descent, and is added to by each holder.* (1893:196)

It is curious that im Thurn makes no further reference in his lecture to the wearer. In his essay on the ascent for Roraima he writes:

> *The Macoosie, smaller, more slightly built men, with limbs of curiously beautiful form and wonderful agility, with unusually good features, cleanly in habit, most*

119. Lonk, *c*.1883–4. (RAI 618)

hospitable, obliging and generous, are by far the pleasantest of all the Indians of Guiana. (1934:7)

Of Lonk himself, the leader of the party of Macusi who travelled with him, he is equally eulogistic: 'One of the finest and best Indians I ever met.' Lonk looks at us from his portrait relaxed and good-natured. There is no fleeing from or uncertainty about the camera here but a confident familiarity with the medium and its technological apparatus.

It is through this genial description of the Macusi, and of Lonk himself, that we gain an immediate familiarity with Lonk, for it creates an extra dimension which goes beyond the written word or unrelated photograph as if one is looking at a portrait of a member of one's own family. He is there, as it were, in the flesh. Brought back from the dead, he lives again before us as he must have for im Thurn. Here lies the spontaneous power and paradox of photography so rarely used by im Thurn's contemporaries and with limited success since. However, having used this photograph as an example of showing a material object (a necklace) in its natural setting, im Thurn then, surprisingly, actually isolates the wearer from his own natural background. Apart from this one, several of his photographs have part or all the background blanked out (this technique of using black paint or varnish on some of his negatives is by no means unknown in anthropological photography (Edwards 1990)). Whether he, or someone else, was responsible for this, im Thurn used these pictures in his RAI lecture, and one is left to surmise whether it was done for aesthetic reasons or for technical reasons (perhaps an out-of-focus background) or for 'scientific' reasons, that is, to isolate the figures for clearer exposition.

Im Thurn created a 'positive image' of the 'native' which was not merely a reiteration of the romantic purity of the noble savage stereotype. It argued for a realism, a cultural relativity, an acceptance which, while much of his writing was in the traditional nineteenth-century descriptive mode, was in line with the move away from the established anthropological categorization of that time.

Photography is a sensitive subject among field-workers; so much depends on circumstance. Research may be undermined by the predatory or intrusive camera and alienation may result. For some it seems not to have been a problem. This could be said of the early pictures of im Thurn, whose rapport is implicit in his work, and we can only speculate on why he apparently abandoned his gift after so relatively brief a commitment.

NOTES

1 Im Thurn's ancestors were from the Swiss Rhineland and he was a second-generation Englishman.
2 Im Thurn's rationalization of his work could be viewed as part of a wider movement which was gathering momentum in anthropological photography at the turn of the century. Many of his ideas are echoed by A.C. Haddon in his essay on photography in the third edition of *Notes and Queries* (BAAS 1899:239).
3 Im Thurn writes of 'visiting a settlement of these people [the Warrau] not many months ago' (1893:199), and it seems likely that these were the most recent and last photographs he took (or that we have record of).
4 When I state 'more fully equipped' I am referring to the additional hand-held camera equipment, as well as his stand camera, which he used for these earlier landscape photographs.
5 The forty-two prints in the RGS archive attributed to im Thurn are predominantly Guianan land-scapes. A few illustrate people, either working in logging camps or in formal groups, and include four views of the Kaieteur Falls, which he visited in 1878. Although it is not, to my knowledge, stated elsewhere, these must all be his own work. This perhaps explains the evident professionalism of his later work, for he was already an experienced and accomplished landscape photographer. The few prints in the Pitt Rivers Museum Archive, presented by E.B. Tylor, come from his later period.

REFERENCES

British Association for the Advancement of Science 1899. *Notes and Queries on Anthropology* 3rd edn. London: BAAS.
Edwards, E. 1990. Photographic 'Types': The Pursuit of Method. *Visual Anthropology* 3(2–3):235–58.
im Thurn, E.F. 1883. *Among the Indians of Guiana*. London.
— 1893. Anthropological Uses of the Camera. *Journal of the Anthropological Institute* 22:184–203.
— 1934. *Thoughts, Talks and Tramps*. London: Oxford University Press.
Tomas, D. 1987. *An Ethnography of the Eye. Authority, Observation and Photography in the Context of British Anthropology 1839–1900*. Unpublished Ph.D. thesis, McGill University.

Photographs of the Sankuru and Kasai River Basin Expedition Undertaken by Emil Torday (1876–1931) and M.W. Hilton Simpson (1881–1936)[1]

Jan Vansina

ON OCTOBER 26, 1907 E. Torday, M.W. Hilton Simpson and the artist N. Hardy arrived at Boma, then capital of the Congo. The purpose of their expedition, organized by Torday and the British Museum, was to undertake ethnographic observations and collect objects for the Museum. Torday was the moving spirit.[2] He had been in the Congo in 1900, spending two terms there, the second as an agent of the Compagnie du Kasai (C.K.), a rubber-gathering and general trading company which operated in the areas where the expedition intended to work. An agreement with the C.K. ensured logistical support for the expedition, which was modelled on the Deutsche Inner-Afrikanische Forschungs expedition, led by the anthropologist L. Frobenius, which had been in the area from January 1905 to June 1906 (Frobenius 1907). This expedition collected some 8,000 ethnographic objects and had successfully recorded ethnographic data by visual means — photographs, drawings and paintings. Torday and the British Museum's keeper, T.A. Joyce, hoped that their expedition would duplicate this feat. It fully succeeded. Thousands of objects were collected and a rich and ample ethnographic record, both written and visual, resulted. The results were published in a scholarly work of two quarto volumes edited by Torday and Joyce, published in the *Annales du Musée du Congo Belge* (1910) as well as several popular volumes (Hilton Simpson 1911; Torday 1925a,b).

The expedition set out at a time when the Congo Free State had become highly controversial in Great Britain and Europe as a result of the Congo Reform Movement, which had brought to the attention of the general public atrocities committed by the government and the trading companies. The C.K. was countering such attacks with a major lawsuit against its accusers, particularly the Presbyterian Black American missionary William Sheppard, who had denounced the C.K.'s atrocities in connection with its rubber-gathering activities. In September 1909, perhaps one month after Torday's expedition left the Congo, the case by the C.K. against Sheppard was dismissed (Shaloff 1970:107–30). In addition, a British investigation conducted by the consular agent, Captain W. Thesinger, was in Kasai at the same time as the expedition. This tense atmosphere was important for it led both Torday and Hilton Simpson to emphasize in their writings that they had not met with any atrocities and they certainly avoided taking photographs which could be used by the Reform Movement. Thus in its way the expedition was, despite its scientific intent, a successful public relations effort for the C.K. and the colonial Congo Government.

The responsibility for the expedition's photography was borne chiefly by M.W. Hilton Simpson. He had travelled in the Barbary States (1903–6) and was an experienced photographer (see Hamouda, this volume), joining the expedition at the suggestion of Joyce (Hilton Simpson 1911:v). The photographic record was predictable given the aims of the expedition. It appears that the taking of photographs was seldom impeded and Hilton Simpson's diaries contain many references to it. On June 5, 1909 he wrote:

> Took a number of photos of people at various kinds of work today; result one half of the village is being shaven ostentatiously by the other half in hopes of getting salt if we photo the process. (Hilton Simpson 1907–9, 7:42; bound in iii)

The photographs of ethnographic items were to illustrate the expedition's scientific publications and be a record for the Museum's archives. Other photographs showing more spectacular or exotic aspects of culture appear to have been intended to illustrate the travel accounts or lectures produced for a wider audience. Others were taken as souvenirs for the members of the expedition themselves, for instance pictures of the boys who served them. The set of photographs examined here deals with the Kuba in two aspects, as an example of the 'ethnographic record' and as expressions of colonial dreams and colonial reality. Further, the photographs reveal a 'hidden history' of the colonial situation and power relations which ultimately made it possible to make field collections and photograph in the way the expedition intended.

The Kuba

The most outstanding achievement of the expedition was a description of the Kuba kingdom with its complex structure of government and the refined lifestyle of its patricians. Torday spent altogether only five months in the kingdom and was ill for much of that time. Nevertheless during that time he not only collected hundreds of objects but also succeeded in making a definitive record of Kuba material culture, thanks to the active collaboration of the king, Kot aPe, who had strong political incentives to make an ally out of him (Vansina 1969:27–38).

The photograph of the man holding the statue (Plate 120) is of great value as a record, both ethnographic and as 'hidden history'. Writing on the photograph identifies the man as the 'banga'; but the caption in Torday and Joyce (1910:64 fig. 41) to a similar photograph of the same scene taken from a different angle, reads 'The Chikala II with the statue of Misha

Pelenge Che' (trans.). The caption in Torday (1925b ill. 50 opp. 60) reads 'The judge in matrimonial affairs (Boushongo)' (trans.) who is the Baang official. Hilton Simpson (1911: opp. 204) reprints the photograph discussed here with the caption 'An elder displaying a statue'. The elder is the Baang or his deputy (Cikl II), the second-ranked official in the Kuba judiciary, a very high and trusted titleholder.

The statue itself, called ndop, belongs to a set. Such statues were memorials of former kings and among the most precious objects at the court. This one, considered in association with the royal genealogy, must date from the eighteenth century. Although in his diary Hilton Simpson tells us (1907–9, 6:16; bound in iii) 'Torday packed the statue of Misha Pelenge Che which he is keeping for himself', the statue is now in the British Museum.[3] The set of photographs to which this belongs shows that the statue has a broken arm which was restored sometime after collection. Comparison with other statues shows that the restorer copied the arm (with bangles) from one of two similar statues. The photograph is of great value as a direct ethnographic record showing details such as the daily costume of court officials, and it is of particular value in that it shows us that this statue was in Africa at that court at that time. The photograph authenticates the statue.

But it tells us much more. Clearly the official keeps his hand on the statue. To steady it? Perhaps. He does it on three of the four pictures in this set, the fourth one showing the statue unattended. Was it a pose required by the photographer? Not really.[4] In these photographs the man has a deep frown; very possibly he keeps a hand on the statue to prevent it being snatched away. Clearly he is unhappy with this situation. Given the importance of the statue one understands him. He disapproved of the photographic session but perhaps reluctantly cooperated. The written record (Hilton Simpson 1911:207–10) would support this interpretation of the tension in the photograph for it relates the negotiations on the acquisition of the related Shamba statue, which was purchased at the same time as that of Mishe Pelenge Che, and illustrates the process involved.

Torday first convinced the king to relinquish some statues but it then took longer to buy out members of the council.

> T wants to get hold of another statue, that of Shamba and the way he set about it is illustrative of the politics here. The root of the matter is this. The king is young and advanced in his ideas; the Kolomos, as a whole, are old and very backward. The king is pro-European; the councillors are anti-European. The King has the appointing of councillors in his hands and he has 3 younger men

120. The *ndop* statue, Kuba, 1908. (RAI 27304)

121. *Mbeem* masquer, Kuba, 1908. (RAI 26644)

in it who constitute his party, 2 against 4. The other 4 old men, as is rather the custom of old men all the world over, think that for them the King would run the country to ruin, and they would therefore like to set him right. Lukengu therefore, is allowing it to be thought that he himself is opposed to the sale of the statue, this being the best way to make them favour the sale; he has told T to catch each councillor separately and square him financially and ask him to intercede with the King on his behalf. This plan has worked well with the premier and another councillor, the only two tried today. The Kolomos did not want Lukengu to sell Bopi's statue to us and asked how we knew of its existence. The chief said one of his wives had left it lying about and it had thus been seen. (Hilton Simpson 1908–9, 5:32; bound in ii)

T . . . squared the remaining elders as to the purchase of Shamba's image. . . . In the evening Samba Samba brought round the image of Shamba. So it is 'got' after all. It was a great wrench to Lukengu to part with it. He said that with the image before him he could see the old King, who, too was looking down on him from heaven. He offered another statue as a substitute, but gave the real one afterwards. T explained that more than probably the image would [be] eventually thrown on a State man, and that it would be better placed with him as historian of the Bakuba. Anyhow it is obtained and it has to be kept a secret like the other statue which already has gone on its way to Europe. (Hilton Simpson 1908–9, 5:37; bound in ii)

Torday was thus able to exploit Kuba political divisions to acquire precious objects for probably the king agreed initially because he needed Torday's support in a crisis with the state authorities (Torday 1925b:143–6).

Plate 121 shows the *Mbeem* official dressed in the mask of royalty, Mwash aMbooy. Hilton Simpson's caption (1911: opp. 204) reads 'The *nyimi* [king] in his ghost dance' and he describes the dance (1911:203–4). The actual mask, called *lapukpuk* at court, was old and renowned and, although neither Torday nor Hilton Simpson appears to have known it, it had been re-worked for the king, who wore it for the dance witnessed by the expedition on October 5, 1908.[5]

Hilton Simpson records the occasion in his diary. During the night, by moonlight, the king in this costume with a huge fan of eagle feathers (representing his authority) walked around the village and danced (Hilton Simpson 1908, 5:36; bound in ii) to express his authority. This is not the only dance in which this masked figure appears, as it also came out with a set of two others during a famous mimed dance organized from time to time at the capital (Cornet 1982:251 ill. 305, 255, ill. 307, 256–62, ill. 314, 263, 272–8). In his book, however, Hilton Simpson talks about the 'heat of the tropical afternoon', thus locating the actual picture.

The following passage in his diary for December 19 describes the scene.

In the afternoon the Baimbi, by request, got himself up in the Mashamboy costume to be photoed, as did another man in another costume. The Moshamboy [sic] in complete costume down to socks and gloves long sleeves garters etc. The mask is ornamented very much with feathers, beads and cowries swarm. The other man had a black costume and weird black and yellow mask. The dancing was witnessed by the King — and it is most exhausting to the dancer who has to take frequent and long rests. (Hilton Simpson 1908–9, 6:17; bound in iii)

The dance captured in this photograph was the 'mime dance', or rather a souvenir of the mime dance. The dancer posed with the king for an 'official' photograph. Torday and Joyce (1910:21, fig. 11) published another photograph taken on the same occasion which shows only the masked person. Both of these photographs illustrate the expedition's power to orchestrate or negotiate re-enactment, but they also recall the mime and its expression of a complex Kuba ideology. However faint it may be, to Kuba and students of Kuba art there is a moving appeal here: a reference to a free monument of thought at the very point of its capture.

Another dance of political significance is shown in a photograph described by Hilton Simpson (1911: opp. 111) as 'A ceremonial dance by an Elder' (Plate 122). Torday and Joyce call it 'Kolomo Bangongo dancing on the occasion of his election' (1910:75, fig. 51) (trans.). The same man is shown sideways in fuller motion by Torday (1925a: opp. 152) where the caption reads: 'An Affair of State. A High Bushongo dignitary proceeding to a state function executes in the street a *pas seul* for the delectation of the populace.' While the ethnographic details show it to have been taken in Misumba, a Ngongo village, it is, once again, a posed photograph. It is likely that the Europeans saw such a march/dance which was then re-enacted for the photograph. The spectators, mostly women and children, are few in number and look at the camera not at the man. In a real situation the focus of attention would be quite different.

This type of scene seems to have appealed to the Europeans. A painting by Hardy actually captioned 'Misumba' (Hilton Simpson 1911: opp. 91) shows an elder stepping with his staff of office held horizontally behind his neck over his shoulders, his hands resting on its ends. This is a posture adopted by men in authority when they assert their status. They will thus parade in the village plaza, going from one end to the other in order to express their will and the general displeasure. Small signs, such as holding a parrot's feather at the edge of their mouth, show their par-

122. Dance of an elder, Misumba village, 1908–9. (RAI 27255)

ticular concern. No one draws near them. In the photograph here the elder dancing is showing off his insignia (sword, fly whisk, feathered hat, skins) and the correct caption is probably one relating to his march on the occasion of his nomination.

Sets of photographs of dancing chiefs and title-holders are quite common among Torday and Hilton Simpson's records. Indeed the cover of the latter's book shows notables dancing. The attraction of this subject seems to originate from a fusion of two forces. One is a Kuba impulse. Such marches or dances are tied to the exercise of both spiritual and factual authority: they are acts of government. The other input, no doubt, was a stereotype well implanted in Europe: African cannibal chiefs dancing around the pot. In Europe the dignity of high office was incompatible with dancing and here the dignity of office had to be expressed through dancing. At the very least this paradox must have struck Torday and his companions. The net effect of their graphic documentation was to reinforce the stereotype that 'Africa dances', a thoroughly exotic notion.

Another image which includes aspects of stereotypical Africa exists in three formats; as a photograph, as a painting by Hardy after the photograph, and as a cracked glass slide. Torday and Joyce publish it (1910;124, fig. 102) as 'Charm at the entry of the Nyimi's [king's] courtyard' (trans.) as one in a series of illustrations of charms (Plate 123). In style the object is not Kuba, but rather Songye (although the photograph is unclear) as is confirmed by the axe handle and the plaiting of its dress, as well as the horn and coiffure. It may thus belong to a set of charms made for the king in 1902 or 1903 by the famous medicine man Iyoong (Vansina 1969:19–20). This was the first time foreign charms had been introduced into the court. Their aim was to stop an epidemic and restore the full sovereignty of the king. The set existed in 1908 and is illustrated by Torday and Joyce (1910;29, fig. 19), 'The Nyimi and the Kot a Mboke charms'

123.   Charm at the entrance of the palace courtyard, Kuba, 1908–9. (RAI 26649)

124. 'The Clockwork elephant.' Itambi village?, 1909. (RAI 14755)

(trans.), as well as by Torday (1925b: opp. 96) with the caption 'The first fetishes introduced in Boushongo country'.[6]

The charm shown at the entrance of a palace courtyard may be in the same style but it is not, however, one of the four in the other photograph. Indeed we know nothing about it in contrast to the excellent documentation of the other photograph. It may be that it was set up on the trestle for the photograph. Equally it may be that this was its normal setting. There is some contradiction between the fact that nothing was recorded about it yet, on the other hand, a slide and a painting were made of it suggesting that some importance was attached to it. Perhaps in this instance it is the image itself and its connotations that caught the imagination. Here we have the quintessential fetish with all its appendages. The image fitted the stereotype and no doubt the slide could be used to illustrate the nature of superstition at public lectures. The irony

is, of course, that charms of state were almost unknown among the Kuba. The image projected was therefore a conscious distortion of observed realities.

Uncharted lands and colonial realities

Between the end of May 1909 and early June the expedition crossed the lands between the Loange and Kasai rivers through Wongo and Lele territory into 'unknown country'. From their accounts we know that its members felt like explorers (Torday 1925a: 234–80; Hilton Simpson 1911:295–345). The supplies of food, furniture, weapons, ammunition and iron rods for currency as well as staff had been obtained by the nearby C.K. post. Going with only twenty Bambala carriers and their own houseboys, they hoped to recruit locally as they progressed.

Despite preparations the expedition did not always meet a friendly reception and measures had to be taken to mitigate the position. The little elephant in Plate 124 is described as playing an important part at Kenge on June 9 and 10, 1909, when the party was 'in a tight corner'. We are told by Hilton Simpson (1911:323) and Torday that on arrival at Kenge the people, disappointed because they had 'brought little or no iron', threatened to attack the expedition. Torday, however, had brought along some toys, including two mechanical elephants (Hilton Simpson 1911:261–2) which he used, with other tricks such as flaming water (whisky), to impress the local people with the power of his magical charms. Torday was not the first to use such tricks. It was common practice, recommended by the highest authorities to their explorer-agents from the very first days of the Congo State (Delathuy 1989:203). Still, the shabbiness of such procedures prompted Hilton Simpson to justify their use (1911:324). These tricks had been used by Torday earlier in the expedition, before crossing the Loange, and their value to the party had become apparent. Now in Kenge (according to Hilton Simpson's diary for June 10), he did it again, in secret, for one of the village headmen:

He entered the tent and as soon as he was in he jumped out backwards with a squeak and then stood with staring eyes, wagging his tongue. (Hilton Simpson 1907–9, 7:45; bound in iii)

Obviously others were told of this 'medicine' and Torday had only to tell the other headman 'I sleep, but the elephant never sleeps' for cooperation with the expedition to begin.

The occasion at Kenge is described in Hilton Simpson's popular account of the expedition (1911:321–4) and this photograph, captioned 'The Clockwork Elephant', accompanies it. A different photograph of the elephant on the table, surrounded by relaxed onlookers, captioned 'A Wonderful Toy' (opp. 256), illustrates Torday's account of the incident (Torday 1925a:255–64). However from Hilton Simpson's diary it seems that this photograph was taken on June 26 at Itambi, a Lele village.

Thus this particular photograph appears to have been taken the last time the elephant 'walked'. Torday, standing as master of ceremonies, shows off the elephant, while the public, unafraid as we see from the mix of adults and children, watch with genuine interest. Some are just curious, some are puzzled and only one woman veers away. But there is no panic, and Torday's guard in white between the tent and the audience could afford to look at his master or the camera.

The elephant was made to walk and created a great impression the people say they saw him wink. (Hilton Simpson 1907–9, 7:63; bound in iii)

The tension stemmed entirely from the written description that accompanied this photograph, not from the photograph itself, as a close reading of the visual evidence shows. The photograph was certainly taken

125.   The original of George Morrow's caricature of Hilton-Simpson and Torday 'frightening the savage Bakongo with a toy elephant' published in *The Sketch*, 6 April 1910. (RAI 27167)

126i–ii.   Inside a Bashilele village, 1909? (RAI 30033, 30032)

to provide just such an illustration to the account, irrespective of the fact that Kenge, where the incident occurred, was a Wongo village and the ethnographic detail in the picture (such as hairstyles and palisading) reveals it to have been taken at a Lele village.

But the description certainly had its effect in Britain where it was the subject of a cartoon (Plate 125) which reduces everything to the basic stereotypes and caricature: smirking European demigods, the elephant, and dancing cannibals with vaguely Zulu armaments. This stereotypic view is present in the photograph and is even more pronounced in the accompanying texts. Consequently, although the two Europeans knew that they were in difficulties and had to extricate themselves in a variety of ways (by instilling fear of their weapons and their guards as well as fear of their 'medicine') it appears in the cartoon representation as if they played no more than a prank in order to tame the unpredictable but jolly savages.

By contrast the photograph of a village (Plate 126i) suggests another aspect to the expedition's experience. It is published in Torday (1925a: opp. 240) and captioned 'A Bashilele Village within the palisade' and a similar photograph (Plate 126ii) taken a few moments earlier and from a slightly different angle is captioned 'Interior of a Bashilele village' (trans.) (Torday and Joyce 1910:154 ill. 191). We are within the 'unknown country', looking at a large village square, a peaceful scene. Four people observe from afar. A lone child sits under the shed. A woman and some children stand to one side and behind the raphia tree beyond which is a tree and some other plants, probably part of the magical garden that protected the village. Clearly a picture taken during the day when most adults were off on their own pursuits. Although the identity of the village is not certain it may be Masuku II where the expedition received a friendly reception (Hilton Simpson 1911:332) and where women who remained in the village were like those mentioned in the diary for June 20, 1909:

> We have taken some photos and no one minds it, but the women are shy of the camera and wax kittenish when asked to pose, so we have not got any to speak of. (Hilton Simpson 1907–9, 7:55; bound in iii)

While the reception at this village was friendly, it was not so elsewhere, as we have seen at Kenge. The contrast between the two contexts suggests the volatile and complex nature of power relations which are belied by the peaceful, 'unmediated' view of this village in 'unknown country'.

While the previous two images suggest in different ways a stereotype of the calm rational superiority of the European explorer, Plate 127 reveals a very different stereotype of Africa itself. The sweet scene 'Babunda playing a drum', taken in April 1910, oozes romantic sentimentality. 'A Souvenir from Congo' could almost be the caption, for it is reminiscent of those postcards captioned 'Souvenir from Rhyl' or those representing Holland in windmills and clogs — it certainly fulfils the same function. Here we have not only a posed picture, down to the last gesture, but, in sharp contrast to the other photographs discussed, one where the actors probably could not even understand the photographer's intentions. The little boy with his hand on his heart, the look passing between the drummers, their gestures — everything is artificial. One neither drums nor sends signals on the slit-drum in this way. It is all fake. But fake for whom and for what? It does not appear in any of the published accounts. Maybe it was a deliberate 'aesthetic' response for European consumption.[7] The composition shows some expression of Hilton Simpson's own aesthetic sensibilities. The back of the kneeling man reminds one of other photographs by Hilton Simpson showing the body beautiful. He may have been making visual reference to other sentimental pictures which were already commonly available. But on the other hand, as a romantic making his way through uncharted lands, he may have felt that this artificial pose reflected a colonial dream — that of the 'noble savage' spoiled elsewhere by European contact. Torday certainly shared such sentiments:

> I should like in all humility, to suggest to the Belgian authorities that the country between Kasai and Loange be made a human reservation and the natives preserved from all contacts with Europeans. . . . (Torday 1925a:237)

By contrast Plate 128 shows the colonial reality. This photograph is of Sam, Torday and Hilton Simpson's houseboy, not yet fifteen when he was hired, the Luba houseslave of a Kuba man in Lusambo. It is one of a genre of 'Sam' photographs — Sam resting, Sam courting, Sam spanking another boy, etc. The picture, taken in December 1907 at the outset of the journey, is labelled 'A "Moluba" given his first set of clothes by Torday'. Proud in trousers, braces, shirt and feathered Panama hat, Sam smokes a cigar and poses. We can be quite certain that he was proud of his outfit, a badge of status, just as we can be certain that this was intended as a caricature, tempered perhaps a bit by the intention that the photograph would also be a memento of their houseboy. Still, the main idea is a caricature: the negro music-hall minstrel with his cigar is suggested. Had the picture been published that would have been its effect. Its message, whether in the caption or by implication, would have suggested how spoiled Africans became when in European company.

127. 'Babunda playing a drum.' 1910. (RAI 25472)
128. Sam. 1907. (RAI 35601)

It was a familiar theme; one finds many instances of it — in Frobenius' work to cite but one book (1907). Yet Sam served faithfully for two whole years, travelling far and wide and adapting to varying circumstances. He was identified with the dawn of the colonial world (Hilton Simpson 1911:39–41, 77–8). Neither Sam nor his master knew that as one of thousands of displaced Luba who were attaching themselves to Europeans he was among those who would be the élite of Kasai in the coming century. The future did not belong to the masked kings — it belonged to the Sams.

NOTES

1 I should like to thank Ms Fiona Stewart for her help, not only with the photographs but especially for the extracts from the diary of Hilton Simpson kept at the Royal Anthropological Institute.

2 On Torday see *Biographie Coloniale Belge*, vol. 4:883–5. Biographical information about Hilton Simpson is available at the Royal Anthropological Institute. Drawings by Norman Hardy (about whom I have no biographical information) appeared in the *Illustrated London News* of 1910 and 1911.

3 For a recent photograph cf. J. Cornet (1982:93 col. pl. 34).

4 The most posed photograph is the one in Torday's *Causeries congolaises* (1925: opp. 160).

5 The mask was still in the capital until recently when the National Museum of Zaïre acquired it (Cornet 1982:259–60, ill. 312, 313).

6 It appears again in Cornet (1982: 292), who found two of the four statues still at the capital in the 1970s.

7 Certainly some of the paintings by the artist, Norman Hardy, who left the expedition after six months, were of this type.

REFERENCES

1955. *Biographie Coloniale Belge* 4. Brussels: Académie Royale des Sciences Coloniales.

Cornet, J. 1982. *Art Royal Kuba*. Milan: Sipiel.

Delathuy, A.M. 1989. *De Kongo Staat van Leopold II 1876–1900*. Antwerp: Standaard.

Frobenius, L. 1907. *Im Schatten des Kongostaates*. Berlin: Reimer.

Hilton Simpson, M.W. 1907–9. *Journal of the Congo Expedition*. Royal Anthropological Institute MS. 65. Typescript diary with contact prints. 7 vols. bound as three.

— 1911. *Land and Peoples of the Kasai*. London: Constable.

Shaloff, S. 1970. *Reforms of Leopold's Congo*. Richmond, Va.: John Knox Press.

Torday, E. 1925a *On the Trail of the Bushongo*. London: Seeley, Service & Co.

— 1925b *Causeries congolaises*. Brussels: Vromant.

Torday, E. & Joyce, T.A. 1910. *Notes ethnographiques sur les peuples communément appelés Bakuba, ainsi que sur les peuplades apparentées Les Bushongo*. Annales du Musée du Congo-Belge. Ethnographie/Anthropologie-Série III. Documents ethnographiques concernant les populations du Congo Belge. 2(1). Brussels: Musée du Congo Belge.

— 1922. *Notes ethnographiques sur les populations habitant les bassins du Kasai et du Kwango orientale. 1. Peuplades de la forêt — 2. Peuplades des prairies*. Annales du Musée du Congo Belge. Ethnographie/Anthropologie — Série III. Documents ethnographiques concernant les populations du Congo Belge. 2(2). Brussels: Musée du Congo Belge.

Vansina, J. 1969. Du royaume au 'territoire des Bakuba'. *Etudes congolaises* 12(2):3–54.

Two Portraits of Auresian Women

Naziha Hamouda[1]

It is difficult, in interpreting and analyzing colonial documentation, to dissociate the author from his work or to disregard a decisive context in the perception of the individuals involved in the encounter. However, it is these two elements which come together as I try to take into account the experience of the people who posed for the photographer of these photographs, the collector and ethnographer M.W. Hilton Simpson. Hilton Simpson visited the Aures Massif region of eastern Algeria with his wife Helen on a number of occasions between 1912 and 1920. The region lies between the high plains of eastern Algeria and the edge of the Sahara. Its valleys run north-east to south-west; Ighzerm' Abdi wadi and Ighzer Amelal are the main valleys, joined by the secondary valleys of Bouzina and Tarhit, and Hilton Simpson travelled extensively throughout the region (Hilton Simpson 1921:10).

It would be a mistake to attribute to Hilton Simpson an ethnographic approach different from that held by his contemporaries, who were deeply influenced by the French conception of the Magreb. This conception, most notably when transmitted in Western media through novel, screen and popular ephemera such as postcards (Alloula 1987), conformed to the internal logic and dynamics of French policy. Its role was to encourage acceptance and to change real conflicts into symbolic representations, usable and assimilable by the people, in order to justify its socio-political project.

If Hilton Simpson was not necessarily bound by specific colonial policy, as were some French ethnographers and administrators, the tone of his writing and choice of subject reveal the influence of such ideological institutions, seeing the peoples of the Aures as exotic, primitive and distanced. His work *Among the Hill Folk of Algeria* is a good illustration of this. Conceived as a popular ethnography (1921:10), its style is perhaps predictable (e.g. 1921:9, 34, 220).[2] But this belies Hilton Simpson's careful and thorough ethnographic observation as an examination of his notebooks[3] and photographs reveals.

Hilton Simpson's photographic documents present little overall diversity in the choice of scenes — women and nature are his favourite subjects, although he also photographed many aspects of culture including work (especially women's work), music and dance. Hilton Simpson had perhaps greater access to women and women's work through his wife, who accompanied him, and also because Auresian women do not face the restrictions experienced by their Muslim sisters in other parts of Algeria (Hamouda 1985:43). Although, arguably, there is a predictability of subject-matter, his approach suggests a desire to document rather than merely to romanticize. His landscape photographs are not chance snapshots but careful establishing images of the land that contained and sustained the culture he was documenting; his book is full of detailed visualizations of both landscape and journeys that give a strong sense of place (e.g. 1921:130, 204); locating and identifying the particular villages, streets and houses and the surrounding countryside.

The two portraits of dancers from Thizi Abed village discussed here represent Hilton Simpson's other favourite subject for photography. As such they might indeed be read as embodying aspects of 'romanticism' and erotic fantasy. While this was perhaps the root of Hilton Simpson's fascination it is too simplistic a reading, but one which was perhaps that of the readership of *Among the Hill Folk of Algeria*, where the photographs are presented as portrait types; indeed the portrait of Algia out fiala discussed below is reproduced in the volume above the generalizing caption 'An Ouled Abdi Dancer and her Finery' (1921: opp. 80). At first glance the central, full-face placing of the figure appears to fulfil this role. However, we are

fortunate in being able to situate these images within Auresian folk memory, thus revealing other facets of them.

At the time of Hilton Simpson's stay in the Aures the valley of Ighzer was famous for its professional dancers, *Theazriyin*. It is from them that the adjective *theaznith* evolved, with its meaning of 'woman' and 'artist'. One of the photographer's first tasks during his stay at Thizi Abed was to attend wedding ceremonies where *Theazriyin* were the main performers. One of the informants who remembered him pointed out that Hilton Simpson used to go to the ceremony whenever he was offered the opportunity and he certainly took a series of photographs of dancers and musicians at another village, Beni Ferah, in a neighbouring valley (Plate 129). This behaviour was not in any way surprising at a time when *Theazriyin* consitituted a subject of popular eroticism, dazzling and charming tourists and city dwellers. Yet in Auresian society *Theazriyin* are an expression of a woman's independence. These women were not

129. Professional dancer from Wed Abdi dances for the crowd awaiting the arrival of the bride. Beni Ferah village, 1920. (RAI 8944)

courtesans (as they were described in the Western literature) but free artists, and perhaps property owners, respected and talented people in their own right (Hamouda 1985:44–5). While Hilton Simpson stresses their freedom in his writings, he also himself perpetuates the Western stereotype with the use of words such as 'voluptuous' and 'unrestrained' (1921:101). Nevertheless, he appears to have responded to the women's independence, strength of character and power of self-presentation: perhaps it was this paradox between the perceived Western view of them and the true nature of their existence which fascinated him.

Algia out fiala (Plate 130), well known for her talent as an artist, was also a businesswoman and a farmer who managed her own personal property. She appears to be posing for the author on the edge of the gorges of Thizi Abed and on the path to *thaqlieth*[4] from the village. The photograph appears to show her completely at ease in precisely the way she is described by those who remember her. Endowed with a dynamic and graceful deportment, Algia out fiala always wore her set of silver: *thimcharfin* (earrings), lay silver collar, lambar collar strung with perfumed seeds, five *hjoub* talismans, two *thibzimin* brooches, a hanging *thesith*, a hand mirror in a small leather case, six pairs of *imakyacen* bracelets and, as required by fashion at that period, rings on her fingers and a chain with a key as a pendant.

One of the admirers of Algia out fiala commented to the author, 'She was very coquettish and dressed up every day, always ready'. However, some elements of her clothing show that she is not dressed in her best (contrary to Hilton Simpson's caption in the book) but rather coming from or going to the orchard. The piece of material she is holding in her hand is used for the foliage collected by the women of Aures for their goats. The *loga* (shawl) around her shoulders is of dark-hued wool, whereas the *thalamt* reserved for ceremonies is made of white silk. Moreover, the *ihar* or main garment seems to be in ordinary fabric, with a belt made of wool and trimmed with glittering threads around the waist. Algia out fiala's casual dress and the way she carries herself, her manner of being, give a personal dimension to this photograph which has otherwise isolated her from any recognizable cultural context. It is a fine portrait.

Aicha Zouza[5] was Algia's niece (Plate 131). Her talent as a dancer and an innovator in dance steps won her a special status among the *Theazriyin*. Admired for her art and her beauty, she was the guest of honour at all the parties in the valley. She told me that she met Hilton Simpson and his wife at one local dance

131.   Aicha Zouza. (RAI 9473)

130.   (*facing page*)   Algia out fiala. 1914. (RAI 8802)

organized by the French officers. 'During their stay in the village of Thizi Abed, his wife visited me after — she liked our cooking.' Aicha Zouza does not remember the circumstances in which she was photographed, but she acknowledged that it was in a lane located at the corner of her house, very close to the *thaqlieth* café of the village.

Oral tradition tells us that at that time the women of Aures, and especially the *Theazriyin*, had such liberty of action that going to the café was a simple act which did not give rise to any special comment. It was in this lane leading to the café that Aicha Zouza posed at ease for Hilton Simpson. Her simplicity was her way of being, of showing herself to advantage. 'I am not so fond of jewellery', she said to me. 'I restrict myself to a necklace of amber and bracelets, the brooch and the earrings I am wearing are made of gold. I was one of the first women to introduce it to Thizi Abed.' A symbol of grace and model of elegance for the young girls of Thizi Abed, Aicha Zouza never passed unnoticed, and Hilton Simpson made sure that he committed her to memory.

The two photographs of the *Theazriyin* show that Hilton Simpson has intentionally chosen to take them outside the circle of the feast. But as we have seen, what begins to stand out are the characters of these two Auresian women, about whose artistic, spiritual and physical qualities oral tradition is so eloquent. Their reputation and consequently their popularity was such that Hilton Simpson could not do otherwise than ask them to pose for him — indeed, perhaps it would have been expected — and for that reason the two scenes have little element of spontaneity about them. Yet is not his decision to photograph the two women in an isolated framework a way of revealing their personality and conveying his admiration for them? In both portraits Hilton Simpson adopts a low camera angle, elevating the two women and giving them stature in visual terms which perhaps mirrors their status in their society. He recognizes the force of their characters, their way of being, producing perceptive portraits which we now know are corroborated by the oral memory of the Auresian people.

The assumptions and interpretations that can be attached to photographs can be as various as those relating to the historical events of the Aures and reflect the rich social history of that region. While such a photographic document is complemented and verified by oral tradition and written material, it in turn complements and verifies information that is obtainable from such sources. As historical data it can act with other texts not only as a point of comparison within a society, in this case the socio-economic status of women with that of men, but also as a living image of what a society was at a given moment.

NOTES

1 Editor's note: Naziha Hamouda died tragically in a motor accident in December 1989, leaving only an early draft of her essay for this volume. So that her work reaches some sort of fruition, this draft has been reworked, drawing on correspondence and conversations with the Editor, Dr Nanneke Redclift and Roslyn Poignant. While it has not been possible to reconstruct the depth of analysis and scholarship which would have truly done justice to Dr Hamouda's ideas, we hope we have not misrepresented her.

2 For example: '. . . like the cannibal tribes of Central Africa and other primitive peoples, the Shawia are very forward and promising when young, often, it must be confessed, quite failing as they grow up to fulfil this early promise owing, no doubt, to the absence of a good native system of education in the remote hamlets of the hills' (Hilton Simpson 1921:220).

3 In the Museum of Mankind, London.

4 *Thaqlieth* means a storehouse where possessions are kept during the transhumance period of the semi-sedentary population in the Aures.

5 Interviewed by the author in September 1985, Aicha Zouza, aged ninety, enjoyed a perfect memory.

REFERENCES

Alloula, M. 1987. *The Colonial Harem*. Manchester: University Press.
Hamouda, N. 1985. Rural Women in the Aures: A Poetry in Context. *Oral History* 13(1):43–53.
Hilton Simpson, M.W. 1921. *Among the Hill Folk of Algeria*. London: Fisher Unwin Ltd.

Photography, Power and the Southern Nuba

James C. Faris

THE PHOTOGRAPHS DISCUSSED in this essay are from an early series of the abundantly photographed Southern Nuba peoples of Kordofan Province, Sudan, and as such form an instructive contrast with more contemporary photography (cf. Riefenstahl 1974, 1976; Faris 1988a, 1989) of these same people. In terms of power and the photographic image, there are at least three 'projects' here that deserve attention. First is an obvious issue of content, the power of the colonial authority over the subject; another, perhaps less obvious project, involves consideration of the structure of the photograph itself; the power accorded the camera loci in these images. A third project concerns the intellectual situating and constituting of the Other, the making 'safe' of the making 'wild' of Nuba agriculturalists for Western consumption in the photographic enterprise.

The six photographs chosen for this commentary are from a collection of twenty nitrate negatives given to the Royal Anthropological Institute by F.S.G. Whitfield in 1982. Whitfield had been a government entomologist stationed at Talodi in the southern Nuba Mountains and took these photographs on February 3, 1929 at Talodi on the occasion of the visit of Lord Lloyd, British High Commissioner of Egypt and Sudan to the Southern Nuba area. Lord Lloyd's visit was important for several reasons, among them being to acknowledge the potential to the colonial enterprise of the newly inaugurated cotton schemes,[1] but more specifically to signal the recently completed road network in the Nuba Mountains and the *pax Britannica* now established over the unruly region.[2] Thus *The Times* report of Lord Lloyd's visit notes '. . . the retinue consisted of His Excellency's Rolls Royce, three touring cars, the baggage lorries, a Sudan Defence Force escort, and a motor machine gun battery' (February 9, 1929:9a), so it must be anticipated that these photographs document overt control in the distinct military-colonial model: '. . . no fewer than 4,000 men were drawn up in semi-military[!] parade to be reviewed by him' (*The Times*, March 5, 1929:18e).

Lord Lloyd is seen at this review (Plate 132) beside a temporary shade decorated with cloth-wrapped uprights, the Union Jack, and other flags of the colonial realm, including the locally despised 'Egyptian Red' (Mohamed 1974:97). Trooping (with more apparent attention to the camera than to Lord Lloyd) are clothed and unclothed Nuba as well as local Arabs of the region (Plate 133). The parade passes on, around a ground with striped lines (Plate 134) in preparation for the 'savage' entertainment arranged for later in the day (Plates 135–7). In these photographs, at least, Lord Lloyd is not being treated to the impressive Nuba

132. Lord Lloyd and visiting officials. (RAI 35236)

133. Procession (RAI 35237)

134. View of the procession. (RAI 35236)
135. Young Nuba men. (RAI 35230)

agricultural prowess — even though the presence of this many local people is probably the consequence of the gathering of the cotton crop (personal correspondence, Mrs Ida Whitfield to RAI, October 2, 1985), and they constitute an example of an essentially agricultural occasion turned into a staged military-control spectacle.

Though we are assured that Whitfield's photographs were '. . . out of pure interest and not on any assignment' (personal correspondence, Mrs Ida Whitfield to RAI, October 2, 1985), his camera was clearly accorded authority, for not only are local people arranged (Plates 133–5), so indeed are Europeans (Plate 132)![3] The camera has thus in these images absolute focal privilege. Only in Plate 136 does the general anarchy (in comparison to the lines and the order in the other photographs of the events of the day) of Nuba wrestling take over and the camera must peer voyeuristically (peeking between other spectators) rather than command. In general, however, it is the site of attention — it is as conspicuous as those photographed — it is demanding of attention, it commands.

Though there is little question of the power relationship and British hegemony, its expression here is even extended to paternal control over the combats of the Nuba. The event — a review parade, wrestling and spear-throwing — involves many traditional elements such as age-grade-specific sports, but they are non-traditionally juxtaposed for the High Commissioner. For example, that adjacent wrestling age grades are joined, as opposed to being traditionally paired with alternate age grades (adumok grades with bells about their waists posed alongside adere grades with no bells, Plate 135) does not suggest self-arrangement.[4] In the same photograph there are also mounted Baggara Arab horsemen just visible behind the wrestlers, not an arrangement much appreciated by those for whom nudity was to be decried or certainly to be avoided as representative of the Sudan, and certainly a vivid expression of the British crusade to inhibit the spread of Islam and control Arabs in the Nuba Mountains (see Ahmed 1971; Faris 1985).

The spear-throwing was sensationally reported by the account in *The Times* of Lord Lloyd's visit '. . . the accuracy and skill shown by the performers, both with shield and with spear, are probably due to the fact that when they are practising at home, the spears are poisoned' (March 5, 1929:18e). In fact, rather than the spectacle argued, spear-throwing (Plate 137) is the less significant, important and honourable of sports; as Nadel states (1947:299) '. . . it is (in the eyes of the Korongo) physically less exacting. The changing from the severe variety of wrestling to spearfighting is

explained as reflecting the gradual loss of youthful vigor . . .'.[5]

The very order and control renders strangely impotent the wrestling and spear-throwing. It is not without significance that it is Nuba fighting and combat competencies that are the object of the photographs, not their agriculture. It is *their* power confined, arranged. They are certified Other by their nudity, by their 'exotic' activity, by the invisibility of their productive agriculture (ostensibly one of the reasons behind the entire occasion), but they are domesticated (by the photographic capture, by the British-imposed order to their sport). This project, this priority, this colonial motion is evident even in the photographs of an amateur, for it was by now well established, dating from the time of the earliest triumph of imperialism and the great confident world's fairs of the turn of the century with their exotic 'theme' pavilions.

Crowds are presented as orderly, events are expansive, even aristocratic, with audiences controlled, the presentation of spectacle so dear to atavistic class structures, especially in the West (cf. Neale 1979). There is ample room for events, and they occur in an atmosphere of structure, if not rehearsal (note the lined grounds in Plate 134). Nothing about the photographic encounter is hidden: the authority is certain, the hierarchy clear and power is situated at viewer focus in a confident, controlled fashion. The relationship between locals and British authority is obvious — both parties appear to understand it (if never accept it; after all, the Nuba continued to revolt periodically) — and this allows something of a confidence to the colonized as well as a temporary arrogance to the colonizer. This situation has dramatically changed in more recent photographic encounters in this region.

The Southern Nuba and their sports have since this time (and even before; cf. Fife 1927) been the subject of continual photographic expeditions (which the flamboyant, sensationalist and celebratory reporting such as that of *The Times* did nothing to discourage). Among others, accounts in English are known from Seligman & Seligman 1932, Corkill 1939, Strachen 1951, Rodger 1955, Luz & Luz 1966, Riefenstahl 1974, 1976 and Caputo 1982, and while the photographic techniques have changed, the subject-matter is essentially unchanging, as are the intellectual notions motivating the photographs. In style, however, in the power accorded or demanded by the instrument, there are stark contrasts. The photograph becomes progressively more autonomous (except for intrusive close-up 'portraiture'), as there is increasingly a lack of focused privilege, increasingly diffuse foci of scrutiny and an attempt to become fly-on-the-wall to the event. There is a deliberate attempt to hide the camera as

136. Wrestling. (RAI 35228)

focus. Today, of course, we are quite accustomed to this, and seldom query the approach or the deliberate use of enabling techniques such as long-focus lenses and high-speed film, or the sinister, insidious and violating intrusion so disguised in more recent times, yet so unapologetic, conspicuous and secure in the photographs reproduced here. Indeed, in comparison, it is the photographs here that appear strictured, the power relations too conspicuous, as we have come to accept in the final decades of the twentieth century; to expect, to allow, to tolerate (and even participate in; cf. Faris, 1988a) the visualist assaults of contemporary photography with its even more intrusive and less honest techniques. It is the view here that this less overt (more 'naturally appearing', capture-of-the-moment) method is far more insidious in its disguise of the power relations.

Anthropology has changed little (the project is still to render Other), and much of the power relations has changed only in form. But the photographic assaults are quite different. Nevertheless, the refined, studied and honed techniques of contemporary photography still insist on their position of documentary objectivity. Indeed, this has been Riefenstahl's argument from her propaganda work for the Third Reich to her subsequent two Nuba volumes (see Faris 1980 for an argument that her aesthetics remain the same throughout). While we may denounce the colonial presence and the clear authority relations, at least nothing is hidden; the camera is clear, for even the authorities are captive. It commands: all subjects are frozen, hailed, and situated at viewer focus in a confident, controlled fashion. And thus a clear political critique is possible, as opposed to the more problematic task in the photography of more recent times; for today's ubiquitous access has produced not only the close-up (often with long-focus lens — a 'safe' close-up) and the action shot (faster and/or longer-focus lens and faster film), but also the dour, resentful subjects that we have become used to.

Clear examples of this recent photography of the Southern and South-East Nuba are those by

137.   Spear-Throwing. (RAI 35230)

Riefenstahl (1974 and 1976). This has produced great local dissent and hostility to photography, except for a few exotic models (see BBC-TV 1982; DeVillez 1982; Faris 1976, 1988a, 1988b, 1989; Iten 1977; Ryle 1982; Usama 1982), as local Arabs object to this representation of Sudan; as local Nuba elders loose control over the youth in traditional bride-service assignments; as those aged, or clothed, or producing, or in school are driven away to cater to the nude, scarred, bleeding, decorated, dancing.[6] It is the latter who are the focus of the documentary film — now paid (cleverly insisting on payment by the hour; see Faris 1983, 1988b) to be objects of erotic and exotic obsession, rather than the commanded as in the interesting historical photographs discussed here.[7]

NOTES

1 Whitfield's assignment in Talodi, in fact, concerned the problem of the stainer beetle to the cotton crop. He was obviously (and we are assured — Mrs Ida Whitfield to author, November 14, 1985) but an amateur photographer.

2 Nadel (1947) notes pacification and punitive patrols against the Nuba were active and necessary up through the 1940s. The specific administration of the Sudan at the time of these photographs was notoriously conservative (cf. Woodward 1979). The Governor-General, Sir John Maffey (1926–33) saw the imposition of Indirect Rule and the encouragement of Native Administration as a way of checking the nationalist influence of educated and progressive Sudanese. Hence the emphasis on traditional practices, the 'tribal' separateness of Sudanese peoples, the celebration of an exotic. But Talodi, the site of these photographs, was not only the home of the difficult-to-pacify and periodically hostile Nuba, but also the site in late 1924 of a rebellion of Sudanese troops stationed there. Thus the controlled, arranged exhibition of a tribal and ethnic and wholly uneducated remote traditional combat can be argued to be of double ideological significance.

3 Plate 132 represents, as can be identified (personal correspondence, Mrs Ida Whitfield to author, November 14, 1985), standing, left to right: District Commissioner, unidentified; sitting left to right: Governor of Kordofan Province, J. Gillan, Lord Lloyd, unidentified Egyptian Palace official. Order, rank and clear power are dramatic here. Note the European officials lined extreme left, the African employees extreme right, and the carpets beneath. The overcoming of the difficulty in assembling these gentlemen (and wives, though Lady Lloyd, who was on this visit, is nowhere to be seen in any photographs here) at this remote location at this date is impressive in itself.

4 Terms used are from the Korongo (Nadel 1947:297), though it may be that many participants are from Talodi and also Mesakin. The three are matrilineally organized Southern Nuba groups from neighbouring hill massifs speaking a common language.

5 It is perhaps worth mentioning that colonial régimes later prohibited the spear combats, and this came eventually to involve stick fighting instead (cf. Rodger, 1955). The 'severe' form of wrestling noted by Nadel may refer to bracelet combats still in fashion amongst the South-East Nuba (cf. Faris 1989).

6 The local government authorities alternatively attempted to ban tourism to the area altogether, required photographic permits which did not allow the photography of 'naked people', or forced tourists to contribute to a 'development fund' for the region. Although they had a different view of how to deal with it, unfortunately many came to share Riefenstahl's vision — especially of the South-East Nuba — as 'wild and passionate . . . Africa had never presented me with a finer visual experience' (Riefenstahl 1976:6–10), and attempted to dress all youth. (See BBC-TV 1982; Faris 1983.)

7 I should like to acknowledge the immense help of Fiona Stewart in preparation of this commentary, and for her generosity in access to RAI archives, especially Riefenstahl to Whitfield, June 7, 1967; and to Mrs Ida Whitfield for her information on the identification of persons in Plate 132.

REFERENCES

Ahmed, Abdel Rahim Nasr 1971. British Policy Towards Islam in the Nuba Mountains. 1920–1940. *Sudan Notes and Records* 52:23–32.

BBC-TV 1982. Southeast Nuba (ethnographic documentary film — Chris Curling Producer; Jim Faris, Anthropologist). British Broadcasting Corporation-Television, Bristol.

Caputo, R. 1982. Sudan: Arab-African Giant. *National Geographic Magazine* 161(3):347.

Corkill, N. 1939. The Kambala and Other Seasonal Festivals of the Kadugli and Miri Nuba. *Sudan Notes and Records* 22:205–19.

DeVillez, P. 1982. Qualifying for a Permit. *Sudanow* 7(3):35.

Edelman, B. 1979. *Ownership of the Image*. Boston: Routledge and Kegan Paul.

Faris, J. 1973. 'Pax Britannica and the Sudan: S.F. Nadel'. In T. Asad (ed.) *Anthropology and the Colonial Encounter* 153–70. London: Ithaca Press.

— 1976. Fascism and Photography. *Newsweek* 88(24):4.

— 1980. Polluted Vision. *Sudanow* 5(5):38.

— 1983. 'From Form to Content in the Structural Study of Aesthetic Tradition'. In D. Washburn (ed.) *Structure and Cognition in Art* 90–112. Cambridge: University Press.

— 1985. 'Nuba'. In R. Weekes (ed.) *Muslim Peoples. A World Ethnographic Survey* 555–9. Westport, Conn.: Greenwood Press.

— 1988a. 'Southeast Nuba: A Biographical Statement'. In J. Rollwagen (ed.). *Anthropological Filmmaking* 111–22. London: Harwood Academic Publishers.

— 1988b. 'Some Aspects of Change in Commodity Production in Southeast Kordofan'. In N. O'Neill and J. O'Brien (eds.) *Economy and Class in Sudan* 212–25. Aldershot: Gower Publishing Company.

— 1989. *Southeast Nuba Social Relations*. Aachen: Edition Herodot.

Fife, C.W.D. 1927. *Savage Life in the Black Sudan*. London: Seeley, Service & Co.

Iten, O. 1977. Bilder und Zerrbilder der Nuba. *Tages Anzeiger* 50(17):6.

Luz, H. & Luz, O. 1966. Proud Primitives, The Nuba People. *National Geographic Magazine* 130(5):673.

Mohamed, Omer Beshir. 1974. *Revolution and Nationalism in the Sudan*. London: Rex Collins.

Nadel, S.F. 1947. *The Nuba*. London: Oxford University Press.

Neale, S. 1979. Triumph of the Will. Notes and Documentary and Spectacle. *Screen* 20(1):63.

Riefenstahl, L. 1974. *The Last of the Nuba*. New York: Harper.

— 1976. *The People of Kau*. New York: Harper.

Rodger, G. 1955. *Le Village des Noubas*. Paris: Achille Weber.

Ryle, J. 1982. Invasion of the Body Snatchers. *New Society* 549:54.

Seligman, C. & Seligman, B. 1932. *Pagan Tribes of the Nilotic Sudan*. London: Routledge & Kegan Paul.

Strachen, R. 1951. With the Nuba Hillmen of Kordofan. *National Geographic Magazine* 99(2):249.

The Times 1929. Reports of Lord Lloyd's visit. February 9, March 5.

Usama, I. 1982. The Children of Kau. *Sudanow* 7(3):49.

Woodward, P. 1979. *Condominium and Sudanese Nationalism*. New York: Barnes & Noble.

James C. Faris   217

The Battle for Control of the Camera in Late-nineteenth-century Western Zambia[1]

Gwyn Prins

THE FIVE PHOTOGRAPHS discussed in this essay illustrate three different dimensions of the principal conflict which occurred in the Kingdom of Bulozi between 1884 and 1916. It was a struggle for metaphysical power between the Lozi *Litunga* (King) Lewanika and the waves of Europeans — traders, missionaries and administrators — who sought to cross the Zambezi and, in different ways, to supplant his power in his realm. The most important of these challengers was François Coillard of the Paris Evangelical Mission, one of the most experienced missionaries to participate in the European expansion north of the Zambezi. He is the photographer of all these images except Plate 140.

Coillard was defeated by Lewanika on March 22, 1886, when against his will and in order to gain access to the country, he made a sacrifice at a royal tomb. Having lost metaphysical predominance, Coillard's mission was thereafter understood by the Lozi nation to be under more than the king's physical control. Among other things, Lewanika used Coillard as his negotiator with the next wave of Europeans, the agents of the British South Africa Company and the Crown.

When in 1897 the first political Resident arrived, the reinforcement of the king's temporal power during the 1890s, which had been made possible by his earlier establishment of spiritual hegemony over the missionary who had challenged and lost in those terms, meant that Lozi society was specially, perhaps uniquely, self-confident among central African peoples in its subtle management of the Europeans during the early colonial period. In this the king had given the lead, but he did not lack general support. After 1897, the king's tactics changed.

It was a story of surprising success. Its essence was that the European and Lozi views of the importance and interrelationships of various types of metaphysical, temporal, customary and formal power differed radically. The Lozi task was to conform outwardly as much as possible to their understanding of what the Europeans expected. That expectation was shaped by Indirect Rule — a hybrid of formal, bureaucratic power above and orderly and cooperative traditional power below. The colonial authority, thus satisfied, would not pry into areas where, hidden from European eyes, Lozi power expressed in different terms and including power over unaware Europeans, could be exercised.[2]

Throughout these crucial years, it is clear that control of photography was perceived by both sides to be a valuable asset. Two of these pictures (Plates 138 and 140) show what the Europeans lost and the Lozi won, respectively — for the Lozi won that battle too. Plates 141i–ii illustrate how historians working in a field

138. Mission Party, 1881.

where the data are as booby-trapped as they are in colonial Africa may draw 'forensic' insight from photographs. That means that 'hidden history' locked into the image, seen without being understood, can be released. But to do this calls for collateral evidence of a rare order; so what is possible here may be the exception, not the rule, for the future use of photographic data by historians.

Coillard was an enthusiastic photographer. His account books record that he spent a good deal of money on photography and he took large numbers of plates during the 1880s and 1890s of which only the earliest and later ones survive in any number: a hippopotamus upset a canoe carrying a substantial part of his collection covering the early years of the Mission in Bulozi. Plates 138 and 139 are from the early period and come from his personal album; Plate 141i was published and Plate 141ii was discovered by chance by the author. For the missionary, this was no idle hobby. Coillard used photography as a weapon in the battle with Satan. He took photographs for two main rea-

sons. One, of which Plate 138 is an example, was for use in Mission propaganda. These images were carefully constructed and when viewed together reveal a scarcely surprising intention of illustrating the positive impact of the Mission's work. Plate 138 was taken in 1881 during the long trek north to found the Mission. In its composition it is a self-conscious study in fortitude.

But the composition is also an eloquent statement about the nature of the Mission. Coillard (standing left) was a man who brooked no opposition. The hierarchical arrangement of the photograph reflects his view of the Mission. In fact the private papers of several of those in the picture reveal that interpersonal tensions were already high in the group; and within a few years, Coillard and/or his wife (seated centre right) had quarrelled irretrievably with everyone else here pictured except the slow-witted Scottish artisan William Waddell (seated far right). But this image, like the Mission party at this time, is totally under Coillard's control.

139i.   Akufuna.

139ii.   Mataa.

139iii.   The Young Lewanika.

139iv.   Matauka.

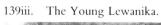

The second reason that Coillard took photographs was in order to exploit their power to bolster his supernatural reputation among the Lozi. He expressed this aim quite openly in his letters and journals. For the same reason, Coillard gave magic-lantern shows of both prepared evangelizing slides and of his own images, transferred on to glass slides. His diaries record with pleasure the galvanizing effect of such displays on ordinary villagers.[3]

Images (i) and (ii) in Plate 139 had an especially potent impact when shown either as prints or projected on a screen (both were done). They are portraits of Tatila Akufuna (i) and his *éminence grise* Mataa (ii), rebels who in 1884–5 attempted to usurp King Lewanika. Their rebellion failed and they were killed, Mataa falling in battle before the royal capital in October 1885. The young Lewanika, photographed after the rebellion, is portrait (iii) and (iv) is his sister the *Mulena Mukwae* (Royal Chief of the South) Matauka.

In March 1886 Coillard showed the prints of the rebels to Matauka. He records that she recoiled. 'These people [the missionaries] are dreadful,' she said. 'They carry the living and the dead in their pockets!' The pictures still created general consternation when projected in 1890. Again, Coillard was in control through his camera. All the subjects are passively posed, like specimens. The hunched, tense Lewanika appears to be oblivious of the camera.

In this regard, the contrast between the image of Lewanika in 1886 and Lewanika in later life (Plate 140) could not be greater.[4] Here the subject commands the portrait. He does it in three ways: the relaxed posture, especially the carriage of the head, signals assurance through the lens; his European dress communicates his *modus vivendi* with the European world; and his *muhata* (fly whisk), which only a chief has the right to bear, states simply who he really is. What had made this transformation? This portrait speaks of a king who has done more than manipulate a missionary.

The answer centres on the Coronation of Edward VII in 1902. Along with many other native rulers from the Empire, Lewanika was taken to London for the occasion. What he thought of what he saw he did not say. But the impact of his visit on his tactics for managing Europeans was clearly to be seen.

What does Lewanika's choice of clothes for the portrait signify? For the Coronation in Westminster Abbey, he was provided with the uniform of a British Admiral of the Fleet. He brought it home and promptly incorporated it into Lozi ritual. Ever since, every *Litunga* has worn such a uniform for the *kuomboka*, the important annual ceremony of transhumance when the king leads the people from their dry-season homes in

140. Old Lewanika

the flood-plain of the Zambezi to temporary shelter at the plain edge during the flood time. The admiral's uniform also figures in the *coliso* — the ceremonies of Installation of a new *Litunga*. What is incorporated is thereby in some part controlled, in some part used.

What does the presence of the *muhata* in the photograph signify? It is symbolic of a more general tactic of which the most potent expression was the authorization, immediately on Lewanika's return from London, after years of stonewalling, of the creation of an 'official' version of Lozi history. Two senior chiefs, Kalonga and Nalubutu, related the *Litaba za Sicaba sa Malozi* (History of the Lozi People) to Adolphe Jalla, Coillard's successor as head of the Paris Mission. The book stresses the antiquity of the Luyi royal dynasty; it stresses the territorial expansion of the Lozi kingdom: it is 'Whig' history. It establishes Lozi credentials for British Indirect Rulers in terms which the king had

141i–ii. The negotiations. i (*above*) as previously published. ii (*below*) the new evidence.

seen in Westminster Abbey and which the British themselves esteemed. Just as the Victorians invented tradition for their present purposes, so the Lozi did for theirs (Cannadine 1983).

The Lozi purpose was to pre-empt uncontrolled probing. The *muhata* was visible; no stranger need ask to know more. The enquirer could be politely directed to *Litaba za Sichaba*. All that mattered, he could be assured, had been told there. Behind these strengthened shutters, the Lozi preserved a private space in the intrusive colonial world. Lewanika's control of the portrait in Plate 140 is a telling witness to his broader political dexterity.

But historians do not all agree. Some would reject wholly the interpretation of Lewanika, Coillard and the Lozi just given here. Instead they would depict a riven Lozi nation, and Lewanika a bloody despot unsure on his throne who, to save his own skin, threw in his lot with the whites. The moment when he sold out, this view maintains, was at the end of June 1890 when, against huge opposition, he granted a Concession to Lochner, an agent of Cecil Rhodes's British South Africa Company. These negotiations are shown in Plates 141i–ii, taken at midday (look at the shadows), probably on Tuesday June 24, 1890.

The reasons why this debate should be so fiercely engaged by historians are not hard to find. At one point, at the end of the 'independence decade' and at the beginning of the 'underdevelopment decade' of modern African historiography, it was for one group of historians important to demonstrate the passivity and powerlessness of Africans faced with the malign and advancing influence of Europeans. This was very much the motif of pro-nationalist historiography. To a second group of historians the issue was no longer as black and white. No longer was it either necessary or desirable to represent African aristocrats as victims of European exploitation. Influenced, particularly in the early 1970s, by the fashion for Althusserian Marxism, they sought to restore dignity to African history by demonstrating the universal presence of exploitation and the universal applicability of a rather rigid sort of class analysis.

These were, in fact, the first indications of the move towards a more sophisticated and culturally sensitive historiography. It portrayed the ordinary man and woman in the bush as double victims — victims both of the colonial juggernaut and of African tyranny. Both the older nationalist and the newer hidden agendas were powerful. Both could become easily impatient with fractious and fragile data that did not conform to their expectation and this, I suspect, may explain the irritation felt when the interpretation offered in this essay was first proposed. It is some

comfort, perhaps, to find that ten years later, the enterprise of African historiography having moved encouragingly into much closer harmony with the methodological and epistemological premises of this piece, the criticism has largely faded away. Evidence and its sensitive use are much more in fashion! How then does the forensic use of photographic material end the argument on more secure grounds than those of academic whim?

In the battle between the irreconcilable historical interpretations, the unique empirical witness of the camera is as much a desirable asset for the historians as, for different reasons, it had been for their subjects. The hidden history revealed by reading these photographs minutely, like a detective, provides powerful support for the general interpretation advanced here. It is only possible because of two lucky chances, but it shows the potential which a photograph has to drive forward an analysis, when it can be embedded in and wired to other types of data.

The first lucky chance was to discover in a cupboard in Switzerland a private notebook that had belonged to Adolphe Jalla, Coillard's subordinate, and in it, a detailed plan of who is sitting where in the photographs (Jalla n.d.).

Thus we know that the royal stewards and the major officers of state are seated at the king's left (right in the plates), the chiefs of Lealui, the royal capital, to his right. Behind the royal musicians stand the inhabitants of Lealui. Immediately behind the photographer Coillard (and therefore invisible) are the royal family members and behind them again, phalanxes of people from all different parts of the kingdom, including those areas which subsequent historians have suggested were in opposition to the whole business.

Plate 141i is quite famous and has been reproduced frequently. Lochner sits facing the king. Lewanika, in European dress, does not meet his gaze: he appears ill at ease (which, from the private diaries of Coillard and Jalla, we know that he certainly was during the negotiations). The royal music has ceased. The people of Lealui are performing the *shoelela* (royal salute). The faces of the senior officers of state are not distinct.

The second lucky chance was to find a packet of negatives in a trunk in Paris. Among them was Plate 141ii, plainly exposed a few moments before Plate 141i. Lochner is not yet there. Lealui inhabitants are still approaching. The band is still playing and — crucially — the faces of the two most senior chiefs can be discerned. Next to the king sits *Ngambela* (Prime Minister) Mwauluka and next to him (in silhouette) is Chief Nalubutu, whose profile is quite distinctive and may be matched to a full portrait of him in another negative in the same bundle.

Given the considerable significance for status which attaches to exact seating in a formal meeting like this, the offices and physical proximity of these two men to the king associate them with his opinions in the proceedings. Had they been in fundamental disagreement, given their power in the land on their own account, they would not have been there. But they are — the two men whom the other historical interpretation identifies as the principal leaders of opposition to what Lewanika was doing. The photographs finish that argument more conclusively than any other form of contemporary data.

NOTES

1 This paper appeared, with the exception of a few additions, in *African Affairs*, 1990, 89 No. 354. We are grateful to the editors for permission to reprint it here.
2 The full story of these years is to be found in Prins 1980.
3 Prins (1980:192–8) links the use of photography to other devices which Coillard used to enhance his supernatural reputation.
4 It has not been possible to identify the photographer by direct evidence. However, comparison with dated photographs of Lewanika establish that this picture was taken during the last decade of his life. (He died in 1916.) For the purposes of the argument advanced about it, it is only necessary to date it after 1903, which it plainly is.

But there is a speculative possibility. A print of this photograph is to be found in the collection of Frank Worthington, now deposited in the Historic Manuscripts Collection of Livingstone Museum. Worthington was the Secretary for Native Affairs during the last years of Lewanika's reign and was himself a competent photographer. He visited Lewanika. He may have made this picture.

REFERENCES

Cannadine, D. 1983. 'The context, performance and meaning of ritual: The British monarchy and the "Invention of Tradition" *c*.1920–1977'. In E. Hobsbawm & T. Ranger (eds.) *The Invention of Tradition* 101–64. Past & Present Society Publication. Cambridge: University Press.

Jalla, A. n.d. *Notes Privées*, p. 96 'Disposition au *pitso* du 22/6/90'. Manuscript in private possession.

— 1954 (1909). *Litaba za Sicaba sa Malozi* 5th edn. Cape Town: Northern Rhodesia and Nyasaland Publication Bureau.

Prins, G. 1980. *The Hidden Hippopotamus. Reappraisal in African History: The Early Colonial Experience in Western Zambia*. African Studies Series No. 28. Cambridge: University Press.

Te Tokanga-nui-a-noho Meeting-house[1]

Anne Salmond

This image (Plate 142) speaks to the heart of Maori history and the meeting between Maori and European in New Zealand. Three women in white stand before the back wall of a meeting-house which is falling into ruins. The *tukutuku* panels, traditionally made by women and here woven as finely as mats, are exposed to the weather and some sections have been torn away. Grass grows on the floor of the house, and the rafters with their diagonal sarking boards have rotted and splintered, and fallen to the ground. The great carved post supporting the ridge-pole rises from the earth with Toi at its base, and his son Rauru above him. For people of Awa descent, they are the oldest ancestors in these islands. The photograph seems to be a tableau of destruction and decay, a traditional society in ruins; but that is an illusion. The house, Te Tokanga-nui-a-noho, still stands at Te Kuiti, although on another site. Since it was built in 1873 for Tawhiao, the second Maori king, it has been moved twice, rebuilt at least once, and renovated and redecorated at least four times (Mead 1969).[2] By 1873 Maori people had been dealing with Europeans for more than a hundred years, and that process continues. The house has witnessed momentous struggles — between settler governments and the Maori King Movement for control over Maori lands; between King Tawhiao and Te Kooti, the east-coast warrior prophet; between the king and Ngati Maniopoto, his hosts at Te Kuiti; and between various tribal factions in the Native Land Court for control over local lands. Like its builders and occupiers, Te Tokanga-nui-a-noho has a formidable power of resilience and renewal.

Large meeting-houses have a long history in Aotearoa; during the first encounters between Maori and European explorers, carved houses were noted and described. Roux in Spirits Bay in 1772, for instance, wrote:

> Among other things their houses prompted our admiration, so skilfully were they made. They were rectangular in shape and varied in size according to need. The sides were stakes set a short distance from each other and strengthened by switches which were interlaced across them. They were coated on the outside with a layer of moss thick enough to prevent water and wind from getting in . . . The interior was woven with a matting on which there were at intervals, by way of ornament as well as to support the roof . . . planks, two to three inches thick and rather well carved. In the middle of the house there was also a big carved pole which supported the weight of the roof (together with two others at the two ends). What surprised us still further was that the whole construction was mortised and very strongly tied together with ropes. (Ollivier 1985:133)

New Zealand.

Carved Whare or Maori Meeting House.

142.   Te Tokanga-nui-a-noho Meeting-house. (RAI 35433)

226

It is clear from the photograph of the Te Kuiti meeting-house (here dated tentatively to 1895) that its construction is not strictly traditional. The diagonal sarking boards, seen more closely in earlier photographs by Alfred Burton in 1885,[3] are sawn in a Pakeha mill; the carvings show the crisp intricacy of steel-tool work, and the central post has two ancestors who carry their names in writing — 'Rauru' on the chest of one, and 'Ko Toi' on small squares at the head of the other. Photographs, like an explorer's journal, are eloquent of physical detail: here the woven *tukutuku* construction and patterns are exposed as the panels fall apart, and one can see painted flowers and stars on the rafters, painting on the carvings, and the inward slope of carved side posts as they lean in from the ground. The women look straight at the photographer, each standing in front of a *tukutuku* panel to echo an old counterpoint of male carving: female *tukutuku* with unconscious precision. Their clothing, hairstyles and expressions can be studied, but that is all. Like the carvings, without background knowledge, on all but physical matters they are mute.

Meeting-houses do speak, but it is in a tribal language. Each meeting-house has a name, of an ancestor or evocative of an important event in the life of the kin-group, and the carved posts and the head at the apex of the porch are named ancestors who carry their lives and their genealogical connections into the fabric of the house. As ancestors for a new house are chosen, alliances are made and broken, insults and compliments are exchanged and the *mana* (power) of those who participate is measured and expressed.

The house, now called Te Tokanga-nui-a-noho, was built in 1873 at Te Kuiti,[4] at the mouth of the Manga-o-kewa gorge. It stood on Ngati Maniapoto land, and was built by outsiders and local experts under the supervision of one exile, the east-coast prophet Te Kooti, for another — Tawhiao, the second Maori king. Ngati Maniapoto had fought against European encroachment in the 1860s Land Wars, and they held out at Orakau under Rewi Maniapoto when the Waikato tribes ceased to fight. In the aftermath the New Zealand Settlements Act of 1863 was promulgated to punish Maori 'rebels', and the Waikato tribes lost 1,202,172 acres (486,500 hectares) of the most fertile lands in the country by confiscation, while Ngati Maniapoto, whose lands were less desirable, lost very little. As a result King Tawhiao was forced to take refuge in Ngati Maniapoto territory beyond the confiscation line, and a centre of resistance was established in the 'Rohe Potae' or 'King Country', where Europeans were forbidden entry and no land sales or leases were allowed. The boundaries of the King Country were defined from Te Kuiti: 'Kuiti to

Te Aroha; Kuiti to Titokura; Kuiti to Mangatawhiri, etc.'[5] and within this domain the King-ites gathered and large and prosperous cultivations of wheat and oats as well as more traditional crops were planted.[6]

In 1869 Te Kooti came to the King Country to seek alliance with Ngati Maniapoto against the Pakeha, and later that year he challenged King Tawhiao and the prophet Te Ra at Maniapoto's great cruciform house of learning. In 1872, after being hounded through the Urewera mountains by Government troops, Te Kooti was invited into the King Country by Rewi Maniapoto, and there he 'laid the sword at the feet of the King' (Binney 1984:364–5). Tawhiao treated him coolly at first, but after a time invited him to live at Tokanga-mutu, a settlement near present-day Te Kuiti where the King-ites held many of their meetings. In gratitude Te Kooti supervised the carving and painting work for a new house by the Manga-o-kewa river which initiated a new tradition of painted art using Ringatu and possibly Tariao[7] patterns of diamonds, clubs, stars, the sun and small naturalistic figures,[8] which in this house included two head-and-shoulders male portraits in traditional dress on the door, and two little figures apparently playing cricket in the porch. The carvings in this original house, some of which appear in this photograph, include many east-coast Bay of Plenty ancestors of Te Kooti and his followers, Waikato and Maniapoto ancestors of the king and local tribes, and also ancestors of Te Arawa and Tuwharetoa tribes in the middle of the island. The meeting-house brought these diverse descent lines together in a physical alliance that gave the building great *mana*, but also a fragility of ownership and social definition. It is perhaps because so many of the ancestors in this house are outsiders, carved by outsiders, that their names (which local people would not necessarily remember) were carved into their chests.

Tawhiao lived in the house intermittently for many years, and it was described as 'The King's House' until about 1883–6, when the Aukati line around the King Country was decisively breached by surveys for the main trunk railway and the coming of the Native Land Court to the district. Ngati Maniapoto's relationship with Tawhiao, always ambiguous, became strained when it was rumoured that the Government would award Maniapoto lands to the king, and Rewi Maniapoto in retaliation allowed the Land Court hearings to proceed. In 1883 Te Kooti also fell out with Tawhiao, predicting that in two years the kingship would end (Binney 1984:391), and it was probably in that year that the house was opened for a second time under the name 'Te Tokanga-nui-a-noho',[9] taken from a house at Aotea in Kawhia harbour which had burned down. This name quotes a lament by a Tainui ancestress as she greeted her husband in her lover's tribal territory:

> He aha koe i haere mai
> I te rourou iti a Haere
> Te noho atu koe
> I te tokanga nui a Noho
>
> (Oh why did you come
> with so small a party of travellers?
> You should have stayed away
> with the large tribe of 'Stay at Home'.)
> (Phillips 1955:143–5)

Te Tokanga-nui-a-noho was first photographed in 1885 by Alfred Burton, who accompanied the third party of surveyors to enter the King Country. The King-ites called Burton's camera a 'taipo' (devilish object), and when he tried to photograph two women at Utapu 'the ladies . . . simultaneously turning round, solemnly assumed a posture of "flexure and low-bending", certainly not suggestive of respect, but rather of the most withering contempt for Pakehas in general, and for this Pakeha and his camera in particular' (Perry 1980:12).[10] In the 1885 photographs the house is shown in good repair, and the name plate under the apical *koruru* mask (identifying that ancestor) says 'Ko Waho', an abbreviated form of the ancestral name 'Rawaho-o-te-Rangi' (Phillips 1938:82). This house is evidently the same building depicted in the more recent photograph, with its characteristic diagonal sarking boards and fine *tukutuku*. Several later exterior shots and one photograph of the porch survive from this period before the house falls into disrepair.

The main trunk railway came through Te Kuiti in 1887, and the local population began to settle around its new railway station; and in 1893 Te Kooti left the King Country to return to the Bay of Plenty. These factors seem to have led to the abandonment of the house on its original site. It was not left for long, however, and when the house re-emerges in the photographic record with a series of photographs by Augustus Hamilton and James McDonald in 1899, it has been substantially rebuilt with a corrugated iron roof, striated boards in place of the diagonal sarking, a new form of *tukutuku* using milled dowls, and an unfamiliar but rotted carving at the base of the apical porch post. The porch carvings have changed places, bargeboard ends have rotted away, the name plate on the gable now reads 'Ko Rawaho', and another name plate inscribed 'Ko Te Tokanganui a Noho' appears in the apex of the porch interior. A series of photographs by a Te Kuiti photographer, Holland, in the early 1900s show the house with a brand-new porch post

and bargeboard end, and set on its present site in the township of Te Kuiti.[11]

Meeting-houses and their carvings are something more than symbols, and much more than representations of the past. Each house is set on a *marae*, a tribal centre where gatherings of the groups are held, and there it gives physical presence to ancestors who take part in tribal affairs and who offer their descendants possibilities of alliance, past reasons for suspicion and precedents for action. The ancestral names and stories appear in accounts told on the ceremonial speaking-ground before the house, in genealogies and place-names and tribal songs and chants, and this lattice of overlapping reference ties the tribe, through its ancestors, to its land. It is said that the house is an ancestral body, with the ridge-pole as its spine, the *koruru* mask at the gable as its head, bargeboards as arms spread wide in welcome, rafters as ribs ending in carved ancestor posts, and the interior as the belly where hosts and visitors can sleep in warmth and safety. Visitors to a tribal gathering sleep on the right side of the house as one enters, and they may seek out a carved ancestor to sleep at his or her feet. The dead of the tribe are placed on the meeting-house porch or inside the house, to be mourned by the living and ancestors alike, and as mourners arrive at the *marae* they greet the ancestral house by name.

The house reaches beyond Te Ao Marama, the world of light and life, casting its genealogical lines back to the shadowy sources of ancestral power; and in its changing life it reflects the fortunes and changing definitions of its owner group. Maori tribal histories, like tribal groups themselves, define the past through the present and the present through the past, and the meeting-house with its *marae* is the pivotal place where this is done. This photograph captures a moment in that constant negotiation, but without a tribal understanding it is a mere formality of expression. The image may say something to an outsider, if only as an exhibition of surfaces and shape, and in that context it can provoke an exchange of questions and answers that open into tribal worlds. It is when a photograph such as this, however, comes face to face with descendants of those depicted, the inheritors of the traditions and the ancestral names, that it most truly speaks. Then alienation may end in recognition, in greeting, or quite often, as I have seen, in tears.

The ambiguity of anthropological photographs, then, is that what appears to have been made visible to all may still be hidden. Sight is not enough for knowing, and the metaphor of knowledge as clear sight can prove deceptive. A photograph may capture the play of light and shadows on physical surfaces, but not the play of meanings. Only the *ariaa* of a thing is taken in photograph — its visible semblance — while its *wairua* (spirit) remains elusive until properly addressed.

Theorists of anthropological photography may see in the camera an instrument of colonial conquest, an analogue of the gun — but that may itself be a sign of European hubris. As the image of Te Tokanga-nui-a-noho shows, apparent ruins may rather be a prelude to rebuilding, and colonists may be left with nothing more than other peoples' shadows in their hands.

NOTES

1 In writing this brief commentary I owe thanks for his help to Professor Bruce Biggs, whose wife Joy comes from an old Te Kuiti family; to Roger Neich and Judith Binney for their knowledgeable assistance and advice; and to Professor Hirini Mead, who with a party of students from Maori Studies at the University of Auckland carried out research on Te Tokanga-nui-a-noho meeting-house in 1969.

2 It seems likely that the Burton photographs of the house in 1885 show it on its original site. According to local Te Kuiti tradition (Bruce Biggs, *pers. comm.*) the house was first sited at the mouth of the Manga-o-kewa gore, where the limeworks now stand: then at a site on a flat by the Manga-o-kewa River exactly opposite and across the river from its present site: and finally on a hill across the railway line in Te Kuiti township. His wife's great-uncle could remember the ridge-pole being shifted to the present site by his father and others when he was a little boy.

3 Photographs of Te Tokanga-nui-a-noho are held in the Dominion Museum Photographic Archives, the Alexander Turnbull Library, the Auckland Institute and Museum, the University of Auckland's Anthropology Photographic Archive, and probably many other institutions in New Zealand.

4 Major W.G. Mair in *Appendices of the Journal of the House of Representatives (AJHR)* (1874) H-2B:1. September 26, 1873: 'There has been some excitement lately upon a rumour that Purukutu had determined to sacrifice a white man, or kupapa (loyal Maori) upon the opening of a house which has been built by Ngati Haua, in their portion of Kuiti, for Tawhiao. Upon inquiry, I do not think that there was any foundation for such a report.' 'Te Kooti is also at Kuiti. He came here to supervise the carvings for the new house, and has been at last noticed by Tawhiao who, it is said, will keep him here for the future.' But also J. Mackay, *AJHR* (1873) G-3:1. July 10, 1873: 'It must always be borne in mind that the Waikato and Ngati tribes have no land of their own at Tokangamutu' (at Te Kuiti). R.S. Bush, *AJHR* (1874) G-2B:4. September 22, 1873: 'After the return of these people, invitations are to be sent to all the tribes of Kawhia and the adjacent districts to visit Te Kuiti, for the purpose of being present at the opening ceremony for Tawhiao's new house.'

5 R.S. Bush, January 31, 1873, *AJHR* (1873) G-1B:8.

6 Major W.G. Mair, June 12, 1873, *AJHR* (1873) G-1:4.

7 Ringatu was the faith founded by Te Kooti, and Tariao is a faith more closely associated with Tawhiao and the King Movement.

8 My thanks to Roger Neich for these details from his forthcoming Ph.D. thesis on Ringatu painted houses.

9 See R.S. Bush, November 22, 1873, *AJHR* (1874) G-2B:6–8: and R.S. Bush, May 12, 1874, *AJHR* (1875) G-2:10. In the first source this proverb is also attributed to the ancestor Hikairo.

10 This gesture, the *whakapohane*, is a mark of supreme insult.

11 Other sets of more recent photographs held in the RAI and the University of Auckland's Anthropology Photographic Archive tell of the house's modern physical history.

REFERENCES

Binney, Judith 1984. Myth and explanation in the Ringatu tradition. *Journal of the Polynesian Society*. 93:345–98.

Mead, Hirini (ed.) 1969. 'Te Tokanganui-a-Noho: the house, the maree, and the cemetery, Te Kuiti'. Typescript in Anthropology Reading Room, University of Auckland.

Neich, Roger, Amaoamo, Tiwai & Tupene, Tuhi 1984. The complementarity of history and art in Tutamure meeting-house. *Journal of the Polynesian Society*. 93:5–37.

Ollivier, Isabel 1985. *Extracts from the journals of the ships Mascarin and Marquis de Castries 1772*. Wellington: Alexander Turnbull Library Endowment Trust with Indosuez N.Z. Ltd.

Perry, John F. 1980. *King Country Journey Alfred Burton*. Catalogue, Rotorua Art Gallery Travelling Exhibition.

Phillips, W.J. 1938. The Te Kuiti House. *Art in New Zealand*. 11:1. 82–9.

— 1955. *Carved Maori houses of the western and northern areas of New Zealand*. Wellington: R.E. Owen, Government Printer.

The Representation of Trucanini

Vivienne Rae-Ellis

BRITISH SETTLEMENT IN 1803 caused rapid destruction of the indigenous population of Tasmania, estimated at about 4,000 at that time. Declining swiftly, the Aborigines were depleted more by introduced diseases than by subsequent warfare erupting between the races. Three hundred individuals who surrendered to conciliator George Augustus Robinson in the 1830s were deported to Flinders Island, and in 1847 the forty-six survivors were repatriated to live in captivity at the Oyster Cove Aboriginal Station south of Hobart. Trucanini, the last Tasmanian to live and die on the island, expired in 1876.

The birth of photography coincided with this precipitated decline. Photographs of Tasmanians are therefore rare. Only two portfolios are known: the earliest, the work of amateur photographer Francis Russell Nixon, first Bishop of Tasmania; and that of Charles A. Woolley, a professional photographer.

In 1858 Bishop Nixon photographed the surviving fourteen or fifteen Aborigines in the squalid conditions of their Oyster Cove camp. Pictured in a familiar setting the Aborigines appear at ease, lounging companionably on the ground in front of rough wooden huts surrounded by their dogs, customarily used as footstools and backwarmers (Plate 143). The educated amateur reveals individual personalities, and his photographs convey the former nomads' air of resigned submission to imprisonment.

Inclusion of Nixon's photographs[1] in the International Exhibition of 1862 held at the time of his return to London (he subsequently retired to Italy) may have led to the suggestion of his friend in Tasmania, pioneer conservationist and author Louisa Anne Meredith, that Charles Woolley should photograph the few surviving Aborigines for inclusion in Tasmania's entry in the International Exhibition in Melbourne in 1866.

Woolley, then thirty-two, accepted the offer from the commissioners who organized the island's exhibit but, unlike Nixon, he rejected Oyster Cove as a setting. He may have been discouraged by government: the authorities would not have welcomed additional criticism of conditions in which the Aborigines were forced to exist. So, transporting his five subjects 25 miles (40 km) to the unfamiliar and artificial atmosphere of his studio in Hobart, Woolley photographed full-length group portraits of Trucanini and two of her companions, fully clothed, in a European setting. In that year Woolley also photographed Louisa Anne Meredith with her family arranged in an identical pose against an identical background in the same studio. When these studies are compared, the portraits of the Aborigines appear as disturbing parodies of the portraits of Woolley's white clients, portraying

143. Tasmanians at Oyster Cove Settlement. From the left: Emma, Trucanini (aged forty-six), Flora (standing) and Wapperty, photographed at Oyster Cove Aboriginal settlement, south of Hobart. Photograph by Bishop Nixon, 1858. (Courtesy of Pitt Rivers Museum, University of Oxford, PRM. B44. 24a)

144.   Trucanini, 1866. Photograph by C.A. Woolley. (RAI 687)

nothing of the former's past or contemporary circumstances. But Woolley, delighted with his creation of black 'Europeans', chose one of these images in preference to his prize-winning photographs for reproduction on his business cards, clearly demonstrating his personal bias in his projection of an Aboriginal photographic image.

At the same time, as requested by the commissioners (who possibly wished to follow the growing tradition of using basic rules for portrayal of racial types), Woolley photographed three sets of full-face, three-quarter-face and profile studies of Trucanini (Plate 144) and her four companions, making a total of fifteen photographs for the official album, the originals of which were to be deposited with the Royal Society of Tasmania at the conclusion of the exhibition. As the Society held all available Aboriginal skeletal remains at that time, the instruction clearly indicated official recognition and acceptance of Woolley's images in 1866. Five of the studies were selected and subsequently displayed in the exhibition. Awarded a prize medal, these portraits of a people hurtling towards extinction attracted widespread attention and were first reproduced internationally as engravings in James Bonwick's *Last of the Tasmanians* (1870), *Daily Life and Origin of the Tasmanians* (1870), *The Lost Tasmanian Race* (1884) and E.H. Giglioli's *I Tasmaniani* (1871). Those publications appearing before Trucanini's death in 1876 firmly established Woolley's head-and-shoulders portraits as the accepted images of the Tasmanian race. Informed contemporary opinion, however, challenges their representational validity.

Whaling master Captain James Kelly, after a long association with the Aborigines, declared in 1874 that no fair judgement of their appearance could be made from 'the few weird-looking old creatures that photography has preserved . . . who seem to have been selected from the most hideous of them' (*The Mercury*, Hobart, July 6, 1874). Kelly's remarks emphasize the point that all survivors were relatively old when photographed. None of the existing images reflect the spirit or physique of younger Tasmanians and their children. Trucanini's youthful beauty was legendary, but little evidence of it remains in Woolley's photograph taken when she was fifty-four, or in those taken in her decline by Alfred Winter and H.H. Bailey (Rae-Ellis 1981:138, 147, 148). In their nomadic state the Aborigines were naked. But Nixon's and Woolley's photographs show them dressed in European clothing, while Woolley posed the Aborigines in a European setting, suggesting that the Tasmanians were successfully Christianized and civilized. Nothing could have been further from the truth. There were no converts

145. Trucanini, *c*.1830. Watercolour by Thomas Bock. (Courtesy of Pitt Rivers Museum, University of Oxford)

among them. Yet the only indication of the existence of indigenous culture in these studies is the shell necklace made and worn by Trucanini.

No archival photograph should therefore be regarded as being a valid representation of the Tasmanian Aborigine. A search for the most accurate available image should include consideration of a second source: the work of colonial artists whose portraits support Kelly's remarks, and offer evidence of the attractive exuberance of young Aborigines never recorded by the camera. Artists depicted Aborigines in tribal dress, featuring tribal settings and artefacts in their paintings. And the portraits of Thomas Bock in particular were widely regarded by contemporaries as being highly accurate likenesses (Plate 145).

When William Lanne (then believed to be the 'Last Tasmanian' male) died three years after the exhibition, Trucanini was recognized as the sole survivor of her people living on the island. The butchering of Lanne's corpse by opposing factions determined to obtain his unique skeleton shocked the public and haunted his lover, Trucanini. Holding firmly to her culture's beliefs, she regarded the skeletal remains as sacred objects, and refused even to utter the names of the dead. But convinced that the same treatment awaited her own end, Trucanini lived on in terror for seven lonely years before nightmare became reality.

Two years after Trucanini's death in 1876 her body was exhumed and officially handed over to the Royal Society on condition that her bones were never to be exposed to public view. A photograph taken of her skeleton illustrates the attitude of successive governments in their treatment and portrayal of the Aborigine. With flagrant disregard for Aboriginal practice and for the agreement by which the bones were made available, the skeleton[2] was placed on exhibition in the Tasmanian Museum in 1905, and the photograph published with an invitation to the public to view this 'absolutely unique exhibit' (Rae-Ellis 1981:169). The skeleton remained on view until 1947, but under pressure from the Aboriginal Movement the relics were cremated in 1976.

Immediately after her death Woolley's photograph (already widely published) was used to convey the official image of the 'Last Tasmanian' and, by implication, the image of the extinct race. A later Tasmanian photographer, John Watt Beattie, compiled and presumably sold commercially a large photographic album containing reproductions of all fifteen of Woolley's official photographs described by Beattie at the time as being 'a very complete collection, embracing almost all photographs taken of the extinct people' (*Walch's Tasmanian Almanac*: 1896). However, at least one of Nixon's photographs appears to have been available in Tasmania after 1876 when the image of the two Aborigines incorrectly identified as King Billy and Trucanini were reproduced by a Hobart furrier, T.E. Barker, as a promotional postcard.

But the authorities and the media persist in promoting Woolley's work. Continuous exposure internationally over the last 120 years has ensured that Woolley's misleading image of Trucanini now symbolizes the vanished Tasmanians in all forms of visual communication. As late as 1973 the dust cover of David Davies's book *The Last of the Tasmanians* featured Woolley's photograph of Trucanini. And following screening in Britain of the Australian film *The Last Tasmanians*, made by Tom Haydon in 1978, in which Woolley's images featured, her photograph was again widely reproduced in international publications reviewing the film.

No effort has yet been made to redress the error by reminding the viewer that Woolley's melancholic image (hauntingly memorable because of the tragic appeal in Trucanini's expressive and much-admired eyes) is the portrait of an elderly woman in despair, recorded for posterity as her four companions faced imminent death, leaving her in fear of surviving alone, the last of her people. When *Australia Post* included Trucanini in its 'Famous Women' stamp series issued to mark International Women's Year in 1975, Woolley's photograph of her was once again chosen for reproduction on stamps destined to receive worldwide exposure in preference to Nixon's younger image or the delightful portrait by Thomas Bock — yet originals of all three were readily available (Rae-Ellis 1981:159).

Nixon, an amateur photographer free from official bias or constriction, chose to make a frank record of the Aborigines, confined as they were in 1858. Woolley, commissioned as a professional photographer, preferred to present them as black 'Europeans', ostensibly participating in an Occidental society. His deceptive official images, reflecting nothing of the earlier Tasmanians and their unique culture or their dismal contemporary circumstances, were those preferred and promoted by successive authorities. The concept of the archival photographic image as an accurate record is widely held, but the danger inherent in uncritical acceptance of that premise is clearly demonstrated in the case of the vanished and misrepresented Tasmanians.

NOTES

1 The definitive sets of originals are kept in the Tasmanian Museum and Art Gallery, Hobart, and the Mitchell Library, State Library of New South Wales.
2 Possibly a composite, with Trucanini's skull connected to the postcranial skeleton of an unknown female replacing that of Trucanini which appears to have been stolen about the turn of the century (see Rae-Ellis 1981).

REFERENCES

Bonwick, J. 1870. *The Last of the Tasmanians*. London.
— 1870. *Daily Life and Origin of the Tasmanians*. London.
— 1884. *The Lost Tasmanian Race*. London.
Davies, D. 1973. *The Last of the Tasmanians*. London: Frederick Muller.
Giglioli, E. 1871. *I Tasmaniani*. Florence.
Rae-Ellis, V. 1981. *Trucanini: queen or traitor?* Canberra: Australian Institute of Aboriginal Studies.
1874. *The Mercury*. July 6. Hobart.
1896. *Walch's Tasmanian Almanac*. Hobart.

The Political Image: The Impact of the Camera in an Ancient Independent African State

Richard Pankhurst

THE RARE ETHIOPIAN PHOTOGRAPH of unknown authorship discussed in this essay captures the spirit of the time in which it was taken, and provides vivid testimony to the importance attached to photography in an independent African state then emerging into the modern world. This picture reflects the political order of its day, and it is only when seen in this context, and in that of other images carrying a political message, that it can fully be understood.

The significance of the camera in early-twentieth-century Ethiopia, the period when the picture was taken, was enhanced by the fact that photography, which was then largely in foreign hands, was relatively new.[1] The first photographs taken in the country were the work of Henry Stern, a German Protestant missionary to the Falashas, or Ethiopian Jews, who arrived in 1859 but was soon afterwards imprisoned for displeasing the then ruler, Emperor Téwodros II (Stern 1868:72).[2] The introduction of the camera was therefore for practical purposes deferred until the reign of Emperor Yohannes IV (1872–89), and more especially of his near-contemporary Menelik II (King of Shewa, 1865–89, Emperor of Ethiopia, 1889–1913) who in the early 1880s arranged for three Swiss craftsmen to come to his court to help with the modernization of the country. One of them, Alfred Ilg, was a keen photographer.[3]

Despite its novelty and alien origin, photography almost at once appealed to Menelik and his courtiers, many of whom were photographed by foreign photographers who arrived in the 1880s. Photography was thereafter easily assimilated into the country's traditional structures.[4] The mourning ceremonial of the Ethiopian nobility is a case in point. It had been customary in funeral processions since time immemorial for mourners to display an effigy of the deceased, together with his horse and other valuable property. With the advent of the camera such articles tended to be supplemented — and the effigy even replaced — by photographic portraits of the departed which mourners held high above their heads, while they wailed, ritualistically, and perhaps recounted episodes of the deceased's life and achievement.[5]

Appreciation of the camera was initially restricted to the aristocracy. The rest of the population was long suspicious of photography — and some country people indeed are so to this day.[6] Acquaintance with the camera, however, soon spread to the urban population of Addis Ababa and other towns. This was largely due to the establishment of local photographic studios, the first of which was founded by an Armenian, Bedros Boyadjian (Zervos 1936:199, 211, 495). Several other photographers, likewise mainly Armenians, also set up studios in the town, while a number of other

146. Emperor Menelik's grandson and heir, Lij Iyasu, with his elderly and much trusted tutor Ras Tessema Nadew, *c.*1909–11. Photographer unknown. (RAI 39956)

photographers appeared in the market area where they took cheap 'minute photographs', thereby introducing the poorer sections of the population to the magic of photography (Pankhurst 1976:952).

Thus by the time the photograph discussed here was taken, the medium had been assimilated into Ethiopian society and growing awareness of the camera can be documented by linguistic evidence. Dictionaries compiled at the turn of the century make no mention of any terms connected with photography, but those of the late 1920s contain two: a purely Ethiopian word, *se'el*, the name earlier used for a painting; and the loan-word *fotograf*, imported from the French (Walker 1928:199; Baeteman 1929:321).

This photograph (Plate 146) was taken sometime between October 1909 and April 1911, at an interesting juncture in the country's history. Menelik, the founder of modern Ethiopia, had long been incapacitated by a serious illness which had caused him for several years to be secluded from his people. Power

was therefore in the hands of his ministers — and of his powerful consort, Empress Taytu, who feared that her spouse's death might lead to her political extinction. A bitter power struggle was thus imminent.

Realizing that his end was approaching the aged monarch defied the empress in March 1909 by nominating his twelve-year-old grandson, Lij Iyasu, as his successor. In October of the same year the Council of Ministers, acting in opposition to the empress, designated an elderly, and well trusted, Ethiopian statesman, Ras Tessema Nadew, as the youngster's tutor and 'Guardian of the Throne', that is, Regent. The ministers' choice of Tessema — though displeasing to Taytu — was generally accepted at court, for he bore the title of *Bitwodded*, literally the emperor's 'Beloved' courtier. His father moreover had been Menelik's own tutor many years earlier. To emphasize the irrevocability of these decisions, which were most displeasing to the empress, a proclamation was issued on October 30, 1910, in the name of the paralysed emperor, in which he was quoted as declaring that he 'entrusted his throne' to Iyasu, and is said to have added: 'Except for Iyasu I have no other child', that is, heir. The aging emperor shortly afterwards suffered a further series of strokes, which left his young heir as nominal Head of State, with his adviser-cum-guardian, Ras Tessema, holding real power. Taytu was thus fast losing the struggle for succession.

Though he was supported by several influential courtiers, it soon became evident that Iyasu was in fact in a weak position. An untried youngster, he suffered from the fact that his father Ras Mika'él, a Muslim chief from Wollo, had embraced Christianity for political reasons, and some Christian churchmen were therefore not convinced that the son would be a reliable Defender of the Faith. Young Iyasu had likewise to overcome suspicion from a section of the all-important nobility of Shewa, some of them Menelik's former courtiers, who feared that their old master's grandson might erode their position by giving land — and preferment — at their expense to people from his father's province.

The photograph of Lij Iyasu, the precocious young prince, with his large, prominent eyes, and the aged regent, with a veritable grey beard, dates from this critical period in Ethiopia's history. The work was no chance snap, but a carefully posed picture, in effect a reconstructed icon, which carried, and was no doubt intended to carry, two crucially important political messages which were delivered visually and without the need for words. The first, which was evident from Iyasu's lion-hair coronet and gold-embroidered clothing, was that the young man was an imperial prince destined to succeed his renowned grandfather Menelik. The picture thus visually confirmed Iyasu's royalty and emphasized his august descent. The second message was embodied in the presence and positioning of Ras Tessema. With his open, honest countenance, and his hand benevolently placed over that of the young prince, his image was an assurance to an essentially conservative Ethiopian public that Iyasu, though still an immature child, with a face unmoulded by experience, would be assisted in the difficult years ahead by an old and wise guardian, who, like his father before him, had long given loyal service to Menelik, and was well known and respected throughout the land. It is probable that the photograph was not taken by an Ethiopian photographer, yet it shows the Ethiopian state's total assimilation of the medium. The sitters confront the camera with the steady gaze of authority and assurance — a self-presentation commanding the camera in the creation of a specifically controlled image.

This photograph, so pregnant with political over-

147. Emperor Yohannes IV with his son Ras Araya Sellasé, c.1880. Photographer unknown.

tones, is, interestingly enough, reminiscent of one of Menelik's predecessor, Emperor Yohannes IV, and of the latter's son and heir, Ras Araya Sellasé, taken over a quarter of a century earlier, around 1880. This picture (Plate 147) shows the great (and in his day much revered) Ethiopian monarch, with his imperial crown and royal robes, placing his hand paternally on the shoulder of his offspring. The pose may owe something to European studio conventions, but is nevertheless carefully chosen with political intent. The photograph visually entrusts the younger man with the aura of kingship.

Notwithstanding the reassurance provided by the presence of the good Ras Tessema in the photograph discussed above, Lij Iyasu's reign was a turbulent one and one in which another, entirely different photograph is said to have soon played an eventful role. Difficulties for Lij Iyasu and his régime began shortly after his photograph with Ras Tessema was taken. The old Ras fell seriously ill in the autumn of 1910, and, after several months largely unable to concern himself with state affairs, died on April 10 the following year. The Council of Ministers at once proposed appointing a successor, but the young prince, who had hitherto meekly accepted his guardian's tutelage, had evidently come to enjoy his new-found freedom, and suddenly displayed unexpected independence. Brushing aside the suggestion of any new guardian he said to his assembled ministers and counsellors, 'My father Menelik gave me a Regent, but God took him away. As for you, you are nothing but my soldiers!', hence his to command (Montandon 1913:381).[7] The courtiers, astonished by the prince's sudden resolve, had no option but to accept the wishes of the prince, who was thus left without any mature adviser or restraining hand. The unbridled youngster, relates Dr Mérab, a Georgian resident, thereafter gave free rein to his 'youthful fantasies', and was 'from morning to evening, and, what is more, from evening to morning, running from one house to another, with the object of amusing himself with young women' (Mérab 1922).

Menelik, who had been totally incapacitated for several years, finally died on the night of December 12–13, 1913, whereupon Iyasu at once acceded to the throne; but, because of his youth and his irresponsible behaviour and the disquiet with which the latter was regarded by some, he was not crowned. Possibly inspired by his Muslim ancestry (Wollo was in any case a province where members of one family were often divided between the two religions) as well as by a vision of an Ethiopia which would embrace all its inhabitants — Muslim as well as Christian — he spent much of his time touring the Muslim provinces, consorting with Muslim chiefs, and, it was widely alleged, with their nubile daughters. These travels were a political mistake: they weakened the prince's already tenuous political position by taking him away from the capital, which was the centre of effective power; and, because they were mainly carried out in Muslim areas, they inevitably disturbed the country's Christian establishment.

Iyasu attempted to strengthen his hand by proclaiming his father, Ras Mika'él, as Negus (or King) of Tegré and Wollo on June 1, 1914. The outbreak of the First World War two months later was, however, to prove disastrous to the young man's fortunes. Influenced by his desire to win the support of the Muslims, as well as by the stifling presence of Italian, French and British colonies or protectorates which entirely surrounded his country, he soon displayed strong pro-German and pro-Turkish sympathies. This angered the British, French and Italian Legations, which felt themselves entitled to interfere in Ethiopian affairs. They made a joint démarche, on September 10, 1916, warning Lij Iyasu's ministers that if their young master continued to support their enemies they would intervene militarily. This threat to the country's independence served as a catalyst, causing a number of the most prominent Shewan nobles finally to decide on immediate rebellion against their still uncrowned monarch. To do so they had, however, to be freed from their oath of allegiance to Menelik's heir and successor. This release could be obtained only through the intervention of Abuna Matéwos, the Head of the Ethiopian Church, who, in accordance with long tradition, was an Egyptian Copt, and had to be convinced, it is said, beyond any shadow of doubt that the young ruler had abandoned the Christian faith.

Photography, it is believed, played a major role at this point. Just as the medium had earlier been used to popularize the young prince by depicting him with his wise old tutor Ras Tessema, so it appears to have now been brought into play to highlight his alleged Muslim sympathies, and thus bring about his downfall.

The issue on which his fate turned was that, though avowedly a devout Christian, when travelling in the Muslim areas and visiting mosques he chose to wear a turban and Muslim-style robes. Thus, it was alleged, he revealed himself to be an apostate who had abandoned the Christian faith and embraced Islam. The story at this point becomes confused and it is to this day impossible to establish with certainty how far Iyasu displayed Muslim sentiments, let alone what were his real motives. If, as is generally agreed, he often dressed as a Muslim this may have been a sign, as many claimed, of conversion to Islam, and hence a determination to abandon Christianity; on the other hand it might equally have been, as many now believe, a purely tactical move to establish a rapport with his country's Muslim population. Whatever the motive may have been, news of the young prince's behaviour created great excitement, especially, it is said, when it was documented photographically.

Local Ethiopian tradition holds that opposition to Lij Iyasu was fanned by sight of a photograph (which the present writer has never been able to trace) of the prince in Muslim dress. It is widely believed in Ethiopia that this was not in fact a genuine reproduction but a 'doctored' picture produced by one Levon (or Léon) Yazegjian, an Armenian resident in Addis Ababa. He is remembered as a clever photographer and an intimate of the prince who, after the latter's fall, rose to an important position in the Ethiopian police.[8] Another version of the story (which was much embroidered in the telling) claims that the photograph was actually the work of British Intelligence directed against Iyasu's pro-German policy.[9]

Genuine photographs of Lij Iyasu showing his Muslim sympathies (genuine or tactical) were, however, also taken. One (Plate 148) depicts the prince, with a Muslim turban and gold?-braided cloak, seated regally on an upright chair, with an important Harar Muslim leader, Abdulahi Ali Sadek, standing

148. Lij Iyasu wearing a turban while on a visit to the Muslim city of Harar. He is seated in the house of one of the principal men of the city, Adulahi Ali Sadik (standing right) and members of the latter's family whose descendants, the owners of the photograph, testify to its authenticity. (Courtesy of Dedria Mohamed and Salah-el-Din Mohamed)

beside him. Behind Lij Iyasu we see five of Abdulahi Ali's children. Their descendants, who own the old, and somewhat tattered, copy of the photograph here reproduced, testify fully to its authenticity.[10] Another photograph of this time (Plate 149) depicts the prince, who was of powerful build, proudly wearing the skirt-like dress of the Muslim Afar, or Danakil, nomads. He stands barefoot, with a typical Afar dagger at his side.

Possibly to counter the effects of such 'Muslim' photographs the Addis Ababa Amharic-language weekly *Aimero*, which was then in the hands of Lij Iyasu's supporters, published a studio portrait, by the said Yazegjian, of the prince (Plate 150), on February 7, 1915, showing a cross very visibly tied round his neck. Further, to increase the importance of this picture and to underline its political-cum-religious message the editors printed above it an effigy of the Lion of Judah, as used in Menelik's proclamations, in which the crowned animal, as customary, held a cross of Christ in its paw.[11]

Another photograph of Lij Iyasu (Plate 151) taken in this period was from the political point of view no less remarkable, for it shows the young man kneeling devotedly beside his renowned father Ras Mika'él, by

then King of Tegré and Wollo, the prince's head resting submissively on the paternal knee. The father, in a gesture reminiscent of Emperor Yohannes IV in the earlier photograph discussed above (Plate 147), proudly places his hand on his son's head. Father and son are dressed in the fine cloaks worn by the higher Ethiopian nobility. Their status is further emphasized by the silk curtain behind them, as well as by their being seated on a costly imported embroidered carpet. Mika'él, perhaps no less significantly, is not wearing

149. Lij Iyasu in the simple dress of the Afar, or Danakil, nomads. The photograph was probably taken during one of the prince's visits to the eastern lowlands which the group inhabits. (Courtesy of the Institute of Ethiopian Studies)

150. Full-length studio portrait of Lij Iyasu as a Christian prince, with cloak and cordon (note the pectoral cross) as published in Lincoln de Castro, *Nella terra dei Negus*. An enlarged section of the photograph showing the head and shoulders — and the cross — was published by the Amharic-language weekly *Aimero* on February 7 1915. Photograph by Yazegjian.

the unfortunate prince on September 27, 1916. That the religious issue was of fundamental importance at the time is evident from the prelate's Manifesto to the 'Princes and People' of Ethiopia, issued on that occasion on which he expressly charged Menelik's heir with wearing 'the dress of Muslim chiefs, taking part in Muslim prayers, and become an apostate to his religion' (Anonymous: 1916).

Though the political intent of the Iyasu–Ras photograph and other representations of Menelik's heir is clearly evident, there is unfortunately no means of telling how widely these pictures were disseminated or how far the message embodied in them travelled in terms of the population at large. Such photographs do, however, appear to have had an important impact in influential circles, and the power of the visual record became thereafter an integral element in the Ethiopian political process. Photography later played a notable part in the overthrow of Emperor Haile Selassie in 1974 when images were used to discredit him and his fast-crumbling regime. 'Doctored photographs', shades of those which had preceded Lij Iyasu's deposition, were exposed for sale and displayed in car windows.[13] The dénouement came in visual form on

151. Lij Iyasu kneeling devotedly beside his renowned father Ras Mika'él, by then King of Tegré and Wollo. Note crown on right. (Courtesy of the Institute of Ethiopian Studies)

his crown, which has been placed beside him on a level with his son's head, on which, it may perhaps not be too fanciful to assume, people may have expected that the imperial crown of Ethiopia would soon be placed.

Pictures of the Muslim-turbaned Lij Iyasu, however, probably carried more weight in Ethiopian Christian circles than either of these two 'Christian' photographs. Genuine or fake, their existence is said to have seemingly proved that the young ruler had embraced Islam, and thus helped to persuade the Abuna to absolve the nobles from breaking their oath of loyalty. The photograph, it is claimed, also had a considerable impact on a populace which, because of the novelty of photography, perhaps regarded it with especial awe.[12] The camera in this manner, it is said, contributed in no small measure to the deposition of

Ethiopian New Year's Day, September 11, when Ethiopian State Television presented Jonathan Dimbleby's film *The Hidden Famine*, depicting starvation in Wollo, interrupted by shots of His Imperial Majesty handing meat to his dogs as well as luxurious living at court. The monarch, constrained to watch this indictment, was forced to abdicate on the following day (Thompson 1975:102; Legum 1975:50; Lefort 1981:69). Photography had come a long way since its first appearance 130 years earlier, but its assimilation into Ethiopian politics has had almost as long and relevant a history.

NOTES

1 Engravings based on these early photographs are reproduced in Stern 1862 and Pankhurst & Ingrams 1988.

2 The impact of novelty was similarly apparent in the early days of the popular Ethiopian theatre, in the 1970s, when audiences attending performances in Amharic of Shakespeare's *Othello* reacted angrily to Iago's treachery. Several women took off their shoes and threw them at the player, whose troubles did not end there, for when subsequently travelling about the town, he was not infrequently recognized and insulted on Iago's account (Pankhurst 1986:169–96).

3 Alfred Ilg, a graduate of Zurich Polytechnic and an enthusiastic photographer, arrived in 1879 and soon overcame the monarch's suspicion of the camera. Shortly after his arrival he was summoned to the royal presence. 'I have heard something about you,' Menelik said, 'which is very bad, and of which I surely would not have believed you capable. At the same time it is so ridiculous, so improbable, that I would not have believed it had I not heard it from trustworthy people.' Ilg at once enquired what the king was referring to, whereupon Menelik continued, 'I have been informed that without my knowledge you made me small, and stuffed me into a black box, together with my whole town, houses, people and mules. And, what is even more unbelievable, I was standing with my legs in the air.' Embarrassed by this report of his photograph exploits, Ilg had 'no other option', his biographer recalls, 'than teach His Majesty the most important laws of optics' — and before long 'the monarch understood the workings of the camera' (Keller 1918:35).

4 Menelik delighted in being photographed. A foreign visitor, J.G. Vanderheym (1896:80–83), who reached the Ethiopian capital, Addis Ababa, in 1894, recalls that the monarch 'begged him' to photograph him, and adds: 'I spent a very interesting morning posing Empress Taytu, the princesses, and the ladies of the court who had dressed in their most beautiful clothes.' On other early foreign photographers see also Pankhurst 1979.

5 One of the first important funerals in which photographs were thus displayed was that of Ras Mekonnen, Menelik's cousin and governor of Harar, who died in 1906 (Guèbrè Sellassie 1930–1:11, 552).

6 Testimony to the widespread fear of the camera is provided by a British traveller, F.L. James (1888:180, 225–6), who relates that when trying to take photographs in the Ogaden towards the turn of the century people ran away from him, and those who consented to sit for their portraits encountered 'considerable abuse' from their friends, who referred to them insultingly as 'dogs and cats'.

7 On the history of this period see also Guèbrè Sellassie (1930–1:11, 540, 623–9) and Marcus (1975).

8 On the history of Yazegjian see Patapan (n.d.:246) and Pankhurst (1981:321–2).

9 The earliest version of this story, apparently based on the reminiscences of Hakim Workneh, a foreign-educated Ethiopian physician and sometime minister in London, appears in 'Princess' Asfa Yilma's biography of Haile Selassie, which claims that the photograph was the work of unspecified 'British agents' (1935:127–8). They are said to have taken 'a big photograph' of a Muslim festival, and then replaced the face of the leader, who was

pronouncing his blessing, by one of the Ethiopian prince, who thus seemed to be wearing 'full Moslem regalia'. Another version is found in the sensational memoirs of Baron Byron de Prorok (1943:162–3) who claims that an informant told him of the arrival in Addis Ababa, in Lij Iyasu's time, of 'a strange, little man, an archaeologist and a linguist' who was 'an ideal member of the British Intelligence Service' and whose description 'fitted remarkably' that of Lawrence of Arabia. He is said to have been 'closeted with the British Minister for several days', after which photographs of Lij Iyasu were distributed. Some showed him 'surrounded by Muslim priests at prayer', others 'in a harem with dozens of white women', but all bore a caption in Amharic, reading 'The Anti-Christ'. These pictures, according to de Prorok, were 'faked by an Armenian called Leon' (i.e. Yazegjian) who perhaps 'felt that his was an act of patriotism', since the Armenians had 'always been persecuted by the Turks'. Qualified support for the story is also given in Greenfield (1963:138). See also Solomon Gashaw 1974 and Kenafe-Regb Zelleke 1981.

10 Grateful thanks for this photograph are due to Ahmed Zecharia, a dedicated scholar of Harari history and culture, who most kindly traced and introduced me to Abdulahi Ali Sadek's descendants, Dedria Mohamed and Salah el-Din Mohamed, who generously gave permission for the publication of this hitherto unpublished photograph.

11 This portrait was apparently part of a full-length photograph of the prince taken by Yazegjian and reproduced in De Castro (1915:11, Plate CXXI opp. 528).

12 'Princess' Asfa Yilma (1935: 128) claims — with obvious exaggeration — that the effect of the 'strewing broadcast' of the photograph was 'sensational. The priests rose as one man to demand excommunication of the vile apostate. It was believed at once that there was a plot to exterminate all Christians and seize their goods. The chiefs renewed their demands that Yassu be deposed.'

13 These photographs were seen at the time by the present writer.

REFERENCES

Anonymous 1916. *Documents relatifs au Coup d'Etat d'Addis Abeba du 27 septembre 1916*. Dire Dawa.

Asfa Yilma 1935. *Haile Selassie. Emperor of Ethiopia*. London: Sampson, Marston & Co.

Baeteman, J. 1929. *Dictionnaire amarigna-français*. Dire Dawa: Imprimerie Saint Lazare.

Byron de Prorok 1943. *Dead Men Do Tell Tales*. London: George Harrap & Co.

De Castro, L. 1915. *Nella terra dei Negus*. Milano: Fratelli Treves.

Greenfield, R. 1963. *Ethiopia. A New Political History*. London: Pall Mall Press.

Guèbrè Sellassie 1930–1. *Chronique du règne de Ménélik II Roi des rois d'Ethiopie*. Paris: Librarie Orientale et Américaine.

James, F.L. 1888. *The Unknown Horn of Africa*. London: George Philip and Son.

Keller, C. 1918. *Alfred Ilg. Sein Leben und sein Wirten*. Frauenfeld and Leipzig: Verlag von Huber.

Kenafe-Regb Zelleke 1981. *The Episode of Eyassu Menelik (1896–1935)*. Addis Ababa: Paper presented to the Seventeenth International Conference of Ethiopian Studies at Lund in 1981.

Lefort, R. (1981). *Ethiopia. An Heretical Revolution?* London: Zed Press.

Legum, C. 1975. *Ethiopia. The Fall of Haile Selassie's Empire*. London: Rex Collins.

Marcus, H.G. 1975. *The Life and Times of Emperor Menelik II 1844–1913*. Oxford: Clarendon Press.

Mérab, P. 1922. *Impressions d'Abyssinie (L'Abyssinie sous Ménélik II)*. Paris: H. Libert.

Montandon, G. 1913. *Au pays Ghimmira*. Neuchâtel.

Ottoway, M. & Ottoway, D. 1978. *Ethiopia. Empire in Revolution*. New York: Africana Publishing.

Pankhurst, R.K.P. 1976. The Genesis of Photography in Ethiopia and the Horn of Africa. *The British Journal of Photography*: 878–92, 910–13, 933–5, 952–7.

— 1981. The History of Ethiopian-Armenian Relations. *Revue des Etudes Arméniennes* XV:355–400.

— 1986. Shakespeare in Ethiopia. *Research in African Literature* XVII: 169–96.

Pankhurst, R.K.P. & Ingrams, L. 1988. *Ethiopia Engraved*. London: Kegan Paul International.

Patapan, H. n.d. *Ardi Et'ovpian ew Haygalut'e*. Venice.

Solomon Gashaw 1974. *Power Struggle in Addis Ababa (1909–1916)*. Addis Ababa: Senior Essay, Haile Sellassie University.

Stern, H.A. 1862. *Wanderings among the Falashes in Abyssinia*. London: Wertheim, Mackintosh and Hunt.

— 1868. *The Captive Missionary*. London: Cassell, Petter and Galpin.

Thompson, B. 1975. *Ethiopia. The Country that Cut Off its Head*. London: Robson Books.

Vanderheym, J.G. 1869. *Une expédition avec le négous Ménélik*. Paris: Librairie Hachette.

Walker, C.H. 1928. *English-Amharic Dictionary*. London: Sheldon Press.

Zervos, A. 1936. *L'empire d'Ethiopie*. Alexandria: pub. privately.

Two Māori Portraits: Adoption of the Medium

Judith Binney

EARLY THIS CENTURY a visionary prophet emerged from among the Tuhoe, the most isolated of the Māori people in New Zealand, living in the mountainous Urewera country of the central North Island. Rua Kenana Hepetipa was not the first, and he would not be the last of the Māori prophet leaders. Prophet leaders became important voices of community protest for, from the middle of the nineteenth century, Māori were being brought within the orbit of European authority. Their economic base was eroded by partial land confiscations and laws which, by more subtle means, dispossessed them. 'Amalgamation' with Europeans was the official policy. The photograph of Rua (Plate 152) was taken in 1908 and it reveals the ambivalence of his world. His coat and clothing are firmly European, but his long hair is not. Nor was its length traditional. His uncut hair was his statement that he was a Nazirite dedicated to God. He considered himself to be the promised King of the Iharaira, the Israelites, the scriptural name his followers had recently taken for themselves. Rua claimed to be the New Messiah, and at his death on February 20, 1937 the people waited in vain for his promised resurrection on the third day.

This portrait was taken by James McDonald. He was at the time a draughtsman working for the Department of Tourist and Health Resorts. In 1912 he would be reappointed to the then Dominion Museum in Wellington as their 'artist and draughtsman', having previously worked there between 1904 and 1906. The photograph is one from a series, which consists of four known posed studies of Rua, one of a group of his major followers, and three additional studies of his pre-eminent wife, Te Akakura Ru, and an unidentified woman. They are all imaged as the elegantly dressed leaders of a proud people, although the reality of their daily lives was harsher. But McDonald was making no attempt to create an artificial environment, for Rua posed for other photographers at that time in similar style. Two series of portraits and group photographs were also taken in 1908 by the professional photographer George Bourne, who worked for the *New Zealand Herald*. Bourne claimed that a full-face study he took of Rua in April 1908 was the first posed portrait that the prophet had permitted.

McDonald himself was a close associate of the well-known ethnographer of the Tuhoe, Elsdon Best, and also of the historian James Cowan, who sometimes travelled with McDonald for the Tourist Department. Both Best and Cowan would subsequently use McDonald's portraits of Rua and Akakura as examples of Māori 'types' in their publications (Best 1934:2; Cowan 1910:39, 148; Cowan 1916:229). The portrait of Rua, together with that of Eria Raukura, was sent to

152.   Rua Kenana, 1908. Photograph by J. McDonald. (RAI 1784)

the Royal Anthropological Institute in this context. The personal image of the leader was appropriated without view to the true context to demonstrate contemporary theories about race.

Nineteen hundred and eight was a high point of Rua's authority as prophet and leader. However, Best dismissed him as a charlatan, claiming, wrongly, that he was of low birth and that he had abandoned many of the traditions and values of his tribe. He could not accept the reality of Rua and his influence. In his ethnographic 'freezing' of the world of the Tuhoe, Best saw them as the last of the traditional Māori. But McDonald's photographs more accurately convey Rua as a leader in a changing world. Rua interpreted Māori history through the prism of the scriptural narratives, with their promises of salvation for God's chosen people.

The second portrait (Plate 153) is of Eria Raukura, or Tutara-kauika, the leading *tohunga* (priest) in the faith in which Rua had been reared, the Ringatū, or the Upraised Hand. It was taken in July 1913, and is one of a series of eight surviving studies of Eria that were almost certainly made by McDonald for the Dominion (National) Museum, which holds the original glass plate negatives.[1] It also reveals a man who was consciously changing his world. Eria, or Elijah, had been baptized in 1881 by the founder of the Ringatū church, Te Kooti Arikirangi Te Turuki, as the major priest of the faith. Te Kooti's predictions had often looked towards his successor, one who would be more powerful than himself and who would complete his work; Eria accepted Rua to be this man. He, in his turn, had in 1906 baptized Rua as the predicted one in the Waipawa river, that is, in the waters that flowed by Te Kooti's tribal home.

In this photograph Eria is studying the Māori Bible. In another in the sequence he stands holding the Bible in his left hand, while his right hand is raised up to instruct. The Ringatū derive their name from their practice of lifting their right hand at the end of their prayers in a gesture of homage to God. Eria had baptized Rua as Hepetipa (Hephzibah) because in 1885 Te Kooti had predicted that his successor, who would bring lasting peace, would be thus named. Hepetipa is the Daughter of Zion in whom the Lord rejoiced and who will restore the land to fertility. The name also means 'chosen by God'.

In the portraits Eria is wearing vestments of his own design: a frock coat, on which the words 'The Holy Church' are stitched on the cuffs. The same words in Māori, '*Hahi Tapu*', appeared in gold braid on the collar. Eria had fought alongside Te Kooti in the last phases of the mid-nineteenth-century wars (as had Rua's father, Kenana Tumoana). Eria had also

lived in sanctuary with Te Kooti in the 'King Country' (the tribal territory of Ngati Maniapoto in the centre of the North Island), where Māori exiles took shelter after the wars, until they were pardoned by the government in 1883. Eria then was able to return to his tribal area, the Urewera and Poverty Bay, where he was held in great esteem. He was believed to possess the dangerous spiritual power of *mākutu*, and it was warned of him, 'Never let his shadow fall upon you'. He died on June 29, 1938, and he was said at his death to be 103.

These two portraits are 'anthropological' in the correct sense: they are records of men in their time and their world. They are not artificially posed images of 'primitives' in a colonial society, but representations which the subjects themselves controlled. Nevertheless, in the early twentieth century the camera was still almost exclusively a European device. At first Rua was reluctant to be photographed for a posed study and particularly, as here, without a hat. (In one of the four in this sequence he does wear his hat.) Bourne had encountered this fear in Rua (Taipo 1908:498). Rua's head, as the seat of his *mana* and his *tapu*, his authority and his sacredness, was exposed to the potentially destructive power of the camera. It was a belief common to many Māori that, by the transference of the human image, the camera sucked out the *mauri*, or life-force of the individual. Bourne assumed as a professional nickname a word used by Māori for the camera: *taipō*, commonly translated as goblin, or devilish object. He was also a magician.

These photographs of Rua and Eria are part of a wider movement in which Māori quickly adopted photography for their own purposes, actively commissioning photographic portraits of themselves and their elders. These portraits, dating from the later nineteenth century, now adorn tribal and family meeting-houses. They are images of the dead *tīpuna* (ancestors), whose *mana* and knowledge are seen as the source of the tribe's present authority and well-being. In this manner the genealogies, which are the backbone of all Māori history, became visual, and the photographs hang alongside the carved images of older ancestors. Photographs of the dead, and their dead kin, were and are brought out and displayed at *tangi* (funerals), which are the most important of all the surviving Māori ceremonies. The portraits and snapshots are transported with the body in the *kawe mate*, the ritual carrying of the body from *marae* to *marae* to the meeting-houses where the dead had belonged. Photographs are sometimes permanently attached to the headstones, which are unveiled at a later occasion. The 'unveiling' of headstones is itself a modern adaptation of the traditional *hahunga* cere-

153. Eria Raukura, 1913. Photograph by J. McDonald. (RAI 7002)

mony, when the bones of the dead were cleansed and displayed and lamented over before their final burial. Photographs brought into a Māori home may be treated as though the person themselves has returned, and they may be cried over as over the dead. A portrait of Pinepine Te Rika, Rua's first (and *tapu*) wife, who died in 1954, was shown by the author in 1978 to a woman whom Pinepine had brought up. She talked and sang to the photograph as if it were Pinepine herself.

Photography was a medium that, although foreign, was transformed into an acceptable means of recording the Māori past, and leaders such as Rua and Eria thus saw it as a way of presenting themselves to their own people, and to a wider audience. One Māori photographer, Canon Hakaraia Pahewa, an Anglican clergyman living in the isolated community at Te Kaha on the east coast, sent many photographs of Māori life from the beginning of this century for publication in the popular newspaper, the *Auckland Weekly News*. He was particularly interested in scenes of communal work: mustering sheep, or cutting up whales for blubber. The inclusion of photographs in written history as a form of *whakapapa*, genealogy of the ancestors, is an important aspect of presenting history to Māori readers. There is today some hostility towards the European historians because the frame-work of New Zealand's written history has mostly been a colonial one. There has either been a focus on the 'old-time' Māori and 'his' adaptation to the changing society, or a concentration on the issues of conflict, and the European lawmakers who invariably dominated. Māori oral histories of the same events in the nineteenth and twentieth centuries are much more accounts of their own strategies for their independent survival, and of their own leaders. Few European historians have conveyed these perspectives, in which photographs can play an important part.

Eria Raukura and Rua Kenana were two men of Tuhoe who sought to retain control of their world. Their religious faith was based in a view of history which found the meaning for events in fulfilment of earlier predictive warnings, or promises. Their teachings were derived extensively from the scriptures, but their lineage as *matakite*, men of foresight, was rooted equally in Māori tradition, whereby the knowledge of the *tīpuna*, those who have gone before, is transferred as visions to the wise among the living. Their vision for their people was the recovery of their autonomous authority within the land of their ancestors. That they chose to have their images recorded was, for them, the statement that their vision would live for the successive generations.

NOTE

1 C256, C257, C258, C259, C261, C263, C264 and C265. C255, C260 and C262 were also originally portraits of Eria but the plates were reused. The photograph in the RAI collection reproduced here is C257. C261, described in the text below, is reproduced in Binney et al. 1987: 31. Other portraits from the 1908 series associated with Rua, and taken by McDonald, are also reproduced in Binney et al. 1987: 14, 20–1, 58.

REFERENCES

Best, Elsdon 1934. *The Maori as He Was*. 2nd edn. Wellington: Dominion Museum.
Binney, Judith, Chaplin, Gillian & Wallace, Craig 1987. *Mihaia: The Prophet Rua Kenana and his Community at Maungapohatu*. 2nd edn. Auckland: Oxford University Press.
Cowan, James 1910. *The Maoris of New Zealand*. Christchurch: Whitcombe & Tombs Ltd.
— 1916. Rua the Prophet. *Wide World Magazine* 38:229–37.
Taipo (George Bourne) 1908. A Dusky Dowie: A Maori Prophet at Home. *Life*, December 1:495–500.

Afterwords:

'Framed Photographs'

Historical Images — Changing Audiences

Iskander Mydin

The practice of anthropological photography, or more precisely photography of anthropological interest, arose in the nineteenth century as a visual parallel of anthropological ideas about culture. This was also the period of the Western forward movement of colonial conquest and consolidation of territories on a worldwide scale. Anthropological photography of non-Western peoples and cultures in these territories therefore emerged at a time of unprecedented social change for non-Western societies as they were incorporated into alien, industrialist-capitalist metropolitan economies.

In encountering countries that were being transformed through the impact of social change, the photographer paradoxically chose to focus on unchanging representations of peoples and cultures. For it was the 'exotic', the culturally different, which fascinated, in both scientific and popular terms. The many reasons for this have received extensive attention elsewhere, including this volume (for example, Gould 1981, Stocking 1987 and Bogdan 1988 explore very different aspects of this continuum). The main themes may be summarized thus: the emergence of an anthropology, with an increasing institutional machinery, articulated contemporary ideas which were predominantly evolutionary, stressing as its object the living primal forms from which Western culture was assumed to have emerged. Not only was this teleological view evident in visual stereotypes such as the ubiquitous 'noble savage' but it was also a thinly disguised motive behind attempts at 'salvage ethnography' in the nineteenth century. Related to this was the 'culture of imagining' (Fleming & Luskey 1986:138) which referred to the consumption of photographic images by a Western audience of individuals, groups and institutions during this period. In its most common or widely practised form, this consumption was seen in market demands of popular ethnography for 'exotic' representations of peoples and landscapes in colonialized territories. The 'exotic' was linked with an unchanging presentation of the subject-matter perceived as undynamic. It is the powerful tenacity of this imagery of the exotic that I wish to consider in this brief essay.

A final important ingredient was the strongly held idea that the photograph was a scientific record of life, time and space. Regardless of the manoeuvre or manipulation of subject-matter by the photographer, the resulting image presented as a 'record' photograph was taken for granted as a truthful representation. When combined with the 'culture of imagining', the photographic task became an almost totalizing encounter; only the sullen gaze or stare of some anthropological subject in these images hints at some element of autonomy retained by the subject in this encounter.

Given that in part the reading of anthropological photographic images is an experiential consumption of culture, what do we make of these images that have survived from the late nineteenth and early twentieth centuries, almost entirely in black and white, in varying conditions of preservation, documentation and, indeed, enmeshed in many different contexts? Photographs have been treated in functional terms, for their historical evidential value. This has been the case with exhibitions based on photographic archives where the ways in which a photograph has been structured to reflect a reality, whether real or apparent, have not been made clear, the stress being on the evidential value of the content. Yet in the salvage, conservation and appeal of these images there appears to be, as I have already suggested, another paradoxical replication of the sustaining motives of anthropological photography in its relation to nineteenth-century cultures undergoing social change.

This is apparent in modern reproductions of nineteenth-century photographic images, in the form of 'coffee-table' books, picture postcards, or as exhibition themes or catalogues, and even in the commercialization of original prints as collector's items within the art market. This is especially so of the work of certain photographers such as John Thomson, Felix Beato, Linnaeus Tripe (for example, see Christies 1989:119–23, 143–6, 194–205), although the tentacles are beginning to reach even the more ethnographically intentioned such as J.W. Lindt and Johnson & Hoffman. In this sense, there can be said to be a growing 'culture of consumption' which is based in the range of responses which these images now evoke. For while the camera is perhaps no longer totally the tool of Western observation, the mechanisms for the marketing, mass production and dissemination of images, especially historical images, are arguably still in an unequal relationship.

Audience responses are as varied as photographs themselves: nostalgia and historical interest, curiosity, anger (at seeing some anthropological subject stripped, measured and photographed) and voyeurism. They may not be mutually exclusive, being rather unstructured mirrors where one response may be reflected in another in the individual encounter with these images. More than anything else, this suggests the intricate nature of the photograph and the need for what Sekula has described as an 'historically grounded sociology of the image' (1988:87). In reading these images, a formalist approach in terms of coherently discerning methodical layers of signification is too rigid or insufficient to allow for the plasticity of representations.

It is a pluralist approach which can be best applied to the idea of the exotic which continues to sustain views of the non-West. Perhaps it would be more revealing, therefore, to approach the 'exotic' not only as an idea but also as a contemporary practice. The 'exotic' as idea can be regarded as the representation of 'allegorical structures'. This refers to a simplification of the way in which the anthropological other was to be pictured, the rendering of complex reality into a visually articulate form which supported a broader world view (Arnheim 1974:155–6). In this way, the consumers of such images could relate to the representations. Perhaps a classic example are the images evoking the past of the American Indians by Edward Curtis, published between 1907 and 1930 (Gidley 1976; Lyman 1982). Representing perhaps the culmination of a genre, these were not realistic views (indeed they were often 're-created') but Curtis's characterization of ideal-types of Indians in pure-form. Elements of this form of 'Indian-ness' did not include the commonplace of Indian experience but exaggerated views of the commonplace, a heightened reality; scenes of Indians standing amid retouched landscapes; for example, a Pima woman drawing water from an irrigation ditch retouched to be a natural pond (Lyman 1982:49, 79–83). The manipulated image articulated a belief that the natural landscape reflected the nature of its inhabitants and vice versa and in the process created an imaginative landscape which when traversed by the camera shaped its contours in terms of pictorialism. Retouching and other techniques of style may be regarded, therefore, not merely as a manipulation but instead as an incidental photographic closure of time and space so that an 'ethnographic present' could exist.

The mechanisms connecting imaginative landscape and so-called ethnographic knowledge, an interaction of 'science', aesthetics and culture, are also found in other 'exotic structures' such as the orientalist perception of the Middle East (Said 1978) and the Tibetan Shangri-La (Bishop 1989). What is important is that it is response which remains powerful in modern contexts, as is demonstrated by the number of television programmes and coffee-table books which use Curtis's images and similar to express the human being's oneness with the natural world, the antithesis of the viewer's urban experience. In general terms this representational response to marginal cultural groups suggests a believed state of innocence and harmony with the environment which is lost in the artifice of Western culture yet which 'they' retain. These essentially nineteenth-century mechanisms are not only absorbed into modern responses to historical images but also inform modern representations which serve modern Western political and environmental preoccupations (Street 1975:120; Ellen 1986; Wright 1990:30). At the same time political realities of the modern world paradoxically strengthen such images as they become a focus simultaneously for outrage and for 'romantic melancholy', a yearning for a paradise lost.

One can identify other responses which feed off related stereotypical representations. Underlying a seemingly unchanging view of the lives and cultures of the other was, as suggested, the medium of 'allegorical structures'. The use of allegory as a means of communicating the meaning of manufactured individuals (such as studio anthropological models), posed scenes and events was linked to the potential saleability of these images. Examples of common allegories include the noble savage, the fecund native, the sexually subversive odalisque and the 'type'. That these are not wholly nineteenth-century structures is evident in their continuing reproduction in contemporary picture postcards of the non-West. But many such images are produced not by the peoples themselves but by a cynical manipulation of traditional culture as a tourist commodity, in a direct lineage from the images of nineteenth-century popular ethnography.

Singapore postcard images are a case in point. On the one hand, historical photographs including picture postcards from archives have been displayed in museums and galleries, while in the street 'exotic' picture postcards are on sale for tourists and locals alike, through whom these representations are disseminated overseas to family and friends. It is a paradox that while the late-nineteenth and early-twentieth-century picture postcards of Singapore reflected to a large extent the reality of the urban milieu of Singapore (for example, the toil of the street working class), contemporary picture postcards present a romanticized view of the ethnic mixture and street scenes through the strategic use of colour, camera angles, card frames and captions. There has emerged a 'neo-exoticism' in the representation of everyday life which is one dimension of the market-place context of Singapore in the ongoing process of the commodification of urban society.

Historical images are also employed to sell present realities, suggesting a place where time stands still (as photographic time must). Historical images are used to represent the imagined 'reality' of present place — as when up-market tourist brochures in the Western world use watercolours and early photographs to sell their wares; for example, a David Roberts watercolour or early photographs of the Valley of the Kings to 'sell' tours of the antiquities of Egypt (a small footnote warns that the image is

in fact not reality!) (*Independent on Sunday* May 12 1991:45). Conversely, as an indication of the plasticity of response on the part of the photographically colonized, the image can be internalized into positive statements of cultural identity, perhaps in the face of present political realities; for example, Lhalungpa (1983), where historical photographs are used as mechanisms in Tibetan identity. While such responses are superficially similar to those of nostalgia considered above, the crucial difference is that the dynamic here is not external but internal.

Yet, at another level, the exotic image is a metaphorical experience. This refers to the photographic manufacture of relationships, both temporal and spatial, that would not be possible or accessible in real life yet are powerful sites of Western fantasy. For example, as Alloula has argued (1987), the traditional veiling of Muslim women in Algeria and the domestic privacy of the harem, led, in the French colonial period, to the creation of the 'phantasm' of unveiled, semi-nude Algerian women in picture postcards which were mass-produced for public view. Through them the viewer was 'arrogating a right of oversight' to himself by claiming a relationship to closed areas of native life. The 'phantasm' was reproduced in the photographic studio with models functioning as surrogates of their referents — the real inhabitants of the harem. But the irony was that the reality of the harem represented a closure of private space, the antithesis of its exposure by photographic voyeurism. The visual legacy is still potent in the new colonialism of the tourist encounter as images of desirable indigenous women have been most successfully used to 'sell' a country's potential for fulfilling dreams of the exotic (Choy 1989:5–6, 21).

In another way, metaphorical experience was also considered as a solution to the colonial dilemma of the maintenance of Western identity in the face of its potential subversion by the native (Monti 1987:4, 130–2). This has been a favourite theme in Western literature of the colonial period, as in the Conradian 'heart of darkness', and in his novels with an Asian setting, notably *Lord Jim* and *Almayer's Folly*.

It was not only in literature but in real life that the theme of Western rationality versus native fecundity and moral and physical corruption became a label to be used in the interaction between, for example, the colonizing male and the native woman. This was seen in the emergence of a colonial ruling caste with native mistresses and concubines whose 'turbid sensuality' was a metaphoric justification. The practice of this sensuality was carried out not only in photographic images (scenes of white men with native women on their laps (see Theye (1989:74–5) for instances from

Cameroon and Eritrea) but also in colonial brothels which offered their customers 'exotic odalisques' (Monti 1987:74–5), a legacy which survives in many well-publicized instances.

A visual reading of 'exotic' images is thus more than a simple act. It involves examining the triangular relationship between the producer of such images, their anthropological and historical subject and we, the audience, who in this case also include the descendants of those anthropological subjects. The relationship is also not fixed as the producer and subject can become consumers (for example, the producer who is also a collector or connoisseur; the subject who re-enacts an extinct ritual for the camera) and the audience who can become producers as well.

In this sense, the 'exotic' has passed from its orientalist phase to a modernist phase but the underlying structure is a mediation between cultural distancing or interaction, through mechanisms which remained strangely familiar. Distancing in the sense that the other can be transformed from living entities to allegorical, metaphorical and aesthetic ideas. Interaction in the sense of consuming or sustaining the consumption of these abstractions and imagined realities; only an historical and anthropological experience of culture can serve as an alternative to this structure. This involves a sojourn into the life-world of a culture to locate and experience its images in perspective.

REFERENCES

Alloula, M. 1987. *The Colonial Harem.* Manchester: University Press.

Arnheim, R. 1974. On the Nature of Photography. *Critical Inquiry* 1(1):149–61.

Bishop, P. 1989. *The Myth of Shangri-La: Tibet, Travel Writing and the Western Creation of Sacred Landscape.* London: Athlone Press.

Bogdan, R. 1988. *Freak Shows: presenting human oddities for amusement and profit.* Chicago: University Press.

Choy, D.J.L. 1989. *Repositioning Malaysia in the 1990s.* Serie B, 59. Aix en Provence: Centre des Hautes Etudes Touristiques.

Christies 1989. *Photography 1839–1989.* Catalogue of the auction sale, November 9, 1989. London: Christies (South Kensington).

Curtis, E.S. 1907–30. *The North American Indian* 20 vols. Cambridge and Norwood, Mass. Univ. Press.

Ellen, R. 1986. 'What Black Elk left unsaid: on the illusory images of Green primitivism'. *Anthropology Today* 2(6):8–12.

Fleming, P. Richardson & Luskey, J. 1986. *The North American Indian in Early Photographs.* New York: Harper and Row.

Gidley, M. 1976. *The Vanishing Race: Selections from Edward S. Curtis's 'The North American Indian'.* Newton Abbot: David & Charles.

Gould, S.J. 1981. *The Mismeasure of Man.* New York: W.W. Norton & Co.

Lhalungpa, L.P. 1983. *Tibet: The Sacred Realm. Photographs 1880–1950.* New York: Aperture.

Lyman, C. 1982. *The Vanishing Race and Other Illusions: Photographs of Indians by Edward S. Curtis.* Washington: Smithsonian Press.

Monti, N. 1987. *Africa Then: Photographs 1840–1918.* London: Thames & Hudson.

Said, E. 1978. *Orientalism.* London: Routledge & Kegan Paul.

Sekula, A. 1988. 'On the Invention of Photographic Meaning'. In V. Burgin (ed.), *Thinking Photography.* London: Macmillan.

Stocking, G. 1987. *Victorian Anthropology.* New York: Free Press.

Street, B. 1975. *The Savage in Literature: Representations of 'primitive' society in English fiction, 1859–1920.* London: Routledge.

Theye, T. (ed.) 1989. *Der geraubte Schatten.* Munich: Münchner Staatmuseum.

Wright, T. 1990. 'Sir Benjamin Stone: Photography and Cultural Theory'. In M. Hallett (ed.) *Rewriting Photographic History.* 28–31. Birmingham: Article Press.

A Political Primer on Anthropology/ Photography

James C. Faris

As soon as you want something, they've got you.

I. F. Stone

ANTHROPOLOGISTS seem to have had considerable problems thinking about photography, as if paralyzed by its 'certificate of presence' (Barthes 1981:87) — its prerogative and its extension. Its use by the discipline has been principally formal, methodological, and/or as adjunct polemic to a humanist agenda. The black, brown, yellow and red subjects of its main practice, however, have been less inarticulate in their increasingly frequent resistance to photography of themselves and of their activities.[1]

Echoing this resistance, anthropology has increasingly retreated to rework histories and comb existing discourses in order to examine its relationship with those photographed, with photography, and with its particular forms of presentation. This activity has generated much criticism, reflexive commentary, the admission of authority from elsewhere[2] (feminism, fiction, autobiography) and not a little indulgence. This volume, part of the critical and reflexive examination, is proposed as a step in another direction from the more confident, celebratory, enthusiastic treatments that have characterized the anthropology/ photography nexus produced thus far (see Singer & Woodhead 1988; Rollwagen 1988; Banta & Hinsley 1986; Heider 1980, and references therein).[3]

Certainly there seems often a resolute assurance in photographic modes — they are commonly accorded a very great authority, they are 'more' — considered more objective, less partial, more revealing of insight. They are considered more humane, as well as more brutal. They are certainly ubiquitous and easily accessible: teachers are eager to use visual materials and films in their classes wherever possible. The question remains, however: is this 'more' not still all aspiration: that desire which leads to capture, enslavement, oblivion, death — is there not a transcendent motivation — a project with a long history in the West?

The focus here will be more tropic than scopic — on governance, project, want, and the dominating appetites of photography and anthropology, and vague suggestions about ways around this. The commentary is designed to be explicitly political. Reviewed will be an assembly of effects and determinations relevant to comprehending the relationship of anthropology and photography — stemming from the discursive practices of both, as well as their possible significances in rationalist philosophical traditions and contemporary media forms. All statements are very preliminary and partial. What, indeed, are the photographic arenas of discourse within anthropology? What are their shapes, their boundaries? The task here is simply to historicize, or better, to situate,[4] but not through the erection of other hierarchies. It will be an approach to the relationship (photography/

anthropology) in a non-designed form of argument, a non-projective, unfocused, seamless politics which operates as intervention at several axes of power to specify the very protocols, the limits and confines of that authority. It is of no concern here whether anthropology/photography may remain henceforth politically problematic, or whether they survive as currently practised. This should not be understood as pessimistic (nor paranoid) — rather, as nontopian. It is an attempt to help comprehend (and perhaps thereby avoid) some of the terrors of power that have, to this point, characterized the relationship, yet it is not an axiomatic suggestion of a posture by which terrors can always be known/recognized.

I. Politics ocular: the eye that governs

While not reducible to it, any attempt to comprehend the union of anthropology and photography must undertake careful consideration of the visualist privilege of the West. This entitlement has a long philosophical history, and has been generally discussed in recent works (Foucault 1973; Rorty 1980; Foster 1988), including some consideration in anthropology (Tyler 1984; see also Pinney, Wright, Edwards, this volume, for some double exposure).

Since Plato's allegory of the cave, wisdom has been accepted in the West in illusions of and allusions to vision — knowing is insight, seeing is believing, light is privileged over heat, and rationalist epistemology rides heavily on ocular metaphor: the mind's eye. This epistemology argues the world exists independently of thoughts about it and is governed by discoverable processes. Through human sensory perceptions (or instruments [scopes] thereby derived from them) and the application of reason and method, it can be represented in a consciousness called knowledge. The enabling implications for the photographic print are plain.

The caveat of reason, of course, provides the philosophical register for a *correct* consciousness, for as the world's processes are not necessarily as they appear, then perception can be deceptive.[5] Some processes need to be uncovered, revealed, posited — and method and logic are required in addition to make the vital discrimination right/wrong, correct/incorrect, the distinction between ideology and knowledge; that is, to situate the notion of *progress* so deeply satisfying to Western history.

With this displacement from reality, reason is frequently expressed in some ratio or even scopic rating. This is the foundation for the teleologies of evolutionary theory and the social classifications of anthropology, including situating the visibly different on whom the discipline is classically based.

Apart from the evidential, however, this introduces a somewhat contrary or limiting possibility for photography, debilitated as it is by its instrumental authority, for as Barthes notes, its '. . . power of authentication exceeds [its] power of representation' (1981:89). As a consequence, this has facilitated and enabled, indeed required, anthropological activity in the photography of others — for its captioning practices, the verbal text, explanations, for more of its particular privilege of representation.

Anthropology, however, is faced with a universe where the *facts* of difference do not depend on method as they must in more contingent disciplines. Others are everywhere; their visibility secures them. The fact does not imply nor obligate this particular ordering, however. Thus the captioning itself creates our possibility, not the object.[6] This is simply to say that non-Westerners exist and can present themselves, at least to themselves — they have no straightforward histories, they are particular. Without contemporary rationalist power/desire (to know), what is their relevance? They are indeed visibly different (as are we all), but why, in what universe, could this difference have significance? And does it necessarily follow that all that can be distinguished visibly should or can be photographed?

But the white (of all lightness) [the West] and the black (of nothingness, of darkness) [the Rest] came to have a sinister sanction, and difference came to be coded for consumption. What *they* might make of difference, of the facts of others, was very occasionally recorded, mostly as an item of quaint charm (in the social administration crisis mode of Kluckhohn & Vogt, *Navaho Means People* (1951), significantly a photographic volume),[7] antique comparative relevance, or as fodder for essentialist argument, for example that ethnic 'prejudice' is universal, that boundary maintenance is thus essential, even biologically based.

Consequently, anthropology, as Western enterprise, as rationalist science, continually restructured difference to establish, preserve and perpetuate the 'ratio' (Foucault 1973:378), to assume West and install the rest, to render the other domestic, to turn difference into distance (argued here to be the anthropological project).[8]

But the other must not represent themselves. Distance requires measure. Otherwise, how can there be rational discourse, correct explanation (or today, convincing interpretation[9]), truth?[10] Measure introduces a dimension, a spatial element which is another privilege of sight (rendered site), but not confined to it (the sightless, for example, have tactile and aural means by which to discriminate space — this is considered again below, and see also Wright, this volume).

Thus anthropology's vision quest, its attempt to render, to usurp the other (ignoring the even more predatory imagery assigned 'sublimated looting', 'capture', etc. [see Sontag 1977]; or the hunting metaphor 'shooting', etc., vital to describing its execution [see Lloyd 1984]), is then ever compromised by the unbridgeable chasm, the distance, the vast spatial separation, the enormous leap constituted by the facts of their culture and local authority,[11] and our view of it, the ratio maintained by rationalism. To the extent that this vision relies then, on photography, only representation (in militant Western terms) is possible.

Some anthropology has been quite comfortable with this — particularly classical British structural functionalism where photographs were principally adjunct to one or another instrumental agenda. The American relativist tradition, however, generally concentrated on means to attempt to focus representation in humanist dimensions. As non-European Americans had long been the objects of conquest and expansion, anthropological photography became an exemplar of salvage, the civilizing mission, and hence archival or nostalgic. These photographers were motivated more by contrition and catharsis than method. The Native American was no longer free (could be no longer free) as subject, but had to become 'perfect' as object, ascetic, actor. Hence, the fakery of Edward Curtis (see Lyman 1982, but also Faris 1990).

Both traditions, however, represented, and photographs were simply part of this larger project. They were seldom independent of intervening discourses. These discursive projects were the focus, the point of view; these were the perspectives inherited from the Cartesian tradition.

II. Politics spatial: reading the tr(sp)ace

Ignoring for the moment some recent museum examples that approximate the size of the galaxy,[12] photographs — whether still or moving — are bounded. That is, they are framed. As such they inject another space — the limits, the edges — proscriptions, prohibitions of the image. These cannot be treated as arbitrary nor as artefact of technique. They define what is to be photograph and what is not. They deny (what was not in the photograph). They decide looking from and looking at. What makes these decisions — who frames and who focuses? How is it that these decisions are possible? What discursive authority, what appeal, determines where the space takes place, and what is thereby excluded, marked, made visible.[13] Must so much difference in the West depend on the insolent features of form, on sighting/siting — the most rigidly dimensional attributes of

photography? This is a discussion in two parts. First there is the issue of the specific framing, the issue of focus, of stage, of whole and parts, of viewer privilege, and of the photograph's intransigent insistence on and simultaneous denial of time. Secondly there is the issue of representation, of representation itself, not 'as of' something else, something more fundamental, something more real, or some metaphorical statement, but of the conditions and possibilities and limitations of meaning. Perhaps, if framing has become so vital with the ubiquitous extension of photography, meaning never arrives and is condemned to dependency and needing (cf. Derrida 1987). What is the function of the spacing, the framing, the making of difference and discrimination, the marking of what is viewed and what not viewed? From this latter point of view, we can treat photographs in semiological terms as indexical, not iconic — that is, they space, mark, trace, they do not stand for.[14] To acquire meaning they must have text (but see below where it is argued that some genre photography indeed may be treated as iconic).

When the anthropological caption is added, we have yet another frame, another boundary, another prohibition, another space made, another universe, another rupture, a double displacement (cf. Krauss 1985b; Derrida 1976, 1987). As noted, for anthropology, photography meant the *necessity* of caption — the space of the photographic print could not be trusted to speak for itself, transparency was not axiomatic, and text had to be added — for content was totally foreign to viewers (as usually was also, of course, anthropological methodology — the framing itself). Consequently a double spacing resulted, a dual displacing motion — on the one hand, evidence rendering the foreign captive (or whatever else chosen — the point is 'we' rule and the viewer is brought close [you are there, participant in the conquest, privileged to the scrutiny of their lives, but very safely so]); on the other hand situating the photographic quotation in humanist terms (in the most 'liberal' of examples), familiarizing and domesticating their presented authority, confronting their evident legitimacy (weakening their own challenge), fixing them in our own denigrating vocabulary — 'ritual', 'myth', 'tribe'; in our own totalities — 'society', 'family', 'domestic', 'religion'; or in our patronage — their sacrifice required for dignity on our terms, the 'indignity of speaking for others' (Foster 1985:80).[15]

Discursive practices secure their fields of objects — it is, of course, *our* social relations that are the focus of the photograph — the object (and viewers) can only have relations, can only appear, in our space.[16] Anthropology is determined to reveal, fix or interpret meaning, it is stuck in the project of representation. It is the science of representation. Indeed, anthropology disappears if it attempts to get out of such representation — it becomes something else. Photographs have become one vital and permanent guarantee and instrumental insurance — after all, everyone can see — but anthropology is *needed* for understanding, for explanation. Difference has been fixed as such distance that photographs need maps to guide viewers — an atlas of terrain (and stratigraphy) provided by anthropology. That no single discourse could possibly scribe all social relations, of course, gave rise to lots of anthropologies, all stemming from the specific discursive enterprises — texts, meanings, representation — by which we situate social relations (psychological anthropology, economic anthropology, symbolic anthropology, etc.).

Many indigenous peoples were captive by the middle of the nineteenth century when photography began, and as such, could be celebrated in the manner of triumph/loss. There came to be a veritable industry in such photography in the United States, to yield an entire tradition of dignified passive victims which became photographic protocol, dominating framing statements to the present day (cf. Curtis 1989). The spacing, the framing evident in such photography, dramatically betray the conditions of its possibility. They are not signifiers, they are signified. This was a tradition in which anthropologists were later more than willing to collaborate — it was (again, particularly in the Americas) anthropological being. It is the humanist itinerary, an acceptance, a partisan embrace, but always carefully and clearly on our terms, 'the oppressed are granted a bogus Subjecthood when such status can be secured only from within, on their own terms' (Sekula 1975:45). Thus, these humanist photographs appeared with text, as icons, as bearers of meaning — they did not really need an(other) anthropology.[17] They are convention.

III. Politics specular: the I that governs

Insofar as discussion thus far has been convincing characterization, we can extend it to its metaphorical diagnostic: anthropology is locked in the image metaphor, trapped in the 'specular' — the cohesive fiction of virtue. Current anthropology is regarded as founded (and foundering) in the 'mirror phase' (Freud, Lacan),[18] that narcissism by which it can but see its reflection, that phase in which projection is the total of activity: the gaze. This is an appeal to the symbolic order, a phallic exercise, evoking of the father's authority, an ignorance of social fiction. The political implications are abundant for both anthropology and

feminism (cf. Gallop 1982). There is in the photograph a denial of modalities of sense other than vision, and the object becomes thereby immaterial (no smell, no touch), available only in image — the eye holding it firmly distant, under the conceit of I.

An aspect of this rule, this control, this consumption is, of course, the fetish, the commodity form of the photograph. Not only is the image seized (variously, depending on national legal forms; cf. Edelman 1979), but its expanding and growing market implies other perversions outside the scope of this essay (cf. Pinney 1989 for a brief statement on the television documentary as commodity). The extension and growth of the photographic, even in anthropology, has become overwhelming — indeed inaugurating ever new contagions. The exponential increase in visual representations has, since television and cheap photographic printing, generated dispassionate and disinterested response as we become ever more saturated. Capitalist production has universalized the prurient gaze of the detached ethnographer (Tyler 1987a: 49). Every innovation facilitates easier capture, quicker seizure (lighter gear, faster film, video) — capital dictates change, with technologies replacing thought (cf. Buck-Morss 1989).

The other can be posed only in our project. No world (yet) exists (that the West knows of) that such project has not shaped, nor can exist without such project. While anthropologists protest against caricatures, the protests rarely seem to matter, and the popular perceptions proliferate. The anthropological ego may have been bruised in what it perceives as a misunderstanding. But is not the ego indeed the problem? If the ego is eclipsed, obliterated, can there be representation of the non-West? If anthropological desire is transcended, what of others? At the very least, they might be left alone.

Is it that anthropology is not listened to, or is it that classical anthropology is the essence of the problem? The Royal Anthropological Institute, concerned with caricatures, recently inaugurated a series of discussions (revealingly labelled 'Anthropology in Focus'), which, according to the reviewer (Banks 1989), were between converts to begin with (talking to the mirror as ego-ed subjects), and he notes that some anthropologists had willingly collaborated in the more extensively communicated and debatable views that brought about the perceived necessity for the discussions. The extraordinarily problematic Yanomami volume (*Yanomamö: The Fierce People*: Chagnon 1968) on violence still ranks as the best selling of *illustrated* and *assigned* texts in anthropology classrooms.

Can there be non-authoritarian photographs? Since the feature which authorites the photograph no longer exists, how, without the visualist sanction, are photographs ceded authority? Photographs 'speak for themselves', are 'worth a thousand words', but it is I (eye) talking [speech here as writing; cf. Derrida 1976] to eye (I). Are photographs paralyzed (and privileged) in their instrumentalism? Can there be anything new — can they add to the world? Or, is the new reality they claim non-additive, is their only possibility a sort of collage, but mocking of reality and the very real extent to which our comprehensions are dictated by old specular discursive projects.[19]

Ego (I) anthropology is a disciplinary apparatus. Its social control is evident in both humanist and essentialist notions, and in the universalist ordering tropes — functionalism, structuralism, etc., by which the other is denied while being championed, the peculiar subsumed, the particular forbidden and the local refused. The revelation and exposure of the photograph becomes the transparent cloth of Emperor Anthro.

IV. Politics and pre-text

It matters little that their presentation of themselves (to themselves) may not be easily photographed,[20] or photographed at all — perhaps others'/another's presentation cannot be satisfactorily traced in photographic terms; perhaps, just perhaps, it is one of the limits of rationalist technology — certainly it is so of rationalist logic. Perhaps this is one inscription of boundaries and limits of the other for us where we had previously assumed none, at least to us.

Photographs just may not be able to assist in their presentations to us — there is simply no debate on the issue, few experiments, and nowhere is there ever the suggestion that photography be abandoned in these endeavours. In this view, photographs may not (just) steal souls — they destroy them as they simultaneously constitute them. Social relations cannot be easily freeze-dried. Without an entire corpus, they are sometimes quite difficult even to 'illustrate' to those foreign to the cultural form in question, and even then, perhaps impossible without additional framing, without some textual form. But here are we not in other conventions, equally problematic? There is, however, at least some promising current discussion on textual forms in anthropology, and as with all critique, there exists the possibility of new or innovative framing.

Inserting a politics of debate, consideration, yes, photography *mis*-presents, is *in*-authentic — not to a truer or more authentic, or other (better) presentation, but to the space for another presentation on different terms, another pre-text. Why cannot other/anothers present themselves?[21] This query is obviously rhetorical, but only partially so. Marx's notion that (peasants) cannot represent themselves so must be represented is, in the view here, not simply arrogant, but a politically paralyzing position.

Is there a possible anthropology? Are questions it might ask, concepts it may have contributed, not worthwhile? Perhaps, but perhaps only insofar as it speaks to itself. Most anthropological concepts ostensibly designed to apply universally do so only in retort to other Western projects which deny or specify humanity outside the West. They battle with each other, each commonly in appeal to some greater Western transcendent. That anthropology informs anti-racist projects (to the limited extent that it may do so) is because it exists in a racist milieu; that it may inform tolerance, appreciation, acceptance, is so because the forms that have generated anthropology generate intolerance, denigration, exclusion. Like psychotherapy, anthropology can but exist and construct from the materials at hand — the templates are Western. They are the two great servants of (and monuments to) our alienation.

What of other experimental work, the photography of performances designed to be public, viewed or indeed photographed by indigenous people? What of the arranging of 'fictions'? These might involve rehearsal, payment of participants, contracts and the like, and certainly these are not without risk. But then at least issues of 'authenticity' would be settled — the most carefully rehearsed, carefully produced performances and productions would be the most authentic. And participants, being paid, would at least have claim to subsistence, and contracts might give them other rights, such as editorial licence. All of this may sound a bit like Hollywood, but whatever other perversities may be implied, a certain amount of honesty applies to these fictions.[22]

The appearance of things (the anthropology/photography nexus) to come can be informed only by very careful meditation and discussion of practices to date, and on careful political discussion and ways to arrange *our* social relations henceforth. This has got to be an exercise liberated from desire, from the symbolic, from the ego — from metaphor and from meaning. It has got to be open, without method, free of will and truth, and the will to truth. Anthropology, perhaps uniquely, is posited to be able to listen, but it has not, at least in the modes, the representations, the shapes having so far characterized anthropology/photography practices. Anthropology thus has not heretofore been a listening mechanism; classically it has been a seeing device, the aural rendered ocular, and hence its naïve embrace of scopic technologies. There does not appear to be a modality free of these privileges, or free of the means by which the West has constituted them.

In these terms, are tourist Nikons worse than 'Disappearing Worlds'? Is Riefenstahl (1974) 'worse' than Faris (1972, 1988a, 1988c; Ryle 1982)? Is '60 Minutes' (or '20/20') 'worse' than the Public Broadcasting System and National Geographic? In the view here, all the parties listed have more in common than they have differences. Their differences are items of Western political disagreements, but their commonality vis-à-vis the subaltern is in fundamental ways uniform. The differences are important, but until a political debate incorporates the Western motions themselves, as opposed to the political differences in Western motions, anthropology/photography is going to continue to be problematic.[23]

But perhaps this volume is a step in another direction — an attempt to examine that classical naïvety, to probe its limits, to unveil its desire — for we are creatures of great imagination, and the world is filled with remarkable alternatives, perhaps worth considering, or even touching, tasting (cf. Stoller 1989); perhaps seeing and being seen in a different way. Perhaps, indeed, seeing in a way that listens.[24]

NOTES

1 Commentaries about resistance are now practically ubiquitous in anthropological film (cf. Rollwagen 1988: *passim*), but there are much older traditions of objection and recognition of the dangers of this form of representation (cf. Lyon 1988). This resistance is even interpreted as challenge, threat (rather than liberation, emancipation), for the other is now emerging as richer, bolder, more complex than previously thought — even as someone who defines his or her own dignity, and voices power in his or her own terms, someone who no longer accepts presentation or discipline by Western representational projects.

2 An interesting recent micro-exchange and contestation may be seen in the reading of the now-famous photograph of Stephen Tyler (as involved in research in India, actually writing culture while Indians look on in the background) on the cover of J. Clifford & G. Marcus, *Writing Culture* (University of California, 1986). Clifford (1986:1) focuses on the ethnographer's centrality/marginality and his activity, noting but one other person in the background of the photograph, an indigenous male (the ubiquitous 'informant'?). Gordon (1988:7), in critique of Clifford's reading/seeing, calls attention to the fact that two females appear in the photograph but are unmentioned, and indicates how indeed one woman is even obliterated by 'writing'! There are, of course, other readings — each involving one or another political decision.

3 After all, in a nation whose entire anthropological academy is in precipitous quantitative decline, one new position/program created with much fanfare was in Visual Anthropology, endowed with television monies (University of Manchester, Granada Centre). And it employed an eye logo not dissimilar to the blinded eye appropriated so ironically from Magritte by the American television giant, CBS.

Some rationalist confidences may also rest with the serial phylogenic order of technological changes in photography (cf. the abundant exhibitions arranged by this feature in celebration of photography's sesquicentennial [viz. Szarkowski's Museum of Modern Art show, 'Photography Until Now', February 18-May 29, 1990]; and the teleology, the progressive motion implied, for instance, in the title of the travelling Peabody Museum exhibition 'From Site to Sight'; see Banta & Hinsley 1986). It might, of course, be argued that such shallow optimism, especially as in the latter case, obscures but vaguely the fears of the past — the agendas of power and racism enabling an anthropology, the predatory and intrusive focus of the photography.

4 The theoretical essay by Pinney in this volume concretely historicizes the photography/anthropology nexus, and correctly calls attention to the parallelism, the problematic association, the caution. One might even extend Pinney's argument: that without an anthropology (the rationalist fix of the other), the photography of non-Westerners, indeed even the filmic documentary (the gaze) of unknown humans in general, might be impossible.

Pinney (this volume) notes the periods of defeat, set-back, insecurity and unease in paralleling the histories of anthropology and photography. For early struggles over the power of framing and photographic access in general, see Jay 1984; Sekula 1975; Snyder & Allen 1975; Gross, Katz &

Ruby 1988; Squiers 1990; and Bolton 1989.

5 The bullets and the bodies are indeed real and exist independently of consciousness. But can an approach to these existences ever be other than political? It is not just that humans are condemned to live in knowledge/ideology, but they are also free to argue for (and act on) other concatenations of cause and effect, or to argue against those received from the past or from contemporary cultural assignments — to always establish other differences.

6 In this sense, then, if emancipated from capital and Western philosophical traditions, could not photographs be argued to be transparent? In the view here, however, not easily; that cameras and film evolved to stop motion; that photography was confined to the visual; that it moved from gaze, from the view; that it obstructed space; that its record was immutable; or even that white skin shade came to be a critical variable in the development of colour film (as opposed to darker shades) make it clear that the photograph, even in its most technical sense, can never be seen as disinterested (cf. Pollock 1990).

7 This notion of the charm of others' identity of themselves, and their comic identification of Westerners, has a long liberal history in novels and travel literature, and more recently in anthropology. There is now a plethora of literature on Their response to Us — reflexivity demands it. But argument that this genuinely constitutes a dialogic condition too often ignores the very considerable power differentials. Consequently these accounts often seem indulgent, patronizing, or confessional at best (cf. Rabinow 1977, with hostility toward the anthropologist/photographer dramatically visible on the cover), or even grotesque at worst (cf. Ben-Ari 1989, on the *angst* of being a repressor of Palestinians).

8 Difference as such has no ratio, unless one really does assume they are all variations of us in some non-trivial sense. There are certainly very successful practising anthropologists who make this assumption: Marvin Harris, etc.,

where, for example, Hindu cattle veneration is really disguised ecological practice; Aztec human sacrifice really a response to protein deficiencies. There are also the equally unsatisfactory reductions of local logics to mere nourishment for the Western-inspired universal in the humanist work of Joseph Campbell or Carl Jung, or, indeed, much of the worst of structuralism.

9 There is considerable debate over 'interpretive anthropology' (cf. Geertz 1973; Rabinow & Sullivan 1979), but at a very fundamental level the 'directed sensibility' in interpretation is something of a bourgeois privilege, a denial of the interpreter's status as a social critic/actor. The photographic analogy is what Sekula (1975:39) has called the 'myth of semantic autonomy of the photographic image'.

10 All philosophies are statements of control, the specifications of motions and fixing of moments by which knowledge is to be possible. That under classical rationalism this movement has taken on teleological dimensions has had a profoundly significant effect on the growth and development of disciplines such as anthropology. The human object was created and situated in simultaneous motion, the other acquired an epistemological significance and thus a natural dimension. The anthropological monograph became the exemplar of the other; objective, dispassionate, intelligent, a record made visual, fixed in space, the document (hence the commonly adjunctive embrace of photography). Non-objective research was presumably that not published, which blurred genre, which challenged boundaries. And 'only descriptive accounts' came to be henceforth denigrated. Geography and evolutionism provided the spatial and temporal parameters, expansionist capitalism the stimulus. This is a significance inadequately discussed in anthropology, though there is currently the inauguration of some debate. Rationalism, of course, has had very dramatic (i.e. visible) success in extending control, over people, labour, disease, matter. The less 'apparent' (in-

visible?) consequences, however, have been devastating.

One anthropology/photography effect has been the dramatic success of documentary film series (for example, in Britain see Singer & Woodhead 1988) and adventure/explorer movies (everywhere; see Rosaldo 1989), but also the means by which anthropological discussion has come to be phrased in ocular metaphor. In a recent flyer for two anthropological monographs from a leading US publisher, the texts offered are discussed thus: '. . . vivid and detailed description of the experiences of a modern anthropologist in the field are interwoven with a clear picture of the effects . . .', and in another, 'is an extremely colorful and detailed portrait . . . helps readers visualize . . .' (Jackson 1987).

11 Of course some anthropologists have turned this chasm into a privilege itself. Noteworthy here are the abundant statements of Claude Lévi-Strauss on the advantage of distance, and even method of its measure, and a 'focus' on the fact of distance itself particularly in the manner of linguistic spacing and marking (cf. Lévi-Strauss 1983).

There are now contests, however, over the shape of this spacing, the parameters of this distancing. Clifford (1988) discusses a debate concerning Mashpee identity, and I (see Faris 1990) recently heard an argument between an anthropological linguist and a Navajo medicine man over whether Navajo had a word that translated as 'religion'. The linguist argued that it did, the medicine man argued that it did not. He gave a metamorphic translation ('the way, moving along in ceremony') of *nahaga*, denied by the anthropological linguist, who insisted on the literal (metaphorical) meaning. This brings up, again, the entire question of torpid, static yet saturating and predatory 'meaning' in the West; see Baudrillard 1988.

12 The hyperbole is only half in jest; see, for example, the new Canadian Museum of Civilization in Ottawa, which must have among the largest photographs extant. These are, of course, simply small

James C. Faris 259

photographs made large, but they introduce special considerations in terms of the space they occupy in reality (the museum wall), and the boundaries, the frame, of the photograph itself, and the act of becoming gigantic. And content in these larger-than-life photographs takes on a host of other significances quite beyond their smaller-sized originals, viz. aesthetics, spectacle, hagiography, and issues of dimension and perspective, etc. (cf. Stewart 1984). The photo-propaganda murals of Herbert Bayer, for example, were at the service of the Nazis in the 1930s as well as for Steichen at the Museum of Modern Art in the 1940s (Buchloh 1989).

The uses of photography in the museum and exhibition framing mechanisms introduce other considerations that are certainly tangentially important. But contemporary anthropological museuming strategies are the subject of such active debate that it is best here to keep the issues separate (cf. Ames 1983; Clifford 1988; Stocking 1985; Faris 1988b; Price 1989).

13 For argument on the spatial obsessions of Western thought (and thus a rather different sort of critique), see Tyler 1987b:34ff. Tyler, indeed, would argue the priority of space to vision in Western thought, and lauds forms of non-written 'vision', or 'saying-showing' (1987b:198), with what appear to be, as I understand his text, paradoxically, consequent hierarchies of determination. He would not be happy with the political approach suggested here.

Of course, there are for anthropology all manner of particular examples of the significance of concrete photographic space (as in specific 'cropping'). See for example Jacknis (1984) on Boas, Salat (1983) on Nadel, and Scherer (1978). Certainly spatial concerns are central to the exhibitional strategies of museums, of anthropological collections, and even, as Tyler has emphasized, writing and publication. These topics deserve more attention than is possible under the concerns here (cf. Torgovnick 1990).

14 There are persistent attempts to suggest otherwise. John Berger (1972; 1980; 1982) is perhaps the most resolute. There are also arguments that cine or moving film escapes this, that it can incorporate, can dissolve boundaries, can dampen proscriptions. But motion pictures are inhibited by even more severe constraints: the phenomenological issues of activity, the point of convergence of the camera(s), and the staging required to have to continually privilege focus. Indeed the more appropriate model and better analogy for the moving picture is with the most rigidly staged and multilayered of all visual productions — opera (cf. Tambling 1987).

15 Here, of course, I speak of but those evidential anthropological photographs and their caption whose structure and framing stem from method and epistemology, not those fabricated, made, altered or otherwise explicitly composed for tertiary purposes.

16 Note that there is no discussion of aesthetic discourse here. While there may be an assumed socio-aesthetic (culture/nature) in many of these photographs, there is seldom any explicit statement — indeed, such a discourse is usually impossible, for then other commentators might infiltrate and deprive anthropology of its hegemony.

There is also the tradition of photographs of others outside their context, such as the scientific studies of Franz Boas (Jacknis 1984) or the staged work of Edward Curtis (Lyman 1982), all of which bear more relationship to catalogue illustration or the fashion photographs of Avedon or Penn (who took Papuans out of New Guinea) than to conventional anthropological photography, for which some allegiance to context is paramount. There are, of course, both methodological and aesthetic (as well as ethical) issues of importance here.

Perhaps only in the photography that has come to be associated with museums and treatises on art and material culture has there developed a distinct photographic aesthetic independent of context. Among

other effects, this tradition, however, basically fetishizes the artefacts/art ('remains') as commodity (cf. Faris 1988b; Price 1989).

17 In fact, such early situating photography (Vroman, for example) largely began to disappear as soon as anthropology began to undertake (take over) research among indigenous peoples, and with rare exceptions (cf. Sandweiss 1985, on Laura Gilpin) there never again developed authored photographic collections of the same order. The space had been usurped from the War Department, from the Geological Survey, from the amateur, from the studio. Indeed, from this time on, non-anthropological photography of indigenous Americans became a distinctly suspect activity. But while many anthropologists photographed, the work never emerged as genre. This is in contrast to landscape photography and to photography of Americans of more recent European origins (and others subaltern or 'marginal'), the latter of which continued, and still persists as a distinct genre registered under the trope of social administration (leaving aside possible voyeurism) and where there are abundant authored and unified œuvres.

There are, of course, interesting examples in new photographic practices, especially from feminists, that are explicitly critical of social relations without necessitating the appearance of victims to gaze (cf. Rosler 1981, 1989), and considerable focus on the self-conscious political choices in self-imagery (cf. Garner 1990).

18 Relevant texts here are Lacan 1977, especially 'The Mirror Stage'; and Freud, *Standard Edition, vol. xix*, especially 'The Infantile Genital Organization'.

19 Hence the interest of surrealists in photography. But as has been widely noted (Krauss 1985a), this was extraordinarily problematic. Surrealism sought light from production and exposure of sign in the real, and indeed a theme of post-modernist critique is the ecstasy/anaesthesy of the projected image. The saturation of the visual representation argued in

the latter has come to characterize an entire nihilistic therapy (cf. Lotringer, in Baudrillard 1988).

20 There is experimental work, such as the Worth/Adair attempts to put cameras in Navajo hands to see what their view of their culture might be (Worth & Adair 1972). What, however, was interpreted by the authors as Navajo cultural expressions must be seen in terms of the fact that neither the camera nor the filmic eye (I) are Navajo. Involving them reveals not how much they are Navajo, but how very much it is our device (see also in this regard Pinney 1989).

In photojournalism, a vicious convention of authenticity rests in the sanctimonious outrage at paying subjects ('cheque-book journalism') depriving those whose souls are stolen, from the most base of rewards, their subsistence. Agreement to be interviewed in most television news broadcasts axiomatically means no pay, but it gives no editorial control whatsoever (see Gross, Katz & Ruby 1988). Refusal to be interviewed, of course, is always presented as some sort of axiomatic guilt.

21 If the other serves anthropology, anthropology can be said to have produced it. When one films neighbours, friends, how do these social relations appear — do they not still remain friends, neighbours? Do they not insist on the presentations of self, on editorial control, on reciprocity (see note 20 above)? And what situates the social relations so labelled are common interests, common residence, love — not a desire to know (them), without disclosure of the pre-text, without complementarity. They are photographed because they are known, loved — not known (or desired) because they are photographed.

22 There has been some work in these directions (cf. Schechner 1982). One interesting experiment, however, foundered on ethnographic 'authority'. In a Performance Group experiment wherein Ndembu ethnography was being dramatized, one female actor queried the sexism of a 'ritual' scene, and suggested changing the performance to eliminate it. But here the opening of ethnography to performance closed down to the 'real' character of Ndembu life (cf. Turner 1982: 93), never mind everything else, of course, had changed quite 'dramatically' in the staging of the activity. The West might rule, but not women.

23 There is some debate in these directions (cf. Faris 1988a:117):

So it is in essence one more film [Southeast Nuba] dictated by the interests of Europeans and their squabbles with one another. That it is an anthropologist's view, informed by intimate knowledge of local people and their language versus the view of a non-anthropologist seems of peripheral significance to me now, for I no longer think the issue is debate about a 'correct' or a 'truthful' view as opposed to an incorrect or untruthful view (one might assume Riefenstahl thinks her view is appropriate), but basically over political perspectives.

And in an interview with Dennis O'Rourke (the filmmaker of Cannibal Tours), he seems to see the film less an indictment of tourists and their Nikons than an exposure of the practice of the filmmaker himself (Lutkehaus 1989).

But current reflexivity has sometimes tended toward a type of global-shopping-mall approach, in which all concatenations of content and form are celebrated (cf. Marcus & Fischer 1986), photographer's flashbulbs as personal decoration in Papua New Guinea, JFK velour wall-hangings at Zuni. These approaches critique the stasis of locality (community) and linear time (for example, notions of ethnographic present, the teleologies of evolutionary theory) and argue the abandonment of such classical space and time tropes. Yet abandonment of specific Western notions should not, in the view here, admit all concatenations in a grotesque amorality and political irresponsibility, but such abandonment should lead us to change the prevailing security of property and place and the received wisdom of hierarchical time (cf. Faris 1988c: 40; and Buck-Morss 1989, on Walter Benjamin's perceptions of the arcade, the mall as ur-project).

Nevertheless, naïve perceptions abound (the 'discovery' of the facts of social construction), and commentary is still filled with enthusiasm over reflexivity and anthropology's potentiality (cf. Adams 1987; Banta & Hinsley 1986; Bruner 1986, 1989).

24 I was asked to write an essay on 'new horizons' in anthropology/photography. Not able to focus on much of promise (and it must be remembered that many new projects are not yet published), I do not, however, see this essay as nihilistic. Nevertheless, it is due to the indulgence and generosity of the editor (whom I thank for her critical suggestions) that it is included at all. And though I certainly know he would not have agreed with any part of it, this essay is dedicated to the memory of Edmund Leach — especially his persistent iconoclasm.

REFERENCES

Adams, M. 1987. Commentary. Looking Beyond the Photographic Image. *Visual Resources* 4:273–81.

Ames, M. 1983. How Should We Think about What We See in a Museum of Anthropology. *Transactions of the Royal Society of Canada*, Series IV, vol. XXI: 93–101.

Banks, M. 1989. Anthropology in Focus: Debating at the ICA. *Anthropology Today* 5(2):19–21.

Banta, M. & Hinsley, C. 1986. *From Site to Sight. Anthropology, Photography, and the Power of Imagery.* Cambridge, Mass.: Peabody Museum of Harvard University, Harvard University Press.

Barthes, R. 1981. *Camera Lucida.* New York: Hill and Wang.

Baudrillard, J. 1988. *The Ecstasy of Communication.* Trans. B. & C. Schutze, ed. S. Lotringer. New York: Semiotext(e).

Ben-Ari, E. 1989. Masks and Soldiering: The Israeli Army and the Palestinian Uprising. *Cultural Anthropology* 4(4):372–89.

Berger, J. 1972. *Ways of Seeing.* Harmondsworth: Penguin Books.

— 1980. *About Looking.* New York: Pantheon.

— 1982. *Another Way of Telling.* New York: Pantheon.

Bolton, R. (ed.) 1989. *The Contest of Meaning. Critical Histories of*

Photography. Cambridge, Mass.: MIT Press.

Bruner, E. 1986. Anthropology and Human Studies. *Cultural Anthropology* 1(1):121–4.

— 1989. Of Cannibals, Tourists, and Ethnographers. *Cultural Anthropology* 4(4):438–445.

Buchloh, B. 1989. 'From Faktura to Factography'. In R. Bolton (ed.) *The Contest of Meaning*, 49–85. Cambridge, Mass.: MIT Press.

Buck-Morss, S. 1989. *The Dialectics of Seeing. Walter Benjamin and the Arcades Project*. Cambridge, Mass.: MIT Press.

Chagnon, N.A. 1968. *Yanomamö: The Fierce People*. New York: Holt, Rinehart & Winston.

Clifford, J. 1986. Introduction: 'Partial Truths'. In J. Clifford & G. Marcus (eds.) *Writing Culture*, 1–26. Berkeley: University of California Press.

— 1988. *The Predicament of Culture. Twentieth-Century Ethnography, Literature, and Art*. Cambridge, Mass.: Harvard University Press.

Clifford, J. & Marcus, G. (eds.) 1986. *Writing Culture. The Poetics and Politics of Ethnography*. Berkeley: University of California Press.

Curtis, J. 1989. *Mind's Eye, Mind's Truth. FSA Photography Reconsidered*. Philadelphia: Temple University Press.

Derrida, J. 1976. *Of Grammatology*. Trans. G. Chakravorty Spivak. Baltimore: Johns Hopkins University Press.

— 1987. *The Truth in Painting*. Trans. G. Benington & I. McLeod. Chicago: University of Chicago Press.

Edelman, B. 1979. *Ownership of the Image*. Trans. E. Kingdom. London: Routledge & Kegan Paul.

Faris, J. 1972. *Nuba Personal Art*. London: Duckworth.

— 1988a. 'Southeast Nuba: A Biographical Statement.' In J. Rollwagen (ed.) *Anthropological Filmmaking* 111–22. New York: Harwood Academic Publishers.

— 1988b. 'ART/artifact': On the Museum and Anthropology. *Current Anthropology* 29(5): 775–9.

— 1988c. 'Significance of Differences in the Male and Female Personal Art of the Southeast Nuba'. In A. Rubin (ed.) *Marks of Civilization* 29–40. Los Angeles: University of California Press.

— 1990. *The Nightway: A History of a Navajo Healing Ceremonial and a History of Its Documentation*. Albuquerque: University of New Mexico Press.

Foster, H. 1985. Recodings. *Art, Spectacle, Cultural Politics*. Seattle: Bay Press.

— (ed.) 1988. Vision and Visuality. *Dia Art Foundation Discussions in Contemporary Culture* No. 2. Seattle: Bay Press.

Foucault, M. 1973. *The Order of Things. An Archaeology of the Human Sciences*. New York: Vintage Books.

Freud, S., 1953–1974. *The Standard Edition of the Complete Psychological Works*. Vol. XIX. London: Hogarth Press.

Gallop, J. 1982. *The Father's Seduction. Feminism and Psychoanalysis*. Ithaca: Cornell University Press.

Garner, G. 1990. Autonomy or Narcissism? Self-Imagery in Photography Since 1970. Paper read to the Society of Photographic Education, National Meeting, Santa Fe, New Mexico, March 17, 1990.

Geertz, C. 1973. *The Interpretation of Cultures*. New York: Basic Books.

Goldberg, V. (ed.) 1981. *Photography in Print*. New York: Simon and Schuster.

Gordon, L. 1988. Writing Culture, Writing Feminism: The Poetics and Politics of Experimental Ethnography. *Inscriptions* 3/4:7–26.

Gross, L., Katz, J. & Ruby J. (eds.) 1988. *Image Ethics*. New York: Oxford University Press.

Heider, K. 1980. *Ethnographic Film*. Austin: University of Texas Press.

Jacknis, I. 1984. Franz Boas and Photography. *Studies in Visual Communication* 10:2–60.

Jackson, H. 1987. (advertisement) Holt, Rinehart & Winston Case Studies in Anthropology. October, 1987.

Jay, B. 1984. 'Photographer as Aggressor'. In D. Featherstone (ed.) *Observations: Essays on Documentary Photography* 7–23. Carmel, Calif.: Friends of Photography.

Kluckhohn, C. & Vogt, E. 1951. *Navaho Means People*. Cambridge, Mass.: Harvard University Press.

Krauss, R. 1985a. 'Photographic Conditions of Surrealism'. In R. Krauss *The Originality of the Avant-Garde and Other Modernist Myths* 87–118. Cambridge, Mass.: MIT Press.

— 1985b. 'Photography's Discursive Spaces'. In R. Krauss *The Origin-ality of the Avant-Garde and Other Modernist Myths* 131–50. Cambridge, Mass.: MIT Press.

Lacan, J. 1977. *Ecrits: A Selection*. Trans. A. Sheridan. London: Tavistock.

Lévi-Strauss, C. 1983. *Structural Anthropology*. Vol. 2. Trans. M. Layton. Chicago: University of Chicago Press.

Lloyd, J. 1984. Old Photographs, Vanished Peoples, and Stolen Potatoes. *Arts Monthly* 83:13–16.

Lutkehaus, N. 1989. 'Excuse Me, Everything is Not All Right'. On Ethnography, Film, and Representation. An Interview with Filmmaker Dennis O'Rourke. *Cultural Anthropology* 4(4):422–37.

Lyman, C. 1982. *The Vanishing Race and Other Illusions: Photographs of Indians by Edward S. Curtis*. Washington: Smithsonian Institute Press.

Lyon, L. 1988. 'History of Prohibition of Photography of Southwestern Indian Ceremonies'. In *Reflections: Papers on Southwestern Culture History in Honor of Charles H. Lange* 238–72. Papers of the Archaeological Society of New Mexico, No. 14. Santa Fe: Archaeological Society of New Mexico.

Marcus, G. & Fischer, M. 1986. *Anthropology as Cultural Critique. An Experimental Moment in the Human Sciences*. Chicago: University of Chicago Press.

Pinney, C. 1989. Appearing Worlds. *Anthropology Today* 5(3):26–8.

Pollock, G. 1990. 'Missing Women: Rethinking Early Thoughts on Images of Women'. In C. Squiers (ed.) *The Critical Image. Essays on Contemporary Photography* 202–319. Seattle: Bay Press.

Price, S. 1989. *Primitive Art in Civilized Places*. Chicago: University of Chicago Press.

Rabinow, P. 1977. *Reflections on Fieldwork in Morocco*. Berkeley: University of California Press.

Rabinow, P. & Sullivan, W. (eds.) 1979. *Interpretive Social Science. A Reader*. Berkeley: University of California Press.

Rollwagen, J. (ed.) 1988. *Anthropological Filmmaking. Anthropological Perspectives on the Production of Film and Video for General Public Audiences*. New York: Harwood Academic Publishers.

Rorty, R. 1980. *Philosophy and the Mirror of Nature*. Princeton: Princeton University Press.

Rosaldo, R. 1989. *Culture and Truth. The Remaking of Social Analysis.* Boston: Beacon Press.

Rosler, M. 1981. 3 Works. Halifax: Nova Scotia College of Art and Design.

— 1989. 'In, around, and afterthoughts (on documentary photography)'. In R. Bolton (ed.) *The Contest of Meaning* 303–42. Cambridge, Mass.: MIT Press.

Ryle, J. 1982. Invasion of the Body Snatchers. *New Society* 549:54.

Salat, J. 1983. *Reasoning as Enterprise. The Anthropology of S.F. Nadel.* Trans. G. Quatember. Aachen: Edition Herodot.

Sandweiss, M. 1985. *Laura Gilpin: An Enduring Grace.* Austin: University of Texas Press.

Schechner, R. 1982. *The End of Humanism. Writings of Performance.* New York: Performing Arts Journal Publications.

Scherer, J. 1978. You Can't Believe Your Eyes: Inaccuracies in Photographs of North American Indians.

Exposure 16(4):6–19.

Sekula, A. 1975. On the Invention of Photographic Meaning. *Artforum* 13(5):36–45.

Singer, A. & Woodhead, L. 1988. *Disappearing Worlds: Television and Anthropology.* London: Boxtree.

Snyder, J. & Allen, N. 1975. Photography, Vision, and Representation. *Critical Inquiry* 2(1): 143–69.

Sontag, S. 1977. *On Photography.* New York: Dell.

Squiers, C. (ed.) 1990. *The Critical Image. Essays on Contemporary Photography.* Seattle: Bay Press.

Stewart, S. 1984. *On Longing: Narratives of the Miniature, the Gigantic, the Souvenir, the Collection.* Baltimore: Johns Hopkins University Press.

Stocking, G. 1985. (ed.) Objects and Others: Essays on Museums and Material Culture. *History of Anthropology.* Vol. 3. Madison: University of Wisconsin Press.

Stoller, P. 1989. *The Taste of Ethnographic Things. The Senses in Anthropology.* Philadelphia: University of Pennsylvania Press.

Tambling, J. 1987. *Opera, Ideology and Film.* New York: St Martin's Press.

Torgovnick, M. 1990. *Gone Primitive. Savage Intellects, Modern Lives.* Chicago: University of Chicago Press.

Turner, V, 1982. 'Dramatic Ritual/Ritual Drama: Performance and Reflexive Anthropology'. In J. Ruby (ed.) *A Crack in the Mirror.* 83–97. Philadelphia: University of Pennsylvania Press.

Tyler, S. 1984. The Vision Quest in the West, or What the Mind's Eye Sees. *Journal of Anthropological Research* 40(1):24–40.

— 1987a. Still Rayting. Response to Scholte. *Critique of Anthropology* 7(1):49–51.

— 1987b. *The Unspeakable. Discourse, Dialogue, and Rhetoric in the Postmodern World.* Madison: University of Wisconsin Press.

Worth, S. & Adair, J. 1972. *Through Navajo Eyes: An Exploration in Film Communication and Anthropology.* Bloomington: Indiana University Press.

Appendix
Photographic Techniques:
An Outline

This volume has not concerned itself with technical aspects of photography, the means by which images of the world are recorded in a two-dimensional form through the action of light reflected from objects on to a film emulsion of light-sensitive chemicals. While they cannot be examined in detail in a volume concerned with the cultural act of photography, technical considerations should not be overlooked for they determine what can be photographed at any given time and thus the shape of the record.

The following outline is intended as a guide to the main processes in use between 1850 and 1930 and their technical limitations. The dates indicate only the main period of use in Europe and North America, and there was considerable local variation due to availability, suitability in certain conditions and personal inclination. However attractive new developments in photographic technology might have been they were not always suitable for use in the extreme climates and conditions experienced by anthropologists. For instance, wood warped and rubber perished in tropical climates, dust abraded moving parts and spoiled negatives, chemicals overheated and deteriorated. The pages of the photographic journals and more specifically *Notes and Queries on Anthropology* and the Royal Geographical Society's *Hints for Travellers* give copious advice on these technical problems.

Equipment

The camera, as an optical instrument, is a direct descendant of the artist's *camera obscura*. The earliest cameras comprised two telescoping boxes, used for focusing and carrying the negative, with a lens. The technology developed rapidly, and cameras became smaller, but they were nevertheless large and cumbersome wooden brass-bound boxes on tripods. In addition, until the advent of dry-plate negatives in the late 1870s (see below) photographers had to carry their darkroom, equipment and chemicals with them. By the 1880s cameras had developed alongside the new negative technology, and folding or bellows cameras became available, some of which, although still heavy and bulky, could be used as hand-held cameras. An integral part of these developments of the late nineteenth and early twentieth centuries was the steady improvement in lenses, shutters and the sensitivity of negative emulsions, and thus smaller plates, leading to increasingly short exposure times.

In 1888 Eastman produced the first mass-market hand-held camera using a film-based negative with the famous slogan 'You press the button, we do the rest'. By the 1920s the small, unobtrusive, manoeuvrable, high-quality, hand-held camera was available. In 1924 the Leica was introduced, a 35-mm miniature camera, with its reputation for high optical quality. It was followed in 1928 by the Rolleiflex, a twin-reflex-lens camera which likewise took roll film. Both these cameras were popular with anthropologists for obvious reasons: 'The small camera can be carried in the pocket or, better, round the neck, without anybody being aware of its presence, and is always ready with the minimum amount of preparation' (*Notes and Queries*, 5th edn. 1929:372).

The photographic process

The photographic image is created by the light reflected off an object, channelled in a controlled way through a lens and falling on light-sensitive chemicals, usually silver salts, which are suspended in emulsion on a support, usually glass or film, or in the very early period, paper (calotypes). As a result of exposure the chemical compounds are altered as the reversed image of the subject is reflected on the plate. The degree to which the chemicals are altered depends on the amount of light reflected off the object, the size of the camera aperture, the length of the exposure time and the sensitivity of the chemicals themselves. The resulting negative is then 'developed' to bring out the latent image, surplus light-sensitive chemicals are removed and the image 'fixed'.

There are 'direct positive' processes such as the early daguerreotypes or modern 'instant' film, but that which concerns us most here is the standard negative/positive process. Negatives are printed by two processes: 'print-out' papers and 'develop-out' papers. The earliest prints were made on print-out papers, produced by the negative being placed in direct contact with sensitized paper which was then exposed to sunlight (or later gaslight) until the image emerged. The time required varied according to the sensitivity of the paper, density of the negative and intensity of the light source. The print was then fixed and toned chemically. With develop-out papers, which came in at the end of the nineteenth century, the latent printed image is developed chemically, a process which is still used today.

Negative processes

Wet collodion plate
This was the dominant negative process from the mid 1850s to *c*.1880. Despite its cumbersome nature and technical complexity it heralded a photographic explosion in high-quality, reproducible images in the mid-nineteenth century. A glass plate was coated with an emulsion of gun cotton and ether which was sensitized in a bath of silver halide. This work had

to be done on site by the photographer. The plate was exposed in the camera immediately for several seconds, the duration depending on conditions, and then developed in the darkroom, all while still wet (hence the name). All the equipment, chemicals and in some cases clean fresh water had to be carried to the field. Additional hazards were dust, which stuck to the plate, and high temperatures and low humidity, which dried the plate too quickly. However, the wet-plate negative had excellent definition and a good tonal range.

Dry gelatin plate
Manufactured rather than prepared by the photographer, the dry gelatin plate first appeared *c*.1878 and was in common use by the mid 1880s. Despite the fact that cameras were still bulky, it revolutionized field photography. Plates were purchased ready-sensitized, the silver halide suspended in gelatin emulsion on a glass support, and could be processed any time after exposure providing they had been properly packed and stored. In their early days dry plates did not have the sharpness of wet plates but they soon became more sensitive and contributed greatly to the increase in amateur photography, including that by anthropologists. Because of its stability this technique was favoured by anthropologists as late as the 1930s and some twentieth-century cameras were capable of taking both plate and film negatives.

Film negative
The first film negative was introduced as early as 1886 as a sensitized gelatin emulsion backed by paper which was soaked off during processing. This process was not widely used by anthropologists, despite the attractions of simplicity and portability, as the result was often very fragile. The first film base to make a major impact was cellulose nitrate, which appeared soon afterwards and grew in popularity after the turn of the century. Despite its problems (it is highly inflammable) it remained the main film-based negative of the interwar years. Safety film was introduced in 1937, first on a diacetate base and in 1947 on the more satisfactory triacetate base, which by 1950 was in almost universal use.

Positive processes

Albumen print
Albumen paper was the predominant printing paper of the period *c*.1850–90. Wet collodion negatives printed on albumen papers have resulted in some of the finest images of the nineteenth century. A thin, good-quality paper was coated with an emulsion of beaten egg white (hence the name) with sodium or ammonium.

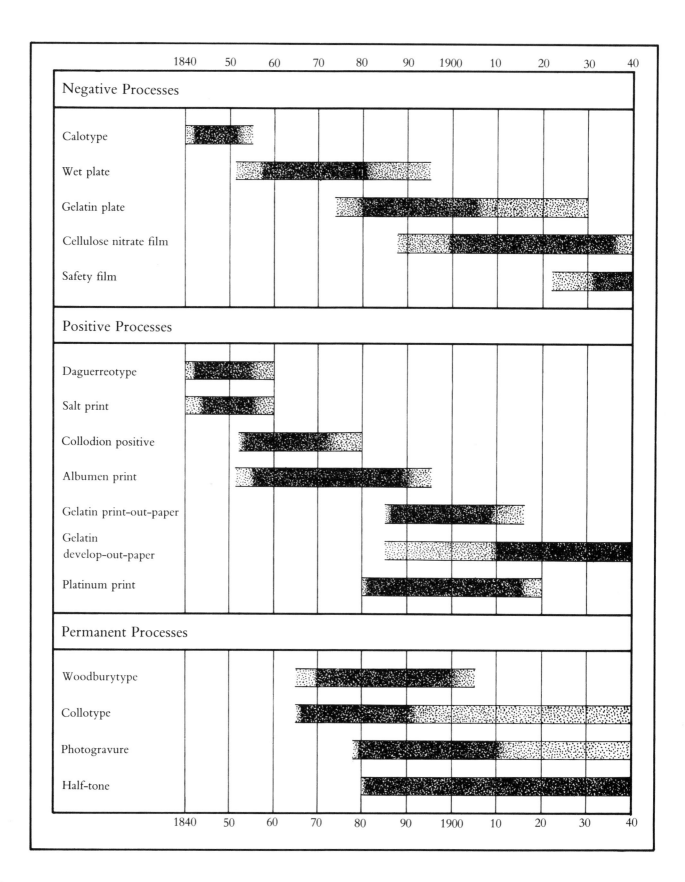

Coated paper could be stored for some years but once sensitized by floating in a bath of silver halides, it had to be used at once. It was a print-out paper in that prints were made through direct contact with the negative exposed to light. The print was then washed, toned (usually with gold chloride), fixed and re-washed. The prints have a low gloss, soft sepia tones and yellow highlights, although this is in part due to the aging process, the original tone being more rich and purple-brown in character.

Gelatin print

The first gelatin paper, introduced in the mid 1880s, was a print-out paper. Good-quality paper was coated with a baryta layer, supporting a silver-gelatin emulsion. The image had a high gloss with warm tones, white highlights and good definition. Matt gelatin papers were also available. Gelatin paper, with its greater sensitivity and image stability, was well established by the mid 1890s. By the turn of the century gelatin develop-out paper with cool black and white tones had been introduced. The latent image was projected through an enlarger and the print developed chemically. From about 1910 gelatin silver-bromide develop-out paper dominated the market and was only recently superseded by resin-coated papers.

Platinum print

This process was less common in anthropological work, although it was widely used in a number of contexts. The photo-sensitive chemicals, platinum salts rather than silver salts, were actually on or in the paper surface. This texture, plus the characteristic soft grey-black tones, made the platinum print aesthetically appealing. It had the further advantage of being very stable although it became less common after the First World War when dramatic increases in the price of platinum made the process expensive.

Colour processes

Despite extensive experimental work colour processes did not become established until the 1930s when direct-positive transparencies, Kodachrome, appeared in 1935, followed by the negative-positive processes, Agfacolor (1939) and Kodacolor (1942).

Permanent and photomechanical processes

It was through 'permanent' processes and photomechanical reproduction that photographic images became widely disseminated, in books, magazines and newspapers and as postcards and other ephemera. A wide range of processes and qualities were in use from the third quarter of the nineteenth century onwards, the most common being the Woodburytype, the collotype, the photogravure and the half-tone, the last of which is still a standard method of reproducing book and newspaper illustrations.

BIBLIOGRAPHY

Coe, B. 1976. *The Birth of Photography*. London: Ash & Grant.
Coe, B. & Haworth-Booth, M. 1983. *Guide to Early Photographic Processes*. London: Victoria & Albert Museum.
Gernsheim, H. & Gernsheim, A. 1969. *The History of Photography*. London: Thames & Hudson.
Lemagny, J.-C. & Rouille, A. (eds.) 1987. *A History of Photography*. Cambridge: University Press.
Munoff, G. 1984. 'History of Photographic Processes'. In Ritzenthaler, M.J., Munoff, G. & Long, M.S. (eds.) *Administration of the Photographic Collections* 27–54. Chicago: Society of American Archivists.
Swan, A. 1981. *The Care and Conservation of Photographic Materials*. London: Crafts Council.
Wade, J. 1979. *A Short History of the Camera*. Watford: Fountain Press.

Index

Indexed in the following pages as entries for groups (marked as such with an asterisk), terms such as 'Pygmy' and 'Hottentot' have been included. These are now seen as somewhat incorrect and pejorative, but, since they are used here in an historically contextualised sense, they are worth including. Broader terms such as 'Plains Indians' are also entered as groups, although accompanied, where applicable, with references to more specific group names. Plate references appear in bold, and entries for journals and newspapers appear in italics.

Christopher Wright
Photographic Librarian, RAI

268

ANTHROPOLOGY AND PHOTOGRAPHY, 1860-1920

edited by Elizabeth Edwards

Since its beginnings, photography has been a valuable resource for anthropologists in the recording of ethnographic data. This book, published in conjunction with the Royal Anthropological Institute (RAI) London, looks at the significance and relevance of still photography in British anthropology from about 1860 until 1920. It examines how photography provides evidence of the past and how this evidence is used in conjunction with more traditional forms of anthropological information. And it considers the reflexive and critical nature of the photographic 'way of seeing' within anthropology.

The book opens with five substantial essays on the nature of photography, visual perception, theoretical and historical approaches to anthropological photography, and the photograph as a document. These are followed by twenty shorter essays by leading anthropologists and historians with special interest in visual representation. The essays examine the content and historical contexts of a range of 157 remarkable photographs, drawn mainly from RAI collections, many reproduced for the first time.

The book as a whole establishes the intellectual and anthropological frameworks for the analysis of specific photographs and articulates a body of ideas about photography and the way in which it was perceived in anthropology. The volume encompasses many ways of thinking from the theoretical to the ethnographic and from the historical to the 'post-modern'. This pluralist approach stresses the complex nature of the photographic message and its interpretation within anthropology in a way that is as relevant to modern material as it is to the historical.

'This book will be warmly received and widely read, and it should be adopted in courses of all kinds, particularly those concerned with the history of anthropology, of photography, and of colonial domination.' – Peter Loizos, *Department of Social Anthropology, London School of Economics*

Elizabeth Edwards is archives curator at the Pitt Rivers Museum, School of Anthropology and Museum Ethnography, University of Oxford.

Contributors:
Judith Binney
Margaret B. Blackman
Nicholas J. Bradford
Brian W. Dippie
Elizabeth Edwards
James C. Faris
Naziha Hamouda
Paul Hockings
Ira Jacknis
Martha Macintyre
Maureen MacKenzie
Iskander Mydin
Richard Pankhurst
Christopher Pinney
Roslyn Poignant
Gwyn Prins
Vivienne Rae-Ellis
Anne Salmond
Joanna C. Scherer
H.L. Seneviratne
Frank Spencer
Brian Street
Donald Tayler
Jan Vansina
Terence Wright

JACKET ILLUSTRATIONS:

front   Mary Deane, daughter of the Census Officer, on board a government steamer with a group of Onges, Little Andaman, 1911. Photograph by H.W. Seton-Karr. Royal Anthropological Institute.
back   Bushongo dignatory performing a celebratory dance, Congo, c. 1908. Photograph by the Torday expedition. Royal Anthropological Institute.

Jacket design by Philippa Stockley

Printed in Hong Kong